HANDBOOK OF MIDDLE AMERICAN INDIANS, VOLUME 8

Ethnology, Part 2

HANDBOOK OF MIDDLE AMERICAN INDIANS

EDITED AT MIDDLE AMERICAN RESEARCH INSTITUTE, TULANE UNIVERSITY, BY

ROBERT WAUCHOPE, *General Editor*
MARGARET A. L. HARRISON, *Associate Editor*
INIS PICKETT, *Administrative Assistant*
ARDEN E. ANDERSON, JR., ROBERT FINK,
    FRANK SCHNELL, *Art Staff*
JAMES C. GIFFORD and CAROL A. GIFFORD, *Indexers*

ASSEMBLED WITH THE AID OF A GRANT FROM THE NATIONAL SCIENCE
FOUNDATION, AND UNDER THE SPONSORSHIP OF THE NATIONAL RESEARCH
COUNCIL COMMITTEE ON LATIN AMERICAN ANTHROPOLOGY

Editorial Advisory Board

IGNACIO BERNAL, HOWARD F. CLINE, GORDON F. EKHOLM,
NORMAN A. MCQUOWN, MANNING NASH, T. DALE STEWART,
EVON Z. VOGT, ROBERT C. WEST, GORDON R. WILLEY

HANDBOOK OF MIDDLE AMERICAN INDIANS

ROBERT WAUCHOPE, General Editor

VOLUME EIGHT

Ethnology

PART TWO

EVON Z. VOGT, Volume Editor

UNIVERSITY OF TEXAS PRESS · AUSTIN

Published in Great Britain by the
University of Texas Press, Ltd., London

Standard Book Number 292–78419–8
Library of Congress Catalog Card No. 64–10316
Copyright © 1969 by the University of Texas Press
All rights reserved.

The preparation and publication of
The Handbook of Middle American Indians
has been assisted by grants from
the National Science Foundation.

Typesetting by G&S Typesetters, Austin, Texas
Printing by The Meriden Gravure Company, Meriden, Connecticut
Binding by Universal Bookbindery, Inc., San Antonio, Texas

CONTENTS *(Continued from Vol. 7)*

SECTION III: CENTRAL MEXICAN HIGHLANDS

GENERAL EDITOR'S NOTE

The manuscripts for the following articles were submitted at various dates over a period of several years. Because of revisions and minor updatings made from time to time, it is difficult to assign a date to each article. In some cases, an indication of when an article was completed can be had by noting the latest dates in the list of references at the end of each contribution.

31. Central Mexican Highlands: Introduction

PEDRO CARRASCO

THE AREA HERE DESIGNATED Central Mexican Highlands includes the southeastern part of the Central Plateau (Mesa Central) plus its eastern slopes with part of the adjoining coastal plain and parts of the Balsas Basin to the south. These are the areas where the Indians speak Nahautl, or the languages of the Otomian or Totonacan families. The area is thus defined from both geographical and linguistic criteria. Its center is the Basin of Mexico and the surrounding valleys of Puebla, Toluca, and Morelos, the core area of the people of Nahuatl or Otomian speech. To the west it reaches to the westernmost groups of Otomian speech in eastern Michoacan which are separated from the Tarascans by a wide area with no Indian population. On the north the boundary almost coincides with the pre-Spanish border of the Mesoamerican culture area except for the few surviving Pame and Chichimeca-Jonaz and the remnants in Queretaro and Guanajuato of the Otomi settled there during the colonial period. The east has no clearly defined border; we include the Nahuatl-, Otomi-, Totonac-, and Tepeua-speakers but not the Mayance Huastec, who are discussed in Article 14. The southeast is bordered by the Mestizo areas of coastal Veracruz. No clear-cut line separates our area from the southern Mexican highlands, but the low density of Indian population in most of the Balsas Basin also establishes a boundary with the high concentration of Indian population of Oaxaca and eastern Guerrero.

This region was the key area of ancient Mesoamerica and the core of the Aztec empire. Its present-day Indians are the descendants of the people whose 16th-century culture has been best described. These are also, however, the Indians who have been most thoroughly influenced by the non-Indian population and by the economic and cultural transformations of the colonial and republican periods. In this region were established the colonial Spanish cities of Mexico City and Puebla, the mining centers of Pachuca and Taxco, the sheep ranches and pulque haciendas of the Tierra Fría, the sugarcane haciendas of the Tierra Caliente in Morelos and the Atlixco-Izucar area. During the republican period it is in

579

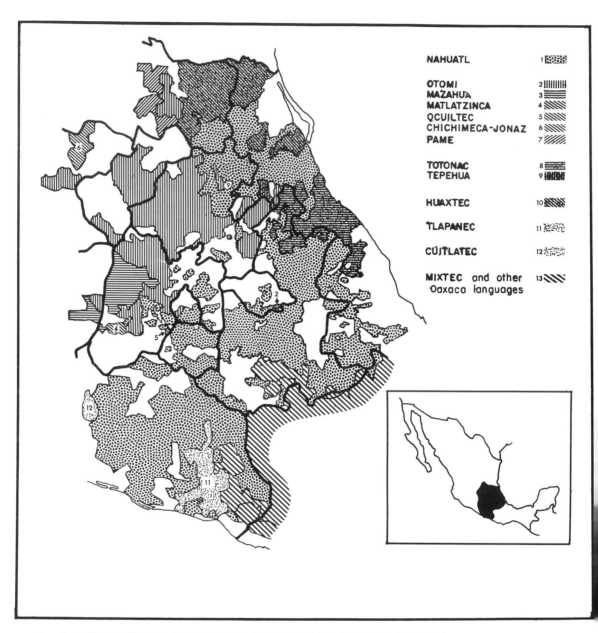

NAHUATL   1

OTOMI   2
MAZAHUA   3
MATLATZINCA   4
OCUILTEC   5
CHICHIMECA-JONAZ   6
PAME   7

TOTONAC   8
TEPEHUA   9

HUAXTEC   10

TLAPANEC   11

CUITLATEC   12

MIXTEC and other   13
Oaxaca languages

Fɪɢ. 1—DISTRIBUTION OF INDIAN LANGUAGES IN CENTRAL MEXICO.
(Drawn by E. Hatch from Mendizábal, 1946b.)

this area that modern industrial development and urban growth have taken place; coffee growing and oil production have rapidly transformed formerly conservative areas. It is thus one of the areas of Mexico where Indians have been subject to the heaviest Hispanization. From the 19th century on, Indian languages have been rapid-ly disappearing as has consciousness of ethnic distinctiveness as Indians are being assimilated into the Mestizo rural population.

DISTRIBUTION OF POPULATION

The distribution of Indian languages is seen in figure 1. The linguistic families included

580

in this region are Uto-Aztecan, Otomian, and Totonacan. Uto-Aztecan is represented only by Nahuatl, the most widely spoken Indian language of Mexico; most of its speakers are in the central Mexican highlands and are found throughout most of the area. The Otomian family includes two sizable groups, Otomi and Mazahua. The other languages of this family have very limited distribution today: Matlatzinca in Mexicaltzingo and San Francisco Oztotilpan; Ocuiltec (or Atzinca) in San Juan Acingo, all three villages in the state of Mexico; Pame in a few spots from east central San Luis Potosi to Northern Hidalgo; and Chichimeca-Jonaz in San Luis de la Paz, Guanajuato.

Otomi is spoken mainly in the western part of the state of Mexico and the Mezquital Valley area of Hidalgo, but there are also Otomi areas in the Sierra de Puebla, at Ixtenco in Tlaxcala and in parts of Queretaro and Guanajuato. Mazahua is spoken only in the western part of the state of Mexico and a few adjoining villages in Michoacan.

The Totonacan family includes Totonac, spoken by a sizable group in the border area of Puebla and Veracruz, and Tepehua, spoken by a few Indians centering in the *municipio* of Huehuetlan, Hidalgo.

The distribution and density of the Indian population can be seen in figure 2. There are five major areas with high concentration of Indian population. The largest, occupying the eastern slopes of the plateau, includes the most conservative cultures, villages of Nahuatl, Totonac, Tepehua, and Otomi speech. A second area is the Otomi-speaking Valle del Mezquital. The western part of the state of Mexico is a third area of strong Indian population where Otomi, Mazahua, and Nahuatl are spoken. Less solidly Indian is the fourth region, in Tlaxcala and Puebla, villages of Nahuatl speech mostly on the slopes of the Popocatepetl and Malinche. The southeastern end of the state of Puebla beyond Tehuacan and the neighboring area of Veracruz form a fifth area of high Indian population of Nahuatl speech neighboring on the Mazatec of Oaxaca. The Popoloca and Mixteca of the state of Puebla are treated with their linguistic kinsmen of Oaxaca in Section 2 of this volume.

THE PROCESS OF ACCULTURATION

Modern Indian cultures are the result of a four-century-long process of acculturation, and the main lines in a discussion of modern basic institutions and regional differences have to be defined in reference to both colonial and present-day acculturation processes.

After the conquest the Indian became part of a plural society, a stratified social system that included not only Indians but Spaniards, Negroes, and Castas (half-breeds), each group with a legally defined social status. Class differentiation, however, also developed within these ethnic groups so that the total stratification was based on the two different principles of ethnic group and class. Changes in the culture and internal social structure of the Indian communities depended on the place that these communities came to occupy within the wider society. The Indians usually became a peasant group, but within this general characterization there have been important differences in the various areas and at different times. The steps in the long process of Indian acculturation can be seen as a sequence of different social structures with the Indian in a distinctive position at each step. And the influence of the total society on the Indian, especially as reflected in government policy, has also been different according to the changes developing in Mexican society as a whole.

Viewing the Indian cultures from the present and without discussing the successive steps of colonial acculturation in detail, we can discuss the total transformation of Indian cultures from the conquest to the present in terms of two great processes.

581

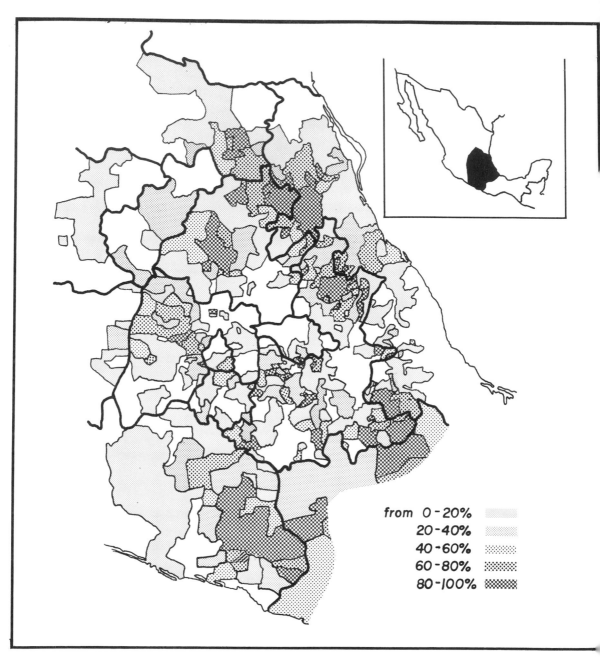

FIG. 2—DENSITY OF INDIAN-SPEAKING POPULATION IN CENTRAL MEXICO.
(Drawn by E. Hatch from Densidad, 1950, map. 1.)

First is the colonial process of transformation of the independent preconquest native societies into semi-autonomous peasant communities, which formed subordinate ethnic groups but were at the same time a basic component of the total social structure. Second is the modern process of progressive assimilation of the Indian into rural Mexican society, with only the marginal survival of colonial type communities in modified form.

Within the wider structure of the Spanish

empire, the colonial society developed a structure of its own. The Spanish policy towards the Indians can be explained by the nature and interrelations of these two structures. From the point of view of the cultural transformation of the Indian, they have to be taken as the conditions, imposed from the outside, within which the cultural and social change took place. In the pluri-ethnic society of New Spain the Spaniards replaced or placed themselves above the native rulers and, although a good measure of indirect rule was practiced, the large native "empires" or confederations were broken down into their constituent chieftancies. The Indian segments of society became thus restricted to the peasant level of organization; of the native ruling group some disappeared, some survived but with a diminished social standing. The Indian communities or *Repúblicas de Indios* were peasant communities with a corporate legal personality, communal ownership of land, autonomous government and responsibility for the payment of tribute and supply of forced labor; they are the Mexican counterpart of the native reserves of other colonial areas. These were the conditions that explain the survival or disappearance of different aspects of native culture and social organization.

The greatest amount of retention is found at the family and village level: the technology of the family or village production unit, family organization, and the private cults and beliefs connected with events in the life cycle or technological activities.

At the village level of organization we find institutions such as local government and ceremonial organization that represent local interests but which are also related to the wider society, indeed are local branches of the wider institutions of state and church. The native forms of local government and ceremonial organization were purposefully changed by the new state and church, whereas the Spanish directives to impose forms of local administration and

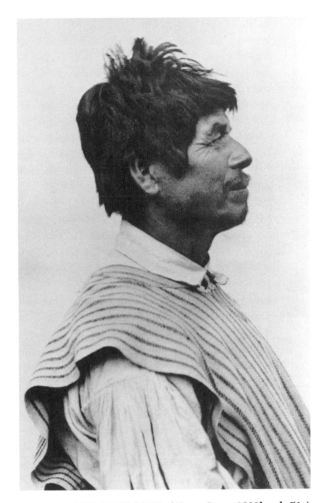

FIG. 3—TLAXCALAN MAN. (From Starr, 1899b, pl. 51.)

religion had to be adapted to local conditions. We thus find in village government and village public cult and cult organization the foremost instances of cultural syncretism.

The disappearance of large-scale native political units and the decline and transformation of the native nobility resulted in the disappearance of all those aspects of culture related to higher levels of organization and the native ruling group: the forms of political, military and religious organization of the native states, the architecture of public buildings, and the luxury crafts whose products were consumed by the ruling groups

583

in their private and public life. As a counterpart to this massive disappearance of upper-class native culture we find the relatively slight impact of Spanish folk or peasant culture. New Spain was a mixed society of a Spanish upper class and an Indian lower class. Spanish culture consequently prevails in patterns of government and state religion and was imitated by the surviving Indian nobility, while the culture of the Indian peasant continued to be basically Indian except in the changes forced by state and church. The policies of political and religious control, however, reached deep into aspects of Indian culture that might be expected to have been left undisturbed. Thus the policy of forced conversion led to the adoption of the standards of the church regarding modesty in dress or the regulation of marriage.

The second great transformation is the modern process of disappearance of the autonomous, communal character of the Indian village and its assimilation into Mexican rural society. The legal bases for this transformation were laid down during the 19th century, first by the abolition of the separate legal status of the Indian and of the tribute system, later by the land reforms aiming at the suppression of the holding of land by corporate bodies. The amount of change, however, has depended on the strength of the economic transformation that resulted from the economic growth of Mexico starting in the late 19th century and on the settling of non-Indians in former Indian communities.

The demands of the total Mexican society on the Indian have changed from colonial to modern times. The Indian is no longer significant as a source of tribute (or taxes) and he is less important than he used to be as a source of labor for non-Indian enterprises. The modern Indian is for the most part a farmer or craftsman producing partly for subsistence, partly for a local market. Both as producer and consumer the Indian's participation in the national market is small.

What we find, then, is the marginal survival of the type of Indian community developed during colonial times free from tribute and forced labor but subject to the influences of the modern industrial civilization and the new national political system. In technology these new influences appear as sewing machines, corn mills (*molinos de nixtamal*), widespread use of factory-made clothes and automotive transportation (used even if not run by Indians). The modern municipal organization of Mexico has everywhere caused changes or additions to the traditional system of local government, and there is often a distinction between the officials that are part of the traditional organization and those whose existence is prescribed by the municipal law of each state. The old religious sodalities introduced in colonial times have usually taken on a folk meaning and have become part of the traditional village organization, and a new set of sodalities is usually fostered by the church. Here and there the spread of Protestantism is another new avenue of change in religion.

The total economic situation is also changing. The land-tenure system has changed in important respects with the loss of importance of the community as the basic landholding unit—loss of communal lands, individual title to land by members of the community, and even the modern introduction of the *ejido* system, since the ejido does not usually coincide with the village community as a whole but forms a factional group within it. The increased industrialization of Mexico has brought about strong competition for some of the traditional crafts and their eventual disappearance, although it also has created a new demand for other Indian products such as new cash crops (e.g., coffee) and thus has increased the Indian's involvement in the money economy. All these factors together with the growth of population and increased scarcity of land increasingly throw the Indian into the national labor market. The combined acculturative effects of all these new

FIG. 4—TLAXCALAN HOUSE GROUP, SAN ESTEBAN. (From Starr, 1899b, pl. 44.)

developments lead to the eventual loss of the cultural traits that are distinctively Indian, including language, and results in the assimilation of the Indian into the general rural Mexican population.

It should be pointed out, however, that the social passing from Indian to non-Indian is only one aspect of a complex process of change. It does not always go at the same pace as the changes in the different aspects of the culture and social organization of the group making the transition. Traits of Indian origin are found at all levels of Mexican society, and the glorification of the Indian component of Mexican culture and history that is part of modern nationalism

has grown at the same time that the groups socially considered Indians with Indian speech and a strong Indian culture have been receding. These are problems, however, that go beyond the subject of this article. We are here concerned with the population that still is socially defined as Indian and has a cultural heritage of predominantly Indian origin. These we find today only as a marginal population socially and geographically.

REGIONAL DIFFERENCES

The most important type of diversity among modern Indian communities is perhaps the one related to the situation

585

that a particular community may occupy within the general process of acculturation outlined before, i.e., the relative amount of pre-Spanish, colonial, and modern social and cultural features. In addition important regional differences are related to environmental adaptation and to the survival of different native traditions from the pre-Spanish past.

Some of the most important and most visible cultural differences among modern Indian villages are connected with differences in the natural environment. In the first place we have those differences pertaining to agriculture and animal husbandry. Crops vary according to altitude and water supply. The most important plants in the native diet, corn and beans, have a general distribution because of the existence of different varieties adapted to the various environments, but otherwise we find the usual differences between crops of *tierra caliente, tierra templada,* and *tierra fría.* Domestic animals are less important in the native economy, but here also is found the concentration of goat and sheep raising in the dry-temperate and cold areas, respectively. Agricultural techniques are also to a large extent related to the environment: slash-and-burn is practiced in the forested areas whether lowland or high mountain, whereas the use of the plow has become general in the highlands. Chinampa cultivation (see vol. 6, Art. 4, fig. 5) has become restricted to the Lake Xochimilco area in the Basin of Mexico but has also expanded to the similar environment at the source of the Lerma River.

Environmental influences are also perceptible in housing, settlement pattern, and dress. The more intensive cultivation of the highlands, related to the natural environment, in its turn results in the higher population density, land scarcity, specialization in crafts and more intense marketing that characterize throughout Mesoamerica the highland cultures in contrast with the lowland.

The differential acceptance of Spanish culture traits is to a large extent conditioned by environment, as for example in the introduction of new crops or the use of wool in clothing. In this respect Spanish influences have added to the aboriginal highland-lowland contrast. Other cases of differential acceptance of Spanish traits may be the result of divergent policies on the part of various missionary orders or bishoprics; this question remains to be investigated.

The survival of diverse pre-Spanish cultural backgrounds can also be seen at the root of some of the modern regional differences. The main one, however, is the continuation although in somewhat changed form of differences conditioned by the environment that had already been at work in preconquest times. Other cultural features that probably continue to illustrate aboriginal regional differences are various types of housing (wattle versus adobe) and corncribs (square, round, radish-shaped) or certain types of garments (*huipil* versus *quexquemitl*). Some types of kinship organization discussed later also must represent the continuation of differing aboriginal patterns. It is not possible, however, to assume that modern regional differences even when relating to surviving aspects of aboriginal culture—for instance, pagan cults—always represent pre-Spanish regional differences. The peasantization of Indian societies after the conquest implied a simplification of the aboriginal cultures, and modern regional differences may well be the result of differential survival and different types of acculturation from a common indigenous base.

Not enough ethnographic work has been done to plot satisfactorily the various cultural regions within the central highlands, but it seems safe to conclude that cultural differences do not coincide with linguistic areas. We will instead have to operate with a series of regions each including a mixed society of both Spanish- and Indian-speak-

586

ers, sometimes with various Indian languages in the same region. To some extent each area may have a somewhat distinct culture, and the most obvious differences will be related to environmental conditions. On the other hand, each area can best be viewed as a regional society within the same cultural tradition, and each will include a similar set of the main types of community —administrative or commercial centers, farming villages, craft villages. Another main factor in defining regional differences will be, then, the relative importance of the various types of community within each region—for instance, the areas with a large conservative Indian population with non-Indian administrative and commercial centers as against the areas of small marginal Indian villages within an area in which non-Indian industrial and political centers predominate.

We shall now review the main aspects of Indian culture, pointing out the major regional differences and outlining processes of change. This article emphasizes the background of those aspects of culture that are most important in contemporary cultures in terms of the various factors making for regional differentiation and change that have been outlined above.

ASPECTS OF INDIAN CULTURE AND SOCIETY
Community Type

The first task in describing and classifying Indian cultures is to see what type of social group we are dealing with by ascertaining its place within the national social structure. Indians everywhere are part of the rural population. Their economic activities are farming, crafts, and wage labor. Some subsistence farming is always practiced, although its relative importance within a specific community differs widely; it is always supplemented by commercial farming, crafts, or wage labor. Village specialization is typical of the rural economy, and most Indian communities can be readily classified

as specializing in one particular line of farming or craft.

Another and most important question is the nature of the Indian group as a type of settlement or administrative unit. From this point of view a contrast can be drawn between what we call village or town cultures and hamlet cultures. A village or town (*pueblo, villa*) is an autonomous unit with its own political administration. It consists of a nucleated settlement with the surrounding land and sometimes with dependent hamlets. When the village is the head (*cabecera*) of a *municipio*, the political autonomy has a strong legal basis, and a number of the local officials will be those determined by the municipal law of the state; when the village is not the cabecera but is subordinate to another town, the local body of officials will be based primarily on tradition, since the municipal law requires a meager administrative body for such a village. In either case, however, from the point of view of the Indian tradition, the village is the political and culture-carrying unit; the most important aspects of Indian culture refer to the village level of integration: village jurisdiction over land, village political and ceremonial organization. In many cases, however, we find municipios and villages in which the non-Indian population is in control of the local administration, usually forming the population of the cabecera or central part of the town. The Indian population, then, is found only in outlying wards or hamlets (*barrios, ranchos, rancherías, congregaciones*). In these cases most features relating to the village level of integration are outside the realm of Indian culture, which pertains then to the family level or to the village subdivision (ward, hamlet, etc.) of which its carriers are members; the aspects of political and ceremonial organization so important in village culture are here very weak or non-existent. This is what we can call a hamlet culture (Tajin, for instance).

During colonial times important groups

587

Fig. 5—WOMAN OF ALTEPEXI, PUEBLA, NEAR TEHUACAN. (Photographed by Donald Cordry, 1963.)

of Indians also lived in large towns, including those that were centers of Spanish urban settlement. In Mexico City, this was the result of the establishment of a Spanish city at the center of the old Indian capital, with the Indian population being organized in outlying barrios with their own separate cabildo. But a Spanish city such as Puebla, founded on a new site, also attracted Indian settlers to dependent barrios, thus creating exactly the same type of social unit (Marín Tamayo, 1960). These Indians, such as those of Mexico City or nearby Xochimilco, engaged in crafts and trades catering to the Spanish urban population. In Mexico City the Indian barrios with their autonomous government still existed at the time of Mexico's independence. It is only during the republican period that the non-Indian nuclei of cities and even of middle-sized towns have everywhere expanded and assimilated the local Indians so that today the Indian population is everywhere rural.

From the colonial period to the present there has also been a constant trend toward the fragmentation of Indian political units (*Repúblicas de Indios*) into smaller and smaller units. Villages that were originally dependencies (*sujetos, estancias*) of some head towns (cabeceras) gradually became administratively independent, choosing their own body of local officials at the same time that most of the important settlements of the early colonial period became non-Indian in character. A constant trend has thus been in operation for Indian society to change from town or village toward hamlet with the corresponding simplification in the patterns of social stratification and political and ceremonial organization.

Material Culture

A comparison of the material culture of the modern Indian with that of conquest times shows a great amount of retention of peasant technology and an almost total disappearance of the material culture associated with the native upper class and its political and ceremonial life. Thus farming techniques, cooking, housing, dress, and craft products such as pottery or basketry used by the peasant family are still largely aboriginal, whereas public architecture and the crafts associated with native upper classes have disappeared. This disappearance was in some cases sudden. For instance, native public architecture, which was primarily religious, went out of existence with forced conversion. In a good number of luxury crafts, however, the continued existence of the native nobility and the demands of the new Spanish state made for a transitional period in which some craftsmen continued to work at their trades, were converted to new products or left their imprint on products of the new technology. Thus feather ornaments were still used in Indian celebrations, and feather mosaics of Christian subjects were made for the church; goldsmiths also could work for the Spanish. The old system of picture writing disappeared from the non-Christian religious codices but was in use for some time in the local administrative records (e.g., Codices Osuna, Tepetlaoztoc, Mariano Jiménez). The stoneworkers put to work in Spanish buildings and churches gave a particular style to the early colonial stone carving.

In spite of the large number of native survivals, the influence of pre-industrial European technology is everywhere noticeable, and in more recent times industrial products are also used. No detailed information is as yet available as to the precise dates and especially the extent to which various technological innovations were introduced in the different areas of Mexico. An often-mentioned early colonial report describes the great skill of Indian craftsmen and the eagerness with which they imitated Spanish products (Motolinía, 1914, pp. 216–17), but this probably applied only to craftsmen in the main urban centers. The Indian nobility imitated the Spanish in dress and entered into new forms of economic activity such as sheep raising. Another avenue of change may have been the Spanish demand for products that the Indian was able to meet. Wheat, for instance, was often demanded as tribute (J. Miranda, 1952, p. 259). And the need for cash to pay tribute may also have been a factor in increasing the commercial involvement of Indians in products of Spanish demand. Old World crops seem to have been widespread rather early.

Metallurgy is perhaps the one field in which change has been most radical. Aboriginal metal work has disappeared and the use of iron is today universal, although in the form of imported tools and rarely of native manufacture.

Agriculture is the basic branch of production of the modern Indian peasant. Slash-and-burn farming continues in the forested areas of the Gulf coast and highland mountain slopes along lines that are basically aboriginal. The old key areas in the highlands, however, have adopted cattle and the plow, substantial additions to the more intensive cultivation of the highland plateau that already prevailed in aboriginal times. Staple crops continue to be the aboriginal corn, beans, chile, and maguey, but Old World crops have been added in all environments. The old chinampa agriculture is still practiced in the Valley of Mexico although in a very restricted area (see vol. 6, Art. 4, fig. 5).

Of the most important crafts, pottery is still basically of aboriginal type (see vol. 6, Art. 5, fig. 11). The most substantial European innovations, glazing and the potter's wheel, are rather exceptional among Indian potters (Foster, 1955). The textile arts have been more influenced by European technology, with the introduction of an important new fiber, wool, the spinning wheel and the foot loom, the latter worked by men so that it also represents a change in the aboriginal division of labor in which weaving was the province of women. All this, however, is an addition to the native spindle

whorl and beltloom that have continued in general use.

An important change in dress took place shortly after the conquest when men adopted pants (zaragüelles, calzones) and shirt instead of the native loincloth. The main force for change may have been the influence of the church, for whom native style amounted to nakedness. The aboriginal cloak (tilma) was kept as well as women's dress that, consisting of a wraparound skirt (cueitl, naguas) and upper garment of the huipil or quexquemitl varieties, met the church's standards of modesty. In the course of the colonial period the use of woolens became general in the highlands for skirts and serapes, the latter a colonial development. Full skirts, blouses, and shawls (rebozos) are of European origin and their widespread use among Indian women probably dates from the 19th century. In recent times factory made clothes have been replacing the local costumes.

In housing tile has been the main Old World innovation. Native types of hut, wattle and thatch are common in the lowlands. In the highlands and in the larger lowland towns the prevailing adobe buildings with flat or tile roofs represent a blend of the native house with the Mediterranean types.

Innovation has been greater in settlement types. In connection with the congregación policy enforced mainly around 1600 most Indian communities were resettled in nucleated towns with a grid pattern around a central square, where the church and other public buildings were located. In some areas, especially the eastern slopes of the plateau and the northern Otomi area, small hamlets and scattered homesteads are widespread, either because the congregación policy was not fully carried out or because a relapse took place to an older pattern.

Economic Organization

The economic system of the early colonial period was clearly based on Indian labor:

590

Indian tribute supported the royal treasury and the encomenderos, forced Indian labor provided a substantial part of the labor needs of Spanish farms, and Indian craftsmen, especially in Mexico City or Xochimilco, were significant in the nonagricultural sector of the economy. Within the Indian communities, independent household production prevailed in farming and crafts, partly for subsistence, partly for the market or for tribute payments in kind. The quantitative importance of labor exchange and work bees is difficult to estimate. In addition there survived a certain amount of land in the hands of Indian caciques whose holdings were parceled out among tenants who paid their dues in a great variety of craft products of their own manufacture, and in labor used to work the landlord's fields, build and repair his house, and provide domestic service (Carrasco, 1963).

Together with this "private" sector of the economy there was a very significant "public" sector managed by the town's officials. All the land in the community was held under communal title and in addition to the lands for family use there were the commons (ejidos) and propios, land worked in common or rented out, the produce of which entered the town's treasury. There was also a certain amount of tribute surplus, and a number of payments in kind and labor were rendered by the members of the community for the support of its civil and ceremonial organization.

An example is the town of Otlazpan in 1549 (today a barrio of Tepeji del Rio, Mexico). Indian householders paid tribute in cash, cacao beans, firewood, and turkeys in proportion to the amount of land they held. In addition there were a number of labor services primarily in working the communal lands and, for women, weaving stipulated amounts of cloth for the officials as well as for the town's treasury. Salaries in cash were paid to the governor, two judges (alcaldes), four councilmen (regidores), and a steward (mayordomo); these

officials also received firewood and had their fields worked for them by the villagers. Smaller salaries in cash were given to a scribe, to church singers (cantores) and instrumentalists (menestriles), as well as to a number of labor chiefs (tequitlatos) in charge of the laborers going to the public works in Mexico City, of the labor drafts for working the encomendero's land, of people taking food to the encomendero's house, of examining marriages, of overseeing the baptism of children, and of gathering people on Sundays and holidays to hear Mass and learn the Christian doctrine. The daily expenditures of the townhall (comun y casa pública) amounted to three turkeys, 500 cacao beans, and one fanega of corn; and every week there was a team, changing every Saturday, of 10 men to bring firewood and 10 women to grind corn. In addition the communal treasury spent at each of the main festivals of the year (St. Matthew and Easter Sunday) 3200 cacao beans, five turkeys, five chickens, and five fanegas of corn (Códice Mariano Jiménez).

The modern economic organization of Indian villages has diverged from the one just outlined in a number of ways. The growth of the non-Indian population, the assimilation of Indians in many areas, and the development of new forms of economic activity at the national level have restricted the Indian population to smaller and marginal areas, and its part in the national economy is far less significant than in the colonial period. The Indian is no longer an important contributor of tribute or taxes; forced labor has disappeared and instead a situation of rural underemployment has developed. Modern Indian communities carry on independent household production in farming and/or crafts for subsistence or for the market. Village specialization in different crafts or farm products and a system of regional markets make for a close interdependence of different Indian villages with each other and with the non-Indian segments of the population. Communal title

591

Fig. 6—WOMEN AND CHILDREN OF ACATLAN, GUERRERO. (Photographed by Donald Cordry, 1964.)

to land has generally been replaced by individual titles, although in a number of villages ejido communities have been set up after the land reforms of the postrevolutionary period. Forest regulations restrict the use of the remaining commons as farming land.

The common lands (propios) of townships and of religious sodalities have generally disappeared. The tribute system is gone and most of the few taxes paid by Indians (such as land taxes) go to the federal and state treasuries. Indian villages thus have a very meager cash income (Mendizábal, 1946b, charts at end of vol. 5). All this makes impossible the type of "public" economy outlined for the colonial period. What remains today is the *tequio* or communal labor for public works and occasional collections for the organization of festivals, but civil and ceremonial officials are not usually supported by the town. Instead they have to sponsor from their private income the public functions they perform. A system of sponsorships (*mayordomías*) thus developed that is connected with the hierarchical ladder basic to the political and ceremonial organization. Survival of the autonomous or self-centered character of the Indian community has come to depend on this sponsorship system that channels surplus wealth toward communal ends, rather than on the communal property of the colonial Indian village. More recent trends of change further destroy the remnants of a communal organization: individual resistance to participation in public works (tequio) and the sponsorship system grows as Indians are more closely drawn into the national economy. But then when the transformation goes this far we usually find that many other aspects of the Indian's culture have changed and the social identification as an Indian has been lost.

Family and Kinship

It is difficult to attempt an over-all view of the evolution of kinship organization from pre-Spanish to modern times. Pre-Spanish kinship still presents a number of problems; little about the colonial period is yet known and the modern data, also quite limited, suggest that different types of organization may have existed from the early period to the present.

Before the conquest extended family households were common. There were no barriers to marriage among close kin other than lineal relatives, at least among some Nahuatl groups. Polygyny was common although in varying degree among the ethnic groups and social strata; the levirate was practiced. The Spanish conquest imposed the marriage regulations of the Catholic church and thus effected a number of important changes. Polygyny was suppressed and marriage was forbidden with kin closer than the third degree, that is, second cousins; the levirate was also forbidden (Doctrina, pp. cxi–cxii). For Indian caciques succession rules of the Spanish nobility (primogeniture) were adopted. (For Huexotzinco, see Carrasco, 1966, pp. 152 and 157). Nuclear family households seem to prevail in colonial village censuses. The age for marriage was late, at least in parts of ancient Mexico, a custom probably related to the importance of the men's house organization and warfare; a change to earlier marriage took place in the early postconquest period. The modern prevalence of the nuclear family and the lack of preferential marriages are thus the result of changes that took place soon after the conquest. The bilateral kindred exogamy that prevails today has a basis in the regulation of the church, although custom seems to favor a wider exogamy than was demanded by the missionary church.

The modern custom of arranging marriages through a go-between, with ritualized visits, exchange of presents, and formal speeches, is probably a survival of old usages (see Fabila, 1949, p. 153 ff.).

At the time of the conquest the ward or barrio (Nahuatl, *calpulli*) seems to have had some basis in kinship, although the precise composition of the group from the point of view of kinship is still debatable. Marriage does not seem to have been regulated by ward membership; patrilineal exogamy was definitely not practiced in the Aztec ruling lineage, but we should not assume that this was the rule everywhere in the central highlands. An analysis of the marriages performed at the village of Chiautla near Tetzcoco from 1585 to 1604 shows that the men of the 11 different wards in that town varied in their choice of wives as far as ward membership was concerned; the variation ranged from a barrio 59 per cent of whose men took wives from their own ward to one in which only 16 per cent did so; the variation in the ward membership of mates seems to be related to the size of the barrio and geographical proximity. The marriage pattern thus seems very similar to that of Tepoztlan in recent times. We might then agree with Monzón (1949) that the old calpulli was an ambilateral clan with some tendency towards endogamy. Modern evidence, however, shows the existence of barrios that are patriclans in Murdock's use of the term among the Totonac of Eloxochitlan (I. Kelly, 1953, p. 181; Palerm, personal communication) and the Nahuatl of San Bernardino Contla, Tlaxcala (Nutini, 1961). The nature of the barrio from the kinship point of view is thus more complex than has generally been assumed, and we should acept the existence of different types of kinship organization both in aboriginal and postconquest times. Much more work is required in colonial history and modern ethnography before this problem can be settled.

The modern barrio, irrespective of its ethnic or kinship basis, is primarily a social division, usually territorial, that functions in the political and ceremonial organization as a unit for the selection of officials and the performance of civil or religious activities.

Ritual co-parenthood (*compadrazgo*) has become an important pattern of social re-lationships among the Indians of the central highlands as in most other regions of Mesoamerica. Some basis for the successful adoption of this institution may have been afforded by a pre-Spanish ritual similar to baptism. Modern compadrazgo in this area has the features typical of Spanish America, but the basis for the successful adoption of this institution may have been afforded by pre-Spanish custom (Chaves, 1865, p. 539).

Village Government

The forms of village government are regulated by the municipal laws of each state which determine the number, title, and functions of municipal officers, the method of selection, and terms of office. The general pattern prescribes popular election of a number of councilmen (*regidores*), a municipal president and an attorney (*síndico*) for short terms of from one to three years. Other officials, such as the secretary and policemen, are appointed and not limited as to terms. In addition to and combined with this pattern one usually finds throughout Indian Mexico a number of customary civil officials and a ceremonial organization whose existence is not prescribed by law. These are the continuation of the colonial civil authorities and religious brotherhoods on top of which the recent municipal organization has been imposed without displacing it entirely.

The civil and ceremonial offices of a town's organization are usually combined in a single scale of short-term (usually yearly) offices, which has been termed an *escalafón* or ladder system. All men of the community have to enter into it and all have a chance to climb up to the highest steps and reach the status of elder. The number of positions is always larger in the lower steps of the ladder; errand boys for ceremonial or civil officials and policemen are usually grouped in gangs from different sections or wards of the town who take turns in performing their duties. The higher offices are those of town councilmen and judges or mayors in the civil government and several ceremonial stewardships (mayordomías) in the cult organization. When a town is subdivided into wards, most often each participates equally in the higher levels of the hierarchy; there are parallel offices of the same rank, one for each barrio, or a single position rotates year after year among the different wards.

Generally a man alternates between civil and religious positions, and after filling an office he takes a period of rest during which he does not actively participate in the town's civil or ceremonial organization, until the time comes again for him to occupy a higher office. As a citizen of the community he has the obligation to serve, and social pressure to that effect is always strong; the individual will also be driven to apply for offices in order to raise his social status.

The group of highest prestige, and in the more conservative communities the ultimate governing body of the town, consists of the men who have gone through the required offices and sponsorships of the ladder. These are usually referred to as *principales* (principals) or, since this grade is reached at an advanced age, *ancianos* (elders). Elders are considered to have done their share for the town and are exempt from communal labor services.

This ladder system is the result of the syncretism of Indian patterns of political and ceremonial organization with the Spanish system of municipal government and guild or religious sodalities introduced in the 16th century (Carrasco, 1961a). The Spanish institutions were adjusted to the main lines of the native class distinctions and political organization, and important changes later took place in relation to the over-all transformation of Mexican society during colonial and republican times.

In the pre-Spanish organization young men entered the men's houses (*telpochcalli* or *calmecac*) where they performed menial tasks in the political, military, and ceremonial organizations and were trained for participation in these organizations at a higher level. Young men could enter into a career of military or ceremonial advancement determined mainly by success in the battlefield. The existence of class differences between nobles and commoners restricted the highest positions to the noblemen. The economic organization of the palace and the temples was marked by a number of occasions for the accumulation and consumption or redistribution of goods. Institutions such as temples and men's houses were supplied with land and tribute that constituted the source of the goods to be consumed or distributed. In addition, individuals achieving an office or performing a ceremonial function contributed to the performance or gave feasts that placed them at the focal point of additional redistributions.

After the introduction of the Spanish system of town government the lower levels of local administration were still a direct continuation of the native organization that was kept for the collection of tribute and organization of public works much as it had been in the past. Even today one finds lesser officials with the title of *tequitlato* (labor boss) and *topil* (literally, 'staff bearer,' usually some kind of errand boy or policeman) that are clearly the continuation of their ancient namesakes (Durán, 1951, 1: 323; 2: 166, 223; Torquemada, 1943, 2: 545; Gibson, 1952, pp. 118–20). The higher offices in the colonial Indian village were clearly derived from the Spanish pattern: a governor (*gobernador*), and a variable number of judges (*alcaldes*) and councilmen (*regidores*). These offices, however, were usually filled by the descendants of the native nobility (*prinicipales*), who would also continue using the pre-Spanish political and ceremonial titles (see, for example, the lists of principales in Códice Mariano Jiménez, 1903). In many towns the native requirement of noble status for high office was sanctioned by Spanish authorities; and although the new offices had yearly terms and re-election for the next

FIG. 7—WOMAN MAKING TORTILLAS, SAN JOSE MIAHUATLAN, PUEBLA. (Photographed by Donald Cordry, 1963.)

two years was forbidden, the evidence is clear that the same group of men repeatedly held all the high offices of the new administration, alternating from one to another. A number of local differences in the system of electing officials have been reported that depart from the Spanish usage and have been interpreted as due to different Indian backgrounds. (Zavala and Miranda, 1954, pp. 80–82; Chávez Orozco, 1943, p. 10; Gibson, 1952, p. 112.)

The old system of achieving prestige through ceremonial sponsorship also continued. Although the offering of sacrificial victims as a way of acquiring status was eradicated, the related practice of feast giving and sponsorship of religious functions is reported in early colonial times by missionaries who saw in it a continuation of the pre-Spanish customs. The well-attested identification of the native gods with Catholic saints, and consequently with their respective rituals, must also have resulted in the transference of the social prestige value of ritual sponsorship and feast giving from the old to the new ceremonials. As in the native period, the occasional achievement of the status of principal by men of commoner origin who had occupied high office is also attested from the colonial period. (Durán, 1951, 2: 125–26, 266; Sahagún, 1938, 3: 299–301; Zavala and Miranda, 1954, p. 61.)

One important change throughout colonial times and the 19th century was the elimination of the nobility as a separate group with inherited rank, private landholdings, and exclusive rights to office, with the consequent opening of the entire hierarchy to the whole town. The process started early in colonial times, first of all because the Spanish conquest destroyed all the large political units, cutting them down to their constituent chieftaincies and depressing them all to the peasant level of organization, with the consequent loss in numbers and importance of the native nobility, especially in the old political centers.

Equally important were the efforts of the commoners to eliminate the restrictions against them and to wrest the control of town government away from the nobility. This process started in the 16th century, but the final disappearance of the native nobility did not take place until the 19th century when independence abolished the legal privileges of the Indian caciques. (Chávez Orozco, 1943, pp. 14–15; Gibson, 1960.)

A second process was connected with the economic aspect of officeholding. As seen before, the tribute surplus and the public lands (or cattle) of the towns and of religious brotherhoods provided in early colonial times a substantial amount of the wealth consumed by the ceremonial organization. The loss of this income increased the importance of the individual sponsorship of public functions. This is how the term *mayordomo,* originally designating a steward or manager of communal holdings, became the usual title of the individual who sponsored with his own wealth a religious festival. Thus today participation in the higher ranks of the civil and ceremonial organization involves a number of expenditures. The operation of the ladder means that all men share in turn the financing of the town's government and ceremonials, and a man's expediture of wealth enhances his social status. No studies of Indian brotherhoods (cofradías) in the colonial period have been made, but the guild organization of the Spanish population in Mexico suggests that cofradía organization was a major source of modern ladder systems (Carrera Stampa, 1954, pp. 64–72, 84–85, 96–97).

The data from our area are poorer on the political and ceremonial organization than on other aspects of culture such as technology or religion. It is difficult to ascertain the relative strength of the ladder type of organization in the various regions. A ladder organization combining traditional ceremonial offices with the civil-legal organization has been reported from Ocotepec

597

in the municipio of Cuernavaca (Basauri, 1940c, 3: 197–98) and apparently similar organizations exist in the Sierra de Puebla in places such as Eloxochitlan (Totonac; I. Kelly, 1953, p. 179) and Atempan (Nahuatl; Nutini, personal communication). In Tlaxcala, Starr (1900, p. 31) neatly described the system in 1900: "Among the towns in Tlaxcala, and to some extent in all the Indian towns of Mexico, there are certain grades of dignity to which a man may attain and to the lower ones of which all men must attain. These grades are related to Church and civil affairs. . . ." Some villages in Tlaxcala still have a well-defined ladder system. Such are Tetlanoca, Ixcotla (Nutini, personal communication), and Tlalcuapan (Carrasco, unpublished notes). But today the most widespread situation is probably that in which the ladder system has become simplified, is losing importance, and is restricted to the ceremonial organization. Tepoztlan is perhaps representative of many other communities in that serving as mayordomo is the usual step before attaining a high civil office. However, there is no group of principales or elders in ultimate control of the political and ceremonial organizations. Important political factions exist, only a few people reach positions of power, and outside political connections are of paramount importance. (Lewis, 1960, p. 52; 1951, p. 221 ff.)

Other examples of a simple civil and ceremonial organization are those places such as Tajin where we deal only with a hamlet culture since the municipal organization has fallen into the hands of the non-Indian population.

Religion

In religious acculturation the distinction between different levels of integration is fundamental. We have on the one hand the rituals and beliefs associated with private or family events, the life cycle or technological activities; on the other hand, the public rituals of the village where, as in the political organization, the communal expressions of the village and the local branch of the national religious organization meet.

Together with the differential acculturation at the separate levels of integration, a foremost factor is the Spanish policy of forced conversion. What factors in Spanish society demanded this policy we must leave out of this discussion and take as a given condition in the acculturation situation. The technique of conversion and the initial Indian reaction to Christianity also deserve close attention but fall outside the scope of this article. Suffice it to say for our purpose that the force of the state was exercised in favor of conversion; the learning of the Christian doctrine and attendance at Christian services were obligatory, while non-Christian practices were forbidden and punished.

Both colonial documents and modern ethnography show that total conversion must have been rare. A good many aspects of Christianity were accepted not necessarily by force but because of the existing pre-Spanish pattern of incorporating new gods and cults within the existing religion, and because the attitude of the Church as the foremost defender of the Indian against the abuses of the conquerors must have made the church politically convenient and Christian doctrine attractive. But this does not mean that the native religion was brainwashed out of existence. Although there were cases of successful indoctrination of the young, and although we may assume that groups such as the Indians in urban settlements (Mexico City, Puebla, for instance) in closer contact with Spaniards and the church were more effectively Christianized, the evidence, colonial and modern, clearly shows that the native religion simply went underground, while the new state religion was outwardly accepted.

A double religious system thus came into existence, a system in which two different sets of practices and beliefs became more or less compartmentalized. On the one hand, there was a large survival of heathen rituals and associated beliefs of a private nature and basically associated with the family level of integration: *rites de passage* in the life cycle of the individual, curing practices or rituals accompanying technological activities. These were performed for the spiritual welfare of an individual or family group and by the people concerned, sometimes with the assistance of a private religious practitioner. The private or family nature of these rituals allowed the continuance of their normal performance since they were less subject to the intervention of the missionaries. On the other hand, there were public performances of the rituals of the Catholic Church: the cult of the saints in the church with the participation of the Catholic priest (never an Indian) and the Catholic sodalities established among the Indians. There was some continuation of public heathen rituals performed by officials (or native priests) of the Indian village on behalf of the community as a whole. There is evidence of the continued observance of some monthly rituals (Procesos, 1912, pp. 1 ff., 202, 200 ff.; Serna, 1892, p. 293), but the secrecy necessitated by the persecution of the native religion made it impossible for these public rituals to survive with the aboriginal form and organization.

Another important process is the syncretism of native and Christian elements, especially important in the identification of native gods and Catholic saints. Both Catholic and native supernaturals were patrons of human activities or of human groups and, although to a lesser extent in Christianity, were connected with natural elements. Their public worship took place at particular temples and on given days of the calendar; they were anthropomorphic and their cult centered about an image. On the basis of any of these points of similarity native and Christian supernaturals were identified. Sahagún thus reports the identification of the goddess Tonantzin with Our Lady of Guadalupe at Tepeyac, of St.

John the Baptist with Telpochtli Tezcatlipoca at Tianquizmanalco and of St. Ann, the mother of Mary, with Toci (Our Grandmother) at Chiauhtempan (Sahagún, 1938, 3: 299–301). In these cases the Christian saints were the objects of a widespread Catholic public cult. In other cases it is seen that the identification of gods and saints also took place in the surviving private rituals of predominantly heathen character. Thus Serna in 1656 reports how the fire god addressed in a number of family rituals was identified as an Old God (Huehueteotl) with St. Joseph or St. Simon whom the Indians had also seen represented as old men. A spell against storms, also recorded by Serna, shows how Our Lady is identified with the native earth goddess and St. James (Santiago) the warlike patron of Spain with Yaotl (Warrior) or Telpochtli (Youth), names of Tezcatlipoca (Serna, 1892, pp. 281, 290). Occasionally an old identification of god and saint can still be detected in modern folklore, as in Coatepec, Guerrero, where a story is told of the infant Jesus that clearly belongs to the old patron Quetzalcoatl (Carrasco, 1945).

Another well-known case of syncretism is that of the modern cult of the dead in which the Catholic prayers for the salvation of the dead have been combined with the aboriginal beliefs in the yearly visit by the dead to their surviving relatives and the offerings and prayers to them.

The development of the dual religion and the syncretism of heathen and Christian elements in the same cults did furnish the basis for the more thorough Christianization of the Indian, through the gradual decline and even disappearance of the heathen private rituals and the growth of the Christian component in the syncretized cults. Important pagan elements are still noticeable in the modern Indian religion (Madsen, 1957), but we have only to compare the modern religion of Milpa Alta or Tepoztlan (Madsen, 1957; Zantwijk, 1960; Redfield, 1930) with that of the neighboring areas of Morelos and Guerrero (Ruiz de Alarcón, 1892) in the early 17th century to conclude that the Indians have been progressively and effectively Christianized and that the missionary policy of allowing a certain measure of syncretism was in the long run successful.

As the Catholic saints prevailed in the public cult, the heathen supernaturals surviving in the private cults lost their connection with the anthropomorphic deities represented in images in the temples, as was the case before, and became nature spirits loosely or not at all connected with the new supernaturals of the public cult. The winds (ehecatl) of modern belief, for instance, are different from the saints of the church rituals, whereas their pre-Spanish antecedents were the hosts of wind and rain gods, retainers of Ehecatl Quetzalcoatl or Tlaloc, and the mountain gods (Tepictoton) that were patrons of certain localities and were the objects of the public cult. On the other hand, as the Catholic cult and sodalities were accepted, the new public cult replaced the old in its different social implications, it supplied the new rites of intensification of the Indian groups, and the sponsorship of Catholic religious functions became part of the economic and political system of the Indian communities. Although the connection with the official church was kept, the local cult and its organization can be said to have been taken over by the Indian, and a distinction has arisen between the church and the local view of Catholic cult and belief.

As a result of these processes, all modern folk religions in Mesoamerica can be analyzed in terms of the extent to which there exists a dichotomy of private versus public rituals as defined above, which may coincide to a greater or lesser degree with an additional dichotomy of heathen versus Christian rituals and beliefs. In the central Mexican highlands there are today two main types of religious configuration. In the eastern slopes of the plateau there is a high survival of native religion. There is the public cult, primarily Catholic, although marked by some elements of aboriginal character such as the *volador*. On the other hand, there is also an elaborate system of private and some public rituals performed on the occasion of life cycle events, disease, and technological activities. This system is connected with nature spirits and shrines in caves, lakes, or other natural places. This prevails, for instance, among the Tepehua (Gessain, 1938, 1953) and the Otomi of San Pablito (Christensen, 1953a). Its nearest counterparts are in the more conservative groups of Oaxaca such as the Mazatec, Mixe, and southern Zapotec or Chatino. A different configuration is that of the groups in the valleys of Mexico, Puebla, and Morelos. Here we have the same configuration that prevails in the more acculturated groups of Mexico, such as the Tarascans or Valley Zapotec; the private rituals are relatively fewer and as much Catholic as heathen in nature. The main native survivals are in the areas of curing and weather lore. (Madsen, 1957; Redfield, 1930; Barrios, 1949; Starr, 1900, pp. 18–22; Gamio, 1922, 2: 404 ff.)

The colonial evidence shows that the present-day pattern of the eastern slopes was once widespread throughout the central plateau, as seen in the abundant data on the survival of heathen private rituals into the 17th century by Ponce (1892) and Serna (1892) for the Toluca area; Villavicencio (1692) for the Puebla region; and especially Ruiz de Alarcón (1892) for the middle Balsas Basin (Morelos and northern Guerrero).

REFERENCES

Barrios, 1949
Basauri, 1940c
Carrasco, 1945, 1961a, 1963, 1966
Carrera Stampa, 1954
Chaves, 1865
Chávez Orozco, 1943
Christensen, 1953a
Códice Mariano Jiménez, 1903
Densidad, 1950
Doctrina, 1944
Durán, 1951
Fabila, 1949
Foster, 1955
Gamio, 1922
Gessain, 1938, 1953
Gibson, 1952, 1960
Gillow, 1889
Inst. Nacional Indigenista (Mexico), 1950
Kelly, I., 1953

Lewis, 1951, 1960
Madsen, 1957
Marín Tamayo, 1960
Mendizábal, 1946b
Miranda, J., 1952
Monzón, 1949
Motolinia, 1914
Nutini, 1961
Ponce, 1892
Procesos, 1912
Redfield, 1930
Ruiz de Alarcón, 1892
Sahagún, 1938
Serna, 1892
Starr, F., 1899b, 1900–02
Torquemada, 1943–44
Villavicencio, 1692
Zantwijk, 1960
Zavala and Miranda, 1954

32. The Nahua

WILLIAM MADSEN

NAHUATL-SPEAKING PEOPLES today constitute Mexico's largest indigenous group, estimated at more than one million.[1] The bulk of the Nahuatl population is concentrated in the states of San Luis Potosi, Hidalgo, Mexico, Puebla, Distrito Federal, Tlaxcala, Morelos, Guerrero, and Veracruz; smaller fringe groups are in the states of Jalisco, Michoacan, Nayarit, Oaxaca, and Tabasco (fig. 1). The largest monolingual group is in the state of Puebla (Mexico, 1944, 1953).

This report is limited to the central states of Hidalgo, Mexico, Puebla, Federal District, Tlaxcala, and Morelos. The coastal states of Veracruz and Guerrero are excluded because there is not enough information on the large Nahuatl groups here to determine their affinities with the Nahuatl culture of the central states. For the purposes of this article, the term "Nahuatl" is broadly used to designate the contemporary peoples of central Mexico who speak the ancient Aztec tongue with minor dialect differences and varying degrees of linguistic acculturation. These people are usually called "los

mexicanos" in the common speech and the literature of Mexico.[2]

The Nahuatl language may be more precisely defined as part of the Nahuatlan division of the Uto-Aztecan stock, according to the Jiménez Moreno–Mendizábal classification (Vivó, 1941, p. 41). The principal dialects are: (1) classical Nahuatl, the language of the ancient Aztec, spoken in modified form in Milpa Alta and Xochimilco, D.F.; (2) the eastern dialect spoken in the states of Puebla and Tlaxcala; (3) the southern dialect of Morelos; (4) the western dialect; and (5) the "t" dialects known as Nahuat (fig. 2) found in southern Veracruz (Whorf, 1946, p. 367).

Modern Nahuatl includes numerous

---

[1] This estimate was made by Whorf (1946, p. 367). Exact figures are not available because recent census counts of the Nahuatl-speaking population of Mexico have not included bilinguals who speak both Spanish and Nahuatl.

[2] I am indebted to Claudia Madsen for research aid and the use of her manuscript on Mexican folk medicine, and to Antonieta Espejo of Mexico's Museo Nacional de Antropología for the use of her material on Nahuatl cooking.

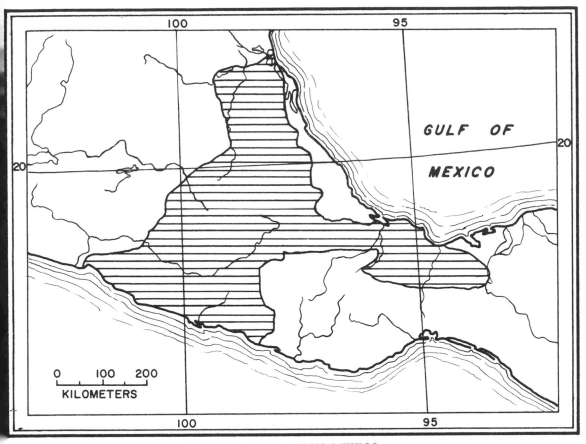

Fig. 1—DISTRIBUTION OF NAHUATL POPULATION, MEXICO.

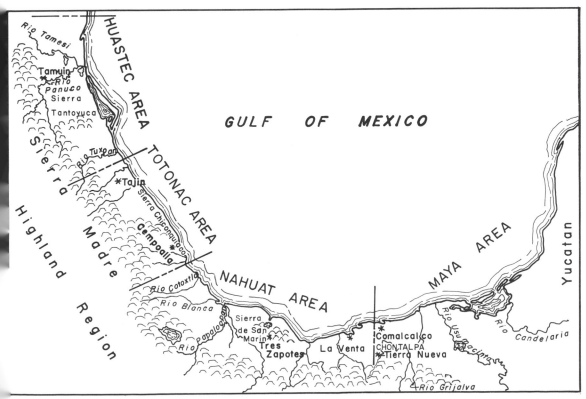

Fig. 2—LOCATION OF NAHUAT AREA ON GULF COAST PLAIN

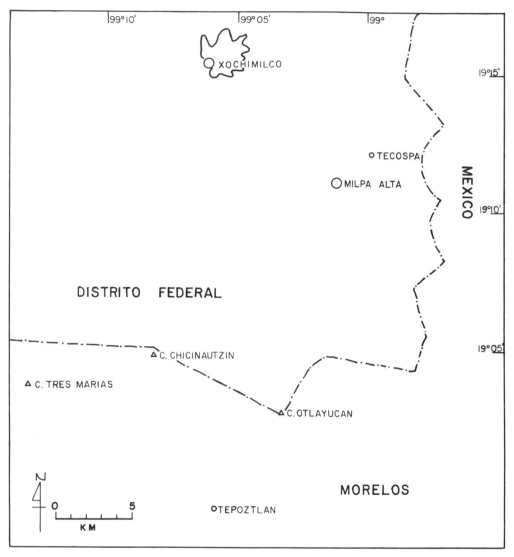

Fig. 3—MILPA ALTA–TEPOZTLAN AREA. (From Atlas Geográfico de los Estados Unidos Mexicanos.)

Spanish loan words even in the Milpa Alta area of "classical Nahuatl" speech where the Indians are completely bilingual. Whorf has observed that the Milpa Alta Indians prefer to use Spanish terms for new things and ideas instead of using the power of free coinage (1946, p. 392). Spanish words have been borrowed for European agricultural tools, crops, garments, money, measures, compadrazgo relationships, disease concepts, herb remedies, political offices,

and administrative divisions. Even native concepts are sometimes designated by Spanish or hybrid terms (Law, 1960, pp. 16–19).

The principal habitat of the Nahuatl peoples is the Mesa Central bounded by the Sierra Madre Oriental and the Sierra Madre Occidental, which come together as a triangle along the southern rim of the mesa. The northern part of the area is tropical forest country of the Sierra Madre Oriental, extending from the southeastern corner

604

of San Luis Potosi south into Hidalgo and eastward into the northwestern part of Veracruz.

The heart of the Aztec area is the Valley of Mexico, including the Federal District and parts of the states of Mexico and Hidalgo. The Valley has an elevation of nearly 8000 feet and a temperate climate. Most of the Nahuatl peoples of the Federal District and the state of Mexico are bilingual. Hidalgo has 35,085 monolinguals who speak only Nahuatl, according to the 1950 census (p. 232).

South of the Milpa Alta area, the forested Sierra de Cuauhtzin forms the boundary between the Federal District and Morelos. The Nahuatl population of this area within the delegación of Milpa Alta, D.F., and the municipio of Tepoztlan, Morelos, has been estimated at 20,000 by Zantwijk (1960, p. 5). The municipio of Tepoztlan has the highest proportion of Nahuatl peoples in the entire state of Morelos. The Nahuatl peoples of Morelos are largely bilingual (Mexico, 1944, 1953).

Puebla has 81,947 monolinguals who speak only Nahuatl—approximately one-third of the total Nahuatl population in the state. The largest Nahuatl group is in the Sierra Norte de Puebla. Another group is in the Valley of Puebla, which embraces the southern part of the state of Puebla and the state of Tlaxcala. The Nahuatl population of Tlaxcala is mostly bilingual.

Contemporary Nahuatl culture must be understood in terms of its historical development, which has been analyzed by Carrasco in Article 31. The Spanish conquest of Tenochtitlan in 1521 profoundly altered the life of the Nahuatl Indians. The greatest accomplishment of the early colonial period was the conversion of the Aztec to an Indian Catholicism characterized by the fusion of indigenous beliefs and Spanish forms. The syncretism of Aztec and Christian religions was symbolized by the miraculous appearance of the dark-skinned Virgin of Guadalupe, who spoke Nahuatl and was called Tonantzin, the appellation of the Aztec earth goddess. Native economy was changed to a lesser extent by Spanish introduction of new domesticated animals, tools, and crops. The European plow drawn by oxen or mules replaced the crude spade used by the Aztec to prepare the soil. Other new animals included chickens, sheep, goats, horses, donkeys, and cattle. Wheat and European fruit trees became important secondary crops raised in addition to native maize and frijoles, which continued to be the basic crops of Nahuatl economy.

HISTORY OF ETHNOLOGICAL INVESTIGATION

Ethnographic investigation of contemporary Nahuatl peoples (fig. 4) has been meager in comparison with research on other Indian groups of Mexico. Starr's pioneer work on the ethnography of southern Mexico at the end of the 19th century contained brief descriptions of Nahuatl customs (1900, pp. 17–33). The first intensive research was Gamio's three-volume study (1922) of the people of the Valley of Teotihuacan, which constitutes a basic source of Nahuatl ethnography.

In 1930 Redfield's study of Tepoztlan presented his initial thesis on folk culture and became a classic concept for anthropological research and theoretical discussion. Folk culture is distinguished from urban culture by the relative social isolation and homogeneity of the folk community, whose members share common traditions and attitudes. Redfield emphasized the cooperative nature of Tepoztecan folk culture, which measured the individual by his contribution to the collective activities of the community.

Seventeen years later, Lewis restudied Tepoztlan and presented (1951) new data with much greater emphasis on economic analysis. His techniques of investigation were vastly different from the informal approach used by Redfield. A team of fieldworkers directed by Lewis administered batteries of psychological tests, question-

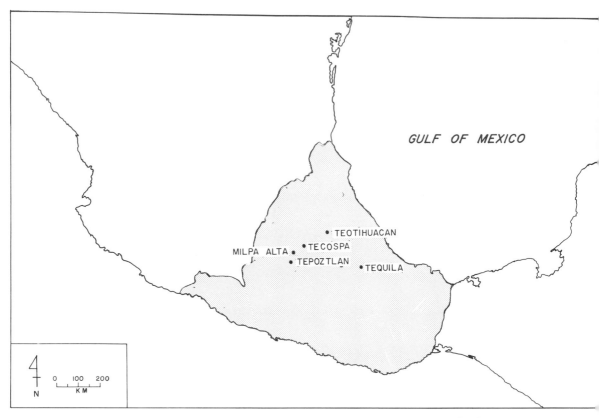

GULF OF MEXICO

• TEOTIHUACAN
• TECOSPA
MILPA ALTA •
• TEPOZTLAN
• TEQUILA

0   100   200
K M
N

Fɪɢ. 4—NAHUATL AREA, SHOWING SITES OF ETHNOGRAPHIC FIELDWORK

naires, surveys, and generally utilized quantitative procedures wherever possible. Student assistants lived with local families and recorded all the intimate details of their private lives. The different emphases and techniques of the two anthropologists produced different results. Lewis corrected Redfield's error in assuming that the terms *tonto* and *correcto* designated two social groups. Perhaps Lewis' major contribution is his illuminating portrayal of the social strife that accompanies modern acculturation in a Nahuatl community. The folk culture portrayed by Redfield has come into direct conflict with western innovations, which are gaining acceptance among the younger generation. Friction has resulted over such issues as Protestantism, women's rights, modern dress, and decreasing respect for the aged.

In 1960 two ethnographic studies were

published on Nahuatl communities in the Milpa Alta area (figs. 3, 4) which has retained a high degree of social isolation from the modern urban culture of Mexico City. Zantwijk's *Los Indígenas de Milpa Alta* deals almost exclusively with Aztec survivals reported by educated informants who were apparently familiar with Aztec history. *The Virgin's Children* by Madsen is an ethnography of San Francisco Tecospa, a small pueblo near Milpa Alta, and focuses on the syncretism of Aztec and Spanish traditions in Nahuatl culture.

A number of supplementary sources have been used in tracing the distribution of the general patterns of Nahuatl culture as well as local differences. Of these sources the most valuable have been the brief ethnographic sketches contained in the medical reports of Mexican doctors who worked in Nahuatl pueblos in the states of Hidalgo,

606

TABLE 1—SECONDARY CROPS LISTED BY MUNICIPIOS

CROP	VALLEY OF MEXICO	NORTHERN MORELOS	CENTRAL AND SOUTHERN MORELOS	NORTHERN PUEBLA	SOUTHERN PUEBLA
Wheat	Milpa Alta Teotihuacan	...	Xochitepec	Tlatlauqui	San Juan Mihuatlan Tlacotepec Coyomeapam
Barley	Milpa Alta Teotihuacan Xalatlaco	...	...	Tlatlauqui	Coyomeapam
Potatoes	Milpa Alta Teotihuacan Xalatlaco	...	...	Teziutlan Tlatlauqui	...
Habas	Milpa Alta Teotihuacan Xalatlaco	...	...	...	Coyomeapam
Alfalfa	...	...	...	Teziutlan	Tlacotepec
Onions	...	...	Xochitepec Tlaquiltenango E. Zapata	...	Zinacatepec
Garlic	...	...	Xochitepec	...	San Gabriel Chilac
Peas	Xalatlaco	...	Xochitepec	...	Coyomeapam
Capulin	Milpa Alta Xalatlaco	...	...	Teziutlan	Coyomeapam
Zapote	Milpa Alta	...	E. Zapata Xochitepec	Tlatlauqui	Zinacatepec San Gabriel Chilac
Plum	...	Tepoztlan Tlayacapan	E. Zapata Xochitepec	Tlatlauqui Teziutlan	...
Chirimoya	...	Tlayacapan	...	Tlatlauqui	San Gabriel Chilac
Banana	...	Tlayacapan Tepoztlan	Xochitepec	Tlatlauqui Hueytamalco	San Gabriel Chilac
Avocado	...	Tepoztlan	...	Teziutlan	Coyomeapam
Watermelon ...	...	Tlayacapan	Xochitepec Tlaquiltenango	...	San Gabriel Chilac

Mexico, Puebla, and Morelos. The medical school of the University of Mexico published a few copies of each of these reports between 1940 and 1951. Basauri's monograph (1940c) on the village of Ocotepec, Morelos, provides an interesting comparison with the Tepoztlan materials of Redfield and Lewis.

Fabila's book on the Sierra Norte de Puebla (1949) and the Cordrys' article on the Cuetzalan region of Puebla (1940) give us a glimpse of the economy, costumes, textiles, and dances of northern Puebla. A program of ethnographic research and community development is now being carried out by the Instituto Indigenista Interamericano in the community of Zacapoaxtla under the direction of Miguel León-Portilla, but the results have not yet been published.

Soustelle's excellent ethnography entitled *Tequila: un village nahuatl du Mexique oriental* (1958) concerns a village in central Veracruz. Unfortunately, comparable studies in northern and southern Veracruz are lacking. Ethnographic research is needed in the states of San Luis Potosi, Hidalgo, Tlaxcala, Puebla, Guerrero, and Veracruz.

SUBSISTENCE SYSTEMS AND FOOD PATTERNS

Maize, frijoles, and chile are basic subsistence crops throughout the area; tomatoes and squash are widely grown. Maguey, the Mexican century plant which yields pulque, is a major crop in the Valley of Mexico. Sugarcane, rice, and coffee are primary crops in central and southern Morelos and in the Sierra Madre Oriental regions of southeastern San Luis Potosi, northern Hi-

607

FIG. 5—SUBSISTENCE FEATURES AND ACTIVITIES. *a*, Corncrib. *b*, Shelling corn on an *olatera*. *c*, Shelling churc corn. *d*, Harvesting tunas. (From Madsen, 1960. Courtesy, University of Texas Press.)

dalgo, and northern Puebla. Secondary crops grown by farmers in various municipios are listed in Table 1.

The wooden plow of European origin is generally used to cultivate level land. The hoe and the coa (Aztec digging stick) are used in conjunction with the plow on level fields but alone on hillside fields.

In the Valley of Teotihuacan three plowings precede the planting of maize milpas. At the beginning of the rainy season, maize is planted by dropping three or four grains in a small hole made with a hoe. During the growing season, fields are plowed twice to dig up weeds and form dirt ridges on either side of the row of corn. When the corn plant is full grown, it is hilled to brace it against the wind (Gamio, 1922, 2: 454–55).

In Tecospa four men work together to plant one milpa in the level crop land around the village. Two men plant maize, a third frijoles, and a fourth squash or habas. The four men who cooperate are usually related by blood or compadrazgo ties. Occasionally neighbors exchange labor at planting or harvesting time. Well-to-do families may hire peons to help them plant their fields. The compulsory system of collective labor is used only on the fields devoted to the support of the church. The seeds are planted in holes made with an iron-tipped coa. During the growing season the ground is turned twice with a plow and a third time with a hoe. The plow is pulled by mules or horses in Tecospa and by oxen in Tepoztlan (Madsen, 1960, pp. 38–39, 44).

In Ocotlan, Morelos, three or four families commonly work together on the milpa of each participating family at planting and harvest time. Labor exchange between relatives is practiced in Tepoztecan agriculture (Lewis, 1951, p. 141; Basauri, 1940c, p. 197).

The slash-and-burn system of agriculture is widely followed on mountain milpas that are too steep for plowing. In the Milpa Alta–Tepoztlan area the forested mountain land is cleared in January and the underbrush is burned later after it has dried out. The ashes are turned under the soil for fertilizer. Because of erosion, the mountain soil is poor and is quickly exhausted by maize when planted annually in the same field. Tecospa mountain milpas are planted with maize one year and frijoles the next year. Potatoes, habas, wheat, and barley are also sown in the poor mountain soil. The hoe and the coa arc thc most common tools for digging holes to plant mountain milpas. During the growing season weeds are cut down with a machete or pulled out by hand (Lewis, 1951, pp. 150–53; Madsen, 1960, pp. 41, 44; Fabila, 1949, pp. 40–43).

After the harvest, green ears of maize (elotes) are put in corncribs to dry (fig. 5,a). The dried ear of corn is shelled by rubbing it over an olotera, which consists of dried corncobs (olotes) bound together by wire or an iron strip (fig. 5,b). The dry maize kernels fall onto a petate. Corn kept for family use is generally wrapped in a petate and stored in attics in Tecospa (Madsen, 1960, p. 44; Lewis, 1951, p. 142).

Maguey is grown in Mexico, Hidalgo, Federal District, Tlaxcala, and Puebla. When the maguey plant is ready to be milked its stalk is cut off with a tranchete (a large, curved knife). The farmer inserts the acocote (a long, hollow gourd) in the center of the maguey, sucks out the juice (fig. 6,a), and spits it into an earthenware container. After each milking he scrapes the cavity inside the plant with a castrador (a flat, metal scraper). The juice is mixed with three or four liters of strong pulque to induce fermentation. The fermented pulque is stored in goatskins and sheepskins (Gamio, 1922, 2: 456; Madsen, 1960, p. 35; Franco Martínez, 1951, p. 14).

Families raise chickens and turkeys throughout the area. Pigs (fig. 6,b) and goats are also common. Draft animals include horses, mules, burros, and oxen. Cat-

a

b

Fig. 6—SUBSISTENCE ACTIVITIES. *a*, Sucking *aguamiel* from maguey plant. *b*, Butchering a pig. (From Madse 1960. Courtesy, University of Texas Press.)

tle and sheep raising is limited. Wild animals are hunted but their meat is not a basic item of subsistence.

Tortillas, frijoles, and chile are universal elements of diet and generally eaten at every meal. The use of meat varies according to locality and family means. In extremely poor farming areas, such as the municipio of Amozoc de Mota in northern Puebla, meat is eaten only at fiestas; ordinary meals consist of tortillas, chile, frijoles, and pulque with the addition of a pasta soup as a main dish once or twice a week (Becerra Cobos, 1944, p. 59). Elsewhere stews or soups with small amounts of meat may be eaten daily or weekly. Pulque is the characteristic drink accompanying meals in the Valley of Mexico and parts of Puebla. A beverage called *lapo* made of pulque, fermented sugarcane juice, and water is the regional drink of southeastern Puebla. Aguardiente, made by distilling sugarcane juice, is consumed in huge quan-

tities in the areas where sugarcane is grown. *Agua loca,* a beverage consisting of aguardiente mixed with chile and onions, is the regional drink of the Xochitepec area in Morelos. Tequila and mescal are widely consumed. Nonalcoholic beverages include coffee, hot chocolate, herb teas, and soft drinks (Chávez Torres, 1947, p. 27; Franco Martínez, 1951, p. 14; Madsen, 1960, p. 35; González Tenorio, 1941, p. 51).

Three meals a day are customary but in some regions only two. Breakfast of tortillas and chile with or without frijoles is taken at daybreak before the men leave for the fields. At noon the men in the fields eat tacos filled with frijoles, leftover meat, or just sprinkled with salt. At home their families may eat tortillas, soup, or nothing at noon. Dinner is usually served late in the afternoon after the men return from the fields. Four or five hours later a small supper may consist of atole (maize gruel) or tortillas and frijoles.

610

Fiesta dishes include mole de guajolote, mole adobo, mole verde, romeritos, tamales, and enchiladas. Mole de guajolote is an expensive and elaborate dish reserved primarily for the annual village fiesta honoring the patron saint. The sauce is made with three kinds of dark chiles (ancho, mulato, and chilpotle), tortillas, peanuts, almonds, raisins, cinnamon-flavored chocolate, and sesame. It may be served with turkey or chicken.

Mole adobo and mole verde are eaten at family fiestas celebrating birthdays, baptisms, or confirmations in the Milpa Alta area. Mole adobo is made with red chiles which are boiled, skinned, ground on the molcajete, and then fried with salt and sugar. The sweet sauce is poured over sliced pork, chicken, beef, or tongue and topped with slices of raw onion. Mole verde is made with pumpkin-seed paste, green chiles, green onions, green tomatoes, garlic, coriander, and broth from the chicken, turkey, or pork. Mole verde and tamales are traditionally served to dead relatives on the Days of the Dead, November 1 and 2.

On the day of the village fiesta, enchiladas are made by filling hot tortillas with mole de guajolote and adding cheese and chopped onion. This kind of enchilada also is purchased by the Nahuatl Indians when they go to market to sell their produce or wares. Enchiladas verdes are made with a sauce of chile verde, green onion, green tomato, garlic, and coriander.

Settlement Patterns

The characteristic feature of Nahuatl settlement patterns is the location of a church in the center of town with streets leading in four directions from the church to the surrounding homes. In the cabecera, the church is situated in a central plaza which serves as a marketplace. The plaza is the social, economic, and religious center of the town. Surrounding the plaza are separate barrios, each of which has its own chapel and patron saint. The Spanish barrio sys-

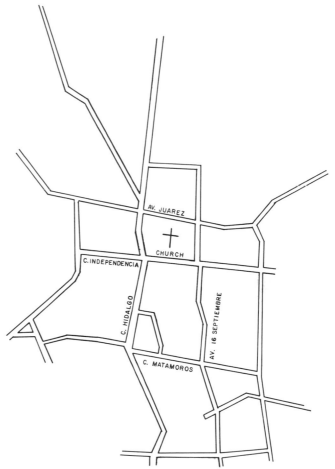

Fig. 7—PLAN OF SAN FRANCISCO TECOSPA, MILPA ALTA, D.F.

tem is absent in pueblitos such as San Francisco Tecospa, which is divided into four quarters surrounding a central church (fig. 7). Each of the four quarters bears a Nahuatl name and recruits its residents for compulsory collective labor on the village land dedicated to the support of the church. Each quarter also erects an outdoor altar in its section of town at the annual pueblo fiesta. These functions of the four quarters suggest that they may be vestiges of the Aztec calpulli system. The town of Milpa Alta has four large barrios grouped around the central church and plaza. Zantwijk describes this arrangement as "the traditional

611

FIG. 8—JACALES AND CIRCULAR GRANARY, MORELOS. (From Wolf, 1959. Courtesy, University of Chicago Press.)

Aztec pattern of four large calpullis grouped around the principal temple and the market" (1960, p. 26). South of the four large barrios in Milpa Alta are two small ones. Tepoztlan is divided into seven barrios, each of which reserves certain milpas for the exclusive support of its chapel. These milpas are worked collectively by the men of the barrio under the direction of the mayordomo for the barrio santo (Redfield, 1930, pp. 75–76). The barrio chapel and its milpas worked by the compulsory system of collective labor for the support of the chapel are reminiscent of the native calpulli.

In the municipio of San Bernardino Contla in Tlaxcala, the barrio is reported to be an exogamous kinship unit whose members may not marry within their own barrio. Nutini believes that the Contla barrios are not territorial divisions but his evidence is inconclusive (1961, pp. 71–73).

In the southern part of the Valley of Mexico and some other areas the family

household is characteristically enclosed by a low wall of stone, maguey plants, or stakes (fig. 8). The most common house is a one-room rectangular dwelling that serves as kitchen, dining room, bedroom, and living room. In addition to living quarters, the family household includes one or more outbuildings—a temascal, cooking shed, corncrib, storehouse, granary (fig. 8), fowlhouse, and a roof shelter for work animals—the number varying according to region and family means. The household also may have a vegetable and flower garden, a patio, and a corral.

Intervillage relationships operate mainly within the framework of the municipio. The municipio is an administrative area embracing a small number (usually less than a dozen) of neighboring pueblos which often have had close ties since pre-Hispanic times. Each municipio has an administrative seat called the *cabecera*, which is commonly the largest town in the district.

The cabecera serves as a market center, a religious center, and a center of judicial proceedings for the dependent pueblitos in the municipio. In the Federal District the *delegación* is the equivalent of the municipio. The various pueblos within the municipio have close social, religious, and economic ties. They trade with each other, attend each other's fiestas, form compadrazgo relationships, and share jurisdiction over the communal lands jointly owned by all the villages in the municipio. The pueblitos share a strong dependence on the cabecera, where their baptisms, weddings, confessions, communions, marketing, criminal hearings, and imprisonment take place.

TECHNOLOGY

Tools

Agricultural tools used by most Nahuatl peoples are the wooden plow drawn by animals, the coa, hoe, machete, and axe. Specialized tools for maguey culture and pulque production are the tranchete (a large curved knife), the acocote (a long, hollow gourd), and the castrador (a flat metal scraper).

Aztec cooking implements are still in use throughout the Nahuatl area, the most characteristic being the metate and meclapil (grinding stone and roller), the molcajete and tejolote (mortar and pestle), comal (clay griddle), olla (earthenware vessel), and tlequil (stone hearth).

The metate and mano grind nixtamal (the cooked maize kernels flavored with lime) into a paste called masa. This is patted into tortillas, which are cooked on the comal over the tlequil. Grinding mills called "molinos de nixtamal" now produce masa in many communities. The molcajete and tejolote pound and mash chile and spices for sauces.

Spinning and weaving tools are the malacate (a spindle whorl), the native belt loom, the Spanish upright loom, and the spinning wheel.

Crafts

Weaving is the outstanding craft of the Nahuatl peoples. Some of the finest serapes in Mexico are woven in the Nahuatl villages of San Miguel Chiconcuac near Texcoco in Mexico and Santa Ana Chiautempan in Tlaxcala. These heavy wool blankets worn by men are woven on the Spanish upright loom, and the weavers are usually men who devote full time to their craft. The municipio of San Bernardino Contla, 4 miles from Santa Ana Chiautempan, is well known in Tlaxcala and Puebla for its serapes, cotones (sleeveless jackets), fajas, and rugs.

Puebla is also famous for its beautiful weaving done primarily by women on the Aztec belt loom. Puebla women weave at home more for family use than for commercial purposes. Among their best garments are the huipil (a square-cut blouse), the chincuete (an ankle-length skirt overlapped into pleats that are tied in place with a sash), the quechquemitl (a short, triangular cape), the rebozo (a stole), and the faja (a sash).

In the municipio of Cuetzalan, Puebla, women weavers often use thread that is handspun and colored with dyes derived from natural sources. When spinning is in process a wooden spindle is twirled in a small clay whorl. The women weave in a sitting position and fasten the warp to a post. The lace-weave quexquemitl is woven of commercial wool yarn on the belt loom by a complicated technique. The warp threads are mounted in 14 groups of five threads each; the weft is a continuous thread wound on a slender stick which serves as a shuttle. The loom carries three shed rods and four heddle rods (Cordry and Cordry, 1940, pp. 36–42).

The fajas woven in the Milpa Alta area are known throughout the Valley of Mexico. They are made by women with wool or cotton thread woven in geometrc patterns on the Aztec belt loom. The weaver sits

613

FIG. 9—WEAVING A FAJA ON A NATIVE BELT LOOM.
(From Madsen, 1960. Courtesy, University of Texas Press.)

back on her heels with one end of the loom tied around her waist and the other end tied to a door post or a tree (fig. 9).

In the Valley of Teotihuacan rebozos and fajas are woven in the town of San Juan Teotihuacan, which has a considerable Mestizo element although the surrounding villages are Nahuatl. The weavers in this town are specialists who have no other occupation. They purchase yarn in Mexico City, dye it, separate the skeins with the malacate, roll up the skeins on a warper, and weave the cloth on an upright loom equipped with foot peddles (Gamio, 1922, 2: 277–81).

Ayates (carrying cloths) and costales (gunny sacks) of ixtle (maguey fiber) are woven at Santa Ana Tlacotenco and San Lorenzo Tlacoyuca in the Milpa Alta area. Maguey fiber rope is manufactured in Tepoztlan and Toluca. In Puebla the Nahuatl

people of San Juan Atzingo are specialists in making maguey fiber rope and costales which are known for their quality and durability. These maguey products are made with only two tools: a malacate and spindle (Franco Martínez, 1951, p. 14).

The barrio of San Sebastian in Tepoztlan specializes in making ixtle rope. This craft is practiced by 10 families who gather the ixtle from maguey plants on the communal mountain lands or buy it. The maguey plant is beaten with a special tool which breaks up the plant so the fiber can be extracted. The fiber is soaked overnight, spun on a simple device, and then twisted into rope on a framework of stakes, according to Lewis (1951, pp. 167–68).

Petates of tule or palm are woven by hand in many parts of the Nahuatl area. Tule petates are made at Acuitapilco in the state of Tlaxcala and at Xochimilco in the Federal District. Some of the best palm petates in Mexico are made in the Nahuatl villages of Puebla.

Pottery-making centers in the Nahuatl area include: Texcoco, San Sebastian, and Chalco in Mexico; Huejutla in northwestern Hidalgo; San Francisco Altepexi, Huejotzingo, Zacatlan, and San Martin Texmelucan in Puebla. Foster states that some of the most graceful of all Mexican pottery is made in Huejutla. The most common forms are water jars with narrow concave bases, high shoulders, wide mouths, and thin walls. Altepexi produces cooking pots, casseroles, and molcajetes. San Sebastian in the Valley of Teotihuacan produces domestic pottery and fake antiquities for tourists (Foster, 1955, pp. 12–21; Gamio, 1922, 2: 277).

The process of manufacturing adobe bricks in San Sebastian in the Valley of Teotihuacan is a common one. The clay is mixed with dung and placed in wood molds until it dries. The bricks are then baked for several hours in a large, brick oven (Gamio, 1922, 2: 277).

a

b

c

Fig. 10—HOUSES. *a*, Stone houses with shingle and tile roofs, Tecospa. (From Madsen, 1960. Courtesy, University of Texas Press.) *b*, Jacal, Tepoztlan. *c*, Adobe house and separate kitchen, Tepoztlan. (From Lewis, 1951. Courtesy, University of Illinois Press.)

Lewis' description of Tepoztlan charcoal-making applies to the entire Tepoztlan–Milpa Alta area (1951, pp. 163–64):

The tools used in charcoal production are an ax, a shovel, a pick ax, and a machete. Charcoal workers generally leave the village for the mountains in the early morning, going alone or in groups of two or three friends or relatives. . . . To make charcoal, oak and sometimes pine trees are felled, cut up into logs a few feet long, and piled upright to form a charcoal oven or kiln. The kiln is then covered with earth on all sides, except for a small opening which is left for a draft of air to enter, so that the fire can be kept smouldering. The kiln is lighted and allowed to smoulder for anywhere from 24 to 48 hours, depending on the size of the wood pile. The worker must continuously be on the watch to prevent too much air from fanning the fire and thus burning the wood rather than producing charcoal. So it is necessary for the charcoal burner to sleep out in the forest for one, two, or three nights.

615

Fig. 11—A SHEPHERD'S HUT. (From Madsen, 1960. Courtesy, University of Texas Press.)

Houses

The most common house is a rectangular, one-room dwelling with a gabled roof covered with zacate, palm leaves, maguey leaves, shingles, or sometimes tiles (fig. 10,*a*). The flimsy Indian *jacal* makes up more than one-third of all the dwellings on the Mesa Central, according to a 1939 census (Whetten, 1948, p. 287). The jacal is usually constructed of canes with a thatched roof (fig. 10,*b*). The more substantial house is constructed of wood, adobe, or stone.

The jacal is made with a framework of otate (*Bacbusa arandinacea*), commonly known as Mexican bamboo, in the municipio of Jaltocan, Hidalgo. Gaps between the

canes are filled with a mixture of mud and dried grass. Floors are made of dirt, and roofs of woven straw. Beams near the roof provide storage space for maize, piloncillo (sugar), and other food. The "attics" are often converted into nests by rats, bats, and poisonous snakes. In the municipios of Tepoztlan and Xochitepec in Morelos, the jacal is similarly constructed of otate canes or cornstalks with a gabled roof of straw (Romero Alvárez, 1952, p. 19; Lewis, 1951, pp. 178–79; Cepeda de la Garza, 1944, p. 10).

In the Valley of Teotihuacan the jacal is made of maguey leaves attached to a pole framework (Gamio, 1922, 2: 585). In the municipio of Tlacotepec, Puebla, the jacal

Fig. 12—HEARTH AND COOKING UTENSILS, TEPOZTLAN. (From Redfield, 1930. Courtesy, University of Chicago Press.)

is constructed of maguey with a thatched-palm roof. The windows are triangular gaps left between the walls and the roof. Six to eight persons sleep on the dirt floor, where petates serve as beds and serapes are used for cover (Aladro Azueta, 1944, p. 33). In the municipio of Hueytamalco, Puebla, the jacal is made of tarros, a kind of bamboo, with a gabled or conical roof of palm or zacate. Windows are unnecessary since there are so many gaps in the walls. There is no furniture other than petates for sleeping (Cantellano Alvarado, 1949, p. 34). In the municipios of San Gabriel Chilac, San Jose Mihuatlan, San Sebastian Zinacatepec, and Tezuitlan in Puebla the jacal is made of canes with a roof of palm fronds or zacate de caña (García Pérez, 1943, p. 31; Areizaga Millan, 1945; Carrillo González, 1950, p. 29; Franco Martínez, 1951, p. 15; Castillo Sánchez, 1944, p. 33).

The second house type, built of wood, adobe, or stone, predominates in the southern part of the Valley of Mexico and parts of Tlaxcala, Puebla, and northern Morelos but it is often found in the same localities with the jacal. In the municipio of Tianguistengo, Hidalgo, houses are constructed of wood or adobe with straw roofs (Bonilla R., 1948, p. 2; González Tenorio, 1941, p. 35). Beds consist of a few boards or sacks laid together on a dirt floor. In the municipio of Acaxochitlan, Hidalgo, houses are made of wood with shingle roofs. This house type also is common in the municipio of Xalatlaco, Mexico (Gutiérrez García, 1946, p. 11; Vara Gómez, 1948, p. 26). The one-room adobe house with a flat roof of adobe or straw is found throughout the state of Mexico. In the municipio of Chiconcuac, Mexico, some houses are furnished with dining tables, crude chairs, sleeping petates, and radios. Separate cooking sheds and corrals are common (Velasco Ramos, 1950; Vás-

617

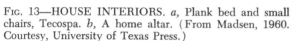

FIG. 13—HOUSE INTERIORS. *a,* Plank bed and small chairs, Tecospa. *b,* A home altar. (From Madsen, 1960. Courtesy, University of Texas Press.)

b

quez Ramírez, 1946, p. 10). In the Milpa Alta area of the Federal District rubble masonry predominates. Separate cooking sheds and storehouses for maize are common. Similar three-part houses are characteristic of Tlaxcala. In the municipio of Xochitlan Romero Rubio in northern Puebla houses are constructed of wood or stones with straw roofs. Adobe houses with straw roofs are typical in Tlatlauqui, Puebla (Arriaga Cervantes, 1944, p. 39; Castellanos Fernández, 1950, p. 21). The adobe house predominates in the towns of Xochitepec, Ocotepec, and Tepoztlan in Morelos. Zacate roofs are used in Xochitepec; tile roofs are typical in Tepoztlan. A separate cooking shed is common in Ocotepec and Tepoztlan (Lewis, 1951, pp. 178–80; Basauri, 1940c, p. 167; Barrera González, 1949, p. 31; Chávez Torres, 1947, p. 26).

Utilitarian furniture is usually limited to cooking utensils (fig. 12), pottery, and

sleeping petates. Families who can afford more furniture (fig. 13,*a*) may have tables, chairs, plank beds, and sewing machines. In every home there is a family altar (fig. 13,*b*) with images and pictures of the santos hung on the wall above a table covered with a cloth and decorated with flowers, candles, and incense burners. The radio is a rapidly increasing item of furniture in the Valley of Mexico. In areas where there is no electricity, candles or gas lamps provide light at night.

The temascal (fig. 14) is widely used and mainly dome-shaped and rectangular. Stones or adobe bricks are the most common building materials. The fireplace usually projects out from the main temascal. A wood fire heats its walls and a pile of stones between the bathing room and the fireplace. When these stones are red hot, they are drenched with cold water to produce large quantities of vapor that

FIG. 14—SWEAT BATHS (TEMASCALES). *a,* Rectangular adobe temascal, Tepoztlan. (From Redfield, 1930. Courtesy, University of Chicago Press.) *b,* Domed stone temascal, Tecosp (From Madsen, 1960. Courtesy, University of Texas Press.)

a

b

FIG. 15—CLOTHING WORN IN CUEZTLAN, PUE-BLA. (From Cordry and Cordry, 1940. Courtesy, Southwest Museum.)

causes the bathers to sweat profusely. Sweat baths are recommended to hasten recovery from childbirth and serious illnesses.

Storage facilities for maize include the corncrib (*cincolote*), a square structure made of poles and used for drying ears of corn (fig. 5,*a*); the circular or vasiform granary (*cuezcomate*) made of clay and covered with a thatched roof used for the storage of shelled corn (fig. 8); the storehouse which contains an indoor corncrib and beams near the roof for the storage of shelled corn wrapped in petates; and similar beam storage space in the family living quarters.

Dress and Adornment

Distinctive Nahuatl clothing woven by hand today is found mainly in Puebla. Throughout this state women wear the native chincuete, a rectangular shaped skirt of dark wool which is gathered in pleats around the waist when it is put on

and tied in place with a bright-colored faja hand-loomed of wool or cotton. With the ankle-length skirt is worn a white blouse (huipil) with a low square neck bordered by a wide band of black or colored embroidery. A white cotton quexquemitl with colored border designs is worn over the blouse in Cuetzalan, Puebla (fig. 15); other regions of the state weave the quexquemitl in different styles. Navy blue rebozos are used in the regions of Teziutlan and Zacapoaxtla, where women wear their hair in two braids tied together in a loop in back with bright-colored yarns. In Cuetzalan women wear their hair piled high on top of the head and cover it with a large white cloth. In all parts of the state women go barefoot.

Cuetzalan men are distinguished by a bowl-shaped haircut with deep bangs in front and a heavy ridge in back. They wear thong sandals, a large faja with elaborately embroidered fringes, and a brown wool overgarment resembling a T-shirt with open sides, in addition to the white muslin calzones, white shirts, and straw sombreros worn throughout Mexico.

In the Valley of Mexico, Morelos, and elsewhere Nahuatl men now wear readymade trousers, shirts, belts, and even felt hats instead of sombreros but they still wear leather sandals, a symbol of Indian culture as opposed to Mestizo shoe culture. Women wear long skirts made of darkcolored yardage purchased in the market and light-colored cotton blouses made of commercial cloth. Aprons commonly are worn over the skirts. The faja and darkcolored rebozo complete the costume. Most women go barefoot. The most common hair style is braids woven with bright strands of yarn. Gold earrings are popular adornments. The chincuete and quexquemitl are still worn in parts of the states of San Luis Potosi and Mexico.

Transportation

Burros, mules, horses, oxen, buses, and

human backs are the means of transportation (fig. 16,a). The Aztec *mecapal* (forehead tumpline) supports burdens carried in a maguey-fiber bag (fig. 16,b) or a crate (*huacal*). Going to market by bus is becoming increasingly popular, especially in the vicinity of Mexico City.

ECONOMY

Division of Labor

The division of labor follows a fairly standard pattern. Men work in the fields, shell corn, sell crops, hew wood, make charcoal, hunt, care for the work animals, build and repair houses. Women prepare meals, clean house, wash clothes, take care of the children, sew and weave, raise fowl and pigs, cultivate the household garden, buy and sell in the market, chop up firewood, gather herbs, and help their husbands in the fields at planting or harvest time if they are needed. In the Milpa Alta area women do not work in the fields if the family can afford to hire a peon; in Tepoztlan wives do not work in the milpas under any circumstances. In the state of Puebla a wife regularly helps her husband plant, harvest, transport, and sell his crops (Arriaga Cervantes, 1944, pp. 24–25; Lewis, 1951, p. 98).

Specialization

Nearly every village has one or more specialists in midwifery, curing, and witchcraft. Some villages have marriage matchmakers, weavers, ceramicists, candlemakers, brickmakers, butchers, ropemakers, carpenters, masons, and woodcarvers. Weavers are full-time specialists in parts of Tlaxcala. The acculturated town of Tepoztlan has an unusual number of trained druggists, silverworkers, millers, teachers, plumbers, barbers, and bakers (Lewis, 1951, pp. 102–03).

Land Tenure

The three main types of landholdings are: (1) communal lands jointly owned by all the pueblos in a municipio; (2) ejido land

a

b

FIG. 16—TRANSPORTATION. *a*, Transporting firewood by burro. *b*, Young pulque vendors; the boy at the right carries a maguey-fiber bag with tumpline. (From Madsen, 1960. Courtesy, University of Texas Press.)

621

nominally owned by the pueblo but actually distributed to local families by officials working under the jurisdiction of the federal government; (3) private property, which includes land devoted exclusively to the support of the church.

Communal lands owned by the municipio may be cultivated by any resident of the villages in the municipio. The land used by each village has clearly recognized boundaries, within which the villager may plant any piece not in use. In the Milpa Alta–Tepoztlan region the communal forest lands are a carryover from Aztec times perpetuated by the Spanish colonial government. They are immensely important in the economy of this region. Recent attempts by some acculturated politicians to sell the Milpa Alta communal lands to a Mexico City lumber company met vigorous and united opposition from all the pueblos in the delegación of Milpa Alta. Nutini reports that communal forest lands owned by the municipio of San Bernardino Contla, Tlaxcala, comprise 40 per cent of the total area. Elsewhere in the Nahuatl area the distribution and economic importance of communal lands owned by the municipio have not been investigated (Nutini, 1961, p. 70; Lewis, 1951, pp. 113–18; Madsen, 1960, pp. 21, 40–41, 121–22).

The relative importance of private property and ejido holdings varies greatly from one region to another. The significance of the modern ejido in village economy depends on the cultivability of the land, its location, the size of individual plots, and local attitudes. In the heavily populated areas of the Mesa Central, the small size of the individual ejido plot makes it a supplementary source of subsistence. The average allotment of ejido crop land made to an individual in the Federal District is less than 1 hectare. In San Francisco Tecospa the ejido is of minor economic significance owing to the small size of the individual allotment, the inconvenient location of the ejido 2 miles from town, and prior concern

with privately owned milpas which provide the main source of subsistence.

In some areas the modern ejido has replaced private ownership of land. In the municipio of Tlacotepec, Puebla, many landowners sold their own land when they had the chance to acquire ejido holdings free of charge. The expropriation of land from nine haciendas and its redistribution in ejido allotments averaging 5 hectares per person has produced large expanses of uncultivated land formerly cultivated under the hacienda system. The average farmer in this area does not have the means to plant 5 hectares and he sees no point in planting more land than necessary to provide for his family. Consequently, a man who receives an allotment of 5 hectares may plant only 1 hectare (Aladro Azueta, 1944, p. 50).

There are no ejidos in the municipios of Teziutlan and Tlatlauqui, Puebla, since the inhabitants of these areas own their own milpas which provide enough food for their daily needs (Areizaga Millan, 1945; Arriaga Cervantes, 1944, p. 39).

Lewis reports an unusually high proportion of landless families in Tepoztlan. In 1944 he counted 384 families who neither own private land nor hold ejido grants. When Redfield studied Tepoztlan in 1926 he reported that most families had at least a small milpa. In the village of Ocotepec near Cuernavaca, Morelos, the average family owns about 3 hectares of agricultural land (Basauri, 1940c, pp. 208–09; Lewis, 1951, pp. 122–25; Redfield, 1930, p. 61).

Trade and Markets

Trade is conducted primarily in markets held on fixed days once or twice a week in the main plaza of the cabecera. Women from all the satellite pueblos in the municipio and more distant places come to the cabecera on the *día de tianguiz* (market day) to sell their produce, buy what they need for their families, visit with their friends and compadres from other villages, and enjoy the enchiladas sold in the market. Important religious fiestas are also accompanied by markets not only in the cabecera but also in the dependent pueblos which hold markets on the day of their annual village fiesta honoring the patron saint.

Each pueblo has a fixed site in the plaza of the cabecera on market day. Similar products are grouped together in a special section. The women set out their goods in attractive arrangements on petates and sit behind them to wait for customers. The first price asked by the vendor is almost always higher than the actual sale price, which is settled by friendly bargaining.

Nahuatl women frequently go to large markets outside of their own municipio. In the Milpa Alta area women sell flowers and nopales in the markets of Mexico City and Xochimilco. The Xochimilco market embraces two square blocks. The flower market is held in the central part while another block is occupied by a quadrangle of store buildings enclosing a huge patio. Visiting merchants, displaying their goods inside the patio and outside in front of the stores, offer meat, ready-made clothing and yardage, huaraches, serapes, rebozos, pottery, herbs, amulets, steaming ears of roasted corn, enchiladas, fruits, vegetables, grains, and spices. The streets surrounding the market are filled with pigs, sheep, ducks, goats, cows, turkeys, chickens, and burros for sale.

Trade is also carried out on a limited scale in the village store, which is common in the Valley of Mexico and Morelos. Six stores in Ocotepec, Morelos, sell sugar, salt, bread, candles, and cigarettes but their main business is the sale of cane alcohol, the favorite intoxicating beverage of the area. These stores are tended by women who simultaneously do their housework in back of the store since they have so few customers (Basauri, 1940c, pp. 147–48).

Itinerant merchants travel from village to village, often by foot, selling chairs, petates, machine-made clothing, serapes, maguey-fiber rope, sacks, and other wares. Corn merchants come in trucks to the pueblos in the Milpa Alta area to buy shelled maize. A milk truck comes to Tecospa daily to buy goat milk, which is sold in the neighboring villages of Tecomitl and San Juan. Weavers from Texcoco come to Tecospa to buy wool for making serapes. Tlahuac bird trappers catch songbirds in Tecospa and sell them in Mexico City. Traveling gopher trappers make a tidy profit at the rate of 2 pesos per dead gopher. Tecospans sell their pulque in the nearby towns of Tlahuac, Tulyehualco, San Juan Ixtayopan, and Mixquic.

Wealth

Private ownership of land and animals is the main criterion of wealth, but land wealth is not a primary goal of Nahuatl culture. The main use for wealth is in fulfilling the financial obligations of being a mayordomo in charge of a religious fiesta.

In the Valley of Teotihuacan the wealth of a Nahuatl Indian family is computed by the number of pigs and chickens they own. "These animals constitute the savings account of the Indian," Noriega Hope writes. "These savings coupled with the Indian spirit of cooperation and aid provide a guarantee that nobody dies of hunger in the pueblos" (1922, p. 255).

Most Nahuatl communities do not have extreme contrasts of wealth, although they usually have a few landless families and a few families referred to as "los ricos." These "rich" families have a few more hectares of land than the average and they may have a sewing machine, a radio, or better than average food, but they avoid any ostentatious display of wealth such as acquiring better houses, better furniture, or better clothes than their neighbors. Any member of the community who does display his wealth by "putting on the dog" draws the censure of his neighbors.

Lewis' statistical study of Tepoztlan shows an extremely wide range of wealth differences. The 38 wealthy families in Tepoztlan eat better food and live in better houses than average but they do not adopt urban dress or spend money on luxuries. Although they hire labor, they work in their fields side by side with their peons (Lewis, 1951, pp. 173–77).

SOCIAL ORGANIZATION

Nahuatl social organization is a highly formalized structure based on a concept of social distance designed to avoid intimacy and friction. This concept is effected through a complex series of respect relationships between wives and husbands, children and parents, younger and older generations, ahijados and padrinos, and compadres. Each of these relationships is governed by special rules of etiquette and mutual obligations.

The Nahuatl family is a stable, cohesive unit in which divorce is virtually unknown. In most families the husband is the absolute master of his home and his authority is unquestioned. He is served with care and respect by his wife and children. The mother also holds a position of honor and respect in her family. Zantwijk (1960, pp. 30–31, 73–74) mentions the following factors which contribute to the importance of the mother's position in the Milpa Alta family: (1) her central role in the home and in the upbringing of the children; (2) her participation in the economic affairs of the family to the extent of handling all the family earnings and being primarily responsible for decisions on how the money is spent; and (3) her unique position as the only object of open affection in a very formalized society.

The traditional pattern of Nahuatl family relationships has become a "social fiction" in Tepoztlan, according to Lewis, who states that: "Although in most homes there is an outward compliance to the ideal pattern, with the wife apparently submissive and serving, there are actually few homes in which the husband is the dominant figure he seeks to be or in which he truly controls his family. Most marriages show some conflict over the question of authority

and the respective roles of the spouses" (1951, p. 319).

The Nahuatl family traditionally includes unmarried children, parents, and grandparents. Although the family of parents and unmarried children constitute the basic economic unit, the grandparents are very much a part of the family social unit. In Milpa Alta it is customary for the three-generation family to live together in the same household enclosure (Zantwijk, 1960, pp. 32–36). Patrilocal residence is characteristic of the Nahuatl area. Newlyweds usually live with the husband's parents for at least a year until enough money has been saved to enable them to establish their own home nearby. In Tepoztlan the biological family consisting of parents and unmarried children constitutes the basic social and economic unit, according to Lewis (1951, p. 58).

Next to the biological family, the most important form of Nahuatl social organization is the compadrazgo system of ritual kinship. A child's first and most important godparents are the padrinos of baptism who become the compadres of his parents. The baptismal godparents have the obligation of supervising the child's training and scolding him for misbehavior. In case the child's parents die while he is young, his baptismal godparents are obligated to bring him up as their own child. Financial aid provided by the baptismal godparents includes paying for the baptismal ceremony and clothing and for the child's funeral if he dies before the age of 12. If a Tecospa child wants to go to school and his parents cannot afford to send him, his godparents will help pay for his schooling. In return, the child helps his godparents when they are sick or short of farm hands, and brings them gifts on special occasions. He must show his godparents absolute respect and never joke or gossip about them. Whenever they meet he kisses their hands.

A respect relationship is also established between the child's parents and godparents.

Compadres lend each other food, money, or labor in time of need and always treat each other with great respect. A man must never quarrel with his compadre or gossip about him. In Tecospa parents choose the couple they respect most to serve baptismal godparents. In Tepoztlan the wealth of the prospective godparents is a primary factor in this choice. Compadres from Mexico City are desirable because it is assumed that they can be of greater financial help (Lewis, 1951, p. 360; Madsen, 1960, pp. 93–103; Gamio, 1922, 2: 243; Foster, 1953a).

Confirmation and marriage godparents rank below baptismal godparents in social importance and have fewer obligations. Other compadrazgo relationships include: godparents of First Communion, godparents of Last Communion, godparent of the scapulary, godmother of a saint's picture or image, godmother of a bridge, godfather of a mule, and godmother of a soccer team (Lewis, 1951, p. 351; Madsen, 1960, p. 93).

The main unit of legal political organization throughout Mexico is the municipio with its administrative seat in the cabecera. The dependent pueblos are governed by an *ayudante municipal* or a *sub-delegado* and other locally elected officials. These officials may govern on their own initiative or merely act as agents for the local council of elders, which has no legal status. The functioning of pueblo government under a council of elders is well illustrated by Basauri's material on Ocotepec (1940c, pp. 197–99).

The legal officials of the pueblo are chosen by the council of elders before the local "election." The council is composed of men over 60 who have passed through an hierarchical system of age grades including: *campaneros* who take turns ringing the church bells; *semaneros* who take care of the churches; *mayordomos* who organize and finance the religious fiestas and supervise the campaneros and semaneros; and *el fiscal*, the supreme authority in religious matters who plans all the fiestas and supervises the services of the mayordomos, se-

maneros, and campaneros. Ocotepec has four mayordomos, one for each of its four barrios. A man must have held all the offices listed above before he can become a member of the council of elders. This council names the fiscal, mayordomos, and legal officials; supervises the compulsory labor on public works; intervenes in the direction of the school; and deals with other political and religious matters at its regular meetings.

San Francisco Tecospa also has a village council in charge of civic and religious affairs but the sub-delegado elected by the community is the real power in local government today. The village council is not a council of elders. Its members are supposed to be elected every three years at a town meeting. Those elected in 1950 resigned en masse because of "too much work" and were replaced by the sub-delegado's appointees.

The compulsory system of communal labor for constructing public works (fig. 17) and for working milpas devoted to the support of the church is widespread. All men over 18 and under 60 are required to donate labor. A man may fulfill his community labor obligations by sending a peon to take his place. In Tecospa the labor for public works is recruited by streets whereas labor for the church milpas is recruited from the four quarters of the pueblo. The compulsory system of community labor is declining in Tepoztlan, where there have been no significant public works in recent years. Communal labor on church milpas is entirely voluntary and is recruited by barrios. There has been increasing difficulty in obtaining barrio cooperation for this purpose (Lewis, 1951, pp. 108–11).

The salient feature of Nahuatl religious organization is the mayordomo system introduced throughout Mexico by Spanish priests in the 16th century. A different set of mayordomos is chosen for each village fiesta or pilgrimage honoring a santo. Mayordomos bear the financial and organi-

FIG. 17—COMMUNITY LABOR ON TECOSPA CHURCH WALL. (From Madsen, 1960. Courtesy, University of Texas Press.)

zational responsibility for these fiestas. Being a good mayordomo is an achievement which brings a man the highest prestige and honor he can earn in a Nahuatl community. It is also a staggering financial drain which may leave his family impoverished for several years, but they do not mind. There is a belief in Tecospa that a satisfied santo repays his mayordomo with good crops.

In Tepoztlan and Ocotepec the mayordomía system is linked with barrio organization. Each barrio chooses mayordomos in charge of the barrio fiesta for its patron santo. Redfield has pointed out (1930, p. 78) that there is an *esprit de corps* in the barrio which is embodied in the barrio santo and expressed in rivalry with other barrios. Each barrio tries to put on a better fiesta than those of the other barrios, and the barrio member likes to boast that his santo can perform better miracles than other barrio santos. In Tecospa there is a similar rivalry between the residents of the four quarters of town to see which quarter can erect the best outdoor altar for the village fiesta honoring San Francisco. The people of Tecospa like to boast that San Francisco is the most miraculous saint in the Milpa Alta area.

Religious fiestas arranged by mayordomos of all the barrios and pueblitos in the municipio are meshed into a unified calendrical system permitting any resident to attend the fiestas of other communities in the same municipio. Villagers also attend some fiestas in neighboring municipios and make pilgrimages to famous shrines.

In addition to mayordomos, the lay officials of Nahuatl religious organization include prayermakers, bellringers, church caretakers, and fund collectors. In pueblos where there is no resident priest, the prayermaker is the worship leader. He leads the chants at fiestas and wakes. The community may also have religious associations whose members meet at regular intervals to worship together.

Group loyalty is largely limited to the pueblo and the municipio. Zantwijk observes that in the Milpa Alta area the "patria chica" is more truly a focus for patriotic sentiment than Mexico as a whole. In general, the Nahuatl pueblos have no close relations with the state or the Republic of Mexico except in administrative matters such as taxation, ejido problems, and violations of the law. There is a widespread attitude of suspicion and hostility toward state and federal agencies even in acculturated communities such as Tepoztlan. The residents of Tecospa are proud of being "inditos" and feel contempt for city Mestizos distinguished by lighter skin and "evil ways" (Lewis, 1951, pp. 43–44; Gamio, 1922, 2:263–64; Madsen, 1960, p. 230; Zantwijk, 1960, p. 69).

The national holidays of September 15 and 16 commemorating Mexican independence are coolly observed in most Nahuatl pueblos with minor fiesta programs put on by the schools. Basauri states that the people of Ocotepec pay little attention to the patriotic fiestas organized by the local school on September 15th and 16th, May 5th, and November 20th. In contrast they show great enthusiasm for all the religious fiestas celebrated in the village. The national holidays are celebrated with outstanding fiestas in Tepoztlan through the efforts of the school (Lewis, 1951, p. 41; Basauri, 1940c, p. 228; Madsen, 1960, p. 112).

RELIGION AND WORLD VIEW

Contemporary Nahuatl religion has been studied only on a superficial level outside of the Milpa Alta area. The unfortunate lack of research on this focal aspect of Nahuatl culture is due partly to overemphasis by United States anthropologists on economic analysis and to the Nahuatl Indian's disinclination to discuss religion or witchcraft with outsiders. On the basis of existing literature, very few generalizations can be made about the Nahuatl world view.

In the Valley of Mexico the Nahuatl universe is ordered by supernatural beings who give and take away the necessities of life. The supernaturals who play the major role in human affairs are the santos. The village patron saint is the most important santo in the pueblo. It is to him the Indians turn when they are afraid of losing their crops or their lives. Every member of the community must contribute time, money, and devotion to the fiestas honoring the patron saint, for he controls the fortunes of the entire village. A man earns prestige only by his contributions to these cooperative community efforts designed to preserve or restore a favorable cosmic order. The individual is subordinate to the group (Gamio, 1922, 2: 214–15; Basauri, 1940c, pp. 216–18).

Most of the santos are dual-natured beings who reward the Indians for good religious fiestas and punish them for neglecting ritual obligations. The most benevolent santo is the Virgin of Guadalupe, who is also called Tonantzin in the Milpa Alta area. She is believed to be the mother of all the

627

Fig. 18—RELIGION AND CURING. *a,* Tecospa boys at the foot of a decorated cross. *b,* Worship at a *posa* in Tecospa. *c,* Chirimía player and drummer in religious procession at Tecospa fiesta. *d,* Tecospa woman demonstrates the egg cure for "aire." (From Madsen, 1960. Courtesy, University of Texas Press.)

"mexicanos." Her dark skin and Nahuatl speech make her a special object of affection. So great has been her influence in Nahuatl religion that Jiménez Moreno aptly designates the Christianity accepted by the Aztecs as "Guadalupinist Catholicism (1958, p. 92).

Many "Cristos" are worshipped in the Nahuatl area. Among the most famous are the crucifixion images of Señor de Chalma, whose shrine is in the state of Mexico and the Señor del Calvario in the state of Puebla. An image of the Señor del Calvario was discovered by Nahuatl Indians in the Tlacotepec district in a mountain cave during the latter part of the 16th century. A local story tells how this Cristo unnailed himself from the cross and moved to the hill now called Calvario where the people built him a temple. One Sunday morning at Mass the white Cristo turned brown, and throngs of people began making pilgrimages to see the Lord who changed his own color to match that of his worshippers (Aladro Azueta, 1944, pp. 10–11).

The Christian supernaturals called "pingos" are devils who live on earth and in hell with their chief who is the Devil. Earth-dwelling pingos usually appear as charros to show they are rich and impress the poor people they are trying to win over. When a man makes a bargain with a pingo he sells his soul and the souls of his family in return for earthly riches. Belief in pingos is general in the Xochimilco–Milpa Alta–Tepoztlan area and probably has a much broader distribution not yet reported (Lewis, 1951, pp. 276–77; Madsen, 1960, p. 133). In the same area there is a general belief in pagan rain dwarfs known in Nahuatl as *yeyecatl* (a word derived from the ancient Atzec *ehecatl* meaning wind or air) or *ahuatoton* (water spirits) from the Spanish *agua* and the Nahuatl *toton*. The dwarfs are also designated by the Spanish terms *enanitos* (dwarfs) and *aires* (airs or winds). These dwarfs produce rain, thunder, lightning, snow, hail, and frost as well as the sickness commonly known as *aire* or *aigre* that occurs when the spirits blow their breath on humans. In Tecospa this sickness is called *moyeyecahuia* or *netenamitili* in Nahuatl and *aire de cuevas* (cave air) in Spanish. The dwarfs are described as little people made of water who stand about a foot and a half high. They live in mountain caves, springs, pools of water, and in damp recesses under volcanic rocks.

Concepts of the afterlife are concrete. Heaven is the skyworld with beautiful flower gardens inhabited by God, the saints, the angels, the angelitos, and the souls of good people. Hell is an underworld where devils burn the souls of bad people and jab them with pitchforks. Only witches and people who bargain with pingos are doomed to hell forever. Ordinary people are sentenced to purgatory in hell for a short time until they have expiated their sins and can get into heaven. Limbo is a place of total darkness where the souls of unbaptized children go to wait for the Day of Judgment when they will become little angels and see light again (Gamio, 1922, 2: 210–12; Madsen, 1960, pp. 209–19).

Individuals who die by violence in a fight or an accident become ghosts doomed to roam the earth by night and frighten the living. The souls of those who die leaving unfulfilled vows, unpaid debts, or undistributed property also become earthbound until their affairs are settled by their relatives. Tecospans believe these earthbound ghosts must carry pingos on their backs who bite them at crossroads causing the ghosts to scream.

The overwhelming majority of Nahuatl peoples are devout Catholics, but Protestant missionaries from the United States are carrying out a vigorous evangelical movement to convert them. Nahuatl Indians in the state of Puebla have become a major target of missionary efforts aimed at destroying belief in the supernatural powers of the saints, particularly the Virgin of Guadalupe (McKinlay, 1945, pp. 63–69).

629

The leading diseases listed by Mexican doctors who worked in Nahuatl communities include *aire* (bad air), *espanto* (fright), *mal de ojo* (evil eye), *mal enfermedad* (bewitchment), and *muina* (anger sickness). The Spanish term "aire" refers to several distinct diseases which produce the same symptoms. In the Milpa Alta–Tepoztlan region aire is commonly used to designate the Aztec concept of illness caused by rain dwarfs, which is called *moyeyecahuia* in the Nahuatl dialect of Tecospa. Symptoms of the disease may be paralysis, palsy, twisted mouth, skin pustules, and an aching in the joints called *yeyecacuatsihuiztli*. Nahuatl terms for ailments sent by rain dwarfs are derived from the ancient Aztec word *ehecatl* meaning air or wind. These illnesses must be cured by a specialist who is called a *tepopoque* in Nahuatl and a *curandero de aire* in Spanish in Tecospa. The standard treatment consists of a series of cleansings performed by brushing the patient's body with a handful of herbs and an unbroken chicken egg (fig. 18,*d*). Both the herbs and the egg cleansing are of Spanish origin (Foster, 1953b, pp. 207–09). A severe case which does not respond to cleansings may require a *tlacahuili*, which is an Aztec ritual offering to the offended dwarfs who appear to the healer in his dreams and tell him what kind of food they want (Madsen, 1960, pp. 181–86; Lewis, 1951, p. 280; Redfield, 1930, pp. 163–66).

A second type of bad air comes from ghosts who cause the sickness called *yeyecatl de motetzahui* (air of a frightening thing) in Nahuatl and *aire de noche* or *espanto* in Spanish in Tecospa. The ghosts who produce this illness are earthbound spirits of people who died by violence or died with unpaid debts. Symptoms of the illness are loss of consciousness, loss of speech, chills, and trembling. Treatments include cleansings which sometimes involve the European technique of rubbing a live, black chicken over the patient's body.

Loose women and whores release a third kind of bad air called *yeyecatlcihuatl* (woman air) in Nahuatl and *aire de basura* (garbage air) in Spanish. Woman air causes eye trouble in newborn babies and fetuses.

A fourth type of aire results from a violation of the hot-cold principle of Hippocratic disease theory. For example, the cold night air causes aire when it strikes the warm body of a sleeping man covered with blankets. This European theory of illness has no Nahuatl name in Tecospa.

Bewitchment is caused by two types of witches: (1) the vampire, called a *tlacique*, who sucks the blood of his victims; and (2) the *nagual* or *itlacatiliz*, who has the power to cause illness from a distance by magical means. The word "nagual" means a "transformer" who has the power to change from human into animal form. In the Valley of Mexico the word is used to designate: (1) a witch who uses this transforming power to spy on his victims; (2) a non-witch who changes into animal form for the sole purpose of stealing food. In Tecospa the nagual witch is also called an *itlacatiliz*, meaning a person born with supernatural power who requires no training to perform supernatural deeds. A. de Molina notes that the Aztec used this word to designate the Christ child after the conquest (1944, p. 41).

Common techniques used by the nagual witch include (1) the European practice of sticking pins in a doll representing the victim; and (2) object intrusion, sending animals, worms, hair, or pebbles into the victim's stomach by magical means. A diagnosis of bewitchment may be made for any chronic illness not alleviated by treatments for other diseases. Stomach disorders are typical of bewitchment. In the state of Puebla bewitchment is treated by another witch who sucks harmful objects out of the patient's body. Bewitchment caused by image magic in the Milpa Alta area is treated by burning the buried doll. In many cases, there is no cure for bewitchment and the patient dies (Benítez P., 1943, p. 36; Castillo Sánchez, 1944, p. 30; García Pérez, 1943, p. 27).

The Spanish concept of evil-eye sickness is found throughout the area, where it is called "mal de ojo" (or "ojo") meaning sickness *caused by* the evil eye. This sickness is not an ailment of the eyes. Rather, it is characterized by continual crying, vomiting, diarrhea, loss of appetite, and loss of weight. Children are the most common victims of the evil eye, which may come from a witch or from a person with "strong vision" who is not a witch. The latter person unintentionally causes evil-eye sickness just by looking with admiration at a child whereas a witch intentionally causes the illness by means of the magical power in his eyes.

Muina (a corruption of the Spanish word *mohina* meaning animosity) is a Hippocratic disease resulting from pent-up anger which causes an overflowing of the yellow liver bile into the blood and the stomach. The excessive bile causes liver trouble and contamination of the blood.

A variety of illnesses are sent by God and the saints as punishments for human misdeeds, such as breaking a religious vow. The only way to cure sickness sent by a saint is to pray for forgiveness and make an offering of flowers and candles.

An aspect of Nahuatl curing which has not been studied is the use of hallucinatory mushrooms to divine the cause of illness. Heim and Wasson report that several kinds of native mushrooms are used for this purpose in the Nahuatl villages of San Pedro Nexapa near Amecameca in the state of Mexico and San Pedro Tlanixco in the Valley of Toluca (1958, pp. 78–84).

Aesthetic and Recreational Patterns

Religious fiestas provide the main opportunity for aesthetic expression and recreation. The village fiesta is the occasion for dance-dramas, music, fireworks, rodeos, markets, gambling, drinking, processions (see vol. 6, Art. 16, fig. 7), feasts, cockfights, and Masses. Traditional music is provided by a chirimitero who plays a small native flute (*chirimía*) and a drummer who plays the *huehuetl* (an elongated upright drum with a skin covering) (fig. 18,*c*), the *teponaztli* (a horizontal wooden drum), or a modern European drum. The fiesta band plays European instruments such as the guitar, flute, saxophone, and cornet.

The most popular dance-drama in the Valley of Mexico is a re-enactment of the battle between Christians and Moors called Moros y Cristianos (fig. 19,*a*) (see also vol. 6, Art. 9, fig. 17). The greatest variety of fiesta dances is performed in the state of Puebla where the repertoire includes Los Voladores (see vol. 6, Art. 9, fig. 30), Los Tocotines, Los Negritos, Los Santiagos (see vol. 6, Art. 9, fig. 16), and Las Vegas. The town of Cuetzalan, Puebla, is famed for its production of Los Santiagos, the dance of St. James on the white horse who leads the Christians in battle against the heathen. The image of Santiago's horse (see vol. 6, Art. 9, fig. 15) is venerated and given a bowl of maize and water daily (Cordry and Cordry, 1940, pp. 13–15).

Private fiestas (fig. 19,*b*) are given in the home to commemorate family birthdays, baptisms, confirmations, weddings, and deaths. In Tecospa the most important person at a party is the mother of the host. Every guest kneels before her to kiss her hand. Nahuatl etiquette is based on the concept that formality breeds respect whereas intimacy breeds contempt. Friends do not drop in at each other's homes just to chat. A family pays visits only on formal occasions such as a birth, baptism, or death.

Gossip tends to center on witchcraft, outsiders, and individuals who flout the local code of ethics. Tourists, city slickers, and strangers who come to a small pueblo are targets of gossip. Anthropologists are commonly taken for land speculators, United

a

b

FIG. 19–AESTHETICS AND RECREATION. *a,* Dance of the Moors and the Christians. *b,* A party toast. The girl in the foreground has been grinding on a metate.

States spies, or agents of the Mexican government. The atmosphere is not conducive to team studies. A local resident becomes a subject of gossip if he steals, neglects his family, shows disrespect for the saints, fails to perform his religious duties, or manifests greed and ambition to get ahead of his neighbors.

Nahuatl humor deals with drunkenness, death, and the strange ways of city people. Fiestas often feature a clown who caricatures the antics of tourists or government officials.

LIFE CYCLE

In the Valley of Mexico birth is sometimes accompanied by a sign indicating the fate of the newborn child. If the infant is born with the umbilical cord wrapped around his neck, he will die by hanging or in some other violent manner. A caul birth is a sign that the baby will be rich (Gamio, 1922, 2: 242; Madsen, 1960, pp. 81, 199).

The first matter of importance after birth is finding baptismal godparents, who become the compadres of the infant's parents. In the Valley of Teotihuacan a baby boy is usually baptized with the first name of his godfather. Here the baptismal fiesta is held 40 days after birth when a Mass is held to solemnize the compadrazgo relationship (Gamio, 1922, 2: 242-43).

After giving birth, the mother stays in bed for two weeks to a month. The baby is his mother's constant companion for most of his first year. He sleeps with her at night and is carried in a rebozo on her back when she goes out of the house. When he is eight months old he begins riding piggyback with his legs sticking out of the rebozo. Then his older brothers and sisters start carrying him and helping tend him. Babies are breast-fed whenever they cry day or night for about two years. The infant is abruptly denied the breast when his mother becomes pregnant again since it is believed that the milk of a pregnant woman is dangerous for a baby (Basauri, 1940c, pp. 186-87).

Little children lead carefree lives playing with animals, rag dolls, balls, and toy trucks made by their father. Nahuatl fathers show great affection for their children and provide them with the best food, clothing, shelter, and medical attention they can afford. The Aztec pattern of teaching children to work when they are very young is still followed. In Ocotepec six-year-old girls help their mothers sweep, wash clothes, sew, and make tortillas. Eight-year-old boys help their fathers weed the fields, harvest the crops, tend the herds, care for the work animals, and carry home wood, charcoal, and water (Basauri, 1940c, pp. 192, 194; Zantwijk, 1960, p. 44; Madsen, 1960, pp. 86-88).

Children are disciplined with Aztec severity after the age of five. Both fathers and mothers beat their children in order to teach them obedience and responsibility. Among the misdeeds meriting punishment are failure to perform assigned tasks, grumbling or rudeness, and mistreatment of younger brothers. A mother slaps her child on the mouth when he talks back to her. The father generally inflicts the most severe beatings. One or two such beatings usually suffice to instill the proper fear of paternal authority so that afterwards a slight rise in the father's voice commands instant obedience. It is generally believed that lack of harsh punishment will spoil children.

There is no problem of juvenile delinquency among the Nahuatl peoples, whose crime rate is low. The most common crime is theft of domesticated animals by outsiders (Cerda Silva, 1957b, p. 224).

Elementary schools including the first four grades have been established to teach the children Spanish, reading, writing, arithmetic, Mexican geography and history. Some Nahuatl villages in Puebla opposed the establishment of these schools and still refuse to send their children because they do not want them to be like educated city people (Arriaga Cervantes, 1944, p. 59).

Marriages are usually arranged by parents and professional matchmakers. When a youth picks out the girl he wants to marry, his parents and godfather ask her parents for her hand. Her parents take the matter under consideration while they find out whether their daughter wishes to marry her suitor. If she says no, the suitor may hire a female matchmaker to press his case. In the event of a favorable reply, a wedding date is set. In Tecospa and Ocotepec the engagement is celebrated with a procession bearing gifts of fruit, cakes, flowers, and candles from the home of the boy to the home of his *novia*. An all-day fiesta takes place at the girl's home where the wedding date is announced. The bride-to-be spends the night before her wedding with her marriage godmother, who traditionally arranges the bride's hair for the ceremony. The wedding takes place in church at dawn in Milpa Alta, where the bride's veil is spread over the groom and the couple are tied together with a white cord wrapped around their shoulders during the nuptial Mass. The religious ceremony is followed by an all-day fiesta at the groom's home. In Puebla wedding celebrations last from three days to a week (Franco Martínez, 1951, p. 16; Basauri, 1940c, pp. 182–83; Madsen, 1960, p. 100; Gamio, 1922, 2: 246; Lewis, 1951, pp. 408–09).

Old age is the time of life when a person receives the greatest respect as well as the liberty of getting drunk in public. An old person's idiosyncracies are accepted with good humor even when they violate local etiquette. Extreme respect for the aged is a dominant feature of Nahuatl society in the Milpa Alta area. Lewis reports that respect for the aged is decreasing in Tepoztlan (1960, pp. 411–12).

Death is the climax of life and requires the most elaborate ritual. The corpse is draped with a shroud and placed on a table. In Ocotepec a cross of lime is placed under the table to absorb contaminating air from the corpse. In Tecospa a special dark sand is sprinkled on the coffin table for the same purpose. In the Sierra Norte de Puebla a cross of sacred marigolds is placed beneath the coffin table (Fabila, 1949, p. 162; Basauri, 1940c, p. 219).

An all-night wake is held at the dead man's home on the night after his death. Guests bring candles and food while the family serves coffee and tequila. The corpse is buried with food and drink for his journey to the afterworld. Wakes are held every night until a series of nine has been completed. On the ninth night after death the shadow soul in the coffin is supposed to leave the corpse and go to heaven. Various local ceremonies are held to help raise the shadow soul and make sure it gets to its proper destination without returning to haunt its old home (Basauri, 1940c, p. 220; Lewis, 1951, p. 416). In the Sierra Norte de Puebla the family and friends of the dead man pray for the repose of his soul for 13 nights after the burial. On the 13th night the entire group goes to the cemetery to erect a black, wooden cross at the head of the grave (Fábila, 1949, pp. 162–63).

ANNUAL CYCLE

A significant feature of the Nahuatl annual cycle is the correlation between the village fiestas and the growing season. Most of the pueblo fiestas in the Valley of Mexico, northern Morelos, and northern Puebla take place in July, August, September, and October when the danger of drought threatens the growing crops. This is the time that the village santo must be placated with an elaborate fiesta so he will repay the villagers with good crops.

January is the time for clearing the mountain fields in the Milpa Alta–Tepoztlan area. In Tecospa level fields are plowed to break up the mounds left by the last crop of maize. In the Sierra de Puebla the soil is turned with a hoe in preparation for planting maize. Wheat, barley, and habas are planted (Fábila, 1949, pp. 41–42).

a

b

FIG. 20—NAHUATL CHILDREN. *a*, Boy carrying his baby brother in a rebozo. *b*, Children with toy house. *c*, Boy and pet lamb. (From Madsen, 1960. Courtesy, University of Texas Press.)

c

Candlemas is celebrated on February 2. Carnival is an unimportant fiesta in most Nahuatl communities but it is the most spectacular fiesta of the year in Tepoztlan, where it is a secular celebration and a profitable commercial enterprise. The Carnival fiesta of Huejotzingo, Puebla, has become a tourist attraction.

In February, Tecospans plant chile and tomato fields. Potatoes are planted in March. Level maize milpas are fertilized with animal manure and mountain fields are burned during February. In the Sierra de Puebla maize and frijoles are planted in February and March.

Planting of maize, frijoles and habas begins in Tecospa in April. Lenten fiestas are rare prior to Holy Week, which is universally observed.

In May and June planting of maize begins in the mountain fields of Tepoztlan and level milpas are prepared for planting. In Tecospa the level fields are plowed a second time about the first of June and a third time in the latter part of June. In the Sierra de Puebla wheat and barley are harvested in May.

May 3, the Day of Crosses, is celebrated in all villages.

In case of drought in the Valley of Mexico, village after village holds a special Mass petitioning its patron saint for rain. Many villages celebrate their annual fiesta honoring the pueblo patron saint during July, August, September, and October.

Harvesting begins in October and continues through November in Tecospa. In the Sierra de Puebla maize is harvested in October.

The ceremonies honoring the return of the dead on November 1 and 2 are universally celebrated. In the Catholic church November 1 is All Saints' Day and November 2 is All Souls' Day, but the belief that dead children return to their homes on November 1 and dead adults return on November 2 is not Catholic. The use of *cempaxochitl*, the sacred marigold, to decorate for the dead and the custom of feeding tamales and calabazas to the dead are Aztec. In some villages of Puebla and San Luis Potosi, marigolds are strewn over all the paths from the cemetery to the homes to guide the returning dead (McKinlay, 1945, p. 64).

November is the main month of harvest in Tecospa. Frijoles are harvested first, then habas, and finally maize.

December marks the end of the rainy season and the time of harvest in Tepoztlan. December 12, the fiesta of the Virgin of Guadalupe, is universally observed but is not a major fiesta in the pueblo. Individuals with vows to fulfill make the pilgrimage to the Basilica de Guadalupe on the outskirts of Mexico City.

The first of the nine Christmas posadas re-enacting the search of Mary and Joseph for lodging is performed on the night of December 16. In the small pueblo these ceremonies take place at the church.

REFERENCES

Aladro Azueta, 1944
Areizaga Millan, 1945
Arriaga Cervantes, 1944
Barrera González, 1949
Basauri, 1940c
Becerra Cobos, 1944
Benítez P., 1943
Bonilla R., 1948
Cantellano Alvarado, 1949
Carrillo González, 1950
Castellanos Fernández, 1950
Castillo Sánchez, 1944
Cepeda de la Garza, 1944
Cerda Silva, 1957b
Chávez Torres, 1947
Cordry and Cordry, 1940
Fabila, 1949
Foster, 1953a, 1953b, 1955, 1960a
Franco Martínez, 1951
Gamio, 1922
García Pérez, 1943
González Tenorio, 1941
Gutiérrez García, 1946

Heim and Wasson, 1958
Jiménez Moreno, 1958
Law, 1960
Lewis, 1951
McKinlay, 1945
Madsen, 1955a, 1955b, 1956, 1957, 1960
Mexico, 1944, 1953
Molina, A. de, 1944
Noriega Hope, 1922
Nutini, 1961
Redfield, 1930
Romero Alvárez, 1952
Soustelle, G., 1958
Starr, F., 1900–02
Toor, 1947
Vara Gómez, 1948
Vásquez Ramírez, 1946
Velasco Ramos, 1950
Vivó, 1941
Whetten, 1948
Whorf, 1946
Wolf, 1959
Zantwijk, 1960

33. The Totonac

H. R. HARVEY and ISABEL KELLY

An IMPORTANT ETHNIC GROUP of ancient and modern Mexico are the Totonac, situated in the states of Puebla and Veracruz. Traditionally, their domain is known as Totonacapan and, except for major shrinkage in the south, modern Totonacapan closely agrees with the distribution reported in early sources (fig. 1).

Today, the greatest concentration of Totonac speech is along the Puebla-Veracruz border and down the front scarp of the Sierra Madre to the Papantla lowlands. A small and rapidly disappearing island is found to the south, about Misantla. Three dialects are recognized (Juan A. Hasler, 1964, personal communication): Munixcan, Zacatlan-Papantla, and Misantla. The first is northern, in the vicinity of Mecapalapa, Puebla; the second, central, extending from the Sierra de Puebla to the Gulf coast; and the third, southern or southeastern.

Field data are not sufficient to permit definition of cultural subareas, but within the central dialect zone there are marked differences between lowland and highland. In the latter, in particular, significant survivals of native social and religious traits are evident.

The Totonac share much in common with Mesoamerican culture, but among the lowland groups a few traits appear unique or rare in Mesoamerica and suggest some affinity with the circum-Carib area (Kelly, 1953, p. 185). Nevertheless, linguistic affiliations do not point gulfwards. Totonac and Tepehua, which are genetically related and geographically contiguous, constitute a separate language family, Totonacan. Linguists are studying the possibility of wider relationships.

Habitat varies widely. The limited area of the Sierra de Puebla known to us is high mesa, deeply dissected, and cool, with mist and rain much of the year. Residual stands of pine and oak testify to major deforestation. In sharp contrast, the coastal zone is low, rolling country, with little level land. Much of the year is hot and humid; a brief, sharp, dry spell generally occurs in the spring. Until relatively recently, this great stretch of lowland was covered with tropical rain forest, but here, too, extensive clearing now has taken place.

These differences in natural surroundings inevitably are reflected in the way of life—in basic economic activities, agricultural cy-

638

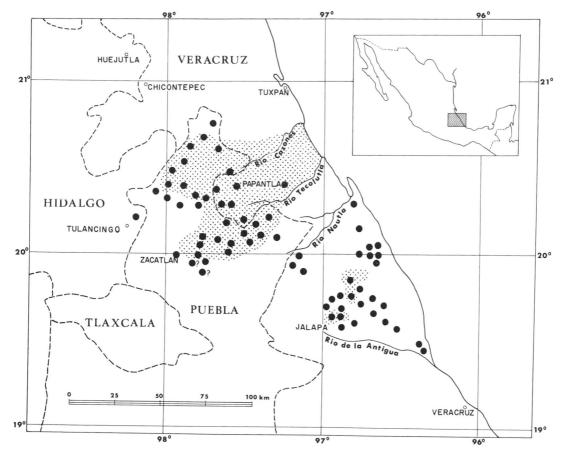

Fig. 1—TOTONACAPAN: APPROXIMATE EXTENSION IN ANCIENT AND RECENT TIMES. Solid circles: occurrences of Totonac speech reported in 16th century sources. Dotted area: the modern extension of Totonac speech (monolinguals and bilinguals) according to 1940 census files. Municipal units with 5 per cent or less of Totonac speech have been disregarded. (A simplification of data in Kelly and Palerm, 1952, Maps 1–3.)

cle, assortment of cultigens, diet, house type, dress, and even in intercommunity relationships. On the whole, the highland is an area of limited resources and consequent poverty. The lowland, by comparison, is generously endowed and relatively prosperous.

Within three years after the appearance of Cortés and his army in New Spain, most of Totonacapan was under Spanish domination. "The Spanish conquest of Totonacapan is almost unique in that the Totonac were received into the Spanish empire as allies, that is, as subjects incorporated into the empire through the will of their own native leaders. This is particularly true with respect to southern Totonacapan . . . [and] the conquest of Totonacapan was singularly free from the violence and cruelty which characterized that of other parts of New Spain" (Kelly and Palerm, 1952, p. 26).

The spiritual conquest of Totonacapan started with the very arrival of the Spaniards, whose missionizing zeal is apparent in their deliberate destruction of idols in the native temples of Totonac Cempoala, at a moment when they could hardly afford to risk the enmity of their hosts. There, in

639

Cempoala, the Spaniards converted a native temple into the first Christian chapel in New Spain.

The arrival of the Franciscans in 1523 marked the first concerted effort to proselytize the Totonac, although their activities were largely confined to the highlands. A decade later the Augustinians arrived, to administer to the northwestern frontier, along the borders of Hidalgo, Puebla, and Veracruz. Gradually, the activities of the religious orders were taken over by the secular clergy, who were under the Tlaxcala bishopric. Notwithstanding the early and unabating interest in conversion, the relative ineffectiveness of the missionizing program is suggested by the paucity of both religious architecture in most of Totonacapan and translations of religious works into Totonac during the colonial epoch (Kelly and Palerm, 1952, pp. 32–33).

In political and economic spheres, the Spaniards took advantage of existing native structure. The old class division with its established lines of authority proved a useful instrument in implementing Spanish policy. For example, native leaders who were cooperative were maintained in their positions and used as intermediaries. The political centers of preconquest times were retained and became the cabeceras or political nuclei of the new administration. The Totonac had grown accustomed—albeit reluctantly —to paying tribute to the Triple Alliance in pre-Hispanic times, and after the conquest they were required to pay tax to church and crown. Despite the retention of many of the familiar components of the native framework, the abolition of the warrior group, the suppression of the native priesthood, and the control of commerce were factors of postconquest times which combined to undermine the fabric of Totonac society.

Of even more direct consequence to native society were the institutions of *repartimiento* and *encomienda* which the Spaniards superimposed on the native structure. In theory, the encomienda was compatible with the preservation of native property rights. In practice, since it proved a mechanism for unbridled exploitation of native labor, it placed an oppressive burden on the native population in many parts of Totonacapan. Its effects are dramatically seen in the population decline in the years following the conquest (Cook and Borah, 1960). Both disease and labor exacted their toll, and many who survived did so only by abandoning their home localities and fleeing to the inaccessible parts of Totonacapan (Kelly and Palerm, 1952, p. 38). Indirectly, therefore, the encomienda served to clear the land of its native occupants and pave the way for Spanish colonization.

Official reaction to the situation toward the end of the 16th century is reflected in the *reducciones* and *congregaciones* which undertook to concentrate the scattered remnants of the native population in fixed localities. These measures were mainly ineffective, but they did, nevertheless, undermine native political organization. For example, native leadership was hereditary, but under the congregaciones native authorities were chosen in free election.

The encomienda system, with all its disadvantages, at least tended to preserve native subsistence patterns. As Spanish colonization proceeded, however, the hacienda system developed and types of economic pursuit shifted. In general, the haciendas specialized in cash crops, such as sugarcane, or in cattle raising. Unlike the encomienda, the hacienda was operated on the basis of paid labor, much of which was imported— Indians from other areas or Negro slaves. Eventually, the hacienda system resulted in the formation of a new social group, the serf.

The adverse effects of Spanish domination were not felt equally in all parts of Totonacapan. In the southeast, and along the coast, contact with the Spaniards was most intensive and most devastating. However, in the large areas where Totonac speech has survived to the present, there

640

was little to attract the Spaniard. Transportation and communication were difficult. Exploitation would have required a major adjustment, hardly necessary when the alternative of familiar environments was so abundant elsewhere. Also, Totonacapan largely lacked the mineral resources so attractive to the Spaniards. Thus, until relatively recent years, much of Totonacapan has remained intact and isolated, and many forms of native Totonac culture have survived.

According to the 1940 data on file in the census office, the number of Totonac-speakers was 90,378, about equally divided between the states of Veracruz and Puebla. Of these, 59,506 were monolinguals. The 1960 census material is still not fully available. A preliminary release gives 29,911 Totonac monolinguals in Veracruz, slightly more than reported for 1940 (Kelly and Palerm, 1952, p. 261). No corresponding figure is available for Puebla, and for neither state has the number of bilinguals been announced.

In the Sierra de Puebla and on its slopes, a considerable Totonac concentration is reported in the 1940 census for the municipal units of Huehuetla (5,954), Olintla (5,600), and Hueytlalpan (4,069), although several others actually contain a far higher percentage of Totonac-speakers in relation to the total population. In the lowlands, the most populous center is the municipal unit of Papantla, with 17,722 persons of Totonac speech.

According to the 1940 information, the related Tepehua language still is spoken by 3,895 individuals and is largely limited to four municipal units: Ixhuatlan (1,563), Zontecomatlan (306), and Tlachichilco (865) in Veracruz, plus Huehuetla (1,067), in Hidalgo.

In 1947 ethnographic investigation of the modern Totonac was initiated by Isabel Kelly and several student collaborators, as part of a joint program of the Institute of Social Anthropology of the Smithsonian Institution and the Escuela Nacional de Antropología of the Instituto Nacional de Antropología e Historia. Two seasons were spent among the lowland Totonac at El Tajin, near Papantla, and one season in the Sierra community of San Marcos Eloxochitlan, near Zacatlan, Puebla. A detailed study covering pertinent historical material, subsistence, and technology of El Tajin was published by Kelly and Palerm (1952) and a brief general ethnographic summary by Kelly (1953) covering highland and lowland Totonac. A short paper on the world view of San Marcos Eloxochitlan (Kelly, 1966) has recently been published. Except for these few works, literature pertaining to the modern Totonac is very scant.

The present article is based almost exclusively on the foregoing published sources, on Kelly's field notes, and on her manuscript which is to constitute the second volume on the Tajin Totonac. Unless otherwise specified, most of the data of the present paper refer to observations made between 1947 and 1951, and to the Totonac communities of El Tajin in the lowlands and San Marcos Eloxochitlan in the Sierra. In 1963 and 1964, Kelly made further observations in the lowlands. There, cultural change has been extensive in very recent times and merits a special field study. For example, a great deal of land formerly in Totonac hands now has been purchased by Mestizos, who have cleared the rain forest. Vanilla production has plummeted to almost negligible proportions. Formerly, most of the Totonac communities of the Papantla area were connected by foot trails; now, they are accessible by car in dry weather, over roads opened in the course of oil explorations of Petroleos Mexicanos. With rural bus service now operating, Poza Rica is replacing Papantla as the urban center where the lowland Totonac sell their produce and buy the necessities which they themselves do not produce.

The linguistically related Tepehua still are comparatively numerous, but they are

641

a

b

FIG. 2—LOWLAND AGRICULTURE, EL TAJIN, VERACRUZ. *a*, Cultivated fields interspersed with vestiges o
rain forest. *b*, Lowland clearing. The felled timber has not burned successfully, but maize will be planted whereve
possible. (Photographed by Isabel Kelly, 1947–51.)

virtually unknown ethnographically, despite a short summary of the Huehuetla Tepehua by Robert Gessain. For want of data, this related group is not included in the present survey.[1]

SUBSISTENCE

By heritage, the Totonac are farmers. Throughout Totonacapan maize agriculture is fundamental, and both maize and squash are grown on a subsistence basis. Other crops vary in importance with locality; beans do not do well in the lowlands, nor chile in the highlands. At low elevation, maize economy is complemented by cash crops and by apiculture, poultry production, and hog raising. In the Sierra, it is complemented by limited poultry and stock production, and by wage labor and minor commercial enterprises. On the whole, animal husbandry is nowhere emphasized in Totonacapan; beekeeping is rare or absent in the highlands, and stock is of little consequence in the lowlands. Nevertheless, in both zones, hog raising on a small scale is a welcome source of income. The plow has intruded itself into highland agriculture, where terrain permits, but the traditional digging stick is still fundamental to the lowland milpas.

Agriculture is more restricted in the highlands, in terms of crop diversity and yield and also in terms of relative significance within the economic system. In the Sierra the growing season permits only one harvest annually and, moreover, cultivable land is scarce. Accordingly, crop production is limited to the basic necessities—maize, beans, and squash—and these are seldom sufficient to supply the daily fare. In the off-season, many men become peddlers of the craft products of the highlands, or seek work, chiefly as agricultural laborers, in the lowlands.

[1] Roberto Williams García's study (1963) of the Tepehua appeared too late to permit inclusion of his data in this article but it is listed in the References.

In contrast, among the lowland Totonac, there is little other than the milpa to compete for a man's time. Several factors—plentiful tillable land, reliable cash crops, occasional surplus of standard dietary items, and a ready local market—combine to make farming a relatively prosperous undertaking. The climate permits two maize harvests annually, and in general the yield is good. The rich crop diversity allows a farmer to exercise considerable choice in the type and proportion of plants he raises. Exclusive of fruits, more than a dozen crops are grown, including maize, vanilla, sugarcane, several varieties of bean, as well as cucurbits and a wide assortment of starchy roots and tubers. Some plants, such as the cultivated chile, are raised for use as condiments; some as native remedies; several grasses are planted for animal fodder and roof thatch.

The milpa system prevails throughout lowland Totonacapan. As in most other tropical rain-forest areas under primitive cultivation, weed incursion seems to be the most restricting factor. Notwithstanding, between crop diversity and maize-vanilla rotation, the lowland Totonac manage to get more mileage out of their milpa agriculture than is usually the case, for "maize requires a clean field; vanilla requires *monte bajo*" (Kelly and Palerm, 1952, p. 100). When a new plot is cleared, maize (fig. 2,*a*) receives priority the first two to four years. From the beginning, there is a constant struggle against the incursion of *monte*, so that after three or four years of planting maize, the farmer capitulates, and the field is given over to monte and to vanilla. After about 12 years of continuous planting, the plot is abandoned completely and lies fallow for perhaps another dozen years. Accordingly, the full cycle comes to 20 or 25 years.

A new field is cleared in the spring, between April and June. The parcel is demarcated and, with a machete, the smaller growth is slashed to a height of about 2 m. The larger trees are felled next, and the cut

a

b

Fig. 3—AGRICULTURE. *a,* "Replanting" a highland milpa whose maize clumps are deficient; note digging stick and gourd to carry seed. (Photographed by Isabel Kelly, 1947–51.) *b,* Lowland vanilla vine with green pods. (Photographed by Eric Schwartz, 1963–64. Courtesy, Mario Vásquez, Planeación del Nuevo Museo Nacional de México.)

vegetation is spread evenly on the ground to dry. Meanwhile, a broad strip surrounding the plot is cleared to serve as a firebreak. Before the onslaught of the first rains, the dried debris is fired (fig. 2,*b*). For heavy growth, 40–50 man-days of labor may be needed to prepare a field. Most of the work is done by the farmer himself, but to cut large trees he may invite several men to assist, on a work-exchange basis.

Almost every family grows maize, usually to the same extent, namely, about 1.5 hectares. Planting takes place twice yearly: in summer, between the end of June and early August; in winter, between late November and early February. Planting is man's work and must be finished in one day. Again the farmer seeks the assistance of his friends —eight or ten; more, if a new field is involved, because rows are carefully spaced at about 1.5-m. intervals, and this is a time-consuming task. For subsequent plantings the old stalks, which are always left standing and which contribute to the disheveled appearance of a milpa, serve as guides and seed is planted between the rows of the previous crop.

From the best ears of corn, which are preserved for seed, only kernels from the center are used. Occasionally, such seed is planted directly, but forced germination is most common. The shelled grains are placed in a wooden tray to which water is added. They soak for a day, then are removed to a box lined with banana leaves; similar leaves are laid on top. The container is left in the sun for a day, and the seed sprouts. In planting, a hole is made with the dibble to a depth of about 20 cm., and several kernels are dropped in and covered with soil. Each clump should produce two to four plants, and deficient clusters are replanted after a week or 10 days.

Once planted, the milpa requires constant attention. Weed growth is prolific and necessitates daily cultivation, a chore shared by most members of the household, male and female, young and old. Furthermore,

during the growing season, a major clearing occurs every month or two. Friends usually are invited to assist, again on a work-exchange basis. The metal *coa* is used to loosen the soil and shear the weeds. Interestingly, the Totonac do not heap soil about the base of the maize plants and so are concerned with high winds which might prostrate the planting.

The mature corn is collected as needed over a period of several weeks. Men and women gather the ears and haul them to the granary. During the main harvesting operation, a temporary shelter is built in the milpa, where ears are accumulated until they can be removed to permanent storage. Maize is stored unshucked. Dry stalks and leaves remain in the field to rot and these, together with the ash residue from the burned debris of clearing, constitute the only fertilizer used.

Maize production, with its time-consuming requirements, dominates the agricultural scene. In contrast, vanilla is far less demanding. It follows maize in the local cycle, and when the milpa is cultivated young trees and shrubs suitable to serve eventually as supports for the vanilla vine are spared. Thus, when the maize yield drops, the field already is well "prepared" for conversion to vanilla. In spring, vanilla cuttings are set in the ground at the base of suitable plants, following which the vine requires no attention for three years, when its blossoms must be pollinated. The vine blooms for about three weeks in late April and early May; as soon as a blossom opens the labellum is slit, and a small, sharp stick is inserted to relocate the pollen. Although the pods (fig. 3,*b*) are not thoroughly mature until December, they usually are cut green in October, to reduce the likelihood of theft. The latter is widespread and not infrequently the cause of bloodshed.

During the first three or four years in the life of a given field, while maize is still the dominant crop, the milpa is the catchall for many other plants. For example, when

645

a
b

Fig. 4—SAN MARCOS ELOXOCHITLAN IN THE HIGHLANDS, PUEBLA. *a,* Approach from Ahuacatlan. *b,* The small, level plaza of Eloxochitlan. (Photographed by Isabel Kelly, 1947–51.)

Fig. 5—TOPOGRAPHY AND VEGETATION. Religious procession enters Eloxochitlan's barrio of Tankan. (Photographed by Isabel Kelly, 1947–51.)

646

sugarcane is grown on a small scale, it is incorporated in the cornfield. Bean seed may be dropped in the same hole with the maize kernels, and various legumes, cucurbits, and chile appear between the rows of corn. Sesame and root crops may be planted along the borders, and, to add to the confusion, sweet potatoes, yams, and manioc may be interspersed in the milpa, along with a host of other plants of lesser importance.

In addition to the milpa, which may be situated at a considerable distance from the dwelling, almost every family has some sort of informal garden in the house clearing. This contains a small assortment of fruit trees and a miscellaneous assemblage of plants such as manioc, sugarcane, chile, perennial cotton, and a few herbs. Most gardens include some flowering plants; flowers are greatly appreciated by both men and women for personal adornment as well as for decoration of the household altar.

Throughout Totonacapan, diet is frugal and high in carbohydrates, low in protein, fat, and most vitamins. Meat (beef or pork) is eaten about once a week in the more prosperous homes; in others, often not more than once a month. Chicken or turkey in hot *mole* sauce is the standard dish for festivals. In the lowlands not even beans are daily fare.

Maize, the mainstay, is prepared in many forms. Tortillas are the chief item of the diet and are eaten thrice daily. Various kinds of maize gruels, particularly a fermented one, are popular. So also are variants of what we should call a tamale; ingredients which accompany the maize paste vary according to what the cook has at hand—beans or other leguminosae, meat, or simply brown sugar. In the highland diet, cucurbits, beans, and wild greens seem somewhat more important than in the lowlands, where there is a much richer assortment of starches, in the form of roots and tubers, bananas, and plantains. In both areas, food is heavily condimented with chile.

SETTLEMENT PATTERNS

San Marcos Eloxochitlan, the one highland Totonac community from which data are available, lies some five or six hours on foot or by horse from the provincial center of Zacatlan de las Manzanas, Puebla, and one hour from Ahuacatlan, the nearest market town. Administrative ties are with the lat-

ter. In this high country, with its deep barrancas, Eloxochitlan clings perilously to the rim of the great cleft (fig. 4,a) which rises near Zacatlan. It is downstream from the latter and on the opposite side of the barranca. A small expanse of level land is occupied by an open plaza (fig. 4,b), and here are clustered a simple, masonry church, of ancient construction; the school; a "municipal building" started in 1906 and not yet completed; and a room with cross-barred wooden doors, which functions as a jail. About this "urban" center lie the three named barrios in which are concentrated the 600 inhabitants. Rarely is a dwelling far removed from the central nucleus, and the settlement pattern is concentrated (fig. 5).

Ordinarily, a ménage occupies a single building, which may shelter stored maize as well as family members. Sometimes there is a separate granary, structurally similar to the dwelling, but with raised floor. A sweat house of stones set roughly in mud mortar, a fowl house and pen, and a corral for other animals complete the domestic installations.

El Tajin is a lowland community some 6

a   b

FIG. 6—LOWLAND LANDSCAPES. a, Papantla-Tajin trail, Veracruz. b, Milpas interspersed with vestiges of rain forest. (Photographed by Isabel Kelly, 1947–51.)

or 7 km. southwest of Papantla, Veracruz, in country characterized by a continuous series of low, rough hills, formerly shrouded in tropical rain forest (fig. 6). Over 80 per cent of its 1,102 inhabitants live widely scattered, in small clearings, well hidden from view and remote from each other. The rest live in the town center, a few minutes by foot south of the ruins of El Tajin. To the south, west, and north the community is bounded by the lands of other Totonac settlements, but to the observer the boundaries are imperceptible. To the east lies Papantla, a large Mestizo urban center, from which Tajin is administered and which, traditionally, is Tajin's main link to the outside world.

Despite the presence of ruins, the formal establishment of the present community is rather recent. Toward the end of the past century, the Mexican government opened a great stretch of the Papantla area to settlement. The zone was surveyed and the area about Tajin was divided into parcels of slightly more than 31 hectares each. Most of these were purchased by Totonac of the Papantla area. At this same time, each major subdivision had land set aside for a town center. The center of Tajin is toward the east end of the tract. Although government action is thus responsible for the morphology of the modern Totonac communities of the Papantla lowlands, the plaza pattern was evidently a characteristic feature in ancient Totonacapan. At least, the old centers of Cempoala and Quiahuixtlan were built around a central plaza.

The distinguishing feature about the town center of El Tajin is the relative concentration of private dwellings and public buildings. Actually, even the "town dwellers" value privacy to the extent that much of the area is left wooded and the houses are secluded in small clearings. Land in the Tajin center is divided into small lots (1250 sq. m.) arranged along narrow "streets," so overgrown as to amount to no more than footpaths. Toward the north end of the cen-

ter, a large, open plot kept clear of undergrowth is the completely unadorned town plaza (fig. 19). On one side of it is a school, built through communal effort; on another side, the municipal offices and jail. Long ago there was a chapel, but it was destroyed by an earthquake, and several decades passed before it was rebuilt on a lot near the plaza, which had been reserved for such use. A few very small stores, randomly located, complete the "urban" scene. Several trails fan out from the center, connecting it with Papantla, with the more remote land parcels of Tajin, and with adjacent Totonac communities.

Those who live in the center have to commute to their fields, sometimes at considerable distance. More than half of these families do not own farmland, but most are able to rent tillable acreage quite nearby. As a general rule, however, the lowland Totonac farmer prefers to live close to his field, and it tends to be the landless ones who live in the "urban" center.

On the outlying parcels, houses are widely scattered and well hidden in small clearings, not visible from the trails. The original subdivision into plots of 31 hectares determines the basic spatial arrangement of the rural part of the community. In all, El Tajin is composed of 107 parcels, nearly two-thirds of which contain both dwellings and fields. Some of the remaining plots are vacant, but many contain fields, with no dwelling units. These lands are worked by people who live on nearby parcels or in the town center.

Fully a fourth of the Tajin parcels are occupied exclusively by one family. The maximum number of families occupying a parcel is eight; the mode is two. When there is more than one household per parcel, these usually are related in the male line.

Economic status rather than family size tends to determine whether the Tajin household inhabits a single-room dwelling or several separate ones, but clustered together. Placement of the various house units

648

Fig. 7—PROCESSING SUGARCANE WITH WOODEN PRESS, EL TAJIN, VERACRUZ. (Photographed by Eric Schwartz, 1963–64. Courtesy, Mario Vásquez, Planeación del Nuevo Museo Nacional de México.)

follows no set pattern. When separate sleeping quarters are built, they usually are somewhat removed from the kitchen, in part because the latter constitutes a fire hazard. Other factors also influence placement: local terrain, position of trees and permanent plants in the clearing, and location of pre-existing buildings.

A one-room house may be partitioned into separate task areas. Sometimes the cooking space is set off by a partition and either or both the resulting areas may be used as sleeping quarters. Sometimes kitchen and living room are coterminus, separated from the "bedroom" by a partition. If there is more than one building, additional structures usually are sleeping quarters.

In addition, the house clearing normally contains various domestic structures, such as granary, sweat house, pigpen, poultry house, and laundry shade. Fences are rare, even in the town center, and their chief function is to protect the haphazard garden from wandering animals. Moreover, a clearing contains a scattering of trees, retained or planted for their shade, fruit, or flowers. A typical house complex of a well-to-do Tajin family is illustrated by Kelly and Palerm (1952, Map 9).

TECHNOLOGY

Tools

Most of the tools and weapons used by the modern Totonac are not of native produc-

649

FIG. 8—FIRING POTTERY IN OPEN BLAZE ON KITCHEN FLOOR, EL TAJIN, VERACRUZ. (Photographed by Eric Schwartz, 1963–64. Courtesy, Mario Vásquez, Planeación del Nuevo Museo Nacional de México.)

tion but are purchased in stores and markets. Game is scarce and little hunted, always with firearms. In the highlands timber is cut with a large, commercial lumberman's saw. In both highlands and lowlands the machete is the most versatile and important tool and weapon: an all-purpose chopping and cutting instrument, in daily use in the home and in the fields. Particularly in the lowlands, training in handling the machete begins in childhood; every man, and some women, wield it with extraordinary skill.

In clearing lowland fields preparatory to planting, both a steel axe and a machete are employed. A dibble is still used for planting. It is a straight stick, 2–3 m. in length, with one end pointed and sometimes fitted with an iron casing. The cultivating instrument is the *coa,* a broad, flat metal blade (Kelly and Palerm, 1952, figs. 10, 11). The highland coa is also metal, but its haft is adzlike. The plow is a common tool in the highlands, but it is considered unsuitable for the milpa agriculture of the lowlands.

Processing and Manufacturing

In general, the Totonac give little time to processing and manufacturing. In the Papantla area, however, subconical cakes of brown sugar, for home consumption and for cash sale, are prepared from sugarcane (fig. 7; Kelly and Palerm, pp. 128–32). Here, too, vanilla pods are sometimes dried so as to command a better price. Drying requires carefully controlled exposure to the sun for about an hour a day over a prolonged period.

In the lowlands candles are made for home consumption. Molten wax of the native bee is spread on a moistened tabletop. A wick, which has been dipped a couple of times in hot wax is placed on the sheet. The sheet is folded over the wick and then rolled between the palms until a candle of sorts is produced. In contrast, when candles are made of the wax of the Old World bee, various wicks are suspended from a hoop and the hot wax dribbled on them (Kelly and Palerm, 1952, p. 98).

Crafts

Totonac craft production has so declined in modern times that only a few hints of former talents can be gleaned from the present scene. The female arts of pottery making and weaving are those which have endured; the male crafts of basketry, woodworking, and tool and weapon manufacture have given way in the competition with commercial products. Paper making seems to have disappeared completely.

Fig. 9—POTTERY BEEHIVES, LOWLANDS, CERRO DEL CARBON, VERACRUZ. (Photographed by Carlos Sáenz, 1963–64. Courtesy, Mario Vásquez, Planeación del Nuevo Museo Nacional de México.)

In highland Eloxochitlan not even pottery manufacture has survived. There, a few nearby centers (of Mexican, not Totonac, speech) specialize in glazed ceramics and supply the entire zone. In contrast, all the elder women and some of the younger ones in the entire Papantla area make vessels for cooking, eating, storage, and other domestic needs. Although commercial containers are used extensively, most households still rely on a few homemade products, and pottery manufacture is considered a primary feminine skill. With such high value placed on ceramic production, it is paradoxical that vessels should be of execrable quality, inferior in virtually every respect. "Tajín pottery is heavy and crude. It is poorly fashioned, poorly finished, and poorly fired [fig. 8]. The color of a single specimen may range from ochre and rosy tan to brown, gray and black; firing clouds are prominent. . . . All vessels are unglazed. Decoration is scanty . . . warping and cracks are the rule, and quite often a new vessel must be mended before it can be put to use" (Kelly and Palerm, 1952, p.

651

a

b

Fig. 10—LOWLAND CRAFTS, EL TAJIN, VERACRUZ. *a,* Spinning. (Photographed by Angelina Macías, 1963–64.) *b,* Weaving with belt loom. (Photographed by Eric Schwartz, 1963–64. Courtesy, Mario Vásquez, Planeación del Nuevo Museo Nacional de México.)

212). Bowl and jar forms predominate, but food dishes, griddles, spindle whorls, candlesticks, and incense burners are common.

One ceramic trait of considerable interest is the technique of jar manufacture. The walls are formed first, as a cylinder, and the rim is shaped. Leaves are then wrapped about the lower portion of the damp cylinder, and the baseless jar is set aside until the exposed area dries. Later, the leaves are peeled off, and the moist clay beneath is carefully drawn together to form the bottom of the vessel (Kelly and Palerm, 1952, pp. 217, 219–20). It is also of interest that among the lowland Totonac, clay pots

function as hives for the native bee (fig. 9; Kelly and Palerm, 1952, pp. 96–97, pl. 4,*d,f*).

Despite the availability of commercial fabrics, throughout much of Totonacapan women continue to weave on the belt loom. In highland Eloxochitlan, weaving is limited to the production of plain woolen material, indigo-dyed, for use as skirts by the women and cotones by the men. The skirt is supported by a woven belt—red, with characteristic motif—somewhat similar to the sashes still used by the older women of the Papantla area. Informants in both zones state that such belts are not produced by the Totonac but are purchased and come ultimately from Mexican communities in the Sierra de Puebla.

In the Papantla lowlands weaving (fig. 10,b) is confined to production of towels; strainers for maize gruel; runners which are coiled and placed on the head to cushion burdens; and "tablecloths" to cover the contents of the wooden tray (fig. 17,b) the woman carries on her head. Occasionally specimens are of native cotton, locally grown and spun (fig. 10,a), but commercial thread is now in general use. The "tablecloths" alone bear designs, formed by lifting loops of weft on the right side of the fabric during manufacture (Kelly and Palerm, 1952, pls. 29; 30,c–g, figs. 58–61). Both technique and motifs suggest European influence.

The art of basketry has all but disappeared, although evidence for it survives in several male-centered activities. In the Sierra, a carrying frame for burdens is in general use. A withe is bent to form a quadrilateral, which then is filled with liana or commercial twine in wrapped stitch.

Two such frames are united on one long and two short sides, to form a container. There is evidence that a somewhat similar frame, its filler of coil-without-foundation, formerly was used in the lowlands.

Wickerwork survives in the form of poorly made sheep muzzles in Eloxochitlan, and in an occasional basket in the Papantla area, likewise of indifferent quality. In the lowlands, however, simple basketry stitches are employed in diverse situations. The upright poles which form the house walls are lashed to transverse supports by wrapped twine. Cradles and circular hanging trays for food storage are filled with coil-without-foundation. Ornamental palm figures (figs. 11,b; 15,b; Kelly and Palerm, 1952, pls. 26,b–f; 27) for altar and other ceremonial decoration and chair seats woven of palm cordage (fig. 11,a) are reminiscent of basketry techniques.

Woodworking must have once been an established art, but little remains today. In Eloxochitlan craftsmen are able to cut planks from a tree trunk; in the lowlands chief reliance is on itinerant workers who

a   b

FIG. 11—LOWLAND CRAFTS, EL TAJIN, VERACRUZ. a, Weaving chair seat with palm cordage. b, Making palm "stars" for altar ornament, as shown in figure 15,b. Cf. Kelly and Palerm, 1952, pls. 26,b–f; 27. (Photographed by Eric Schwartz, 1963–64. Courtesy, Mario Vásquez, Planeación del Nuevo Museo Nacional de México.)

a

b

come from the Sierra. Throughout Totonacapan, few possess or even know how to use modern European hand tools for working wood, and the machete is the all-purpose instrument. In El Tajin there is no full-time carpenter or woodworking artisan. Nevertheless, several local men know how to make particular objects, such as one-piece stools, chairs, tables, sugarcane crushers (fig. 7), bakers' paddles, stirring sticks, jar covers, trays, chests, and grave markers, as well as masks and other ceremonial paraphernalia.

Housing

The characteristic, and presumably ancient, Totonac house is rectangular in plan. Its gabled roof, with two long and two short sheds, rests on a forked-post frame. Its walls, of vertically set light poles, are not structural and support no weight (fig. 12; Kelly and Palerm, 1952, pp. 176–86). Materials vary with locality. In highland Eloxochitlan the thatch is grass, often combined with maize stalks; in the Papantla lowlands, the thatch is usually of palm, the walls, of vertically disposed lengths of bamboo.

There have been innovations in both areas. Sometimes the Sierra house displays a shake roof (fig. 3), and the dwelling of greatest prestige has cribbed walls of squared logs or of planks, and on them, without other support, rests the roof, often of tile. This superficial approximation to our log house is popular in much of the Sierra de Puebla and is not confined to the Totonac.

In the Papantla area prestige is associated with the house which has squared posts and beams, plank walls, and tiled roof (fig. 16; see also Kelly and Palerm, 1952, pl. 9,f). The dwelling is dark, for Totonac houses are windowless. Moreover, it is uncomfortably warm much of the year. In contrast, the bamboo walls of the traditional palm-thatched dwelling permit light and

air to enter between the interstices, so that this residence is comfortable in hot weather but drafty in winter. Sometimes one or more walls are mud-plastered, giving the impression of adobe construction. The palm-thatched, bamboo-walled house usually has a bamboo door; the plank house, a wooden one.

Several advantages favor the survival of the traditional, palm-roofed house (fig. 13). Made exclusively of local materials, it is relatively inexpensive. Much of its construction can be handled by one man, but friends are usually invited to assist. For this the host either pays them or gives each his labor in return at some future time. Buildings are owned independently of the land, and the palm house is comparatively easy to dismantle and move.

Sometimes the interior is partitioned into separate task areas. Furniture is minimal. Long benches and small stools, the latter made from single blocks of wood, are standard equipment. The Sierra bench is no more than a squared trunk, supported at either end by a large stone, but that of the Papantla zone is a thick plank, with four splay legs. In both areas the stool may be simply a short length of tree trunk, sometimes cut at a fork so that, inverted, the branch stubs serve as legs. Handled and animal-effigy stools are common. Today the slatback chair with woven palm seat is used throughout the lowlands (fig. 11,a). Every Totonac house contains some sort of table; that of the Papantla zone is of cedar planks, with four legs, usually squared (fig. 15,b).

Kitchen arrangements differ widely between highland and lowland. In the former area, all cooking is done on the house floor, where three or four stones constitute the hearth. The metate sits nearby on the earth floor, and the woman kneels to grind and prepare meals. Throughout the Papantla lowlands, food is prepared on the floor only when the container is extremely large and heavy—as, for example, when maize is

655

. 12—LOWLAND HOUSES, EL TAJIN, VERACRUZ. a, Attaching withes to support roof thatch.
hotographed by Isabel Kelly, 1947–51.) b, House assemblage. Unused pottery stacked against house
ll. (Photographed by Eric Schwartz, 1963–64. Courtesy, Mario Vásquez, Planeación del Nuevo
seo Nacional de México.)

a

b

FIG. 14—LOWLAND HOUSE KITCHEN, EL TAJIN, VERACRUZ. *a*, Preparing food on raised hearth. The warped griddle is homemade. *b*, Raised hearth with ridges to support cooking vessels. Homemade griddles in rear. (Photographed by Eric Schwartz, 1963–64. Courtesy, Mario Vásquez, Planeación del Nuevo Museo Nacional de México.)

steeped for the family tortillas and when gruel and tamales are made in quantity for guests. Other cooking is done on a raised, mud-plastered hearth, which is built against one wall or in a corner (fig. 14). U-shaped ridges support the pots; in addition, three small, homemade clay jars are often inverted and used as firedogs. The metate occupies a special table or trestle, handy to the raised hearth; here the housewife stands, both to grind and to cook. In the lowlands the commercial handmill often supplements, but does not replace, the traditional stone metate.

In all of Totonacapan, a simple palm mat —not of Totonac manufacture—is spread on the earth floor as sleeping accommodation. A raised bed is known but is not in general use. Its frame of four forked posts, connected by crosspieces, supports planks in the Sierra, lengths of split bamboo in the lowlands. Nowadays, about Papantla, canvas or burlap cots and even commercial beds with springs and mattress are being adopted. Occasionally, the several types of sleeping facilities are found within a single household, in which case status hierarchy

is nicely reflected. The family head occupies the bed or cot; the sons sleep on trestle beds; the daughters are relegated to the floor.

Aesthetic expression focuses on the religious altar or shrine (fig. 15), found in almost every house interior. For the most part, the altar is a colorful creation and, within the basic pattern, displays considerable individuality. Usually it consists of a cloth-covered table, crowned by a tissue-paper-decorated canopy and adorned with images of Christian saints, candlesticks, vases of flowers, and assorted oddments. The area beneath the table is used for storage, not infrequently of archaeological stone "idols."

Most Totonac interiors have a cluttered appearance, precisely because of scant storage facilities. "Almost every house is literally strewn with odd possessions for which there is no adequate storage space" (Kelly and Palerm, 1952, p. 192). Little-used objects are stashed in an "attic," formed by placing long planks across the rafters; from these swing forked-stick hooks, which are useful for hanging clothing and other objects. For kitchen storage, hanging shelves

657

FIG. 13—TRADITIONAL PALM-THATCHED HOUSES OF LOWLANDS, EL TAJIN, VERACRUZ. Walls of vertical bamboo. (Photographed by Carlos Sáenz, 1963–64. Courtesy, Mario Vásquez, Planeación Nuevo Museo Nacional de México.)

a

b

are suspended from the rafters, and about the hearth many items are tucked into the wall interstices. Pottery vessels not in daily use are stacked on wooden racks against the exterior wall of the kitchen, fig. 12,b).

The sweat house, the only masonry structure possibly reminiscent of former architectural prowess, occurs throughout Totonacapan. There is, however, wide variation. The sweat house may be built at ground level or excavated into a slope. The floor plan is usually square or rectangular, rarely, with rounded corners. The earth-covered roof ranges from flat to two sheds to almost dome-shaped. In highland Eloxochitlan one corner is completely walled off to form the fire chamber, and this has a separate exterior opening; water is thrown against the heated interior wall to produce steam. In the Papantla area the hearth is within the bathing chamber. Moreover, the Papantla sweat house usually has a slightly elevated floor of planks or lengths of bamboo, but the Sierra structure has an earth floor covered with a layer of ferns or other plants.

The sweat bath is still used routinely in Eloxochitlan but is losing ground among the young people of the Papantla zone. There, within the past 15 years, a new style of sweat house has been adopted. Flexible wands are stuck in the ground to form a dome-shaped frame, under which the fire is built and over which mats or blankets are thrown when the bath is in use.

Dress and Adornment

Throughout Totonacapan, the men wear a homemade, pajamalike outfit, consisting of white muslin trousers (calzones) and shirt (figs. 7; 12,a; 18; 19). The highland men add a black wool cotón, likewise homemade. Its body resembles a poncho, with rectangular sleeve pieces added. Occasionally, the lowland man wears a small wool poncho, purchased in Papantla. Commercial palm hats, usually with high crown and broad brim, are general. Many men go

Fig. 16—LOWLAND DRESS, EL TAJIN, VERACRUZ. Woman modeling 19th-century raiment. Tubular muslin skirt is handsomely embroidered in red. In rear, plank house with tile roof. (Photographed by Angelina Macías, 1963–64. Courtesy, Mario Vásquez, Planeación del Nuevo Museo Nacional de México.)

barefoot. In the highlands, when footgear is used, it is the leather-thong sandal, with tire-tread sole. In the lowlands shoes are more common than sandals. For dress, many Papantla calzón-wearers use above-ankle-height shoes, with relatively high heel.

On festive occasions, lowland men wear garments and hats of finer quality, and sometimes a gay-colored shirt. They bedeck

659

G. 15—LOWLAND FAMILY ALTARS. a, El Tajin, Veracruz. Paper-covered canopy; free-nding, three-dimensional images; chromos in shadow boxes. In front, a special table with memade clay candlesticks; on floor, homemade pottery containers for incense. b, Cazuelas, racruz. Palm figures hang from rafters; space beneath altar is for storage; colorful paper cut-ts are a recent innovation. (Photographed by Carlos Sáenz, 1963–64. Courtesy, Mario Vásquez, neación del Nuevo Museo Nacional de México.)

a   b

FIG. 17—LOWLAND DRESS, EL TAJIN, VERACRUZ. *a*, Small boy wears magenta rayon dress for festivals. *b*, Mode[r] fiesta garb of white organdy, machine-embroidered; gold necklace and earrings. Colorful rayon parasol has replaced t[he] old-style, black cotton one of 15 years earlier. (Photographed by Angelina Macías, 1963–64. Courtesy, Mario Vásqu[ez], Planeación del Nuevo Museo Nacional de México.)

themselves with bright, solid-color kerchiefs and adorn their hats with fresh or plastic flowers.

In the highlands Eloxochitlan and Tonalixco women wear a full skirt of black wool, home-woven and home-dyed. They say that in other villages of the area white muslin is used. The upper part of the body is covered with a white muslin quexquemitl, under which younger women use a white muslin blouse. Sierra women generally are barefoot.

The everyday raiment of the women of the Papantla lowlands is a white muslin skirt and blouse (fig. 14,*a*), the former us-

ually gathered and tied with tapes. Older women cling to a tubular muslin skirt whose fullness is collected on one hip and secured by a red, woven belt, obtained years ago from highland traders. Over the blouse hangs a bright-colored square of cloth, which is tied at the nape and covers the chest. An apron, often of gaily flowered cotton, is worn over the skirt.

On festive occasions, lowland dress is elaborate (fig. 17,*b*). A decorated blouse, sometimes hand-embroidered, is worn over one of white muslin, and an organdy skirt, factory-embroidered in white rayon, is used over several layers of muslin skirts. The square hung over the chest is of imitation silk, and an organdy quexquemitl, with lace or factory-embroidered trim, covers the head or is thrown over the shoulders. Some women wear shoes with their festival raiment.

The lowland Totonac are far more clothes-conscious than are those of the highlands. They alone have special raiment for festivals and they invest heavily in it. Apparel is washed frequently and an effort is made to present an immaculate appearance. Time is lavished on toilette. Most men carry a pocket mirror for primping. Women's hair is usually braided and embellished with ribbons, combs, clips, and sprays of flowers. Gold jewelry (fig. 17,b) is esteemed and is an important part of the wedding gift.

Western garb is not used by either sex in highland Eloxochitlan, but is fast being adopted in the lowlands, where prestige attaches to city-style trousers and shirt, despite the fact that the loose-fitting muslin garb is well adapted to the climate, less expensive, more easily laundered, and more comfortable for working in the fields. Many women, too, now favor Western dress, which is considerably less expensive—and less decorative—than is the organdy dress.

Transportation

Until very recent years, traffic throughout Totonacapan was largely pedestrian, and a familiar sight in the lowlands was the single-file procession on the trail, with the man at the head, the women and children behind. Nowadays, a small plane reaches all important points in the Sierra and, in dry season, throughout the Papantla lowlands, settlements can be reached by car, over roads opened by Petroleos Mexicanos for oil exploration.

Highland Eloxochitlan had neither pack nor riding animals at the time of our study. In 1947 and 1948, many Tajin families, however, were well provided (Kelly and Palerm, 1952, pp. 84–86), but probably there are fewer animals today as a result of the increased availability of rural bus and truck service.

In burden carrying, regional differences are evident. In the highlands, the head tumpline is commonly used by both sexes, as is the carrying frame. In contrast, the latter has virtually disappeared from the low country, where a woman rarely uses a tumpline. Instead, she carries loads—firewood, sugarcane, water jar, wooden tray—on the head; in fact, the bright red wooden tray (fig. 17,b), used to transport all manner of small items, is so ubiquitous that it qualifies as an indispensable feminine accessory.

The Eloxochitlan infant is carried in a muslin sling which hangs from the mother's left shoulder, but on long trips he is relegated to the carrying frame. In the entire Papantla area there is no device—neither sling nor carrying frame—for transporting an infant. A baby is simply carried in the arms. The shoulder-borne litter is used in both regions for transporting the sick, wounded, and dead.

Weights and Measures

All the weights and measures used by the modern Totonac are of European derivation.

Reckoning by volume, which is more easily measured than is weight, is used extensively for maize and other produce. The common unit is the *cuartillo*, which in the Sierra is of 2 liters; in the lowlands, of 3. Only in the highlands is there mention of the *chavo*, which is a quarter-cuartillo, used for small-scale transactions in chile, tomatoes, and so on. In the Papantla area, 4 cuartillos make an *almud*; 3 almudes, an *arroba*; 12 amudes, a *fanega*. Both almud and fanega are terms known in Eloxochitlan, but the measures are not used there, perhaps because the comparative poverty makes large-scale negotiations infrequent. In the highlands and in the lowlands, acreage is most frequently expressed in terms of cuartillos, which refers to the volume of maize required to plant the plot in question.

Linear measures include the *vara* (yard), used in house-building and sometimes in sewing. Smaller units are the *codo* (elbow), calculated at half a vara and used in connection with locally woven textiles. The *cuarta* and *jeme* are the standard Spanish units, used likewise for fractions of the vara. A traditional linear measure in the Papantla zone is the *garrocha*, of 12 cuartas (each of 20 cm., hence 2.4 m.). A plot of land 50 by 50 garrochas is the *destajo*, which amounts to nearly 1.5 hectares. Nowadays, the garrocha deliberately is being reduced to 10 cuartas, so that a *destajo* by such reckoning is the equivalent of an hectare. Many now use the two latter terms interchangeably. Contact with city markets, especially in the lowlands, brings increasing use of the metric system.

Some merchandise is reckoned by the piece. In Eloxochitlan 60 bundles of thatching grass constitute a *tercio*. This term, in the Papantla area, applies to 50 units, such as sugarcane, or withes, poles, or thatching bundles for house building. Here, 2 tercios make a *carga*, and both terms are applied to firewood, but with definition less fixed.

Liquid measures, for honey and alcoholic beverages, are the 5-gallon tin, demijohn, wine bottle, and liter. In the highlands, a beverage is sold by the *topo*, said to be a fifth of a liter. In the Papantla area brown sugar is marketed in parcels containing two subconical cakes, placed butt to butt and wrapped in cornhusk. This unit is called the *mancuerna*, and its weight varies from less than a kilogram to about 1.5 kg., according to the size of the sugar mold used.

ECONOMY

In general, the highlands are not as self-contained economically as are the lowlands, and only in the latter area may the Totonac be considered relatively prosperous.

In the highland community of Eloxochitlan land is scarce and produces but one annual harvest, and frequently that is insufficient to meet family needs. In marked contrast, throughout much of the lowlands, land has been plentiful and reasonably productive. Except for middle-elevation Olintla, where coffee production is important, the highlands have no cash-producing crop to match the vanilla or sugarcane of the Papantla lowlands.

Of necessity, in the slack agricultural season, the Eloxochitlan highlander seeks other means to supplement his slim income from farming, and so must depend on wage work or some small-scale commercial enterprise—both of which take him to other areas. The Papantla Totonac, however, has no such need and seldom leaves his home territory. His comparative prosperity is visible in many ways: in the prevalence of pack or riding animals; the opulence of festive raiment; the expense of a wedding, on which the groom's family may spend between 2000 and 3000 pesos; and in the not infrequent occurrence of polygyny.

Division of Labor; Specialization

In the economy of the modern Totonac, in theory, a division of labor along sexual lines prevails. In actual practice, however, very few family or household-centered activities are exclusively performed by one or the other sex so that the division of labor, which, although explicitly conceptualized, is by no means rigidly followed.

The Totonac man of the Papantla area devotes himself primarily to the care of the milpa: clearing, planting, cultivating, and harvesting. He markets his crops and does whatever processing may be necessary, such as drying vanilla or preparing brown sugar. He cares for any pack or riding animals he may have and is responsible for the construction and upkeep of his house and its wooden furnishings. He keeps his tools in working order; does what little basket making and weaving of tumplines may be required; makes palm ornaments for the domestic shrine; and attends to a host of other small tasks.

There is little economic specialization. Nearly all men are maize farmers, and even the storekeepers, barbers, and carpenters in El Tajin derive most of their income from the milpa. By request, many men make articles for sale to neighbors, such as casting nets, sugarcane presses, belt looms, chairs with woven seats, and dance masks. Within the context of spare-time activity, therefore, limited craft specialization is evident.

The lowland woman cares for the children and runs the household. She cleans, cooks, hauls water, launders, feeds the fowl, cares for the small garden, and gathers wild plant products, such as chile and the miniature tomato. She makes pottery, weaves, makes and mends clothing. She sells the pots and textiles she herself makes. She also sells eggs, poultry, and such produce as sweet-potatoes, manioc, chile, and wild tomatoes when small quantities are involved.

Some responsibilities are shared. The thoughtful husband returns from the milpa with a load of firewood, but not infrequently his wife has to forage for it. Most women and girls work daily in the maize field and participate in all aspects of local agriculture except clearing and planting. Widows, in particular, may take full responsibility for the milpa, hiring laborers as needed. Both sexes care for the bees and the hogs, haul cane to the crusher, and bake wheat bread. In case of emergency, a man may help his wife by preparing tortillas or even hauling water, but such endeavors amuse the neighbors, and men less frequently than women depart from their defined roles. Curers and healers include both sexes but only old women are midwives.

The division of labor is more marked with respect to activities which are not family-centered. Large-scale commercial transactions are the province of the man. Only he is storekeeper, although his wife normally assists. Men alone butcher and prepare cracklings and are part-time barbers and carpenters. All public offices are held by men and they alone participate in the com-munal labor program; women have no voice whatsoever in local government. Only men represent the church and are religious singers. They also are the secular musicians and the dancers.

The pattern in highland Eloxochitlan agrees on the whole, but there are some differences. Because the land yields but one harvest a year, agriculture is less time-consuming and less rewarding. Some men devote considerable time to cattle—buying, selling, trading—but there is no dairying. When the harvest is in, many men turn peddlers or day laborers. In fact, in one highland Totonac community, "Tepango de Rodríguez, commercial activities are probably more important than is agriculture" (Kelly, 1953, p. 176). Dedication to crafts is negligible, but the Totonac trader sells objects produced in Mexicano-speaking communities of the Sierra de Puebla.

The Eloxochitlan woman seldom works in the milpa, but she helps harvest and shell corn. If the family has sheep, she and her children herd them. She makes no pottery, but she prepares the wool (purchased in Ahuacatlan) and weaves the man's cotón and the material for her skirt. An adolescent girl, still unmarried, presents herself at the church each Monday before dawn, to receive instruction in religious doctrine and to help sweep the church. Upon occasion, all young, unmarried girls and all widows are required to work in a communal labor force, but under the religious rather than the political authorities. They are given the "lighter" tasks, such as hauling sand and lime.

Property

There is a shortage of cultivable land in highland Eloxochitlan and, to make matters worse, residents of adjacent mestizo and Mexicano settlements have been trying aggressively to purchase local property. In 1951, officially, Eloxochitlan was an ejido, but in reality it was composed of small private holdings. Only five or six persons, con-

663

sidered the wealthiest, had 25 or 30 not very productive hectares—somewhat less than the size of Tajin's standard parcel of land.

Twenty years ago, comparatively good land was abundant in the lowlands and most Totonac farmers were property owners. Even then, some ejidos had been established in the Papantla area, but El Tajin was not among them. Recently, in the non-ejido communities of the lowlands, the situation has changed dramatically. Mestizo investors have purchased Totonac property and have cleared vast tracts of forest, primarily for the purpose of establishing grazing land. Today, Tajin has many landless families, and in another generation the situation will be acute.

Theoretically, in Eloxochitlan children inherit on an equal basis, but sometimes the widow receives all the property. As a rule, an aging couple summons local officials and witnesses and in their presence specifies the desired division of property, denying a son or daughter who has been neglectful. The dwelling usually goes to a son. Reputedly, disputes over inheritance are common.

In El Tajin the situation is quite different. Patrilineal inheritance of land, houses, and other property predominates, perhaps owing to the fact that a daughter often marries outside the community and goes to live with her spouse. Until recently, many land parcels in Tajin were held by the descendants of the original owners, who purchased in the latter part of the past century. In fact, title often remains in the name of the purchaser, long since deceased. To avoid the bother and expense of having title transferred, the heirs have continued to pay taxes in the name of the earlier owner.

Production and Consumption Unit

Throughout Totonacapan, the economic unit is the household. Its composition varies from a single nuclear family of three or four persons to a large patrilocal extended family, composed of several nuclear families and representing three or even four generations. This domestic group is both the production and the consumption unit and is linked closely to the local pattern of subsistence agriculture.

In highland Eloxochitlan there is no surplus, and all families must buy maize and beans long before the new harvest. In the lowlands, in spite of crop diversity and good yield, there is a tendency to plant only a sufficient amount for home consumption. Thus, in 1940, of 518 Totonac households in several communities of the Papantla area, only one dedicated itself exclusively to growing a cash crop, and nearly half the others planted no cash crop at all (Kelly and Palerm, 1952, pp. 99–100). To some extent, this may reflect the fact that vanilla and sugarcane do not do well everywhere in the lowlands.

The lowland Totonac household tends to be self-sufficient in that it grows most of its food staples. Certain other necessities, such as pottery, special kitchen utensils, furniture, and clothing are produced by members of the domestic group or by neighbors. Inasmuch as most lowland families sell some produce—even if it be no more than wild tomatoes and chile—many small items which might otherwise be made in the household are purchased from neighbors or itinerant traders, or are bought in the stores or market of the nearest urban center.

There is a considerable amount of cooperation within the household. In accord with the division of labor as described above, some tasks are allotted to each sex, some are shared. The woman's participation in the milpa is most important economically and tends to encourage polygyny. From an early age, children learn to help, thus lightening the parents' load and at the same time preparing themselves for adult responsibilities. In part, because children are genuinely helpful, parents are sometimes eager to remove them from school. However, in recent years, in the lowlands, there is increasing interest in academic preparation, and some

Totonac families, at considerable expense and inconvenience, send their children to school in Papantla. Throughout Totonacapan an adolescent girl is reasonably skilled in basic feminine responsibilities, and, by the age of 16, a boy is practically able to do a man's work.

Trade and Markets; Labor Export

Despite the persistence of a subsistence economy, the Totonac are becoming increasingly dependent on a cash market. Objects of native manufacture have been or are being replaced by commercial products (see Technology). In the lowlands, store-bought beds and other furniture (e.g., rocking chair), as well as city-style clothing, enjoy prestige.

Probably every Totonac community has a small internal market for produce such as maize, eggs, or even hogs and other animals; some, in homemade pottery, textiles, and other spare-time manufactures. As far as we know, there is no sizable native market controlled by Totonac, although the surrounding Totonac communities are often the mainstay of the Mestizo-Mexicano market of the nearby municipal center. From the latter comes the meager merchandise stocked by the so-called "stores" in the rural area.

Large-scale coffee production by the Totonac of middle-elevation Olintla probably gives that district a distinctive and profitable economic cast. In highland Eloxochitlan there is no real cash crop and no excess of any staple. Here the Totonac often operate as middlemen. Many men and women go on foot to villages at slightly lower level, where they buy fruit and chile for resale in the Ahuacatlan or Zacatlan markets, both of which are predominantly Mestizo and Mexicano. Men who work part of the year as itinerant peddlers go to the lowlands to hawk Sierra craft products—such as metates, glazed pottery, glass objects and, until recent years, woven belts for women and carved images of Christian saints—none of

Totonac manufacture. The vendor returns with a cargo of small, hot chile from Papantla, to be sold in the Sierra. Other highlanders go to the coast to cut timber for a price or to hire out as agricultural laborers.

In the lowlands the Papantla market is a Mestizo institution whose prosperity depends largely on sales to the Totonac of the rural hinterland. No Totonac man sells his produce in the market, and even the women dispose of their minor products on a house-to-house basis. The men deal directly with the important Mestizo merchants in Papantla or Poza Rica. At times, and in the case of vanilla alone, they sell to intermediaries and to "the agents of the big dealers in Papantla [who] infest the trails, trying to persuade passersby to sell to them" (Kelly and Palerm, 1952, p. 125). Vanilla lends itself to such traffic, for it can be marketed in small quantity in varying states of maturity. Moreover, early sale is advisable to reduce the danger of loss through theft.

Wealth and Its Uses

The highland Totonac of Eloxochitlan is in no position to amass wealth. Moreover, he must spend—sometimes trifling amounts, sometimes staggering sums—for ceremonies and offerings which amount to payment of perennial blackmail to various supernatural beings (Kelly, 1966). If he fails in these obligations, the offended deities inflict illness, death or other disaster on the family. To make matters worse, five mayordomías are associated with the Catholic church. These change hands yearly, and the recipients are obligated to spend on such a scale that normally they must borrow money, mortgage or sell their land. In short, in an area where bare subsistence presents a problem, the harried Totonac is under constant pressure to spend for matters related directly or indirectly to religion, be it his old, native pantheon or the Catholic Church.

The Totonac of the Papantla lowlands is in more comfortable circumstances, and his use of wealth is very different. In Tajin al-

Fig. 18—THE IMAGE OF SAN JOSE VISITS EL TAJIN. A cantor heads the procession; in the rear, women and dren with flowers and lighted candles. (Photographed by Eric Schwartz, 1963–64. Courtesy, Mario Vásquez, Planea del Nuevo Museo Nacional de México.)

most nothing remains of native religion, and adherence to Catholicism is quite perfunctory. To be sure, a man may give a festival in honor of a visiting Christian saint (fig. 18), in the conviction that his harvest will benefit, but ordinarily spending is secular rather than religious. Some do not stint on festival raiment, although it is thought prudent to avoid ostentation and thus reduce the danger of theft. A wedding represents a considerable expense for the groom's family. Large sums are spent in connection with death, starting with hospitality at the wake and continuing for friends who foregather the 80th day after death, in honor of the deceased. Annually, at Todos Santos, the

666

Days of the Dead, every family spends generously for the pleasure of its demised relatives. Finally, a man in comfortable circumstances may gain prestige by becoming the financial sponsor of a group of musicians or dancers.

SOCIAL ORGANIZATION

Family and Kinship

The basic structure of modern Totonac society shows relatively little regional variation. A thorough-going bilateral organization prevails, but within this frame there is emphasis on the paternal line, resulting from the rule of patrilocal residence and, in the lowlands, of patrilineal inheritance of property.

The patrilocal extended family presumably is the traditional unit; it still exists but today, by actual count, the independent nuclear family is dominant. Within the family, considerable emphasis is placed on the conjugal relationship, and in general, women enjoy high status in the society. Outside of the immediate family, kinship plays a reduced role in social relations. Rather, individuals are linked together as ritual kin and by almost formalized friendship ties.

Marriage is a focus for considerable elaboration and seldom is casually contracted. Marriage arrangements are negotiated between the respective families and often these negotiations stretch out over a long period of time. Initiative is taken by the groom's parents who, in the course of four formal visits, arrange the betrothal with the girl's family. Most of the expenses associated with marriage are assumed by the groom's family and, in the lowlands, the costs can be sizable. Frequently, before their betrothal, the young couple is not acquainted.

In the highlands, in particular, girls frequently marry very young, sometimes before the onset of their first menses, and the first overture toward marriage is often made when a boy is barely 9 or 10 years old, the girl a year or so younger. Allegedly, there is a shortage of females and it is thought that a bride may not be available should one delay. In this region, formal betrothal may "precede marriage by several years" (Kelly, 1953, p. 181). In the Papantla lowlands formal betrothal seldom is arranged more than a year prior to marriage, and the couple may even be slightly acquainted prior to the initiation of proceedings. There, also, marriage takes place at a somewhat more advanced age, and proof of virginity is normally required.

Some contrasts in practices relating to marriage between the highland and lowland Totonac reflect economic differences which distinguish the two regions. In the lowlands, polygyny occurs to some extent, whereas strict monogamy prevails in the Sierra. In the former, a man's agricultural output may be limited only by the amount of assistance that he can muster from his family, so that a second wife and expanded family can be economically advantageous. Likewise, in the lowland communities, there is greater instability in marriages.

In the highlands marriage between cousins, especially second cousins, is said to be fairly common. In Tajin, however, cousin marriage is rare and the practice is condemned. In both regions, the levirate and sororate are widely practiced. There is no barrio organization in the lowland communities, but a bride will usually be selected from a nearby community, and hence local exogamy tends to be the dominant pattern. In the highlands, where barrio organization exists, exogamy is usual but not obligatory. Marriage between ritual kin is prohibited in both areas.

Although, in both regions, marriage arrangements are formally negotiated by the parents of the future spouses, in the lowland Tajin community the couple may be slightly acquainted through chance meetings, and the prospective groom reasonably certain of acceptance before he asks his parents to make formal request. It is during the fourth and last of their visits to arrange the betrothal that the girl's parents state their terms. Some request music and dancing at the wedding festival. A few of the stipulated gifts are standard: a painted calabash shell to use as a drinking cup (fig. 17,b), a wooden chair, a woven palm mat, and a painted wooden tray (fig. 17,b). If the boy's family is moderately prosperous, the following are also stipulated: a gold necklace (fig. 17,b), gold earrings, two or more gold rings, an organdy skirt, blouse, and quechquemitl, hair ribbons and other hair ornaments, perhaps shoes, plus an umbrella (fig. 17,b) to be used as a parasol on trips to Papantla.

Once the gifts have been agreed upon,

commercially available items are then purchased in Papantla by the boy's family and are delivered the following Saturday, when a feast is served by the girl's family, using food provided in advance by the boy's relatives. The next day the families meet to set the date of the wedding, taking into account aspects such as the age of the couple and the church calendar. During Lent, for example, weddings are prohibited. Throughout the waiting period, normally less than a year, the boy supports his prospective bride and delivers firewood and food to her parents' home weekly.

Following the civil and religious ceremonies in Papantla, which are attended by relatives and friends of both families, the wedding party returns to the house of the groom's family for the festival. For large weddings, the returning procession can be very picturesque. It winds along the trail, single file, headed by the groom, followed by the bride in her white veil, then the parents, godparents, and finally the other guests. A few men on horseback bring up the rear. Almost everyone is dressed in gleaming white. To this, a touch of color is added by the bright-red wooden trays which the women balance on their heads. The green forest forms a backdrop.

The wedding feast is lavish and is followed very often by a whole night of music and dancing. Throughout these festive hours, the bride and groom remain solemnly seated, side by side, without exchanging a word. Consummation takes place the second night and in the morning the bride is expected to produce evidence of virginity. The same morning, she must be the first in the household to arise, and she presents a cup of maize gruel to her parents-in-law, as a gesture of respect and submission.

Despite the emphasis upon virginity, the costs involved in sponsoring a traditional wedding are such that a boy's family may encourage him to attempt seduction of his prospective bride or elopement with her to avoid the expense. In either instance, the girl's family loses its bargaining power and must be satisfied with any gifts proffered. Elopements, in the Papantla lowlands, are by no means rare, especially if the boy's family is poor and a good chance exists that any formal overtures toward marriage might be refused.

Following the wedding, the couple lives with the husband's parents, even if the groom has the means of building his own house at the time. Later, a separate dwelling is built, generally on land provided by his father and close by. The result is a cluster of dwellings whose occupants are related in the male line.

Secondary marriages are contracted with a minimum of formality. Before a man takes a co-wife, consent of the first wife is indispensable. Should she protest, he risks losing her; if she complains to the authorities, he may have to make a property settlement. Often, however, a woman will urge her husband to take a second wife. The latter assists in the milpa, while the first wife runs the house. Sometimes, polygyny is simply inspired by a desire for more children.

Selection of a second wife follows no set pattern. There are a few cases where a man has taken as co-wives his wife's grown daughters by a previous marriage. There are also instances in which the co-wives are sisters or distant relatives of one another. Widows, especially, are frequently taken as second wives. According to individual circumstances, co-wives may share the same house or occupy separate establishments. A widow or widower must wait a period of 80 days before remarrying.

In the highland community of Eloxochitlan no expensive and elaborate gifts are given at the time of marriage. The bride's family supplies her with new clothes, and the groom's family does the same for him. Later, his parents or those of both may give the couple two or three hens to start their poultry stock. Here, likewise, the expense of the civil and religious ceremonies and of the marriage feast is borne by the groom's parents and the godparents, and the latter are selected by the groom's father.

Native kinship terms are rapidly disappearing from the current of everyday speech throughout Totonacapan. For the most part, usage of Spanish terms represents a form substitution rather than a conceptual or semantic shift. That is, the Spanish system of kinship terminology is similar to the Totonac system, particularly in regard to terms for consanguineal relations. Insofar as native terms can still be elicited, there appear to be no major differences within the Zacatlan-Papantla dialect. Terms in southeastern Totonacapan may differ somewhat and nothing is known of those from the northern dialect.

Briefly, cousin terms are of the Eskimo type, and speaker's sex and relative age are both recognized in sibling terminology. The criterion of sex is recognized in the terms for all lineal relations except grandchildren. It is also recognized in the terms for parents' siblings, but for other collateral relatives, such as cousins and siblings' children, it is ignored. Unfortunately, little is known of the extensions of these terms. For affinal relations, child's spouse and spouse's parents are terminologically equivalent and the term applies to both sexes. There are separate terms for spouse's siblings, and these are distinguished according to sex.

It is within the context of the localized family that kinship terms are most used. One's spouse's immediate family may also be designated by kinship terms, but for more distant relatives, personal names are used. As a gesture of courtesy and affection, kinship terms may be used in addressing nonrelatives.

Whereas kinship plays a small role in social relationships outside of the immediate family, individuals are linked in almost formalized friendship ties and in ritual kin, the two categories overlapping. During adolescence boys and girls, but particularly the former, establish a few close friendships with agemates of their own sex; as they

grow older, these friendships continue to constitute some of the closest affective ties outside of the immediate family. Friends visit one another and give mutual aid in economic pursuits and in financial crises. Close friends may become ritual kin. Between *compadres,* there is great "respect," exchange of gifts, and considerable economic assistance.

In highland Eloxochitlan compadres are acquired for certain church rites: baptism, confirmation, first communion, and marriage. In addition, a compadre is sought when one purchases the image of a saint for the domestic shrine. Interestingly, compadres are sought in connection with two major native ceremonies: the appeasement rite for the Owner of the forests, following the construction of a new house, and the definitive celebration to satisfy the Mothers of the hearthstones (Kelly, 1966). There are four compadres of the house, who participate in the construction and, with their wives, in the ceremony following; there are eight or more for the hearthstone ceremony, and they and their spouses donate the large amount of new raiment received by the individual for whom the rite is held.

There is also an impressive array of compadres in the lowlands. Those associated with church rites are substantially the same as in the Sierra. In addition, if a visiting saint comes to Tajin and a family decides to give a festival in his honor, the host seeks compadres to help with expenses. There are also compadres of the cross, which is set up in the graveyard 80 days after death. If one goes to the coast for his first bath in the waters of the Gulf, he seeks a compadre. Sometimes a new cane crusher or a new fishing net has such sponsorship (Kelly and Palerm, 1952, p. 81).

Territorial, Political, and Religious Organization

At least some highland communities have barrios. Eloxochitlan, for example, is composed of three named barrios, which are

669

Fig. 19—THE EL TAJIN VILLAGE PLAZA IS CLEARED THROUGH COMMUNAL LABOR. (Photographed by Gabriel Ospina, 1947–51).

usually exogamous but not invariably. A man normally belongs to his father's barrio, and as a consequence there is comparative stability of the male component. There is a marked feeling of barrio loyalty, but if a man so desires he may assign his son to one of the other units. Occasionally, an adult man shifts barrio affiliation—if he has squabbled with fellow members, and sometimes if he or his wife has inherited property elsewhere. Nevertheless, simple change of residence does not alter barrio membership. A woman belongs to her father's barrio until she marries, whereupon she is considered a member of her husband's barrio. Apart from its exogamous aspects, the barrio organization figures principally in connection

with the communal work group. It has no association with the mayordomías.

It is principally in the highlands where some of the ancient political and religious structure appears to have survived. In Eloxochitlan, despite formal administration from the Mestizo municipal center of Ahuacatlan, the local political hierarchy is rather elaborate, and almost every adult male either holds or has held public office. Here, too, community activities of church and state, so to speak, are intertwined in the election of the mayordomos and in the whole matter of communal labor.

The organization of the public labor force in Eloxochitlan is intricate. When barely adolescent, the individual begins his service, under the aegis of the church. The church continues to supervise communal labor given by unmarried girls and widows, but when a boy marries or when he reaches the age of 18, he shifts to the secular labor force, which is administered by political authorities.

In El Tajin the political structure is far less complex and seems to be rather simple and democratic in operation, with considerable local autonomy, despite official subordination to the Papantla municipal seat. The institution of *faena,* public labor (fig. 19), is prominent, but only married men are recruited and women are fully exempt. Apart from the demonstrable material benefits to the community, the communal labor program brings together periodically the male heads of households, in a situation not unlike a town meeting, so that news is exchanged, important issues discussed, elections held, and a community feeling generated. Such a function is of extraordinary importance to a community with a dispersed settlement pattern.

RELIGION AND WORLD VIEW

Many traits of the old religion survive in the Sierra. Despite four centuries of indoctrination, Catholicism appears in Eloxochitlan as an overlay, adapted to native patterns rather than the reverse (Kelly, 1966).

Fragments of myths relate to the classic Mexican sequence of the four "suns" or worlds. The present era begins with the rising of the Sun. Subsequently and paradoxically comes destruction by flood, with one human and a rabbit the lone survivors. Some informants anticipate the next "cleansing of time" in the year 2000. Accounts of the appearance of the Sun and Moon and of the flood may give explanations for natural phenomena: why highland and lowland differ; why a certain bird has a red head; why the dog "speaks with its tail"; why the ant has a constricted waist; why cucurbits are "watery."

The Eloxochitlan Totonac designate the pre-Sun world as that of the "ancient ones." Illuminated by stars alone, it is inhabited by tiny people, who are hunters and gatherers. The Sun-elect is conceived when a woman inadvertently swallows a brilliant trinket which she finds in the water. She dies giving birth, and the infant Sun emerges from her navel. In four days (or four years) the Sun is a large boy; in another four, a grown man. He plants a milpa, engaging peons who survive today as the animals who eat the planted seed corn. His conversion into a heavenly body follows that of a well-known tale: he builds a great fire, throws himself on its coals, and thereupon soars heavenwards as the Sun. The Moon-elect, an inveterate woman-chaser with scant prestige, falls into the hot ashes. He also rises, but not as high as the Sun, and he gives less light.

With the appearance of the Sun, the people of the ancient world are converted into "stones, trees, all the animals, the metates, and the cooking pots." Eventually, when the Sun terminates, these objects will resume their former identity and eat the present population—a notion reminiscent of beliefs reported in the Popol Vuh and for several modern Maya groups. Even now the stones present a hazard. Mindful of their earlier existence, they try to move. Such an enterprising stone is "shot" by a falling star, drawing blood. Dangerous snakes are similarly dispatched by stars.

The universe is divided into horizontal layers (Kelly, 1966), with difference of opinion concerning the number. The Sun and the "principal saints" are in the highest level of the sky, the Moon and lesser beings below them. Beneath the earth are four bearers. With the assistance of four hills, they support our world on a litter-like platform. To either side of the earth is water. Beyond, both east and west, where the Sun rises and sets, is land inhabited by "the short ones," tiny people who take refuge underground each day, when the hot Sun approaches. When the Sun and Moon quar-

671

rel, an eclipse occurs. When the earth bearers shift their burden, there is an earthquake.

The Sun, identified with the Santisimo Sacramento, is the supreme deity. There is no hint of the benevolent "goddess," wife of the Sun, and of their son, reported in the old sources for the lowland Totonac of Cempoala. The several manifestations of the Virgin seem to be considered separate beings, without evident native counterparts. Old Thunder is older than the Sun and tries daily to impede the latter's rising. The Thunder beings—usually called the Sanmigueles in Eloxochitlan—are of a less important category but are the direct producers of thunder, rain, and wind.

There is an Owner of the underworld, and various other "owners" are associated with nature: the Owners of the soil and the planting, of the harvest, of the cliffs, of the forests, and of the water. Most of these are identified with Christian saints. The Owner of the underworld and the spirits of the dead are responsible for much illness, but the other beings also are malevolent. They exact certain deportment, ceremonies, and "substance" or offerings, and the same is true of the 14 Mothers of the hearthstones (spirits of deceased midwives). As a consequence, the impecunious Eloxochitlan Totonac lives in a state of chronic blackmail by supernatural beings (Kelly, 1966).

Illness also results from sorcery, in which case a witch may persuade the spirits of the dead or one of the several "owners" to act on his behalf. There are various kinds of shamans, male and female, each type designated according to specialty and techniques used. The transforming witch, or nagual, is well known, but allegedly from neighboring communities only. A curing shaman diagnoses illness through consultation with the Mothers of the hearthstones: "he asks with his soul" and reads the reply in the smoke of the incense. The most common specific cause of illness is loss of the soul which re-

sides in the head (see Life Cycle). Intrusion of a material object is less common, as is damage to one of the 12 "companions." Inasmuch as illness, death, crop failure, and bad luck in general result from supernatural intervention, appeasement of the beings considered responsible is the only logical recourse.

Major ceremonies which are predominantly native include: the placation of the Mothers of the hearthstones shortly after birth and again after reaching adulthood, observances connected with planting and harvest, and those which follow the construction of a dwelling.

In the harvest and house-dedication ceremonies, a turkey is slaughtered and the blood dripped on copal. Moreover, in the dedication rite, a young male turkey is buried alive beneath the floor. Other ritual elements recur generally in native observances: censing with copal; offerings of entire copal bars; libations with various alcoholic beverages; extensive ceremonial drinking; use of wax and of both wax and tallow candles; offerings of tobacco; fairly elaborate food offerings, including tamales of various kinds, coffee, bread, and alcohol. The ceremonial use of a sedum (*Sedum batteri* Hemsl. det R. T. Clausen) is prominent. Four is the common ritual number, but 7, 9, and other numbers crop up.

No such wealth of native lore survives in the Papantla lowlands, but vestiges suggest there once may have been considerable resemblance to the Sierra. Specific similarities are seen in the account of the rising of the Sun and Moon; identification of the latter as a male, addicted to women; conversion to stone of the inhabitants of the pre-Sun world; survival of a rabbit following a flood. Likewise, certain tales explain natural phenomena, such as topographical details, the peculiarities of various animals, and the production of two ears or less by each maize stalk. Anecdotes refer to the Thunder beings, to the Old Man of the forest (Eloxochitlan's Owner of the forest), and to encounters with specters and transforming witches.

There is no mention of a laminated universe; the earth is flat, the heavens domed. Daily the sun rises in the east and sets in the west, passing beneath the earth and emerging in the morning from an opening at the east. At the western extremity of the world is "Jerusalén," the abode of the spirits of snakebite victims, dancers, musicians, midwives, and childbed casualties.

Of the ancient pantheon, the beings which survive vigorously are the Owner of the forest, the Great Thunder, the Thunder beings, and the 12 Old Women (Eloxochitlan's 14 Mothers of the hearthstones). There are vague references to the Owners of the earth, of the water, and of the harvest, suggesting somewhat the same assemblage reported for the Sierra.

As in the highlands, the supernatural beings may be responsible for illness, primarily through soul-loss. Other causes are: contact with the spirits of the dead, sorcery, fright, and the evil eye. Witchcraft occasionally takes the form of disease-object intrusion. Diagnosis is through descrying: a practitioner peers into a container of water, adjacent to which is a lighted candle. Sometimes small stones are placed in the liquid. In diagnoses and curing, Catholic prayers and intervention of Christian saints are emphasized; sometimes the Thunder beings collaborate. Treatment involves "cleansing" by stroking with flowers, foliage, or candles; for the evil eye, with an egg. Censing with copal is standard procedure. So, also, are libations of cane alcohol at the "four corners," either of table or of house. Sometimes the individual is sprayed with alcohol from the mouth of the practitioner. Occasionally, an ailing person seeks treatment in a spiritualistic center in Papantla or with one of the physicians there or in Poza Rica.

Current ceremonies which seem native are those connected with postnatal observations and the 12 Old Women (see Life Cycle). Elements of ritual which overlap with those just mentioned include, in addition, use of the wax of the native bee and a food offering in the form of a special, oversized tamal.

Palm "stars" are made for certain ceremonial occasions, particularly Christian festivals, when the family altar is decorated (fig. 15,b; Kelly and Palerm, 1952, pls. 15,a; 26,b–f). The most common ritual numbers arc 4 and 7, but 8 and 12 also occur. Reference to 20- and 80-day periods strengthens the assumption that the Totonac shared the Mesoamerican calendar.

AESTHETIC AND RECREATIONAL PATTERNS

Arts and Crafts

The early sources indicate that the Cempoaltecan Totonac were highly skilled craftsmen, but little remains of such a tradition (see Crafts). Although the culture provides little scope for artistic expression, some young men in both highland and lowland have marked skill in drawing. Occasionally, a Tajin boy will sketch a design which one of his womenfolk will use as an embroidery pattern. In nearby Cerro del Carbon one unique house has a façade of whitewashed planks, on which sprightly animal figures are painted.

Music and Dance

Totonac music awaits study. Except for Catholic chants, vocal music seldom is heard. Probably the cane flute and gourd rattle used in certain dances are native, but other instruments—including, presumably, the double-headed miniature drum—are Old World. In highland Eloxochitlan essentially indigenous ceremonies are accompanied by violin and guitar. Informants consider the music Totonac, but the opinion of a specialist is needed.

Musical talent is manifest; many men in highland and lowland play acceptably by ear. Bands and "orchestras," each with a financial sponsor, are established institutions in the Totonac communities of the Papantla area. Members meet regularly for practice, using written music, and the groups are engaged to play at certain festivals, locally and in neighboring settlements.

The principal native ceremonies in Eloxochitlan involve dancing, presumably of indigenous style, with both sexes participating. Two more formal, named dances, by men alone, are performed during the January festival (see Annual Cycle). These are the Negritos and the Españoles, Moros y Tocotines. The Volador dance is well known in Eloxochitlan but, in 1951, it was said that the last local performance had been in 1930. No standing organization is associated with the named dances, and there is no performance outside the community. It is said specifically that individuals who have not danced in recent years are under civic obligation to do so in January celebrations. Costumes are rented in Ahuacatlan, where the same stock is accessible to Totonacos, Mexicanos, and even Mestizos.

Lowland dancing is focused on the established, named dances. As with musicians, a group is organized by an individual who advances funds for equipment and who contracts for performances. Tajin dances include: Negritos, Moros y Españoles, Santiagueros, Guagas, and Voladores. Except for the last-named dance—now publicized and commercialized—groups usually have a semisacred mask, to which they make "the promise." This stipulates avoidance of women for four days prior to performance, under threat of illness or death of one of the group. Barring this feature, lowland dances seem to have lost whatever esoteric associations they once may have had.

Both music and dance are significant in the lowland social fabric. Not only may a prosperous person gain prestige through sponsorship of either kind of organization, but the latter also functions somewhat like a men's club, whose members have common interests and responsibilities. Through regular practice and occasional performance there is social intercourse between men who otherwise might have scant contact, and this network not infrequently cuts across village boundaries. Some groups are stable and endure for years, with occasional replacement of an individual, but others are fluid and disband and reorganize because of death, illness, differences of opinion, jealousy, or other conflict.

Humor, Games, and Gossip

Humor is similar in highland and lowland. A play on words—in Totonac, Spanish, or both—is frequent and much appreciated by men, particularly if there is sexual connotation or reference to bodily functions, such as urination or evacuation. Women claim to regard such puns as indelicate. Minor mishaps which cause personal discomfiture and loss of dignity are considered amusing by both sexes.

There is little in the way of organized, competitive games. Some 20 years ago, baseball gained a tenuous hold in the lowlands. Intermittently, Tajin has a team which plays those of neighboring communities.

A favorite game among Eloxochitlan boys and men consists in trying to toss a coin inside a small circle drawn on the ground. Children throw simple palm figures into the wind and, from fresh cane, make a projectile-type toy. Occasionally, a devoted Eloxochitlan father fashions a rough, one-piece wooden doll for his young daughter.

Lowland children also have few toys. Little boys make clay dolls and animals and bake them on the cooking hearth. They also manufacture popguns and tops. Girls wrap sticks with rags to form dolls. Most play is imitation and make-believe: domestic chores such as hauling wood or grinding maize, playing "store" or "school," riding "horseback," and so on.

In the lowlands, gossip is the spice of

life. News and chat are exchanged the day of communal labor, when men from far-flung parcels congregate at the community office. The small stores—which sell soft drinks, beer, and cane alcohol, as well as staples—tend to be social centers, where men congregate to talk and drink. Sometimes a drunken lowlander becomes contentious, squabbles, and draws his machete. In this connection, it may be noted that the local rate of homicide is very high.

Women do not loiter in stores nor do they have an institution parallel to public labor, but among neighbors there is a certain amount of casual visiting. In conversation, details concerning weather, crops, and domestic animals loom large, but of most interest are vital statistics: births, seductions, marriages, and domestic rifts.

Patterns of Etiquette

In highland Eloxochitlan, no reunion—social, political, or ceremonial—is complete without consumption of alcohol, and drinking involves considerable etiquette. Irrespective of age and presumably of social and economic status, a woman usually is addressed as "nana," a man as "tata." As a particular sign of respect, there is token hand-kissing: a man may clasp his comadre's hand, bow, lift it, and deposit the kiss in midair. Handshaking characteristically consists of slight and fleeting contact of the palms, but with outsiders contact is more substantial. If a stranger approaches, ordinarily he is not asked to enter the house nor is he offered a seat.

Although alcoholic consumption is less formalized in the lowlands, there, too, a certain amount of etiquette is associated with drinking. Formerly, it is said, kinship terms were used in address, even among persons not related. In reference, teknonymy is still important. Until recent years, a child who approached an elder person ducked his head, anticipating a benediction and the sign of the cross. Hand-kissing scarcely ex-

ists. Handshaking, of the slight-contact type, is common. Lowlanders have had far more contact with outsiders and to visitors seem more urbane than their highland relatives. Guests commonly are invited into the house and are offered seats, sometimes atole or other refreshment. In many ways, the lowland Totonac are thoughtful, considerate, and generous hosts, and when a guest leaves, he may be given a small gift—an egg, a bit of fruit, a spray of flowers.

Perhaps because houses are so dispersed, one has the impression of less visiting than in the Sierra. If a man comes to call and finds the host not home, he is expected to depart immediately. Strict lines of deportment apply to women, especially nubile girls. The latter must not be left alone in the house or go forth unaccompanied, even to gather firewood or haul water. It is bad form for anyone, but especially a man, to ask concerning the feminine members of another household.

Narcotics and Stimulants

Eloxochitlan men smoke sparingly, usually leaf tobacco, occasionally commercial cigarettes. An unmarried girl does not use tobacco, but during pregnancy it may be a craving. Elderly women often smoke. As in the Papantla area, tobacco is thought to protect one from snakes and the spirits of the dead, and it forms part of the offerings for the supernatural being associated with the forests. In the lowlands, both sexes smoke, often commercial cigarettes. Men sometimes prefer cigars, home-rolled, of leaf tobacco purchased in Papantla. Several decades ago a pipe was current (Kelly and Palerm, 1952, fig. 18).

Practically every gathering in Eloxochitlan involves social or ceremonial drinking (Viquiera and Palerm, 1954). Favorite occasions for drinking include a simple trip to market, performance of communal labor, any and all dealings with political or judicial authorities, and virtually all ceremonies, including those ostensibly associated with the church. On some occasions, such as a house dedication, all participants, of both sexes, are expected to become tipsy. Most women drink, particularly the elderly.

The standard beverage for secular and ceremonial use is cane alcohol (*refino*), which is sold in Eloxochitlan. For important occasions, scheduled to permit advance preparations, "tepache" is manufactured by treating pulque, purchased in Zacatlan, for eight consecutive days with additions of brown-sugar syrup and refino. Other beverages mentioned are mescal, mistela, a commercial anise drink, and beer.

In the lowlands tippling is predominantly a male diversion. Young women seldom drink, but a few elderly widows are confirmed alcoholics. Drinking patterns differ markedly from those of the Sierra, where consumption of alcohol not only is socially sanctioned but is obligatory. The Tajin man drinks on special occasions, such as a trip to Papantla, festivals and funerals, and the gathering for communal labor. Unlike Eloxochitlan, where authorities provide refino from public funds for those of the labor force, in Tajin a man engaged in communal labor purchases a drink at his own expense, in one of the little stores. In addition to refino, a potent local beverage—home-fermented cane juice, known as pulque de caña—sometimes is available. Refino seldom is offered to a woman. At feasts, two commercial liquors—jerez (theoretically sherry) and an anise drink—are provided for the ladies.

Fiesta Patterns

There are two distinct fiesta patterns in Eloxochitlan: certain church festivals in which the public at large participates, and private or family celebrations which touch comparatively few people.

Most, but not all, the church festivals are financed by the respective mayordomos, who often mortgage or sell property to meet their obligations. However, the feast of Santos Reyes, the first week of January, has no mayordomo and is the responsibility of the community. Similarly, two days of the Corpus Christi observances are at community expense, and every inhabitant, including women and children, pays a fixed quota. These major church festivals last several days and follow a set routine: the priest comes from Ahuacatlan to celebrate Mass, and the religious images in the Eloxochitlan church are carried in procession through the village. On the secular side, fireworks, feasting, and generous consumption of refino and tepache provide entertainment.

Family festivals are quite different. In them elements of ancient ritual predominate and a shaman presides. Observations which precede planting of a milpa and those designed to cleanse the hearthstones shortly after birth are not festive. Rather, they are prophylactic ceremonies, to avoid the ire of certain supernatural beings. Attendance is extremely limited.

There is wider participation, but by invitation, for the definitive cleansing of the hearthstones during adulthood, for the maize or harvest ceremony, and for the dedication of a new house. Besides the shaman, two musicians attend and from four to 15 married couples participate. There is dancing by both men and women and elaborate offerings, with feasting and imbibing.

Following civil and religious marriage ceremonies in Ahuacatlan, a wedding party returns to Eloxochitlan for a feast which has a few native ceremonial survivals. Food and drink are provided for invited guests, and the scale of entertainment depends on the financial standing of the godfather and the groom's father.

FIG. 20—DAYS OF THE DEAD, EL TAJIN, VERACRUZ. *a*, Altar (left) and offering for the dead (right). Small colored balloons are an innovation. Split-stick candlesticks are set in floor in front of offering. Offerings include food on altar and table, and on the latter are new ribbons, handkerchiefs, maguey-fiber bags, and towels. *b*, Three cantors kneel to chant in front of offerings. (Photographed by Eric Schwartz, 1963–64. Courtesy, Mario Vásquez, Planeación del Nuevo Museo Nacional de México.)

a

b

The Tajin social season has two established peaks, one in spring, one in fall. The first is to celebrate the annual visit, for several days, of the image of San José (St. Joseph, fig. 18), borrowed from the neighboring community of Joloapan. The saint is received with great respect and is fêted extensively in the hope that, thus gratified, he may send rain. One or more families in comfortable circumstances receive the image in turn, and each sponsors a feast attended by perhaps a couple of hundred local residents. Musicians and dancers may offer to perform in the saint's honor, particularly if someone of the host family belongs to such a group.

In the fall, the Days of the Dead are the occasion for widespread feasting. Then, every family prepares an elaborate offering (fig. 20,a) for its deceased members—invariably including tamales, white rolls in fanciful forms, chocolate, and fruit, as well as handkerchiefs, hair ribbons, and similar items for the pleasure of the spirits. Cantors are engaged to chant (fig. 20,b). Later, after the visiting spirits have withdrawn, relatives visit one another and exchange food gifts.

Corpus Christi is not observed in lowland Totonac communities, but most families go to Papantla at least once to attend the secular fair held for several days at that time. At the insistence of municipal authorities, dancers from outlying Totonac settlements perform in Papantla at Corpus.

Weddings are important family festivals. Some are lavish, with feasting, drinking, and music. Expense is borne by the groom's family and the godparents, and attendance is by invitation. Death and some mourning observances involve so much feasting and entertainment that they might well be considered festivals.

LIFE CYCLE

Three events in the life of a Totonac are marked by ceremony: birth, marriage, and death. There are also suggestions that once puberty may have received more formal

recognition than today. Marriage is treated elsewhere (see Family and Kinship).

In highland Eloxochitlan, prophylactic observances follow birth, the timing dependent on the family's economic condition. A cantor offers candles, copal, and cane alcohol to the Christian saints, so they may protect the infant from the spirits of the dead, known as the "evil airs." Later, when funds permit, a shaman is engaged to appease the Mothers of the hearthstones (see Religion and World View). He offers candles, copal, and cane alcohol to cleanse symbolically the firedogs of both dwelling and sweat house. The house is swept and the accumulated rubbish deposited in the mother's sleeping mat, together with the broom and a piece of copal. The resulting bundle is placed high in a tree and left to disintegrate.

In the lowlands, interesting survivals appear in birth observances. When the umbilical cord is cut, the infant must be "married," to avoid illness. The fictitious spouse is selected by the baby's parents, without prior notification—any person of the opposite sex, not a relative, qualifies. Either four or eight days after birth, a gift of food is presented as formal notification, and the recipient sends the newly acquired "spouse" a return gift, usually a cake of soap and swaddling rags. There is no further obligation. If the infant cries constantly, presumably the ritual mate is not satisfactory and another is selected.

The major postnatal ceremony, however, is held on the eighth day following birth. It also is prophylactic, to protect the mother and child from the displeasure of the midwife and the 12 Old Women, who are the spirits of the deceased midwives of all time. A special tamale is prepared and cut in 12 pieces. A ceremonial table is spread, with further food offerings, accompanied by candles, copal, and cane alcohol. All who had close contact with the birth are sprayed with alcohol from the mouth of the presiding midwife and censed with copal. Alcohol is poured on the floor, and sweepings from the birth area are abandoned in a field or in the forest.

Every Totonac of highland Eloxochitlan, male or female, must be the central figure of a ceremony for the definitive cleansing of the hearthstones. Ideally, this takes place when the person is 15 or 16 years old, thus suggesting relationship to puberty. However, because of cost, the rite may be deferred for many years. Eight to 15 godfathers, each with respective spouse, are sought to help defray expenses. A shaman is summoned to make offerings to all the saints in the church and to the Mothers who reside in the hearth. In addition, there is praying, feasting, and drinking. The godparents present the individual with new clothing, following which he or she dances in turn with each godparent of the opposite sex. Then, the hearth Mothers "are happy," for they have been cleansed and have received their offerings or "substance."

No ceremony is associated with puberty in the lowlands. When a boy reaches about age 15, however, it is thought that his "voice is heavier." For a girl, the onset of puberty is more sharply defined. She is removed promptly from school, is given a metate, and the family decides if she is to continue with Western-type dress worn by young girls or if she is to shift to "native garb," a muslin blouse and full skirt, with white organdy for festivals. During her first menses, the girl's mother sees that precautions are taken to avoid swelling of the hands and feet, and the girl may not launder nor carry a heavy burden at this time. Afterwards, she is never left alone in the house nor may she leave home unaccompanied.

A variant of the "tonal" concept is current in highland Eloxochitlan. Every human has 12 "companions," usually animals, of which four are the principal ones. If one of the four is injured or killed, the person suffers correspondingly (Kelly, 1966). Moreover, every human has two souls, one in the head and one in the heart. The former participates in one's dreams and sometimes is "grabbed" by the evil airs. At death, both souls leave the body. Those of children go direct to the sky, to be born anew. Those of adults go to the underworld, which is precisely like our world, but with day and night reversed. After some time elapses, most souls rise, for rebirth. However, murder victims and anyone who died by drowning or in childbirth are not reborn. They remain for all time with Old Thunder—the women as his wives, the men as his agricultural workers. No adult may present himself in the afterworld without a spouse, and in the coffin of a young betrothed person of either sex is placed a candle, which has been blessed by the priest. In the hereafter, the candle is accepted as a substitute for a mate.

A corpse is bathed, dressed in new raiment, and his used clothing is deposited in the casket, together with seven tortillas, a bottle of water, and 14 copper coins. The family tries to provide a wooden coffin, otherwise, in the afterworld, the demised will live in a house with a leaky roof.

Food and alcohol are provided guests who attend the wake, and a serving is placed on the altar for the deceased. Some days later, the cantor is summoned, and food is prepared for him, the grave diggers, and other guests. There is no 80th-day celebration, as in the lowlands.

The Tajin Totonac say that the spirit of the dead does not leave the house for nine days, perhaps not definitively, for 80 days, at which time food no longer is served for the deceased. Concerning the destination of the spirit after death, there is confusion. In special instances it goes west, to accompany the sun (see Religion and World View). Infant spirits are reborn.

As in the Sierra, an unmarried person is buried with a candle, which latter substitutes for a spouse. In the casket are placed 12 miniature tortillas, a cane containing water, and a crayfish or so. Family and friends are fed at the wake and alcohol is provided. The fourth day after death, a spe-

679

cial food offering is prepared, from ingredients solicited among friends and family. Then the cantor receives 12 tamales, following a purification rite for members of the immediate family. There is another ceremony, with guests and feasting, the ninth day after death, and still another the 80th day.

ANNUAL CYCLE

The Sierra agricultural season occupies eight or nine months of the year. Planting is in March or April; the first cultivation, in May; the second, in June; the harvest, in November. Harvest is followed by several months without agricultural chores. This time, in particular, is when a good many men go forth to seek work elsewhere (see Economy; Trade and Markets). Animal husbandry is somewhat desultory and does not interfere with their departure. In contrast, a woman's work is less seasonal and she is occupied throughout the year with routine domestic chores.

The Eloxochitlan ceremonial calendar includes several church festivals, which do not fall entirely within the months of agricultural activity. In chronological order, the major observances are: Santos Reyes (Holy Kings, Epiphany, January 6); Santo Patrono, or San Marcos (St. Mark, April 25); Corpus Christi, or the Santísimo Sacramento (movable; celebrated full scale once every three years); Virgen del Carmen (July 16); San Salvador (August 6); and Virgen del Rosario (October 7).

In addition, prior to planting and, if funds permit, following the harvest, essentially indigenous rites are performed by a shaman to insure good crops. These are sponsored by private individuals and do not involve community participation. Other family festivals—birth, marriage, definitive cleansing of the hearthstones, and dedication of a new house—are independent of season.

In the Papantla lowlands, agricultural activities are continuous throughout the year,

and there is no month in which one crop or another is not planted, tended, or harvested. Maize, for example, is planted twice yearly, from November through January, and from late June through early August. The summer planting is harvested in December and January; the winter planting, in June. Beans may be planted any time of the year, often with indifferent success.

Spring is the busiest season, and time must be carefully allocated. The milpa must be weeded. Vanilla cuttings must be planted and blossoms on mature vines individually pollinated. Cane planted in October is cut in May and made into brown sugar. A bean crop may be harvested and another planted. Under the fallowing system followed in the lowlands, a spent field is allowed to return to forest, and in spring, a fresh field is cleared to replace it. At this time a man needs additional agricultural hands and, in turn, must lend assistance to others. Even communal labor may be suspended in spring to permit maximum time for personal agricultural demands. By fall, the pressure is relaxed. Apart from routine cultivation of the milpa, considerable time is spent simply guarding the vanilla crop against theft. In winter, vanilla vines are trimmed, granaries repaired, maize and beans harvested.

The agricultural cycle affects the man's activities directly, but the women who work in the milpa experience parallel periods of pressure and relaxation. Even if a woman does not help in the fields, the agricultural schedule is reflected in her program, for she is responsible for feeding the neighbors and friends who come to assist in clearing, planting, and harvesting. Furthermore, every spring the women normally give a hand in pollinating vanilla.

The socio-religious calendar is tied, in part, to agricultural demands, for in the spring the image of San José (St. Joseph) visits the settlement, to be fêted in the hope of breaking the drought. The chief social event of fall focuses on the Days of the

Dead (November 1, 2), when every household prepares food and other offerings for its demised members. Scattered throughout the year are family-centered celebrations, such as weddings and mourning observances. These may call for decoration of the household altar, for which the men make palm ornaments, and for the services of musicians and of religious singers (fig. 20,*b*).

A few other activities may be noted. In spring, the arroyos often dry; then the women must go farther from home to haul water, and the men take advantage of the low water to fish. Pottery making is concentrated between the Days of the Dead and mid-March, when temperature and humidity favor slow drying of the vessels.

REFERENCES

Cook and Borah, 1960
Gessain, 1953
Kelly, I., 1953, 1966
—— and Palerm, 1952
Viquiera and Palerm, 1954
Williams García, 1963

34. The Otomi

⌐⌐⌐

LEONARDO MANRIQUE C.

OTOMI FAMILY is a term which designates a linguistic group whose components have had a highly diverse history and cultural tradition. An ethnographic description of them will probably indicate as many differences as similarities, in spite of the relative homogeneity which the Indian groups of central Mexico have recently attained through "national culture."

The Otomi family comprises today seven languages: Otomi (proper), Mazahua, Matlatzinca, Ocuiltec, Southern Pame, Northern Pame, and Chichimec Jonaz. The Matlame, which according to Mendizábal and Jiménez Moreno (1937) belonged to the same family, disappeared, probably during the 16th century; the Southern Pame is now spoken by less than ten persons. The degree of kinship and the external relationships of the languages of the Otomi family may be consulted in Volume 5, Article 7G (Manrique, 1967).

The classification of an individual as a member of a particular group often depends on the Indian language he speaks. In the case of the Otomi family this criterion is insufficient; there is a large number of Indians who neither speak nor understand the language of their ancestors. Nevertheless, they consider themselves Indians and they share a series of cultural traits, some of which existed prior to contact with European culture, while others were acquired early during the colonial period. For this reason it is very difficult to compute the size of the population of the groups since the census, for various reasons, does not supply sufficiently dependable data; the figures in Table 1 should be taken as approximate.

HISTORY

According to Kirchhoff and to Driver and Massey (1957, map), Otomi family groups occupied a greater area when the Spaniards arrived in Mexican territory than they do now (figs. 1–3). J. Soustelle (1937b) states that the Otomi proper were then in a period of expansion at the expense of the nomadic populations ranging to the north.

In the 16th century the Spaniards aided Otomi (proper) expansion already begun, so as to insure themselves of a sedentary, agricultural, and submissive population in a

682

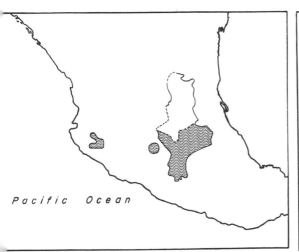

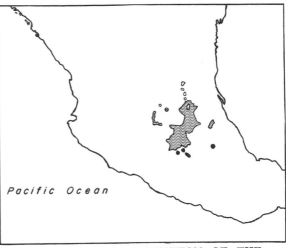

Fig. 1—PREHISPANIC DISTRIBUTION OF THE OTOMI FAMILY. (From Driver and Massey, 1957.) *Shaded area,* Mesoamerican groups. *Outlined area,* Non-Mesoamerican groups.

Fig. 2—PRESENT DISTRIBUTION OF THE OTOMI FAMILY. *Shaded area,* Descendants of Mesoamerican groups. *Outlined area,* Descendants of non-Mesoamerican groups.

region then subject to raids of the nomads. The most important townships founded at that time with Otomi settlers and small groups of Spaniards were: Queretaro, San Juan del Rio, Toliman, San Miguel Allende, Xichu, Tierra Blanca, Santa Maria del Rio, and San Luis de la Paz; in this last place the Chichimec Jonaz adopted a sedentary life and settled in La Mision, where they still live. Also during the 16th century the mines of San Luis Potosi and Zacatecas were discovered, giving rise to the policy of establishing friendly townships in hostile territories which resulted in Tlaxcalteca Indians being taken to San Luis Potosi.

During the 17th century the need to offer security to the pack trains loaded with products from the mines led the Spaniards to try to control the nomadic Pame through the founding of missions such as Cadereyta, Maconi, Jalpan, Rioverde, Ciudad del Maiz, and Gamotes. But the bands which were not subdued constantly attacked the new outposts, maintaining a state of endemic war. Constant hostilities and lack of a regular agriculture provoked uprisings among the recently established Indians; the new settlements frequently disappeared and had to be founded all over again (Soustelle, 1937b, 508–10).

TABLE 1

	Estimated Population	Number of Speakers of Native Language
Otomi	300,000	250,000
Mazahua	70,000	65,000
Matlatzinca	500(?)	500
Ocuiltec	1,500	400
Southern Pame	300	8
Northern Pame	2,500	2,000
Chichimec	600	400
TOTALS	375,400	318,308

683

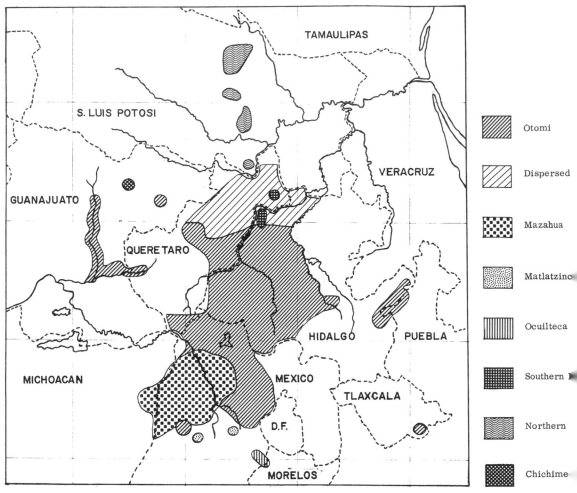

FIG. 3—PRESENT DISTRIBUTION OF THE OTOMI FAMILY. (Adapted from J. Soustelle, 1937b.)

During the 18th century the interests of the new cattle ranches joined those of the mining industry and gave the policy of subjection a purely military character. At this time, economic control passed from the hands of the Spaniards into those of Mestizos. The "civilized" Indians (some of whom were important as collaborators in colonization during the two preceding centuries), as well as those recently made sedentary, were relegated to an inferior position, dispossessed of their lands in favor of the ranchers and compelled to work in the mines. Many missions were destroyed and the Indians persecuted despite the efforts of the missionaries, and in their place military posts (*presidios*) were established. The nomadic Pame, faced with the alternative of submission or extermination, often selected the latter. The territories which up to that time had been exclusively or predominantly Indian were occupied by an increasing number of Mestizos.

The War of Independence and the liberal period of the *Reforma* changed the political status of the country, but they actually worsened the situation of the Indians by accentuating the differences and consolidating the *gente de razón* (the non-Indians) against the *inditos* or *naturales* (Indians).

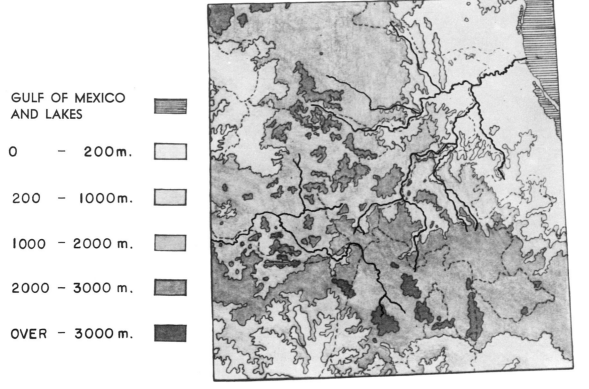

GULF OF MEXICO
AND LAKES

0   —   200 m.

200   —   1000 m.

1000   —   2000 m.

2000   —   3000 m.

OVER   —   3000 m.

FIG. 4—SHADED RELIEF MAP OF OTOMI AREA

During the 19th century the groups which had remained more or less nomadic or constantly rebellious and which had escaped extermination quickly adopted Mestizo techniques in farming and assimilated Mestizo culture, losing a large degree of their distinctiveness. The groups which had been sedentary for a long time (Otomi, Mazahua, etc.) were also assimilated in the north; in the central and southern zones they retreated from the cities (sometimes forming neighborhoods on the periphery). The invasion of Otomi lands by Mestizos caused some of them to infiltrate the Pame of the Sierra Gorda.

After the Revolution of 1910 the Indians obtained endowments or restitutions of their lands in the form of *ejidos*. At the same time increased communications and rural education intensified the move toward "national culture" begun the previous century. Today all groups of the Otomi family present, at first sight, a quite homogeneous aspect and similar to that of other Indian groups in central Mexico.

HABITAT

The habitat of the Otomi family (figs. 3–5) is restricted to the Central Plateau of the Mexican Republic to approximately between 19° and 23° N. latitude. They never inhabit altitudes under 1000 m. above sea level nor, except in a few places, are they found at elevations less than 1500 m. The differences in terrain and vegetation distinguish various regions (figs. 6, 7).

A. *Sierra de las Cruces*, west of the Valley of Mexico, is a mountainous region of over 2500 m. Rainfall is relatively heavy. In the forested areas *ocotes* (*Pinus*), *abetos*

685

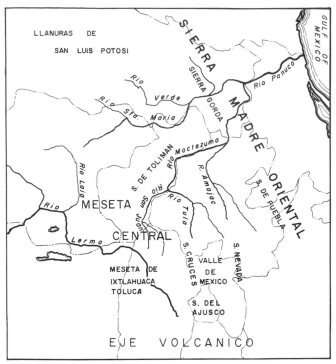

FIG. 5—PRINCIPAL RIVERS AND OROGRAPHIC FEATURES OF OTOMI AREA

(*Abies*), and *encinos* (*Quercus*) predominate. The terrain is very irregular. This region is populated by Otomi, but in the south where it joins the Sierra del Ajusco and descends toward the Balsas Basin, are San Juan Atzingo and Toto, the only Ocuiltec settlements.

B. *Meseta de Ixtlahuaca–Toluca*, a flat region west of region A, lies approximately 2300 m. above sea level. Precipitation is regular during the summer, but in the dry season the plains are covered with gray dust. In the very few places not planted, bushes and a resistant grass grow. The southern part of this region, where the Lerma River originates, has lagoons a few centimeters deep. The Otomi inhabit the region east and north of the city of Toluca, the Mazahua inhabit the remainder, and the only town which retains some part of Matlatzinca (San Francisco Oztotilpan) is at the foot of the Nevado de Toluca.

C. *Western escarpment of the Mesa Central* is of irregular topography, and has regular humidity and milder temperature than region B. The vegetation is subtropical. Culturally it is a prolongation of region B.

D. *Plains of Queretaro and Hidalgo* is a region a little less than 2000 m. altitude, its scant humidity and precipitation making it a semidesert steppe during most of the year. Pasture predominates, with some cacti and few bushes. Riverbanks are always green; in the rainy season the land is covered with crops or with a grass of short season duration. In the central part, the Sierra de Toliman runs from north to south. It is highly fractured and of like climate, although cooler and more humid than the plains. It constitutes the habitat of an Otomi group.

E. *Sierra Gorda*, geographically, is a part of the monocline which forms the Sierra Madre Oriental, bounded by the Moctezuma River to the south and the Santa Maria to the north. Since, however, its topography, climate, and vegetation are similar to other parts of the Sierra Madre which extend farther north and which are inhabited by the Pame, the term is here applied to the entire region. Its altitude ranges from 1000 to 2000 m. In the valleys the climate is temperate, rainfall rather scant, and vegetation poor, lacking large trees. In the south it is inhabited by Otomi who extend from region D, and by the Southern Pame, of Jalipan and Pacula; in the north the Northern Pame range in scattered groups.

The regions previously mentioned are more or less contiguous, but there are four other isolated regions.

F. *Valley of the Rio Laja* is similar geographically to the plains of Queretaro, but with the advantage of permanent water in the river, which makes small-scale irrigation possible. It is inhabited by Otomi.

G. *Plains of Guanajuato*, in topography and vegetation, are a prolongation of the plains of Queretaro, but there is no contin-

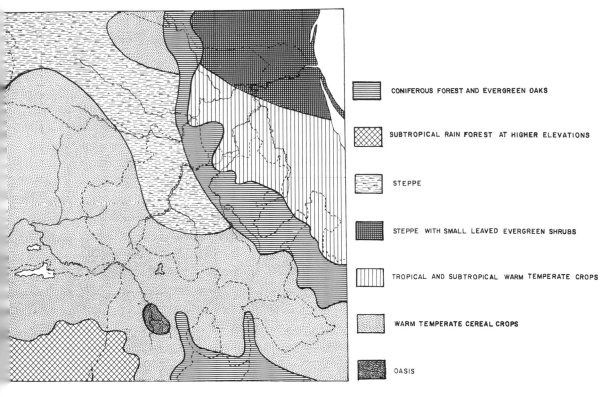

CONIFEROUS FOREST AND EVERGREEN OAKS

SUBTROPICAL RAIN FOREST AT HIGHER ELEVATIONS

STEPPE

STEPPE WITH SMALL LEAVED EVERGREEN SHRUBS

TROPICAL AND SUBTROPICAL WARM TEMPERATE CROPS

WARM TEMPERATE CEREAL CROPS

OASIS

FIG. 6—VEGETATION ZONES, OTOMI AREA

uous Otomi occupation between the two regions. Region G contains the only Chichimec settlement and some Otomi settlements.

H. *Sierra de Puebla* is similar physiographically to the Sierra Gorda, but precipitation is much greater, and consequently vegetation is high-altitude subtropical. Otomi live in some regions of this Sierra.

I. *Ixtenco* is a single Otomi town in the state of Tlaxcala, at the foot of Malinche, in elevated plains (over 2000 m.), with regular humidity and rains in the summer.

ETHNOLOGICAL INVESTIGATIONS

The ethnographic description in this article has been limited to the period from 1900 to 1950. Descriptive works for this period are scant or deficient. The most complete one is by Jacques Soustelle (1937b), who describes the habitat and component languages of the family and establishes their relationship. His description of the material culture, however, especially refers to the Meseta de Ixtlahuaca–Toluca; he ignores the groups which inhabit other regions. He hardly takes into consideration social organization or spiritual culture, but he offers a good historical basis which, for the period preceding contact, has been described by Carrasco (1950).

We have descriptions of Otomi groups in other areas—the Valle del Mezquital (Séjourné, 1952), San Gregorio (Jenkins, 1946), and San Pablito (Christensen, 1953a)—but they are very short and emphasize the more conspicuous local aspects, neglecting others less notable but nevertheless important for the ethnologist.

The Instituto Indigenista Interamericano has in its library unpublished reports by its investigators on other Otomi groups (R.

687

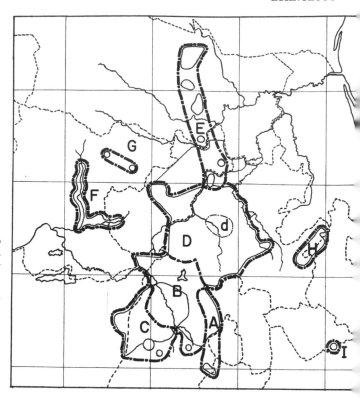

FIG. 7—OTOMI FAMILY CULTURAL REGIONS. A, Sierra de las Cruces. B, Meseta de Ixtlahuaca-Toluca. C, Western escarpment of the Mesa Central. D, Plains of Queretaro and Hidalgo. d, Mezquital. E, Sierra Gorda. F, Valley of the Rio Laja. G, Plains of Guanajuato. H, Sierra de Puebla. I, Ixtenco.

G. Guerrero: 1950a,b; Morales, 1950). The students of the Escuela Nacional de Antropología have recently studied San Pablito (Montoya and others, 1961).

Maza published a description (1947) of the Northern Pame of Santa Maria Acapulco that suffers because the writer was not a specialist at that time, although his other works on the history of the same group (1953) are of high quality.

Nothing similar had been recorded on other members of the family at the time of writing, except for two works of great importance: an ample and highly detailed study on the Chichimec of San Luis de la Paz (Driver and Driver, 1963), and a short but complete description of the Ocuiltec (Rodríguez Gil, 1907).

All the work mentioned, as well as the field notes of R. J. Weitlaner (1958a) and Manrique, 1957, 1959), have contributed to the present article.

688

SUBSISTENCE SYSTEMS AND FOOD PATTERNS

The subsistence of the Otomi family is based primarily on agriculture and secondarily on domestic animals. Only in a few places do hunting, fishing, and gathering have some importance; here they constitute an occasional supplement or emergency substitute rather than the source of a regular supply.

Agriculture

Agricultural techniques vary according to acculturation and terrain. There is also a close correlation between techniques and crops. The most acculturated Indians, when they have good lands (sometimes irrigable on a small scale), plant commercial crops (wheat, barley, coffee) with non-native techniques; these they do not consume except in small quantities. The other Indians, who are the majority, plant only maize, or

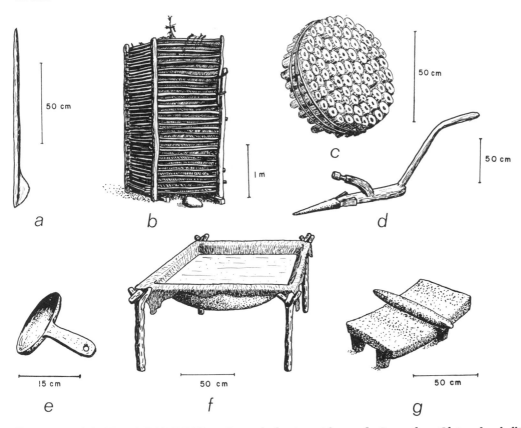

Fɪɢ. 8—SUBSISTENCE FEATURES. *a,* Pointed planting stick, *coa. b,* Corncrib. *c, Olotera* for shelling corn. *d,* Wooden plow with metal share. *e,* Instrument for scraping center of maguey. *f, Tinacal* for fermenting *aguamiel. g,* Milling stones (*metate* and *mano*).

maize, beans, and squash in the same field, according to the ancient Mesoamerican techniques.

Maize and Indian Technology. Maize is planted, almost exclusively, with the *coa* or planting stick, or with their modern substitutes (crowbar, steel shovel with pointed handle), although sometimes the plow is used. The coa is made of wood and has a flattened end and a pointed one (fig. 8,*a*). First, the underbrush which has grown during the fallow season is cut and burned, and stones and other debris are thrown out of the field, using the flat end of the coa. Second, after the first rains have fallen (generally between April and May) comes the sowing (*siembra*), in which a man, with the pointed end of the coa, makes a hole at each step, followed by a woman (Otomi from the Meseta de Toluca) or a boy (some Pame, Chichimec), who drops from three to five seeds of maize in each hole and fills it with earth with the foot. In some holes may be dropped also bean seeds, in others, squash seeds, but never the three together. Seeds are carried in separate little sacks hung from the shoulder. In certain places the planter both makes the holes and drops the seeds.

The Chichimec and some Otomi use the pointed end of the coa a few days after planting to make a hole near where the seeds have been dropped "to help the plant shoot forth."

The third stage is the care of the plants when they reach some 60 cm. high (the

689

limpia or *chapaleo*). The flat end of the coa (or a hoe, among the western Mazahua) serves to clear underbrush and to hill up earth around each plant, to prevent damage from the wind. Effort is made to retain humidity if there has been little rain, or to drain water if it has rained heavily. This procedure may be repeated when the plants are higher. The third stage is almost exclusively men's work, but among the Northern Pame women and children may help.

The agricultural cycle is closed with the harvest, which may come from September to December, according to the variety of the corn and the particular year. The *elotes* (tender maize) are gathered between July and October. The harvest is gathered in many parts with the aid of a short stick, which may end in an iron point, and which the harvester carries tied to his arm so as to pick it up again easily when he lets it go to use both hands. The cut ears are thrown into an *ayate*, which hangs from the harvester's neck, or into a basket suspended from his back (Chichimec). Women and children often take part in the harvest, in addition to men.

The storage of the ears for complete drying before shelling is variable. The Mazahua and Otomi of the Meseta de Toluca build every year a corncrib of sticks, whose crib walls permit free circulation of air (fig. 8,*b*). The corncrib is disassembled when the maize is shelled. Among some Northern Pame, the ears are kept in a similar construction (*chapil*), but it is erected in a corner inside the house. The Southern Pame store ears in *tapancos* (see Housing); the Otomi of the Sierra de Puebla, in granaries built identically to dwellings. Other groups use variations of these methods.

When the maize is well dried, it is shelled. The Otomi prefer to do it by scraping the ears against an *olotera* (fig. 8,*c*), a bunch of corncobs bound together; in other parts, two ears are scraped against each other. In the Meseta de Toluca the grain is stored in a structure made of clay inside the house

(see Housing); the Southern Pame store it in tapancos, or in sacks kept in a corner of the dormitory.

The stubble is left standing until dried completely, then cut down with a machete and stored. To keep it out of the reach of animals, the Otomi erect a platform on four poles, on which the stubble is kept; the Chichimec pile the stubble inside a circular stone fence; and in other places it is hoisted into the forked branches of nearby trees.

WHEAT AND MEDIEVAL EUROPEAN TECHNOLOGY. Wheat and barley are two commercial products widespread in the plains. For cultivation their plow, of the Spanish medieval type, made out of wood with a metal share (fig. 8,*d*), is pulled by oxen.

Sometimes the underbrush is burned beforehand. The seeds are broadcast, generally in the dry season in the same fields where maize has been planted. After sowing, a harrow which levels the terrain and covers the seeds is pulled over the field.

When the plow is used in the cultivation of maize, the land is prepared in the same way as for wheat; the seeds are not broadcast but planted, from three to five grains, at each step in furrows a meter apart. The seeds are covered by plowing again, not with the foot.

Wheat does not require special care during its growth, except for sufficient irrigation. Maize is cultivated by hand or with the plow, and earth is piled up at the foot of the plants by passing the plow first in one direction (to make the *rayas*) and then in another (to make the *surcos*).

Wheat is harvested by grasping a bunch of spikes in the left hand and cutting a few centimeters below with a sickle. The spikes are placed on the roof or across the house to dry, then threshed by being scraped against a coarse stone or stamped under animals' feet. The seed is stored the same way as the corn.

The stubble is left standing until it dries, then cut and heaped into piles.

MAGUEY. Maguey (*Agave*) is useful in

690

its wild varieties as well as in its cultivated ones (maguey *manso* or *blanco*), but here we focus on cultivated magueys as a source of food. Its other uses are considered in the sections on Housing and Crafts.

Maguey is grown not from seed but from cuttings of small plants growing at the base of large plants. In some places special plots are assigned exclusively to maguey, but commonly the new shoots are planted on the border of paths or on the boundary of the plots. Each plant takes from five to seven years to mature, when a woody stem (*quiote*), which carries the flower at its terminal, issues from its center.

The maguey's fermented sap provides a beverage (*pulque*) common to all the Otomian family except those who inhabit the north half of Sierra Gorda. The first step in the manufacture of pulque is to cut off the quiote and scrape the center of the plant with a special instrument (fig. 8,*e*) to form a cavity where the sweet sap (*aguamiel*) accumulates. The aguamiel is extracted by using the fruit of a cucurbit (*acocote*) as chemists use a pipette, and is transported to the place of processing in leather bags or small barrels of special shape (*castañas*). When pulque is made only for family consumption, the aguamiel is put in large pots, but when it is made in great quantity, it is fermented in *tinacales*, cowhides suspended from rectangular wood frames (fig. 8,*f*). Fermentation is induced by a starter of excessively fermented pulque. Pulque is consumed in various degrees of fermentation (and of correspondingly alcoholic concentration), but in general it is preferred not too fermented. In the same areas where pulque is common, *mescal* is also concocted. The center of the maguey is roasted in an underground oven, making a fibrous, sweet mass which is sucked as a tidbit.

OTHER CROPS. Nowadays beans are also planted in separate fields (*mateado* or *de tabla* beans). Other products are almost always commercial. For example, the Otomi from Sierra de Puebla cultivate peanuts (*Arachis hypogaea*), coffee, and plantain (*Musa paradisiaca*); the Southern Pame grow common vetch, tomato, chickpea.

Fruit trees are not an important source of food and they receive little attention. The Otomian area, however, does grow *capulín* (*Prunus capuli*), *tejocote* (*Crataegus mexicana*), *zapote blanco* (*Casimiroa edulis*), and oranges.

Domestic Animals

Domestic animals do not contribute an important part to the diet, for their meat is consumed only during festivities or ceremonial meals (see Food Habits). Cattle are very scarce and are mainly used to pull plows, but when they grow old they may be killed and eaten. Cows are milked only occasionally for children and sick people (Maza, 1947; Driver and Driver, 1963).

Sheep are common in the highest and coldest zones, such as the Sierra de las Cruces and the mountains of the state of Hidalgo, but some are found in nearly all towns. Although sometimes sacrificed and eaten, sheep are raised especially for the wool used in wearing by the Indians themselves, or for sale.

Goats are more abundant in the places which are warmer and somewhat dry, where sheep are not raised. Generally the Indians sell the meat to Mestizos; they themselves do not eat it except occasionally and in very small quantities. In Ciudad del Maiz goats are sold on the hoof to merchants who take them out of the region. The Chichimec also use the milk of the goats (Driver and Driver, 1963).

In all the towns one or several hogs are kept by each household. Generally their meat is sold to Mestizos and their lard used in the kitchen, but in some towns they are sold on the hoof to merchants outside the community. Pork is consumed almost exclusively during ceremonial meals (see Food Habits).

Although chickens and turkeys are seen in all communities, Indians hardly ever eat

691

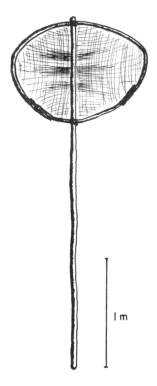

1 m

FIG. 9—CRAWFISH NET, LERMA

eggs but sell them instead to Mestizos. Chicken is occasionally consumed; turkey is a regular part of ceremonial meals. In the Otomi town of San Pablito, in the Sierra de Puebla, chickens are raised exclusively for their use in witchcraft (Christensen, 1952b; Montoya and others, 1961).

Among the various domestic animals that do not provide food are horses, burros, mules, dogs, and cats. The most common is the dog, always one or two in each house; they are guardians and pets of the home and sometimes assistants in the hunt.

There are not many burros, and it is very difficult to find mules or horses. They carry burdens and occasionally riders, but never pull (except among the Chichimec, who yoke burros to plows).

Still rarer are cats and bees. The former have been reported only among the Chichimec (Driver and Driver, 1963). We have information only on one or two beehives

692

(fig. 19,b) in two Northern Pame communities (Agua Puerca and Ciudad del Maiz) and among the Chichimec.

Hunting

Game animals have long disappeared from the most densely and continuously populated zones, and now are found only on the escarpments of the Mesa Central, especially in the Sierra Gorda. Hunting today is mainly a form of amusement for Mestizos and for the few Indians who can afford shotguns or rifles.

The animals hunted most frequently are deer and rabbits. The former are hunted at night, when they are dazzled with a flashlight before being shot, and provide much appreciated skins and meat. Rabbits are taken during the day with shotguns; usually only the meat is used.

Toward the end of the last century, deer were hunted at Ocuilan and south of the Sierra Gorda, as well as other animals in the latter region and at other places, for their skins. Now the Indians crudely tan, to keep or sell, the skins of animals which are hunted only when they have attacked the smaller domestic animals (coyotes), the fowl (foxes and *cacomixtles*), or the crops (badgers, gophers). The same thing is done with the skins of these and other animals (skunks, snakes) which are killed when seen by chance.

The Chichimec trap a wild variety of rat whose meat is considered to be very good for women who have just given birth (Driver and Driver, 1963).

Fishing

The habitat of the Otomi family is so poor in fishing resources that fishing is important in only two places: the lagoons at the head of the Lerma River (Meseta de Toluca) and San Pablito (Sierra de Puebla). Fishing in the lagoons is limited to the women's work of catching crustaceans (*acociles*) by nets (fig. 9) which are laid in the bottom and lifted when full of crawfish.

In the Sierra de Puebla, men fish in groups when the river is running low, poisoning the water with poison made from plants. When the river is running high, they use a hook or fishing net (Christensen, 1933b). Crabs are taken at night by attracting them with lights.

Gathering

There are three wild plants useful for the entire Otomi family: nopal, maguey, and quelite. There are domestic varieties of all three, but their use is the same and less abundant (except the maguey) than that of the wild ones.

Nopal (*Opuntia*) offers meaty leaves which are stripped of thorns, cut into little segments, and cooked with condiments; its fruits (*tunas*) are eaten raw, but the Chichimec and some Northern Pame also boil them to make desserts (*miel* and *queso de tuna*). Popularly the numerous varieties are distinguished by such names as *cardón, duraznillo, nopal blanco*.

The leaves of quelites are eaten cooked with condiments. Some varieties offer tender spikes (*huautzontli*) which are cooked like the leaves, or seeds, which, when ripe, can be used to prepare a dessert.

The gathering of other plants has a limited distribution. The Ocuiltec and some Otomi groups of the Sierra de Hidalgo gather various kinds of edible fungi.

The Chichimec eat raw the fruit of the *biznaga* (*Echinocactus*); they make atole with the seeds of the *pirú* (*Schinus molle*); they cook the flowers of the *izote* (*Yucca brevifolior*); they eat the fruit raw and make soup out of the flower of the *garambullo* (*Lemirocereus*); and they grind the fruit of the mesquite (*Prosopis*) and roll it into balls which are dried in the sun and may be eaten that way or made into atole (see Food Habits).

The Northern Pame gather the poisonous fruit of the *chamal* (*Dioon edule* Lindl.). They cut the fruit into little pieces and boil them with lime water, separating the poison which rises to the top in the form of gum. The pieces are then ground and made into dough for tortillas, tamales and atole.

The only insects whose gathering is worthwhile are the larvae which attack the magueys; they are eaten raw, toasted, or fried.

Food Habits

Almost all the communities have three meals a day: the first one taken by the entire family between 7 and 8 in the morning, before the men leave to work in the fields; the second one by the women and children who stay at home, between 1 and 3 in the afternoon (the men eat earlier in the fields); the third meal by everyone at sundown.

The Ocuiltec are in the habit of having two meals a day, the first between 7 and 9 in the morning, the other at 6 in the afternoon (Rodríguez Gil, 1907), although today many have become adjusted to the general practice. The Chichimec have only one meal a day (Driver and Driver, 1963).

Tortillas and beans seasoned with chile (*Capsicum*) are eaten at every meal, along with pulque or coffee sweetened with *piloncillo* (dark sugar). In some places a rice or commercial noodle soup has been introduced into the midday meal. Cooking is an exclusively feminine chore.

To make tortillas, *nixtamal* (corn cooked in water with lime or ashes) is first prepared, then washed to remove the cuticle, and ground several times to make a smooth and homogenous dough. Today the first grinding is frequently done at home with a hand grinder or the corn is taken to the mechanical grinder found in almost all the towns, but the last grindings are always done on the metate or milling stone (fig. 8,g). Small pieces of dough are slapped between the palms of the hands until a disc is formed which is cooked on a flat clay surface (*comal*). The tortillas are flexible and 2–5 mm. thick, according to local custom and the use to be made of them.

693

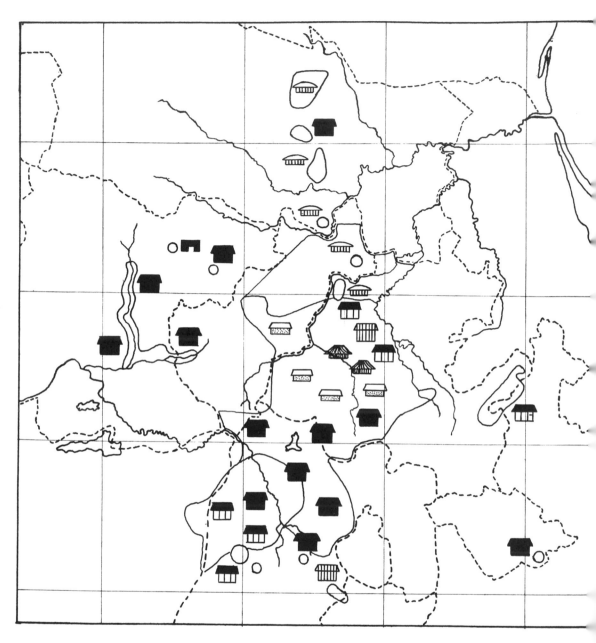

F<small>IG</small>. 10—DISTRIBUTION OF HOUSE TYPES

Adobe house with hip roof   Apsidal house

Adobe house with flat roof   Stone house

Plank house with thatched roof   House thatched with long grass or maguey leaves

House with shingled roof

The beans are cooked in water and are seasoned with chile or herbs. Each person is served on a plate a portion of beans which he takes up with pieces of tortilla and puts into his mouth.

The most common daily beverage is coffee, but it may be substituted by drinks from other plants. In the dry lands pulque is drunk instead of coffee. Beverages are served in individual jugs.

The monotony of this daily diet is broken once in a while by nopales, quelites, some other gathered plants, elotes (tender corn) baked or boiled, eggs, meat, tamales and atole.

Tamales are made by wrapping a piece of maize dough with lard and a little chunk of pork in cornhusks and steaming them. Atole is prepared by dissolving maize dough (or chickpea flour, *pirú*, etc.) in water and boiling it.

In the ceremonial meals of baptisms, weddings, and mayordomías, beans and *mole* are eaten. Mole is prepared with turkey or pork and a highly seasoned sauce made with tomatoes and various kinds of chile. Pulque, bottled beer, and hard liquor are drunk on those occasions. For the ceremonial meals at funerals, tamales and mole are made. The Pame of Agua Puerca (San Luis Potosi) prepare beef broth for this occasion.

Narcotics and Stimulants

Pulque is the intoxicating liquor most favored by the Otomi family. To the northeast its use is less and less frequent, until at the northern extreme of Sierra Gorda it is completely replaced by rum. Another beverage common to the entire area is beer. Men gather at the stores to drink and talk, and frequently they become intoxicated; women drink to inebriation only at festivities.

Aside from the beverages, tobacco is the only general stimulant. Factory cigarettes are commonly smoked, but some Pame buy tobacco leaves which they tear up and roll in wrappings of cornhusks.

There are some data on the use of narcotic fungi (as part of the magical ceremonial) among the Otomi of the mountains surrounding the Valle de Toluca. In the region of Santa Ana Hueytlalpan, Hidalgo, a few sorcerers take the seeds of *ololiuhqui* to foretell the future (Weitlaner, personal communication; according to his description it could be a sort of *Ipomoea*).

SETTLEMENT PATTERNS AND HOUSING

Settlement Patterns

These are quite varied. According to Soustelle (1937b), the general trend is to live in dispersed towns, as long as the availability of water permits it. But it seems more probable that settlement patterns are a result of historical accidents: some Mesoamerican groups kept their semidispersed pattern of one house inside of each lot (Ocuiltec, certain Otomi, Mazahua, and Matlatzinca), while others were compelled to concentrate in towns or on the periphery of Mestizo centers, adopting the Spanish standard of a compact hamlet surrounded by cultivated fields. The congregated nomads sometimes adopted the Spanish hamlet, but at other times they formed dispersed or semidispersed districts or groups of huts in the environs of towns (Mision de los Chichimecas, near San Luis de la Paz, Guanajuato; group of houses of Agua Puerca, near La Palma, San Luis Potosi). These basic patterns have been altered by the plundering of Indian lands, and the consequent further concentration or dispersion.

Today settlement shows a hierarchy. Here we describe four levels of the hierarchy; the first two are purely Indian, the other two are not but are included to show the relationship of Indian towns with the rest of the country.

ISOLATED HOUSES AND RANCHERÍAS. Each house, frequently 500–1000 m. from its

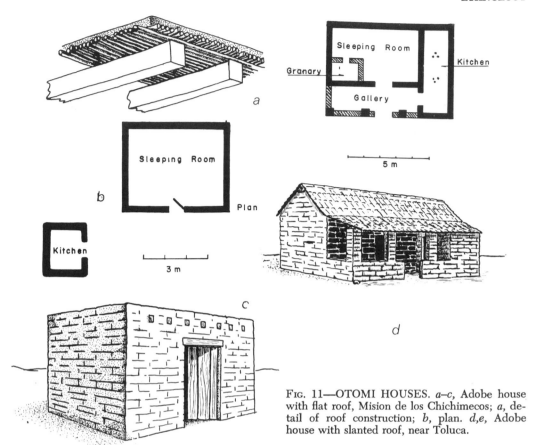

Fig. 11—OTOMI HOUSES. *a–c*, Adobe house with flat roof, Mision de los Chichimecos; *a*, detail of roof construction; *b*, plan. *d,e*, Adobe house with slanted roof, near Toluca.

neighbor, is surrounded by a plot for cultivation. Very often the plots have unowned areas between them. Administratively they depend on a town and do not have their own authorities. They produce for their own consumption and for a slight surplus to exchange for items they do not manufacture (tools, footwear, metates). There are no established shops; purchases and sales have to be made in the town, some 4–8 km. away. There are no religious buildings, but in some rancherías there might be a room set aside for "the school." The rancherías surround the town and thus have closer relations with other nearby rancherías and with the town itself than with rancherías lying on the far side of the town.

INDIAN TOWNS AND INDIAN NEIGHBORHOODS IN MESTIZO TOWNS. Houses, 50–200 m. apart, lie within ample contiguous lots (separated by paths) which are frequently cultivated. In addition plots of cultivated land lie outside the town. Politically and administratively they depend on a town or on a Mestizo center; they have their own authorities, but these are of a low level (*jueces auxiliares*). Although a large part of production is for internal consumption, specialized craftsmen often supply the markets of the rancherías, of the Mestizo nucleus, and even of other towns (for example, the serapes of the Mazahua town of San Andres Jilotepec, Mexico, the *arpilla* of the Barrio of San Jose, Ciudad del Maiz, San Luis Potosi; see *Crafts*). There are shops which supply articles of daily use (soap, sugar, coffee). It is not infrequent for the neighborhoods—less than 3 km. from downtown—to have a chapel and a school; the towns farther away from the Mestizo center almost always have one or more chapels, a school, and a building for the local government.

MESTIZO CENTERS AND TOWNS. These are settlements of the Spanish type. The lots are smaller, the houses closer together. There are streets, a central square, religious buildings and schools, and a municipal building. Production is to a large extent for the market, supplying the dependent neighborhoods and towns. Commerce is more active and diversified; generally on a given day of the week the Indians take their merchandise to the *tianguis* (market) and buy what they need from the stores. Often these towns are the seat of municipal government (see Political Organization). They are connected by roads and more or less regular bus service with the regional urban centers and, through them, with the whole country.

REGIONAL URBAN CENTERS. They are typically urban, although modest in size. The regional centers are the foci of concentration and distribution of Indian products (agricultural and artisan) and the direct suppliers of Mestizo centers and towns. Administratively and politically they are also the limits of Indian activity; the natives who transcend permanently these regional confines ordinarily lose a large part of their indigenous way of life and become assimilated into the population of the cities (as masons, peons, laborers, housemaids).

Housing

The house types of the different Otomi groups reflect their cultural history as well as adaptations to climate and to available materials (fig. 10). There are seven common types.

The *adobe house with slanted roof* (fig. 11,*d*) is characteristic of the Meseta de Ixtlahuaca–Toluca. The foundations are stone; the walls are adobe; the roof is shingle or, more commonly, tile, laid on a structure of beams; the floor is earthen. The win-

FIG. 12—PLANK HOUSE WITH GRASS ROOF, JILIAPAN

FIG. 13—SHINGLE HOUSE, SAN JUAN ATZINGO

dows—in the few instances—and the door are wooden. A single structure contains bedroom (with interior granary), kitchen, and corridor. Its annexes are the granary for corn (fig. 8,*b*), a platform to store stubble, and an oven for tiles.

In Alaquines (San Luis Potosi), Ixtenco, and part of the Sierra de las Cruces, the

697

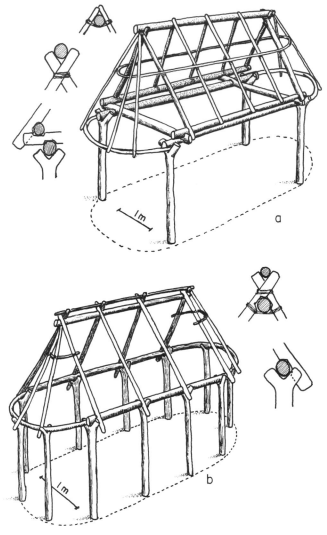

FIG. 14—APSIDAL HOUSE FRAMINGS. *a*, Jilia-pan. *b*, La Palma.

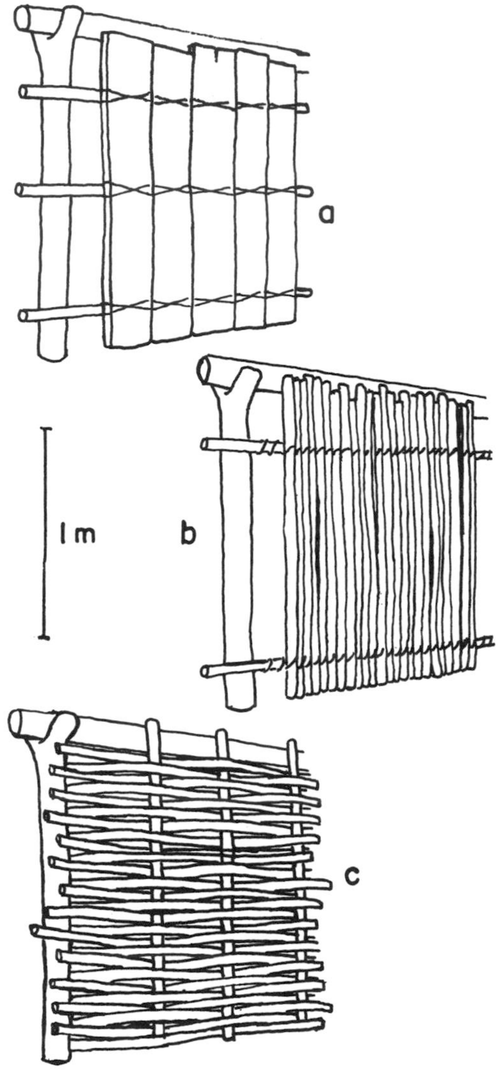

FIG. 15—HOUSE WALL TYPES. *a*, Vertical planks. *b*, Vertical rods. *c*, Interwoven sticks.

structure is a single rectangular room which serves as dormitory. The kitchen is separate.

The *adobe house with flat roof* (*cuarto*; fig. 11,*a–c*) is found only as a dormitory among the Chichimec. It has an earthen floor, stone foundations, adobe walls, stick roof over roof beams covered with clay. There are no windows; the door is of wood. Annexed to it is a kitchen with walls of stone or adobe and a slanted roof of vege-

table material (*izote* or maguey leaves or both).

The *plank house with grass roof* (fig. 12) is typical of the Sierra de Puebla and the western watershed of the Mesa Central, although also sometimes found in the south of Sierra Gorda (Jiliapan and Pacula). The basic structure is of six posts, one at each corner and two to uphold the ridge of the roof. The walls (without foundations) are

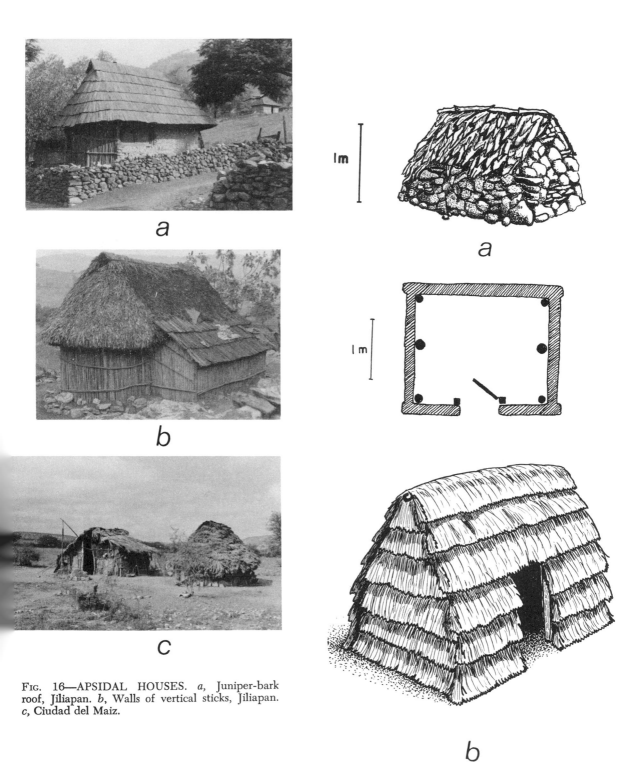

FIG. 16—APSIDAL HOUSES. *a*, Juniper-bark roof, Jiliapan. *b*, Walls of vertical sticks, Jiliapan. *c*, Ciudad del Maiz.

FIG. 17—HOUSES, VALLE DEL MEZQUITAL. *a*, Stone walls, maguey-leaf roof. *b*, Zacate thatch.

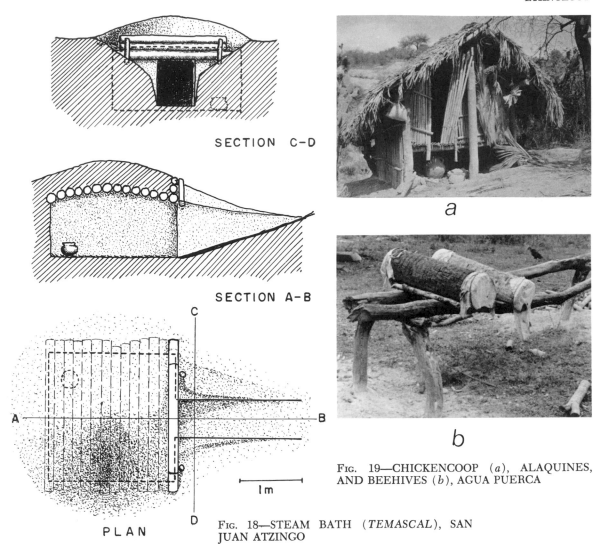

SECTION C-D

SECTION A-B

PLAN

a

b

Fig. 19—CHICKENCOOP (*a*), ALAQUINES, AND BEEHIVES (*b*), AGUA PUERCA

Fig. 18—STEAM BATH (*TEMASCAL*), SAN JUAN ATZINGO

adze-hewn planks, tied to three horizontal beams (fig. 15,*a*). The roof (which has two larger slopes and two smaller ones) is covered with *zacate* (herbaceous plants) or—in some houses of Jiliapan—bark from *enebro* (*Juniperus;* fig. 16,*a*); it is affixed with pegs to the beams. The floor is earthen. Usually the *tapanco*, a horizontal partition covering only part of the room area and placed at the lowest point of the roof, divides the upper area into a kind of loft. Used for storage, it is reached by a tree trunk with carved steps.

In San Pablito, Puebla, three of these structures are used as bedroom, kitchen, and granary, respectively. Besides these there is almost always a steam bath and an oven for toasting peanuts. In Jiliapan they are only used as bedrooms.

The *shingle house* (fig. 13) is characteristic of San Juan Atzingo, where walls and slanted roof are made of shingles. A single structure, without foundations or windows, serves as bedroom, kitchen, and warehouse. Some houses have a steam bath on the same lot.

700

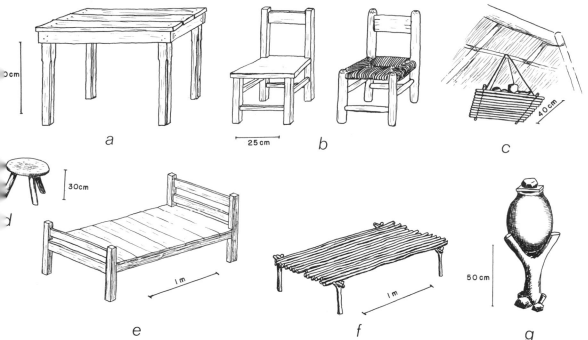

FIG. 20—HOUSE FURNISHINGS. *a*, European-type table. *b*, Chairs. *c*, Storage tray (*zarzo*). *d*, Stool. *e*, European-type bed. *f*, Native bed (*tapesco*). *g*, Outdoor forked stand with water jar, La Palma.

The *apsidal house of sticks* (*casa de culata*) (figs. 14–16) is found throughout the entire Sierra Gorda. It may have two apses or, infrequently, only one. It has an earthen floor. Mostly the walls are vertical sticks driven into the ground and tied to horizontal crossbeams (fig. 15,*b*), but they may also be horizontal sticks interwoven with vertical poles (fig. 15,*c*). The height of the walls varies according to local custom (from 1 m. in Ciudad del Maiz to 1.7 m. in Jiliapan). The thatched roof sometimes comes down almost to the ground.

In some places (Ciudad del Maiz, Jiliapan) each house consists of two structures, used as bedroom and kitchen respectively; in others (Agua Puerca) it is more common to use a single building as both kitchen and dormitory, separating the two areas by interior walls about the height of the exterior ones. Annexes (oven, corrals) are infrequent.

The *stone house* (fig. 17,*a*) is common where wood is not abundant. It has a rectangular ground plan, earthen floor, stone

FIG. 21—NATIVE STOOL, JILIAPAN

FIG. 22—CHILDREN'S HAMMOCK, AGUA PUERCA

701

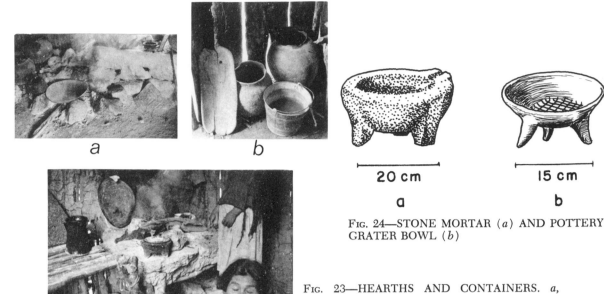

a   b

c

FIG. 24—STONE MORTAR (a) AND POTTERY GRATER BOWL (b)

20 cm   15 cm

a   b

FIG. 23—HEARTHS AND CONTAINERS. a, Three-stone fireplace on floor, Agua Puerca. b, Batea, pottery jars, and metal pail, Ciudad del Maiz. c, Platform hearth, Ciudad del Maiz.

walls without mortar, slanted roof made from zacate or maguey leaves.

Houses of zacate and of maguey leaves (fig. 17,b) are found in the Valle del Mezquital, Hidalgo, where walls are made of the same combination of maguey leaves or of bunches of zacate as is used for the roof. These houses are rectangular, with earthen floor and slanted roof. In Cardonal the maguey leaves are interwoven, giving the house the aspect of a large basket.

Men build their own houses, shortly before or after getting married, and repair them when needed. Communal work is not used, salaried work rarely.

Imitation of Mestizo houses and use of new materials (for example, zinc sheets for the roof) have produced infinite variations.

Among the *annexes* is the steam bath (*temascal*), almost always a semisubterranean structure (fig. 18), of airtight walls and roof. A fire burning inside for several hours heats the interior and the special stones. The ashes are then taken out, the

floor is covered with green leaves, and cold water is poured over walls and stones to produce steam.

The Pame of Alaquines, San Luis Potosi, erect chickencoops with pole walls, slanted roofs, and floor made of sticks, raised some 50 cm. above the floor (fig. 19,a). Beehives are lodged in hollowed tree trunks (fig. 19,b).

Furniture and Kitchen Utensils

In the entire area small European-type tables and chairs are common: one in the living area and one in the kitchen (fig. 20,a). There are also from two to six chairs (fig. 20,b), and even more low stools carved from a section of tree trunk (fig. 21) or made of a round or oval board with three legs fitted into it (fig. 20,d).

Mats are always used to sleep on. In many places they are placed directly on the earthen floor and during the day kept rolled in a corner. In Sierra Gorda they are placed over European-type beds (fig. 20,e) or over

FIG. 25—POTTERY. *a*, Making a comal, coiling method, Agua Puerca. *b*, Making a water jar (*olla*), Agua Puerca. *c*, Open firing, and *d*, Pulling out a fired jar, Jiliapan.

tapescos (beds made from sticks placed over forked branches driven into the floor, fig. 20,*f*). The Ocuiltec place the mats on a wooden platform 2 m. square, 40 cm. above the floor, on which the whole family sleeps. Small children almost always sleep in *ayates* suspended from the walls like hammocks (fig. 22), but the Otomi of central and eastern Hidalgo suspend the ayate from a rope which may be hooked to a crossbeam or the branch of a tree, or from a *mecapal* (tumpline).

Valuable or infrequently used clothing and small objects are kept in wooden trunks or in commercial cardboard boxes set on the floor or on chairs next to the walls. Food supplies are stored in pots and tins on shelves suspended from the lowest part of the roof; they are also kept in *zarzos*, small square platforms made of sticks and hung

703

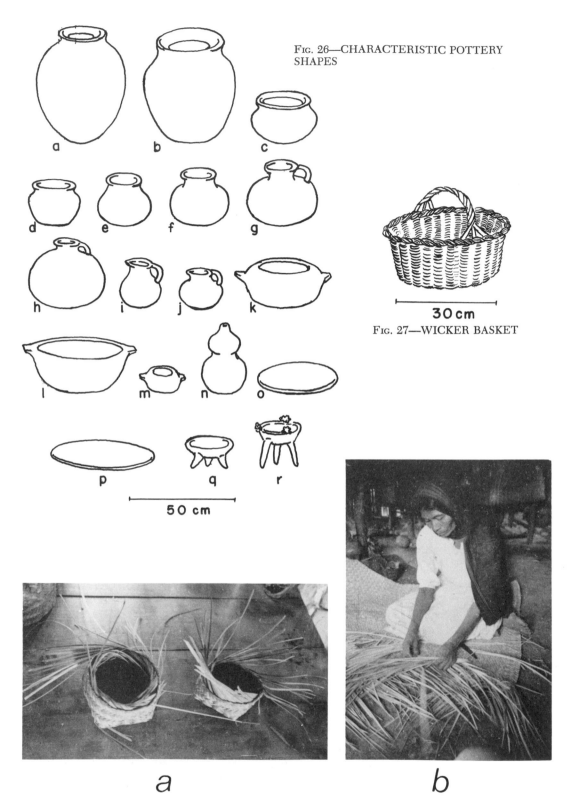

Fig. 26—CHARACTERISTIC POTTERY SHAPES

a

b

c

d

e

f

g

h

i

j

k

l

m

n

o

p

q

r

50 cm

30 cm

Fig. 27—WICKER BASKET

a

b

Fig. 28—BASKET (a) AND MAT WEAVING (b), AGUA PUERCA

from the ceiling (fig. 20,c). Water is stored in large pots in a corner of the kitchen. The Pame of Ciudad del Maiz place the pots outside on three forked branches driven into the floor (fig. 20,g).

Everywhere hearths consist of three stones set directly on the floor (fig. 23,a); here tortillas are cooked before each meal and the pot of nixtamal boils for many hours. Commonly other dishes are cooked on a second hearth either like the first or, especially in Sierra Gorda, made of three stones on a platform made of sticks covered with clay (fig. 23,c). The stones are sometimes replaced by burners made with the same clay.

In every kitchen are pots, pans, jugs, and plates of all sizes, made locally, plus knives and plates commercially manufactured. There is at least one metate—generally of Middle American type (fig. 8,g) but without legs and with a short mano (huilanche) among the Northern Pame—and a mortar, the most common made of stone (fig. 24,a). In some Otomi areas (central and western Hidalgo) they use pottery grater bowls (fig. 24,b). Now one finds in almost all houses, metal pans, buckets, and spoons made in factories. Large, shallow wooden containers (bateas or canoas) are used for washing clothes; smaller ones are used for making maize dough (fig. 23,b).

TECHNOLOGY

Crafts

This section is limited to a brief description of the most frequent techniques and their specific characteristics.

POTTERY. Ceramics are made in numerous towns. The most common technique consists in mixing the clay with a temper of finely ground gypsum or lime, letting it settle for some time, and building the object by coiling (fig. 25,a,b), smoothing it with a piece of cloth and with a polisher of hard stone.

The Otomi wash the interior with litharge

FIG. 29—SPINNING WITH SPINDLE WHORL (*MALACATE*)

to make them impermeable; the Pame only burnish them. The decoration (generally phytomorphous motifs) is done with commercial varnishes when the objects are glazed, and with kaolin (white), ocher (red), and sugar (black) when they are not varnished.

The pottery is fired in adobe ovens by the Otomi, and in open fire by the Pame (fig. 25,c,d). The most characteristic shapes are shown in figure 26.

Indian pottery is exclusively women's affair; the potter's wheel, operated by men, is a Mestizo innovation.

BASKET WEAVING. In the Meseta de Toluca wicker baskets exactly like European ones (fig. 27) are made. The Chichimec make conical handbaskets from common reed-grass. The Northern Pame follow the pre-Hispanic technique to make *tenates* (fig. 28,a) and mats (fig. 28,b). Various Otomi groups, such as those of the Mezquital, weave coiled baskets.

Many families throughout the area make hats by braiding four strips of straw into a band which is then coiled and sewn into the desired shape. The woven, waterproof capes (Soustelle, 1937b, pp. 69–70) are falling into disuse as a result of the competition from the low-priced industrial products.

20 cm

Fɪɢ. 31—CARDS FOR WOOL

Fɪɢ. 30—TWO-BAR BACKSTRAP LOOMS. *a*, For weaving *ayates*, San Jose del Sitio. *b*, For weaving decorated bands, San Felipe, Mexico. (Photographed by Jacques Soustelle, 1937b.)

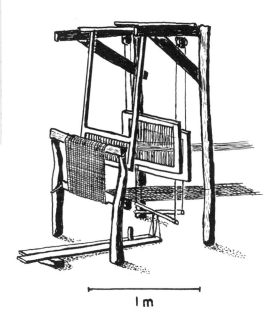

I m

Fɪɢ. 32—STATIONARY LOOM, CIUDAD DEL MAIZ

Tᴇxᴛɪʟᴇs. The pre-Hispanic technique of weaving, exclusively by women, is retained only among the less acculturated Otomi and very sporadically among the other groups. The products are almost always for family consumption. Wool, cotton, and ixtle (see Cordage) are spun by hand with the aid of a spindle whorl (*malacate;* fig. 29). Weaving is done on simple two-bar (backstrap) looms when ayates are woven (fig. 30,*a*) and with a more complicated system of heddles to create different sheds for more elaborate weaving like bands and small bags (fig. 30,*b*). For weaving ayates and the narrow strips of cloth used for skirts two warps are raised together; for more elaborate work the warps are raised separately (Soustelle, 1937b, pp. 77–85).

Weaving with European techniques is

done exclusively by men. Wool—the only fiber used—is combed between two wooden cards with steel teeth (fig. 31); spinning is done with a distaff. A stationary loom is used for weaving; the hoists for the warping threads are operated by treadles. With this procedure only serapes to be sold are manufactured.

A similar loom (fig. 32) is used in Ciudad del Maiz to make *arpilla,* a loose fabric made from ixtle with which shopping bags are made. The Indians of the nearby towns prepare the ixtle from wild plants and sell

706

FIG. 34—SCRAPING *IXTLE* FOR CORDAGE

FIG. 33—SPINNING *IXTLE*, CIUDAD DEL MAIZ

it to Mestizo merchants of the downtown area, who give it out to the Pame of Barrio San Jose to be spun (fig. 33) and woven.

CORDAGE. Everywhere men make threads and cords from ixtle, mainly for their own use, although sometimes for sale. Ixtle is obtained by slightly baking the leaves of different magueys (*Agave*) and scraping them over an inclined board to eliminate the pulp. Generally the scraper is a blade of metal or stone with a special handle (fig. 34) and the board is placed high up, but the Ocuiltec rest the board on the floor and scrape with a long wooden spade. The fiber is washed and bleached in the sun.

The fibers are twisted two-ply between the palms of the hands, one end held by the big toe. The thread, which only has four fibers, is used to sew hats; the cords are

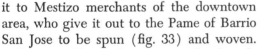

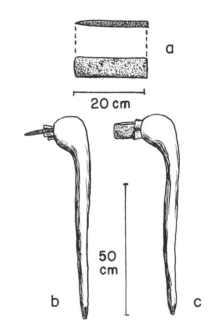

FIG. 35—CONVERTIBLE AXE-ADZE. *a,* Blade. *b,* Hafted adze. *c,* Hafted axe.

707

FIG. 36—JILIAPAN MAN

FIG. 37—OTOMI WOOLEN BAG, TOLIMAN.
(Photographed by Jacques Soustelle, 1937b.)

made by repeating the twisting process until the desired weight is obtained.

OTHER CRAFTS. In the places where there are adobe houses, the builder makes the adobes with rectangular molds. In many houses of the Meseta de Toluca clay tiles are made in wooden molds, colored by being baked with alternate layers of clay and flowers (Soustelle, 1937b, pp. 61–62).

Net making is men's occupation wherever fishing is done.

The Otomi of the forest zones (Sierra de las Cruces, Sierra de Toliman) derive income from manufacturing charcoal, carving beams and planks with axe and adze (the Ocuiltec used a convertible tool, fig. 35), and splitting shingles with wedges.

The women of San Pablito, Puebla, manufacture paper for witchcraft from the bark of certain trees (*Ficus, Morus* and *Garrya*?), pounding it over a board with a stone beater (Christensen, 1953a).

Other crafts include carving *tecomates* (fruit of *Lagenaria*), making leather bags, making metates and mortars from volcanic stone, but their distribution in the area here is too irregular and scarce, and their techniques are too complicated to warrant description here. In many Indian towns specialists use the tools and the techniques imported from Europe during the colonial period.

DRESS AND ORNAMENT

Dress ranges from garments almost identical to those of pre-Hispanic times (women of San Pablito, Puebla) to those of the Chichimec which are not distinguishable from clothes of the poor people in the cities.

The common native shirt of coarse cotton

708

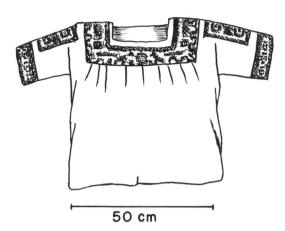

Fɪɢ. 39—OTOMI WOMAN'S EMBROIDERED SHIRT, SAN FELIPE

Fɪɢ. 38—LEATHER KNAPSACK, JALPAN

has a round collar and long sleeves; it is sometimes open the whole length of the front, with buttons (fig. 36), sometimes open only in the upper part. It is being replaced in many areas by colored shirts bought ready-made. In the past, the Chichimec wore a short garment made of coyote leather, the Ocuiltec one made from deerskin, but both disappeared some 60 years ago.

The majority of the Otomi wear coarse cotton trousers held to the waist by a band and tied to the thigh. The other groups and some Otomi have adopted the commercial trousers made of light tweed or drill cloth. When the leather garment mentioned above was worn to cover the chest, the Ocuiltec and Chichimec also wore pants of the same material.

Hats are often made at home but now increasingly bought in stores. Sandals have soles of leather or old automobile tires.

The woolen serape is frequent. The Otomi of San Pablito use an ayate made of cotton with embroidery in the corners; those of Sierra de las Cruces wear one made from ixtle.

Almost always a small woolen bag (fig. 37) or an ixtle or leather knapsack (fig. 38) is taken along to carry food and small objects. The Ocuiltec carried in it pebbles for the sling.

Nowadays the hair is worn short, without ornament. Earlier the Pame of the south and the Chichimec wore their hair long. The latter painted their teeth black.

Women wear a shirt of coarse white cotton with embroidery on the collar and on the short sleeves (fig. 39). Otomi women may wear the shirt with nothing over it when they are in the house, but outdoors they add a kind of poncho, quechquemitl (fig. 40,a; Soustelle, 1937b, pp. 91–95; I. Weitlaner, 1953, pp. 241–57). Around Toluca a colored shirt of shiny cloth has been adapted from the *catrina* cloth of the latter 19th century (fig. 40,b). Other places have a similar shirt but made from cotton print, with sleeves to the elbow but no pleats.

Indian skirts are fashioned from a piece

709

a

b

FIG. 40—WOMEN'S DRESS. *a*, Ocuiltec woman wearing *quechquemitl*, San Juan Atzingo. *b*, Mazahua woman.

FIG. 41—MAZAHUA WOMAN'S WOOLEN BAG. Length of scale at top, 5 cm.

of handwoven wool almost 5 m. long, the ends sewn together to form a tube. The material is pleated around the waist, to which it is held by a sash. Now ready-made skirts and blouses or whole dresses are increasingly popular. An apron seldom accompanies an Indian skirt but is never absent when another type of skirt is worn.

Head and feet are almost always bare, but where the footing is thorny or stony, women wear sandals. For going out, the shawl (rebozo) is almost invariable when the quechquemitl is not worn.

Throughout the area women wear their hair long, almost always combed in two braids, sometimes interwoven with wool cords. The only ornaments, besides the cords for the hair, are silver earrings and necklaces of glass beads.

Fifty years ago, Mazahua and Ocuiltec women carried large woolen bags (fig. 41).

Very young children wear a small shirt and diapers, and a cap on their heads. Later on they wear clothes similar to those of their parents, but simpler.

CARRYING DEVICES, TRANSPORTATION, AND COMMUNICATION

Small objects, seeds for planting, and food

710

for the men who go to the fields are carried in small woolen bags (fig. 37) or knapsacks made from ixtle or leather (fig. 38). Larger objects go into baskets in the Meseta de Toluca, and, throughout the area, into *ayates* or *guangoches,* which are rectangular cloths made from loosely woven ixtle, the opposite corners bound to form a bag which is hung from the shoulder or the back. For loads the ayate cannot accommodate, cribbed boxes (*huacales*) are used in the central and southern regions (fig. 42,*a*); semicylindrical or semispherical structures covered by a net (*huajacas*), in the north (fig. 42,*b*). Heavy loads are suspended from the back by a tumpline (*mecapal*), which the man rests against the forehead, the woman against the chest (fig. 43).

In the central part of the area, water is carried in large, three-handled jars (*cántaros*) suspended from a tumpline. Elsewhere women carry a cántaro or a tin can on the head (fig. 44) or supported on the hip. Men suspend vessels from a shoulder pole.

The most frequent way of carrying children is to straddle them over the back and support them with a shawl which is bound over the breast; some Otomi carry them on the ayate itself which serves as a cradle (see Furniture and Kitchen Utensils). The Chichimec carry them on huajacas.

Most travel is on foot, even for long distances. There are very few beasts of burden and they are almost never ridden. At Lake Lerma flat-bottomed canoes are used. Motor vehicles are more and more frequent, both buses which have scheduled service and trucks which offer occasional service.

Today the mail keeps those who live in the towns in touch with their relatives who have emigrated to the cities.

The resolutions of the local authorities are communicated verbally through policemen or government messengers (*topiles*). To call an urgent meeting (for example, when a fire occurs) church bells are rung in some localities. The Ocuiltec use special

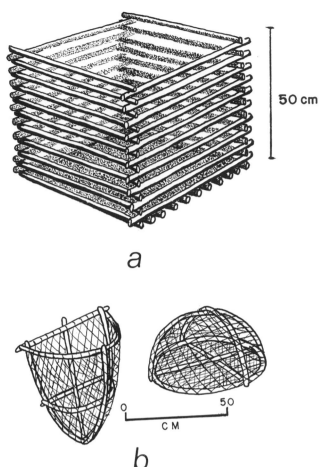

FIG. 42—CARRYING DEVICES. *a,* Cribbed box (*huacal*) for heavy loads. *b,* Frame and net *huajacas.*

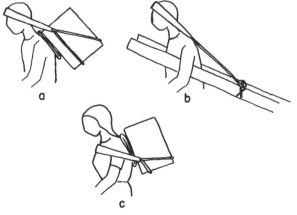

FIG. 43—TUMPLINE (*MECAPAL*). *a,* Man carrying a *huacal. b,* Ocuiltec man carrying lumber. *c,* Woman carrying a *huacal.*

711

FIG. 44—WOMEN CARRYING WATER, LA PALMA

shouts and whistles; they announce a *faena* (see Units of Production and Consumption, Forms of Work) by beating a drum, and announce fiestas by beating a *teponaztle* which is kept chained in the sacristy of the church (Rodríguez Gil, 1907).

WEIGHTS AND MEASURES

The metric system is in common use, but some units of weights and measures of the colonial period, now current for lesser transactions, still survive. They vary slightly in local usage, but the most common are:

> Weight:
>   *libra* = 0.5 kg.
>   *arroba* = 12.5 kg.
>   *quintal* = 46 kg.
> Volume:
>   *cuartillo* = 0.5 liter
>   *fanega* = 55.5 liters
>   *carga* = highly variable
> Linear:
>   *vara* = 85 cm.
>   *legua* = 4 km.

The monetary system is that used throughout Mexico, in addition to the denomination *reales* (12 centavos).

Some items are sold by *docenas* (12 units) and by *gruesas* (12 docenas).

ECONOMY

Division of Labor, Specialization

In all communities men are in charge of farming, building and repairing the home, repairing footgear, caring for cattle, making cordage, and carrying heavy loads. Wherever nets are made, hunting is done; and where European textile techniques are followed, men are in charge of these tasks.

Feminine chores common to all groups are housecleaning, washing and repairing clothing, cooking, caring for children, caring for domestic fowl, carrying light loads, fetching water (fig. 44), buying and selling. Weaving by Indian technique and pottery making are also feminine tasks.

Basket weaving (except hat making) is women's work in Sierra Gorda, but elsewhere is entrusted to men. Women fish in the lagoons of Lerma, men in San Pablito, Puebla.

Specialized work, such as carpentry, fabrication of metates, and the weaving of waterproof capes, is allotted to men.

Children of both sexes are entrusted with herding and with helping their fathers to carry firewood, their mothers to fetch water (see Socialization).

Practically the entire population is fundamentally agricultural. The specialists noted (see Crafts) devote only half-time or less to their specialty; other crafts, such as pottery and cordage, are mastered by all families.

Units of Production and Consumption, Forms of Work

The basic unit of production and consumption is the nuclear family, even when there are aspects of an extended family. Production is mainly for family consumption, either directly or by acquisition through exchange of a small surplus of the production.

712

The most frequent work unit is the family. Each family head, with the cooperation of his wife and unmarried children, cultivates the land which supports them. Cooperation in the nuclear family is basic to the division of labor by sex and age, and to certain artisan productions. For example, in Santa Maria Acapulco, San Luis Potosi, men gather the palm leaves with which women make mats (Maza, 1947).

For some agricultural tasks that must be attended to promptly, and for house construction sometimes the cooperation of relatives and friends is sought. This help is compensated by reciprocal assistance and occasionally by money.

Obligatory communal labor (*tequio* or *faena*) serves common needs such as construction or repair of roads and public buildings like schools or chapels.

Wage labor is scarce in these communities and is very seldom expended on agricultural work, even less for artisan work. More frequently Indians work as peons in Mestizos' agricultural enterprises to supplement family income.

Export of labor also adds to family income. A temporary export of male labor comes when fields do not require care and the men go to work at the nearby sugar mills (Sierra Gorda), or as peons to the cities, and sometimes as day laborers to the United States. The export of female labor is usually a permanent emigration of women to the cities as servant girls, who send part of their earnings back home.

Property and Land Tenure

An individual is the owner of his personal effects and the house which he has built and occupies. When he dies, the youngest son or daughter inherits the house, and the rest of the property is divided equally among the descendants, men or women, and the widow.

Generally, all married males have a piece of land which they cultivate. The two most common forms of tenure are the *ejido* and the small property. *Ejido* land belongs to the community, but in many cases titles of plots for individual use are granted. Lands producing firewood and pasture are common to all. The small property, purchased or inherited, is generally distributed among the male descendants; by law, title to the ejido plot is inherited by one son.

Commerce and Markets

Commercial activity in the area is related to the hierarchy of settlements described under Settlement Patterns. Goods produced in the smallest communities go directly to the nearest centers and from there to those next in the scale; goods that come from outside follow the same route in reverse. These products are distributed through various shops and the *tianguis,* a market held in the Mestizo centers or towns on a given day of each week.

Wealth and Its Uses

From the position Indians occupy in the total Mexican society, differences in wealth among them are not great. Wealth consists of monetary capital, normally used to acquire prestige by paying the cost of a mayordomía (see Religious Organization).

SOCIAL ORGANIZATION
Family and Kinship

The basic family unit is the nuclear family, many of which form part of an extended family with loose ties (Manrique, 1961).

Kinship terminology is mainly Spanish but occasionally Indian. The entire Otomi family has a bilateral system, although Chichimec, Mazahua, and Otomi apply the system of generations (relative age) in limited form to the generation of ego. Terms for father, mother, grandfather, grandmother, uncle (consanguineal and by affinity), aunt (consanguineal and by affinity) do not distinguish paternal or maternal descent. There are different terms for brother and sister, which among Chichimec,

713

Otomi, and Southern Pame are extended to cousins; the Ocuiltec, Northern Pame, and an alternate Chichimec term do not distinguish the cousins' sex. Other terms are not common to the entire region but only to the majority of the groups. The same word is used for the brother of husband or wife and the husband of the sister, another for the sister of husband or wife and the wife of the brother. There are words for son, daughter, father-in-law, mother-in-law, son-in-law, daughter-in-law. Usually, the sex of grandchildren and children of the cousins is not distinguished. Paternal and maternal surnames are inherited; all persons know their two surnames, but frequently use only the paternal one.

Maximum family authority is in the hands of the father or, in an extended family, the oldest man—grandfather or uncle (Manrique, 1961). It is thought that children should help and obey their parents, brothers should help each other, and cousins should be regarded somewhat as brothers. If children become orphaned, their grandparents, uncles, or godparents are supposed to take them in.

The strongest and most universal relationship of ritual kinship is the one established through baptism. The parents of a child ask a married couple, selected from among their friends, or relatives in some cases, to be baptism godparents. When the ceremony takes place (see Fiesta Patterns), a kinship is established between godparents and godchild, ritually considered the same as that between parents and children, and also between parents and godparents who now call each other compadres. This prohibits marriage between them and theoretically bestows on the godparents the obligation to treat the godchild as a son. In fact, however, this entails merely giving small gifts, supplying clothes for the marriage of their godchildren, or paying for their funeral.

There are also marriage godparents (frequently the same as the baptism ones) and confirmation godparents, in accord with the Catholic ritual, as well as godparents *de reliquia* (in San Pablito, Puebla) and of *de evangelio* (Ocuiltec), according to a magic ritual. None of these relationships confers the same obligations as the baptism godparentship.

Local and Territorial Units

Frequently rancherías (see Settlement Patterns) are formed by groups of houses of nuclear families that form one or more extended families. Similarly in many towns and neighborhoods the houses of an extended family tend to group together in favor of patrilocal residence.

Political Organization

The municipal political organization, varying slightly as to the Constitution of each state, is the same everywhere. Generally, it includes a *presidente municipal* and four or five *regidores,* for the political center, and as many *jueces auxiliares* as there are settlements outside the center. The presidente municipal directs and coordinates the tasks of the other members of the council and is in charge of the civil registry wherever an official specifically charged with keeping it does not exist. The regidores are in charge of various aspects of municipal administration. The jueces auxiliares, representing the superior authorities, arbitrate small local problems or refer serious ones to the authority at the center.

These members of the council, who do not receive a salary, are elected by their constituents in their own settlements for periods of one to three years. Normally the jueces auxiliares, the highest authority in the Indian communities or neighborhoods, require the approval of the predominantly Mestizo council of the center. Besides, there are various aides (*policías, topiles, alcaldes*) who serve as messengers. All men of a community are expected to serve as messengers at least once (for one year); there is one for each section or neighborhood.

In communities where there is an ejido, a *Comisariado Ejidal* (president, vice-president, secretary, committee members, etc.) functions side by side with the constitutional council. It controls and directs the agricultural work of the members of the ejido and administers bank credit, thus constituting a second political force.

Various northern Pame communities still retain a *Gobernador de los Indios*, whose functions are now more religious than political. Each year he is named by popular election.

Religious Organization

The vast majority of the Indians are nominally Catholic, but there are also some who call themselves Protestants. There is no permanent priest or pastor in any Indian community. In this respect the neighborhoods, because of their proximity to the center, are in a better situation, but generally religious instruction and observance are very slack.

Each community celebrates annual fiestas for certain saints. One or more mayordomos are appointed, who pay for the expenses of the fiesta (decoration, priest's services, music, ceremonial meal) and take care, for a year, of the altar and the image of the saint being honored. Since the mayordomía confers prestige, it is very often expressly requested.

The Otomi and Mazahua of the Meseta de Ixtlahuaca–Toluca have private family chapels which are demolished and rebuilt every so often. Each new building is accompanied by conspicuous consumption of food and drink (Soustelle, 1937b, pp. 543–47).

Certain communities (Otomi from Santa Ana and Toliman, Ocuiltec from San Juan Atzingo, etc.) have chapels with apparently Catholic brotherhoods, but their purpose seems to be, rather, an exchange of gifts among the brothers.

Nowadays there is no longer a relationship between the political hierarchy and the religious organization, as in parts of Oaxaca or Chiapas, since the Gobernadores de los Indios have lost political power. The two or three cases in which political authority has a direct role in the few religious activities are definite exceptions.

RELIGION AND WORLD VIEW
Myth and Ritual

As yet there is no serious study on the religious ideas of the present-day Otomi, but certainly most beliefs coincide with the teachings of the Catholic Church, either deriving from them or reflecting their influence. The legends on the origin of the world are more or less complete versions of the biblical narration; and in the story of the deluge, mention of Noah is almost never omitted.

The identification of pre-Hispanic deities with Catholic ones goes all the way from calling Christ and the Sun by the same term, or the Moon and the Virgin Mary (Northern Pame), to making offerings of evident pre-Hispanic origin to Catholic images.

Supernatural beings which lie outside the Catholic framework will be dealt with in the section on Folklore.

For Catholic supernatural beings ceremonies have been established by the church, such as the Mass celebrated by the priest (see Fiesta Patterns), but as long as they are identified with pre-Hispanic deities, appropriate offerings are made to them: double ears of corn, cigarettes, maize, wax candles, etc.

Pagan ritual has more manifestations in San Pablito, Puebla, than in any other place; there it takes the name of *costumbre*. In the costumbres, figures are cut out of paper manufactured in this locality, and frequently a black chicken is sacrificed (Christensen, 1953a). These propitiatory ceremonies are principally dedicated to the fields—to protect the sown fields and to obtain abundant crops—to the waterhole so that the water should not be harmful, to the water-spirit if it has not rained or if it has

715

rained too much, to any dead person so that he should not return, to the steam bath so that it should heal the sick (see Sickness and Curing), etc. In other places ceremonies are fewer and simpler. In Jiliapan, Hidalgo, the only procedure is to play music, shoot skyrockets, and adorn the waterholes on Easter Saturday, so that the water should be abundant and pure.

Propitiatory rituals more in accord with Catholicism seem to exist. If it does not rain, an image of the Virgin Mary is carried through the fields; if it rains too much, the priest is asked to bless a wax candle which is taken to be buried in the field; if locusts are to be driven away, some are caught and, after the priest has blessed them, set free so that they may escort their companions elsewhere.

Folklore

SUPERNATURAL BEINGS. Throughout the area they speak of *brujas* who come during the night and suck blood, especially of young children and old people. Although details vary, it is thought that for flying they turn into turkeys or rid themselves of their eyes and legs. They may be seen as fireballs, because of the light they keep lit, in the head or in the abdomen. Elsewhere are non-evil brujas, who fly and perpetrate some mischief but who do not suck blood.

Everywhere, except in the far northeast, it is known that *nahuales* exist, and these may take the form of any animal or object. Some persons say that they steal people, and that if their relatives look for the abducted one, he is turned into a chair, a stool, or an animal so that he may not be recognized, but they do not cause the victim any other harm. In other parts it is said that they make tamales with the meat of the abducted person (especially a pretty girl), and that if anyone eats one of those tamales, he also turns into a nahual.

The Chichimec talk of little dwarfs who lock people in caves in the mountains but

do not harm them. Their relatives may rescue them by excavating from the outside. They also know of a personage who has the head of a horse, dresses in black, and rides a black horse.

The Otomi of San Pablito say that there are various spirits (of the water, of the steam bath), *semillas* of plants and animals (beans, maize, tomato, plantain), and good souls and bad souls. All these beings have a special form in the paper figures for magical ritual. The Chichimec have a powerful water spirit, called *chan,* who frequently takes the form of a great serpent; it is he who bestows power on medicine men.

In some zones it is believed that each class of animal has a patron or owner (*dueño*). For example, the deer's is San Onofre.

STORIES AND LEGENDS. As there is no compilation of the legends of the Otomian family, very brief summaries of the most interesting are presented here.

1. A newlywed girl did not want to eat anything which her husband ate, but instead she wanted to go to her parents' house "to eat that to which she was accustomed." At first the husband would not let her go, but finally one day gave her permission. When the girl arrived at her mother's house, she asked her for blood. The mother had none at the time so allowed her to "suck a little from her father," but the girl sucked too much and the father died.

There are many other legends about brujas, ascribed to specific persons, but their content only illustrates what has already been said about brujas.

2. One night two friends passed a place where they had always seen a rock but this time found a store. One of them went in, and at that moment the store disappeared and the rock closed, leaving him inside. The other friend was blamed for the murder of the first one and was thrown into jail, but he remembered the date and a year later asked to be taken to the rock. He found his friend and set him free.

3. Various persons know the enchanted caves which hold huge treasures and which open for one day each Easter Saturday. Anyone may enter them, but if he takes part of the treasure, he cannot leave and stays a prisoner an entire year. There are many variations on this story about enchanted caves.

4. The Chichimec tell that San Luis de la Paz was founded on the spot where an eagle stood, and that this happened with many other cities, including Mexico.

5. The Ocuiltec say that there used to be two *teponaztles* in their town, but that one day the older went to Tepoztlan, Morelos, where it now is. That is why they chain the other one, which is kept in the sacristy of the church, so that it should not escape and go with its mother to Tepoztlan.

TRADITIONS REGARDING OLD CUSTOMS. Aside from actual memories of customs decades ago, some places have legends regarding the ancestors. For example, the Pame of Jiliapan have traditions regarding cannibalism, nomadic life, etc. (Manrique, 1961).

SICKNESS AND CURING

Sickness has many "causes" and cures.

1. Witches produce illnesses by introducing foreign objects (thorns, stones, animals) into the body. The only effective cure is to have another witch extract the object.

2. Brujas who suck blood may even cause death. There are no therapeutic methods, but prophylactic measures may be taken. Any kind of small seed can be broadcast around the outside of the house, and the bruja takes so long picking it up that it does not have time to enter the house.

3. A strong, sudden emotion may cause *espanto* (some places distinguish less severe degrees: *susto* and *asombro*). It is cured with a *limpia* or *barrida*, which consists of passing over the body of the sick person aromatic plants, wax candles, eggs, or black chickens which pick up the illness, to the accompaniment of music and singing (San Pablito) or prayers (elsewhere). The variety of procedures is almost infinite.

4. *Ojo,* or evil eye, is produced by the stare of a person who has "strong sight." It may be cured with a limpia or the application of holy water.

5. Belief in "cold" or "hot" objects which might cause sickness or make difficult its alleviation, is similar to that found throughout Latin American. It appears to be of European origin.

6. Some illnesses are attributed to the *aire* and are usually cured with limpias.

7. In almost all settlements there is at least one midwife. She usually gives the mother a steam bath in the temascal (sometimes improvised) before the parturition, another one after. She also massages the abdomen "to arrange the child." The temascal is also used for other cures.

8. Many people have a knowledge of curative herbs and how to set dislocations and fractures ("to fix the bones"). It is not uncommon for one person to have several of these specialties.

An Indian rarely consults a doctor, but regularly takes analgesics and pharmaceutical preparations against coughing.

Sanitation is generally precarious. Although waterholes are fenced against animals, there is no prevention of contamination through infiltration. There are no latrines; body needs are relieved in the field or between cultivated fields. Bathing is not very frequent (once every week or two), but face and hands are washed upon awakening in the morning and before each meal. The mouth is rinsed after each meal. Houses do not offer adequate protection against wind and cold (except those of adobe), but these are sometimes too humid and poorly ventilated.

AESTHETIC AND RECREATIONAL PATTERNS
Plastic Arts

Products of the textile art, such as Otomi bands and bags, are among the most beau-

F<small>IG.</small> 45—LOS MALINCHES DANCER,
LA PALMA

tiful because of their color and infinitely varied decoration. Ceramics, famous for their decoration more than for their shape, frequently have great beauty.

Music and Dance

The most common instruments are the violin and the guitar, played simultaneously, but larger ensembles may include wind instruments and drums. Phonograph records are being played more and more.

The music throughout the area is clearly European in origin, generally *sones*. Music is always played to enliven fiestas and for the final dance. In some places music accompanies funerals, especially those of children. In San Pablito it is an essential part of curing ceremonies.

Religious dances are very infrequent. The Northern Pame perform the dance of Los Malinches, attired in ordinary clothes but with a crown on the head (fig. 45), a rattle in one hand and a bunch of feathers in the other. In Ciudad del Maiz Los Caballitos is danced, with the figure of a horse attached to the belt to indicate riding (fig. 46,*a*). The Chichimec have a dance in

which they wear long satin garments of brilliant colors with rows of applied beads, headdresses of feathers bound with a cloth band, and a bow (fig. 46,*b*).

The secular dance is usually a sort of clog dance, in which the man does not touch his partner.

Song, Poetry, Narration, Conversation

In the region of Ixmiquilpan–Zimapan, Hidalgo, the sheepherders sing while watching over their flock. Themes deal with love or with deserted husbands. Most compositions have two, three, four, or six distinct verses (Soustelle, 1937b). Around Santa Ana Hueytlalpan, Hidalgo, women almost always sing when they have had quite enough to drink at parties. There is no defined melody nor verse. In other areas the little singing is exclusively as couplets to the *sones* that are played.

Poetry, found only in the region of Ixmiquilpan–Zimapan, is simply the recitation, without music, of the lyrics of the songs (Soustelle, 1937b).

It is common for men and women to gather in small groups in front of the houses to converse and gossip. Men get together at the stores to talk, drink a little, and play cards. Women converse when they meet at the places where they wash clothes.

Games

Boys make slingshots, throw a ball at each other without rules or score, and compete in long-distance racing and in climbing trees. Girls play *matatena* (jacks), hide-and-seek, and play with dolls. Adolescent boys play adult games or practice basketball at the backboard in the school yard. The most common adult entertainment is the game of cards.

Etiquette

There are established forms of greeting and leave-taking, in Spanish as well as in

Indian languages. When two people who know each other meet, they stop to greet; people who do not know each other greet but without stopping.

As a sign of respect, godchildren kiss their godparents' right hand. The Chichimec have a ceremonial greeting by which the visitor deposits a kiss between the host's hands placed together, palms up.

It is customary to invite the visitor to take a seat; if he should arrive at mealtime, he is also asked to dine.

Custom dictates that emotions be concealed, that indifference be feigned, except when one is drunk.

Fiesta Patterns

Religious fiestas are generally begun in the morning, with Mass celebrated by the priest, who has come for the occasion. At noon a meal is offered by the mayordomos (see Food Habits, Religious Organization). During the afternoon a game of horsemanship or some competition may be organized, in which Mestizos take part, almost exclusively. At sundown the musicians, who have been playing intermittently throughout the day, transfer to the place where the secular dance is held. There the entire town meets, young people to dance, old people to look on and converse, and children to run around everywhere.

There are almost no celebrations which are entirely secular. Baptisms, weddings, and deaths all have religious undertones; private festivities on these occasions are less ostentatious, but they follow more or less the same pattern: religious ceremony, meal, dance.

LIFE CYCLE

Birth

The pregnant woman should abstain from eating foods considered "cold." During delivery she is helped by a midwife or another woman. Kneeling or squatting, she holds

FIG. 46—DANCERS. *a*, Los Caballitos, Ciudad del Maiz. *b*, Chichimec dancer.

on to a rope hanging from the ceiling, her waist strongly girded. A few days after parturition, the child receives a warm bath, the mother a steam bath in the temascal.

Baptism is celebrated in accordance with Catholic ritual and with a ceremonial meal, when the priest comes through town (see Family and Kinship and Fiesta Patterns).

At first the mother's diet is limited to toasted tortillas and atole but soon includes other nourishment until it returns to normal.

719

The newborn is fed on mother's milk; at six months he begins to take very diluted maize-dough water, then adds bean broth and tortilla chunks, until he eventually eats the usual diet. At this time (about one year) he is weaned, often by putting bitter substances on the nipple.

Socialization

Begun about the time of weaning, toilet training is completed when children are three years old.

For the next two or three years they have much freedom and few duties. At age five or six both boys and girls begin to tend the family's animals, but still play a good deal while they work. When seven or eight they must also help in fetching water (girls) and firewood (boys), thus beginning the division of labor by sex.

Between eight and 10 years of age, boys begin to help their fathers with agricultural chores, girls their mothers in household chores. When 12 or 14, girls are capable of assuming charge of the household, and boys are able to cultivate the fields by themselves.

When boys reach between 14 and 18 years of age, according to the place, they begin climbing the ladder of administrative posts by serving as topiles (see Political Organization); that is, they commence to fulfill adult status. Ideally, to be elected to a higher office, a man is supposed to have occupied all the lower ones, but today this is not essential. At approximately the same age (14 to 18 years) women are also considered adult and therefore marriageable.

Formal Education

Some children, between seven and 14 years of age, go to school (which follows the official program of rural schools throughout Mexico). Most schools go only to third grade, a few to fourth or fifth. They are scarce, and many Indian communities lack them or a teacher. If they have no teacher,

they pay a Mestizo to teach the children Spanish, and reading and writing, almost always with very poor results.

Marriage

Young people of marriageable age have a chance of talking to each other when the girls go to fetch water. When they have agreed on getting married, the groom's family asks for the girl, sometimes via special petitioners. Usually the petition is repeated from three to five times, always on a given day of the week; this is required by custom, since on the first visit the girl's family ordinarily refuse consent or wish to discuss the matter with relatives. Each time gifts of cigarettes, liquor, and food are taken. If an agreement is reached, the date of the wedding is set.

When a civil registry exists and a priest is nearby, the civil and religious ceremonies are commonly performed, but seldom in remote places. The most important part of the wedding is the ceremonial meal, in which the couple's parents or grandparents give them advice and admonish them.

Today, the robo de la novia is more and more common and takes various forms. If a young man does not obtain the girl's consent, he sometimes resorts to abduction. If two young people wish to marry but their parents do not approve, they elope. If the families are in agreement but wish to avoid the considerable expense, an abduction is simulated. In all these cases, it is common for the youngsters to return when the first child is born; they are then admitted into the community as if the standard marriage had taken place (Manrique, 1961).

Among the Pame of Agua Puerca, San Luis Potosi, trial marriage allows a girl to live for three months at the house of a young man. If they get on well, they continue to live as man and wife; if they don't get on well, the girl simply returns to her home. The trial may be repeated several times.

Sexual relations outside marriage or before it are exceptional, unless in the trial marriage. The family, generally, is quite stable.

Residence is, almost without exception, patrilocal. At first the newlyweds live in the kitchen of the boy's parents' house, but soon afterwards build their own house (see Local and Territorial Units).

Death

When a person dies, the news is announced verbally to relatives and neighbors, or bells are specially rung. Commonly the deceased is dressed in his best clothes (often the same ones he wore for his wedding, deliberately kept for the funeral) and placed in the center of the room, on a table under which is a cross painted with lime. In some localities an altar, bearing the family *santos* (almost always printed images), is erected next to the wall, near the corpse's head.

Relatives and neighbors immediately get together. The men take aguardiente and cigarettes and the women food, placing it near or on the table on which the corpse rests. These items are consumed by all while they keep vigil for the rest of the day and an entire night. Next day, before starting for the cemetery, the corpse is placed on the bier (or wrapped in a mat, as in Agua Puerca) along with some of his tools and a little food, water, and a few coins, as if for a trip.

Burial generally takes place in the afternoon. Children (and often adults) are accompanied with music all the way to the cemetery, where prayers are said by a professional *rezandero*, and the corpse is buried with a fairly complicated ceremony (Rodríguez Gil, 1907).

A rosary is said for nine nights. At the end of the novena the lime-painted cross, left throughout the vigil, is taken to the grave; at the same time a wooden cross is erected on the grave.

On November 2nd an altar is prepared in all the houses to receive ceremonial food and drink, cigarettes, and candles as offering to the dead. In many places, the offering is prepared on November 1st for dead children and remains the following day for dead adults. The offerings are consumed on November 3rd, some of them frequently given friends, relatives, and visitors. The Pame of Agua Puerca observe complicated ceremonies and repeat the offerings from November until the end of the year.

ANNUAL CYCLE

The annual cycle throughout the area is conditioned by agricultural chores and religious festivities.

Soustelle (1937b) has described the rhythm of building and tearing down the granaries for drying maize, and the platforms for stubble in the Meseta de Ixtlahuaca–Toluca. Where these customs do not exist, the rhythm is less marked but quite regular.

It is impossible to describe a calendar of religious fiestas, for they are different in each place. The most important ones are held for the town's patron saint, Easter, and Christmas.

There are no Indian calendars in use today although Indian names for the months and days of our calendar have been recorded, almost always translations or hybrid words (Manrique, 1957).

REFERENCES

Carrasco, 1950
Christensen, 1953a, 1953b
Driver and Driver, 1963
—— and Massey, 1957
Guerrero, R., 1950
Guerrero, R. G., 1950a, 1950b
Jenkins, 1946
Manrique Castañeda, 1957, 1961, 1967
Maza, 1947, 1953
Mendizábal, 1947a, 1947b
—— and Jiménez Moreno, 1937

Montoya, Montes Vázquez, and Morales, 1961
Morales, 1950
Muñoz, 1950
Rodríguez Gil, 1907
Sejourné, 1952
Soustelle, J., 1937b
Starr, F., 1899b
Weitlaner, I., 1953
Weitlaner, R. J., 1958a
Williams García, 1950a, 1950b

SECTION IV: WESTERN MEXICO

35. The Tarascans

⊒⊒

ONTEMPORARY TARASCANS occupy the west-central section of northern Michoacan, Mexico. They mainly occupy an area (fig. 1) extending from Lake Patzcuaro on the east to the line of the railroad to Los Reyes on the west. The northern boundary lies roughly along the highway from Lake Patzcuaro to the railway with some settlements north of the highway in the lake area; the southern boundary lies slightly north of an east-west line through the volcano of Tancitaro and Uruapan. This region may well coincide approximately with the area of Tarascan speech before the expansionist period of the so-called Tarascan Empire (Kirchhoff, 1956).

CULTURAL AND LINGUISTIC DISTRIBUTIONS

At the time of contact, Tarascan speech and presumably Tarascan culture extended from Lake Chapala in Jalisco to south of the Balsas River and from slightly west of the Tepalcatepec River into part of Guana-

juato (figs. 2, 3) (Brand, 1944; West, 1948, Maps 7, 8). This distribution is somewhat more extensive at the north than Brand shows and follows the 1750 distribution of Tarascan speech given by West (figs. 4, 5). Unless evidence for a resettlement of Tarascans in Guanajuato is discovered, the West distribution is more likely. It should be noted that at contact the area of Tarascan speech included enclaves of Matlazinco and Nahua speech; it is probable that the area of Tarascan political domination included additional areas of non-Tarascan speech.

Since contact times the area of Tarascan speech has shrunk considerably, a process that is still continuing. (As late as 1850 Tarascan persisted in Tierra Caliente near the Balsas River.) Tarascan place names, however, remain, and elements of Tarascan culture are found beyond the region of modern Tarascan speech. Aspects of colonial and modern Tarascan architecture appear in many of the Mestizo towns of the area, and in places Tarascan architecture

725

terminates with a fairly sharp boundary, for example, along the south shore of Lake Chapala.

Tarascan culture at contact was a distinctive version of the basic Middle American culture of the Mexican highlands. Linguistically the Tarascans were equally unique. Few suggestions of affiliation with other speech families have been proposed. Recently, on the basis of lexicostatistics Swadesh (1960) has suggested a remote relation with his Macro-Mixtecan with a minimum separation date of 64 centuries. Tarascan speech apparently has been remarkably homogeneous, and only minor dialectic variations occur today.

Geographical Sketch

The principal area of contemporary Tarascan culture lies in the so-called Sierra region and in several adjacent valley and lake-basin areas, the principal ones being the basin of Lake Patzcuaro and the adjoining regions to the north and northeast, and the Cañada, a valley along the main highway between Zacapu and Zamora. Virtually all are in Tierra Fría.

The Sierra region (figs. 6–9; see also Vol. 1, Art. 2, fig. 6) is a high volcanic plateau containing large composite volcanoes of Tertiary age, numerous more recent cinder cones and lava flows, and more or less level depressions, cols, and basins filled with ash and cinder fall and aeolian and alluvial deposits. Because of the porosity of the soil, the Sierra has very few perennial streams or permanently flowing springs. Water therefore is a problem for most Sierra Tarascan settlements except those situated near lakes. Town elevations in the Sierra range from 1,580 m. (Atapan at the extreme west) to 2580 m. (Cruz Gordo in a detached portion of the Sierra region east of the capital city of Morelia). Several volcanoes reach elevations of over 3050 m.; Cerro de Tancitaro at the west and Cerro de San Andres at the east are over 3810 m. Many of the volcanic

slopes are too steep for cultivation. Slopes of the younger cinder cone formations are very loosely consolidated and too porous to retain moisture, but the crater floors of many of the more accessible cinder cones often are cultivated. Most cultivated soils are fairly level alluvial fills forming extensive plains or flat valleys, often with no exterior drainage. Extensive areas, however, are covered by lava flows of varying age. The majority of these support only forest growth, but occasional *joyas* or "holes" in the lava where older surfaces are exposed are prized agricultural land. Most Sierra Tarascan settlements are within or near the region of coniferous forest, mostly pine but some fir. The Sierra contains some 60 per cent of present Tarascan-speakers.

The lake region consists of the islands and adjacent shores of Lake Patzcuaro and the smaller lake Zirahuen to the south. Closely surrounded by Sierra type of terrain, the lake communities are actually at higher elevations than are some so-called Sierra villages. The lake levels fluctuate but in 1942 the surface of Lake Patzcuaro was 2,034 m. and that of Lake Zirahuen 2,089 m. Minor climatic and subcultural (economic orientation, dress, architecture) differences are the main justification for separating the lake people from the Sierra. The region contains 19 per cent Tarascan-speakers living in 13 pueblos and 13 ranchos.

The Cañada, through which runs the Patzcuaro-Zacapu-Zamora highway, is a unique valley about 2 km. wide and 10 km. long, ranging in elevation from 1,785 to 1,939 m. Rich alluvial soils, abundance of water, and sheltered position have made this a highly productive orchard and wheat-raising area. Often called the Once Pueblos (today actually nine), it contains 9 per cent Tarascan population.

The remaining modern Tarascan-speakers are found in scattered islands, mostly south of the main areas of concentration, including two towns, Caltzontzin and Villa Silva, settled recently with refugees from the area devastated by the volcano of Paricutin. A few Tarascan-speakers are in predominantly Mestizo towns such as Uruapan, Zacapu, Zamora, Coeneo, and Patzcuaro. In a number of former Tarascan towns Spanish is today the predominant speech. In a few places, such as Tzintzuntzan and the Sierra pueblos of Paracho and San Juan Parangaricutiro (destroyed by the volcano of Paricutin) the majority of the residents appear to be of Mestizo origin. (Most of the preceding information is from West, 1948).

Major Postcontact Events

The Tarascans remained neutral during the siege of Tenochtitlan, despite efforts by the Spanish and the Aztec to obtain their support. Following the fall of Tenochtitlan, save for one minor military clash, relations were formal. The one Spanish display of force was the Olid expedition in 1522. In 1525 Fr. Martín de Coruna destroyed all the temples and idols at Tzintzuntzan and the Caltzontzin ("king") invited a permanent religious establishment. In 1526 the first two Franciscans arrived and established a convent in Tzintzuntzan. Other establishments followed quickly, first about the Lake Patzcuaro region but eventually extending from Uruapan to Zinapecuaro (Ricard, 1933, pp. 93, 96). The Augustinians established their first convents in 1537 at Tiripitio and Tacambaro, ultimately occupying most of the area north and west of the Franciscans and on into the Balsas drainage (*ibid.*, pp. 94, 97). Nevertheless, in the early years there were probably never more than five or six missionaries in all Michoacan (*ibid.*, p. 99).

The relatively orderly and peaceful development of Spanish-Tarascan relations was broken by the expedition of Nuño de Guzmán in 1529. The "king" Caltzontzin was tortured to death for his supposed hidden treasure, heavy food levies were imposed, and thousands of Tarascans were forced to accompany the expedition as porters. Relatively peaceful relations were soon re-established, although the diocesan headquarters, established in 1536, were moved first to the new town of Patzcuaro and finally to Morelia (the present state capital) because of the persisting hostility in the neighborhood of the ancient capital of Tzintzuntzan.

The effects of the two missionary orders on the Tarascans require additional study, overshadowed as they are by the attention given the first bishop of Michoacan, Vasco de Quiroga. The Augustinians in particular seem to have paid considerable attention to the development of handicraft skills, building on local patterns. Whatever the source of influence, the introduction of hat-making techniques, the encouragement of woodworking and lacquer work, and attempts to rationalize the native market system are fairly evident even from analysis of the present-day handicraft and market system.

Study of the effects of the *encomienda* and *repartimiento* in this region is also lacking. Many Tarascan town names do not appear in the list given by Cook and Simpson (1948) for about 1565. Although some of these towns are of later establishment, the Cook and Simpson list does not contain many names given in the *Relaciones Geográficas* of 1579 and in other sources of about the same date (West, 1948, p. 25).

By far the most important influence on the Tarascans in the 16th century was that of the first bishop of Michoacan, Vasco de Quiroga, who took office in 1537–38 and continued to 1565, and who was one of the group of humanists associated with the first bishop of Mexico, Zumáraga. These men saw in the New World an opportunity to revive the virtues of primitive Christianity. Following closely the ideas of Sir Thomas More's *Utopia*, Quiroga's first and best-known undertaking was the establishment of the famous Hospital de Santa Fe in the Valley of Mexico. This served as the model first for the second Hospital de Santa Fe on the shores of Lake Patzcuaro and then for hospitals in all the villages of Michoacan (Ricard, 1933, p. 190).

A new social and religious organization centered on the hospital, new rules of conduct affected every aspect of life. The effects of this program are evident in many phases of contemporary Tarascan life, and it is clear that the Michoacan experiment resulted in the most far-reaching acculturation of perhaps any group in Mexico. Modern Tarascan life shows fewer survivals or adaptations of aboriginal ways of life than possibly any other persisting Indian group in Mexico. (See various works by Zavala, especially 1937 and 1941 for discussions of Quiroga and additional bibliography.)

Nevertheless, heavily influenced by European culture and missionary administration and teaching as the Tarascans were, their modern culture is neither a 16th-century fossil nor a modification of contemporary Mestizo culture. In the period since the 16th century, Tarascan culture, although far from isolated from its cultural surroundings, has acquired an integration and dynamic of its own and is highly selective in its reaction to and acceptance of stimuli from the industrial civilization developing around it.

Events affecting the Tarascan area since the 16th century have been little studied. Hacienda systems developed in places, particularly along the northern edge. The War of Independence must have been heavily felt, for important routes between Guadalajara and the Bajio and the Balsas Basin crossed Tarascan territory from north to south, and a route to Colima crossed from east to west.

In the 19th century the Maximilian intervention evidently made a substantial impression, for it formed a memory time-marker for a few elderly persons as late as 1940. Late in the century a commercial lumber industry developed and brought railroads into parts of the Sierra, accelerat-

ing Mestizo penetration of such towns as Nahuatzen. Nahuatzen, although in appearance a typical Sierra Tarascan town with predominantly Tarascan style of dress and noted as a center for characteristic "Tarascan" textiles, especially embroidery, nevertheless contained few Tarascan-speakers in 1940.

The most catastrophic event of the present century was the revolution and its aftermath. The Tarascan territory was long the center of conflict between *agraristas* and *cristeros*. Cheran, in the heart of the Sierra, was burned to the ground twice during this period, and other towns suffered similarly. Starvation was common; thousands of Tarascans migrated to the United States in the disturbed period beginning in 1916 or possibly earlier, many never to return. Others returned only after the onset of the depression of the 1930's. In the 1940's one met at every hand persons who had been born in the United States, or had been long resident there, or had relatives still living there. It is evidence of the vitality of Tarascan culture that the majority of the returnees reassimilated rapidly. The cultural effects of the migration seem surprisingly small.

Following the revolution, establishment of the Federal rural school system accelerated the spread of Spanish speech. Cultural effects seem less, for certainly as late as 1940 the rural educational system was more designed to facilitate the emigration of Tarascans than to prepare children for the rural life of most Tarascans (Beals, 1946, p. 175).

The period of the cristero revolt and the subsequent conflict between church and state in the 1930's was one of considerable tension. Many communities supported the church and clandestinely arranged and financed the secret performance of sacraments in private homes. Despite the strongly Catholic sentiments of most Tarascans, considerable conflict exists with the clergy over efforts to modify or eliminate folk as-

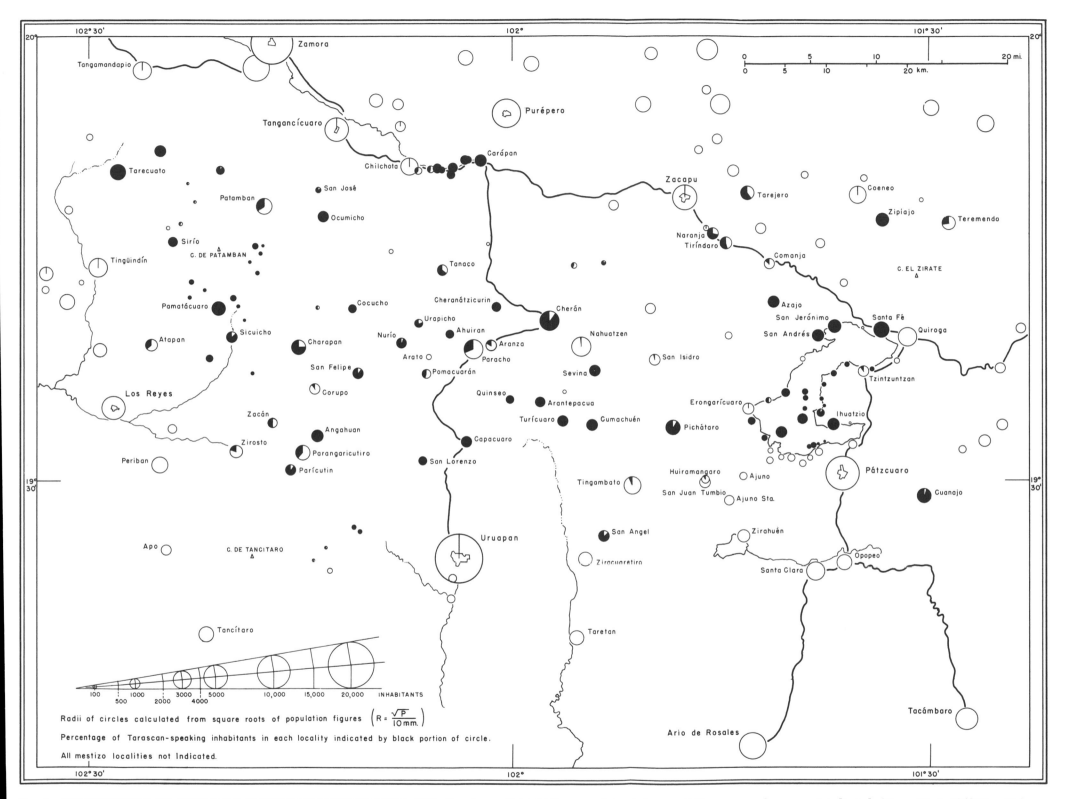

FIG. 1—DISTRIBUTION OF TARASCAN SPEECH BY SETTLEMENTS, 1940. Based on official 1940 census data. A few small Tarascan ranchos are not indicated. (From West, 1948, Map 12.)

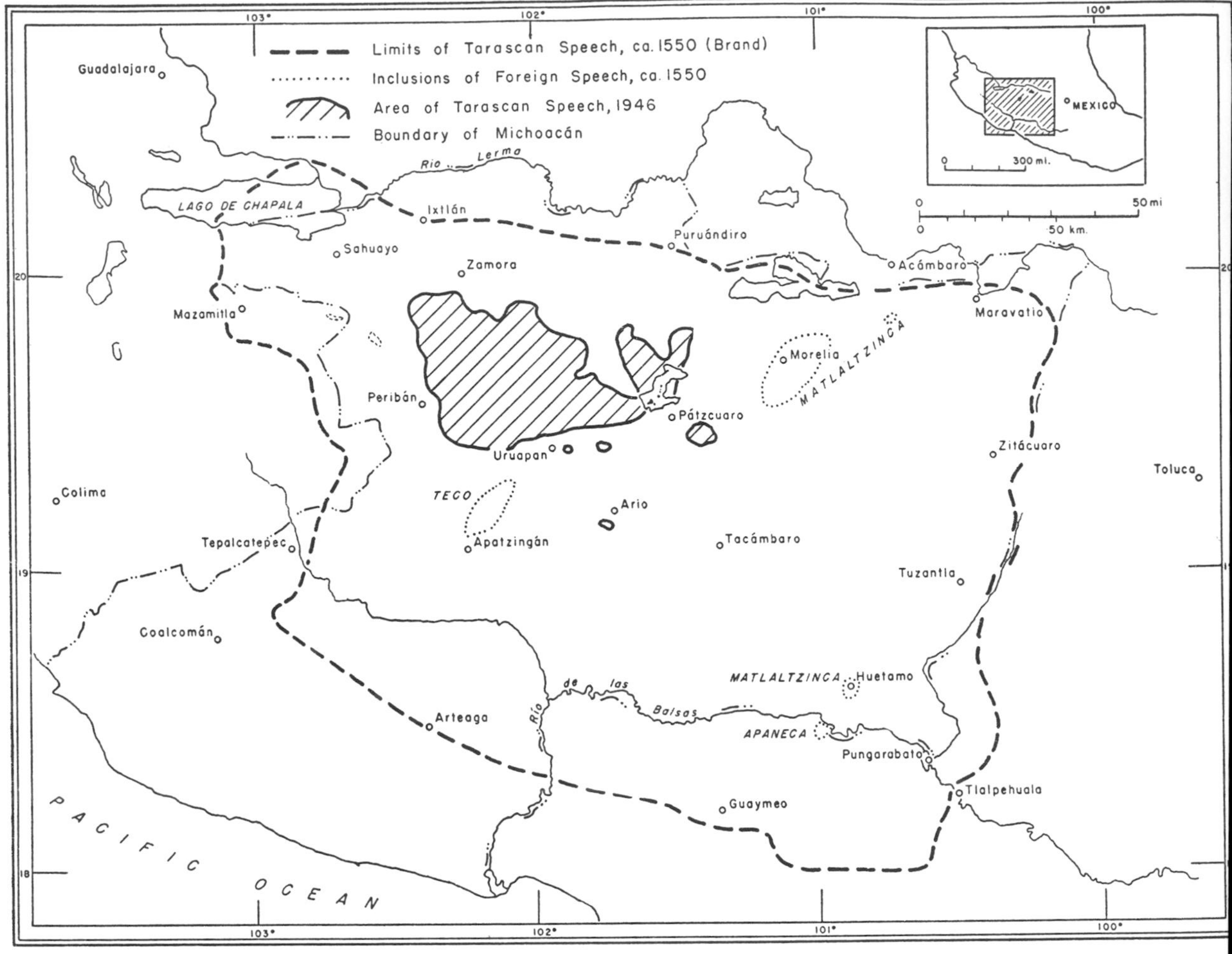

FIG. 2—PRECONQUEST AND MODERN BOUNDARIES OF TARASCAN SPEECH. (From West, 1948, Map 7.)

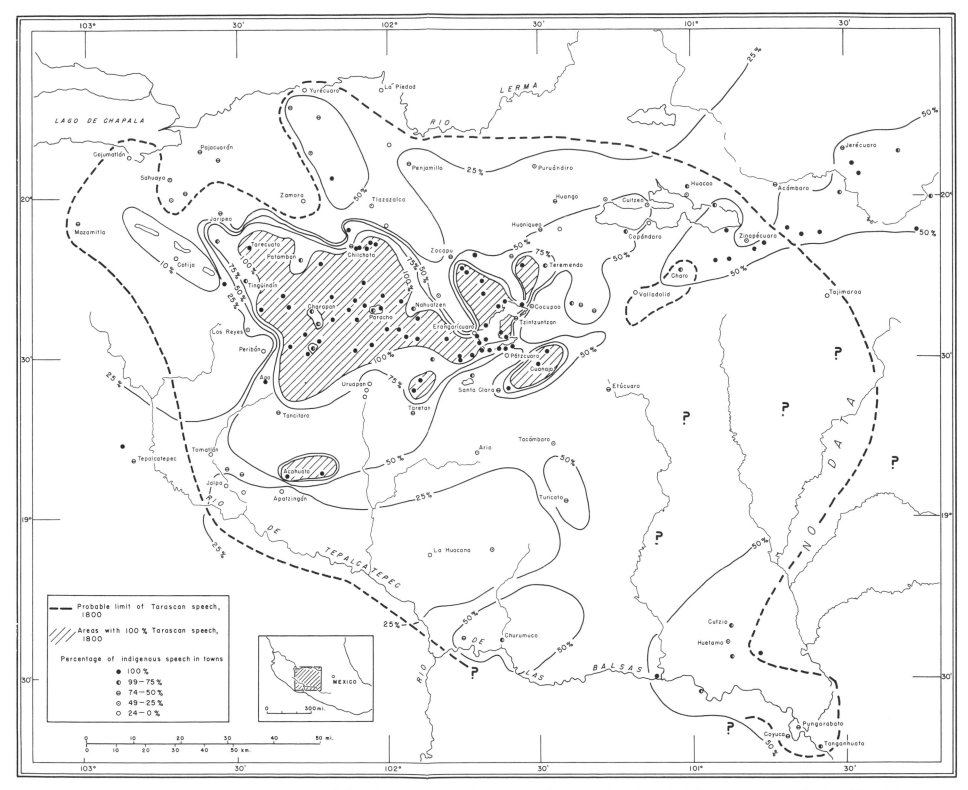

Fig. 4—AREA OF TARASCAN SPEECH ABOUT 1800. Isopleths indicate percentage of Tarascan-speakers to total number of inhabitants at any given locality. (From West, 1948, Map 9.)

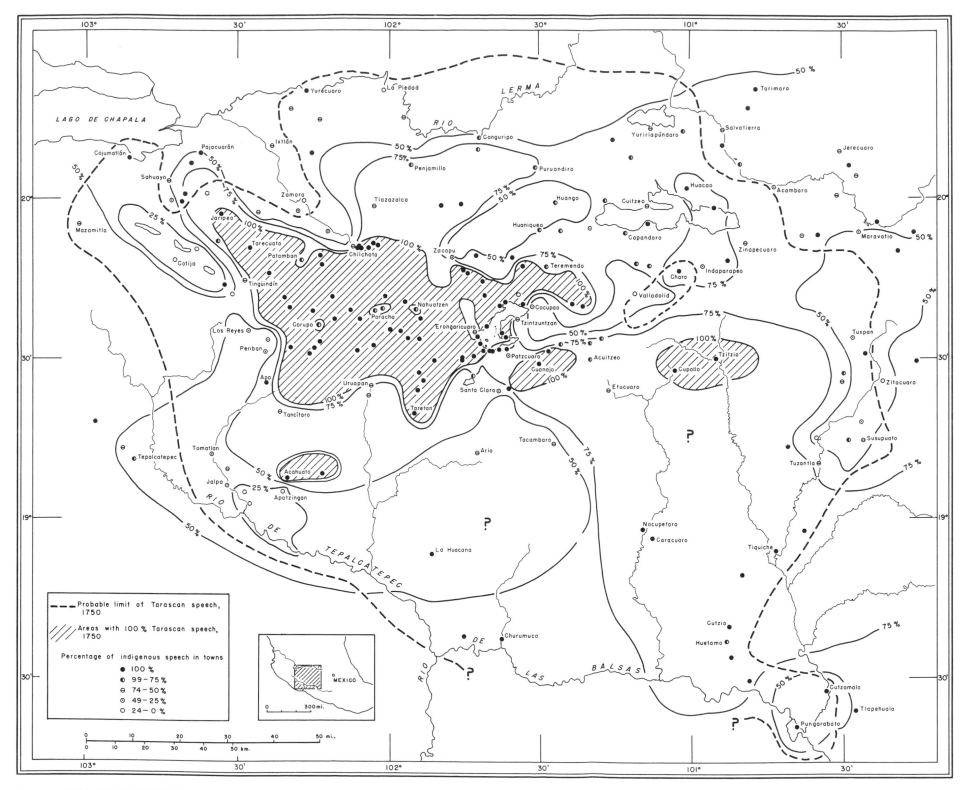

Fig. 3—AREA OF TARASCAN SPEECH ABOUT 1750. Isopleths indicate percentage of Tarascan-speakers to total number of inhabitants at any given locality. (From West, 1948, Map 8.)

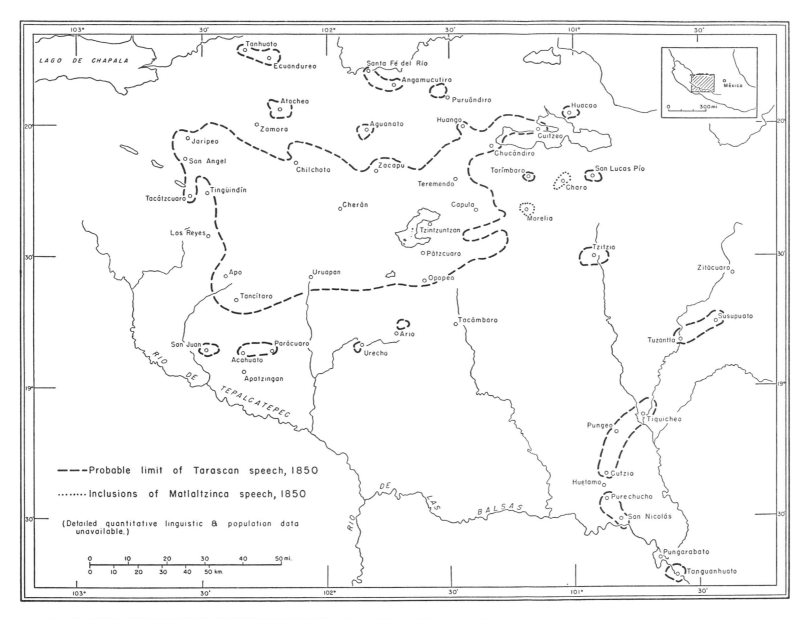

FIG. 5—AREA OF TARASCAN SPEECH ABOUT 1850. (From West, 1948, Map 10.)

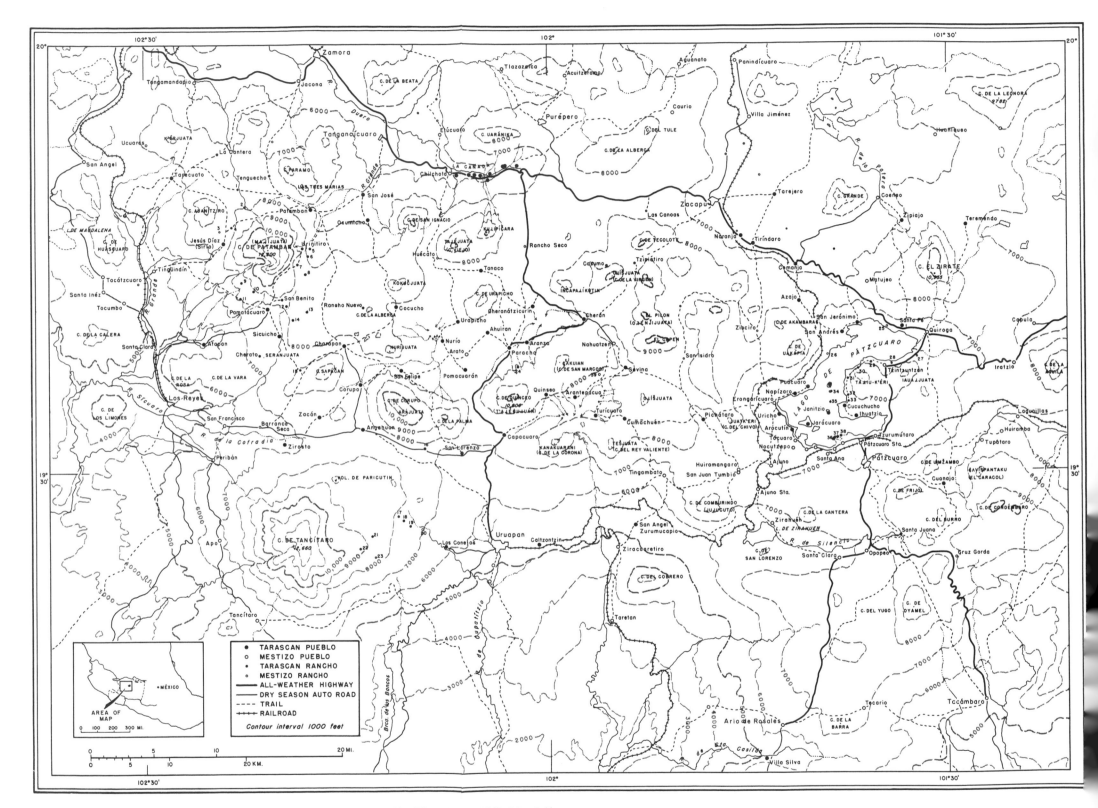

Fɪɢ. 6—TOPOGRAPHIC MAP OF THE MODERN TARASCAN AREA. (From West, 1848, Map 1.)

a

b

c

Fig. 7—PHYSICAL LANDSCAPE, TARASCAN AREA. *a,* Lake Patzcuaro, looking north; note volcanic islands in middle of lake and the Uranden Islets immediately offshore. *b,* Mixed pine-oak forest at edge of maize field, Charapan. *c,* La Cañada, looking west, or down valley. (From West, 1948, pl. 1, *d,e,f.*)

pects of Tarascan religion. More recently it has polarized about the agrarian and sinarquista movements (Beals, 1946, pp. 119–20, 134–36; Carrasco, 1952).

The completion of the Mexico City–Guadalajara highway and its branch to Uruapan in the late 1930's and early 1940's also had significant effects on many parts of the Tarascan area. The highway traverses several parts of Tarascan-speaking territory, including the heart of the Sierra region. Construction of truck roads and dry-weather roads into many communities accompanied the highway development. Not only were many Tarascans exposed to a flood of new influences, but visits to major urban centers

became a commonplace, especially for younger men.

The Tarascans also have been the object of many recent governmental programs designed to stimulate culture change. The earliest was undertaken in the Cañada by Moisés Sáenz (1936; Basauri, 1928b). The region about Paracho in the heart of the Sierra was the setting for the first experiment in teaching the elementary grades in the native language (Swadesh, 1940; Barlow, 1948; Castillo, 1945). In more recent years the CREFAL (1959), a UNESCO-sponsored training project, has operated from Patzcuaro with several extensions affecting lake and nearby sierra Tarascan

Fig. 8—THE NORTHWEST BARRIO OF CHE-RAN. A highway curves along the edge of the barranca. Typical cultivated fields slope gently up to the cinder cone, which rises 1000 feet above the town. (From Beals, 1946, pl. 1, *lower left.*)

towns. Efforts of numerous Mexican government agencies and officials have resulted in improved water supplies, health projects, resettlement of victims of the Paricutin volcano eruption, and agricultural reforms. All too frequently these enterprises involved ill-informed attempts to change the body of custom recognized by the Tarascans as *los costumbres* and thus created unnecessary resistance and hostility toward all types of change. Despite acceptance of some technical innovations and some increase in the recognition of the value of education, the main core of Tarascan culture seems to have suffered little change.

POPULATION

The slow drift toward Mestizoization of many Tarascan towns, particularly in pe-ripheral locations, and the gradual decline of Tarascan speech, make discussions of Tarascan population difficult, further hampered by changes in the criteria used in the various Mexican censuses.

The aboriginal population of all the diocese of Michoacan has been estimated at 200,000 by Mendizábal (1939), the figure used by West (1948, p. 12). This figure included the non-Tarascan populations of Michoacan as well as Colima and seems absurdly low when it is considered that the Tarascans held their own against the pressures of the Mexica and were expanding their own imperial system. Cook and Simpson (1948, p. 29) believe a figure of 1,000,-000 may be an underestimate. West's (1948, pp. 11–24) review of the data presents some problems. For 1750 he had a total of 55,000 Tarascans, but only 6700 for the Sierra. Between 1750 and the present, Tarascan-speakers became restricted to Tierra Fría, mainly the Sierra; for this region he shows a figure in 1900 of 41,368, more than the total of the official census for all Tarascans. From 1900 to 1921 all sources show a decline in Tarascan speech: 33,598 for official census figures, 32,262 for population of the Sierra area according to West's calculations. Whatever the magnitude of the decline in this period, most of it can be attributed to the effects of the Revolution and the large migration to the United States associated with it.

The downward trend was reversed following the 1921 census. Official census figures show 44,350 for 1930 and 53,795 for 1940. Later figures are based on such different criteria as to be unusable. West's figures for the sierra for 1930 and 1940 are 40,002 and 43,243.

West (1948) also provides detailed figures by settlement for the number of Tarascan-speakers and the distribution of monolinguals. Tarascan-speakers in various communities range from 0 to 100 per cent. The census data for 1940 indicate that 38 per cent of the Tarascan-speakers were

9—TZINTZUNTZAN, MICHOACAN, FROM THE AIR. This view, looking south, shows the eroded slopes of ▄uaro (left center), and Tariaqueri (right center) hills, between which the village nestles on the lakeshore. Most of ▄ lake is out of sight to the right; its southern extremity reappears (middle upper right), beyond which lies Patz-▄o town. (Courtesy, U.S. Army Air Force and Mexican Army Air Force. From Foster, 1948, pl. 3.)

monolinguals, but most field observers believe that this is too high and that the percentage of monolinguals may be as low as 30. The areas of high monolingualism are mostly in the more isolated parts of the Sierra. An exception is La Cañada where, despite a position on the old Camino Real and the modern highway, nearly 60 per cent were monolingual in 1940. It should be noted that the relation between the number of Tarascan-speakers and the number of monolinguals is quite variable. In some of the western Sierra towns that show 100 per cent Tarascan speech or percentages approaching this figure, more than 75 per cent are monolingual. On the other hand, Cheran with 88 per cent Tarascan-speakers or Sevina with 99 per cent each has less than 25 per cent monolinguals. In less than 50 per cent of Tarascan settlements do all the residents speak Tarascan whereas nearly 25 per cent of the population in the area are Mestizo. The percentage distribution of Tarascans by region has already been given in the section on geography.

HISTORY OF ETHNOLOGICAL INVESTIGATION AND SOURCES

The Tarascans were virtually ignored between the 16th century and the late 19th century. Beginning in the 1880's Nicolas León concentrated on the group. Most of his works dealt with archaeological or ethnohistorical subjects but he also wrote several short notes on the contemporary Tarascans (1887a, 1887b, 1889a, 1889b, 1902b, 1906, 1934). Bourke (1893) published a short note on distillation processes, Starr (1899a) includes some Tarascan objects and Lumholtz (1902) makes brief observations. After another period of obscurity, folkloristic notes began to appear by writers such as J. Alvarado (1939), Alcaraz (1930), Francisco León (1939), Adrián León M. and Contreras (1944), Toor (1925), Storm (1945), and Zuno (1952), mostly at a popular level. Serious studies in cultural geography began in the latter 1930's with Stanis-

732

lawski's analysis of town "anatomy" (1950) and political geography (1947) and Brand's historical and modern geographical work (1943, 1944; Brand, 1951).

Shortly before these dates several general surveys appeared in Mendieta y Núñez (1940). To a large extent these studies rest on government statistics and reports, popular materials, and superficial surveys; none involved intensive modern ethnographic work.

Intensive and extensive ethnographic work began in 1940 with the formulation of the Tarascan Project, a cooperative enterprise of the National Polytechnic Institute, Mexican Bureau of Indian Affairs, and the University of California (Rubín de la Borbolla and Beals, 1940; Paul Kirchhoff took an active part in the planning, although his name does not appear in the published description). When difficulties developed in financing, parts of the project were carried forward by the Institute of Social Anthropology. Results included monographs on a large Sierra Tarascan community, Cheran (Beals, 1946), which included comparative notes from a number of other communities collected by student collaborators; on a Mestizo-Tarascan community on Lake Patzcuaro, Tzintzuntzan (Foster, 1948); on a Mestizo town, Quiroga (Brand and Corona Núñez, 1951); a general survey of Sierra Tarascan house types and house use (Beals, Carrasco, and McCorkle, 1944). Out of the field work related to these studies came articles on games (Beals and Carrasco, 1944), pottery (Pozas, 1949; Foster, 1960b), ritual (Rendón, 1950), diet and nutrition (Beals and Hatcher, 1943; Rendón, 1947), a review article (Foster, 1946) and, based on later field work not directly associated with the project, an important study of folk religion (Carrasco, 1952b) and another of social structure (Foster, 1961). Significant articles unconnected with the project included studies of Tarascan art (Medioni, 1952), analysis of changing dance functions (Kaplan, 1951), and lacquer work (Zuno, 1952). A number of studies connected with applied programs have ethnographic interest, the most important being Aguirre Beltrán (1952) on problems of the Indian population in the basin of the Tepalcatepec River, where a major development program is under way.

The studies listed are generally of good quality and have removed the obscurity surrounding Tarascan culture before 1940. Nevertheless, much more could profitably be done. No village in the western part of the Sierra, where a high incidence of Tarascan speech and monolingualism is found, has been reported on even superficially. The one study of a predominantly Tarascan village of the lake region is only partly reported (Carrasco, 1952b). Indeed, the only extensive published ethnography of any of the 60 Tarascan pueblos and 55 ranchos listed by West (1948, p. 1) is Beals' monograph (1946) on Cheran. The extended and complex regional market and trading system has been examined only fragmentarily. Recent studies are only partially reported (Friedrich, 1958; Kaplan, 1960). Problem-oriented research that makes use of the easily accessible Tarascan communities is likewise minimal.

The relatively abundant popular accounts of the Tarascans have only minor and occasional ethnographic value. They are not included in the references listed at the end of this article.

SUBSISTENCE SYSTEMS AND FOOD PATTERNS

Tarascan subsistence systems are complex and must be viewed regionally (Beals, 1946, and West, 1948, are the main sources for this section). No one community shows all the characteristics here described. Farming, the major enterprise, produces not only a substantial part of the basic food supply but also surplus and special crops for cash sale. The same is true of livestock raising. These activities are supplemented by fishing (fig. 10), forest exploitation, handicrafts, wage labor, and trading. Trading activities are of two types: a lively internal market system, linked with major markets in Mestizo towns, especially Patzcuaro (fig. 34) and Uruapan, and an external trading system.

The market system provides for the sale of products and the purchase either of necessities produced in other villages or of articles drawn from the national economy. The external trading system may include some sale of local products outside the area but mainly concerns the purchase of products of either local or distant origin, their transport (often over long distances), and their resale. Probably a majority of Tarascan families buy a significant part of their food supply for cash.

The principal subsistence crops are still the aboriginal American trio of maize, beans, and squash. Several varieties of maize are grown (Anderson, 1946; West, 1948, pp. 34–35) depending on elevation, soils, and food preferences. Communities differ in their preferences for white or yellow field maize, the major food. "Black" (actually dark blue) and red maize is usually cultivated in garden plots and is reserved for foods for special occasions or eaten fresh. In a few places, e.g., Nahuatzen, black maize is field grown fairly extensively. In most communities growers consume their own maize. Surpluses often go toward fattening animals, especially swine, but in good years may be sold. Only a few specially favored districts at lower elevations around the fringe of the Sierra are regular maize exporters. Maize is always stored on the cob, never in grain. Maize fodder is important for feeding animals.

Most if not all Tarascan communities are self-sufficient in the production of squash. Three types of cucurbita are known, *C. pepo*, *C. moschata*, and *C. ficifolia*. *Moschata* may be a post-Spanish introduction. Two varieties of *ficifolia*, usually called chilecayote, command first preference, in contrast to most of Mexico. They are sun cured for two or three weeks and then

FIG. 10—LAKE PATZCUARO FISHING SCENES. *Top,* Drawing in the seine. *Bottom,* Seine stretched to dry; the man holds the tip of the *bolsa.* (From Foster, 1948, pl. 8.)

stored. They are ordinarily planted not in the same hill with maize but on field borders or in gardens.

Although all Tarascans grow some beans, an important element in the diet, many communities are not self-sufficient. Especially in the Sierra, where beans often do not grow well or require too much labor, they are commonly imported. Some 20 varieties of *Phaseolus vulgaris* are cultivated; all but a few appear to be modern introductions. *P. cocineus* L., a large sweet-flavored bean, may be old but is little cultivated today. In Tierra Caliente lima beans may be old. "Wild" beans are reported but are little used.

Several other field-grown native crops are of minor importance. Historically the most interesting is amaranth (*Amaranthus cruentus*), usually called in Mexico alegría or bledos. Three varieties are grown; the grain is used in a few special foods, usually for fiestas. Some sweetpotatoes and jícamas (*Pachyrrhizas erosus*) are grown in the Cañada but probably most of these rather popular (but not highly significant) foods are imported from outside the Tarascan area. Two tubers, the potato and an oxalis, are of recent introduction. Neither is grown or consumed extensively.

In addition to native field crops, wheat, barley, oats, broadbeans, chickpeas, and lentils are grown. Only wheat is extensively cultivated. In the Sierra it is generally grown on poorer soils, the main production being in the lake and La Cañada districts; in the latter area it is usually irrigated. Although some wheat is consumed in a rather wide variety of dishes, it is primarily a cash crop.

Barley and, to a much lesser extent, oats are produced primarily for animal feed. Barley is often used as a rotation crop. Other European field crops are little grown and are unimportant in the diet.

In addition to the field crops, many plants are grown in garden plots around houses. Special varieties of maize, to be eaten fresh

or in *elote*, are the most important part of the garden crop. The second is cabbage, which has been thoroughly incorporated into the Tarascan diet and is an essential in some of the most common and characteristic Tarascan dishes.

Depending on elevation and, for chile peppers, the availability of irrigation water, many other plants are grown. Among native plants are chayote (*Sechium edule*), the small green husk tomato (*Physalis angulata*), and a variety of herbs for medicinal or flavoring purposes. Most European vegetables are known but are little used. Almost every house garden also has ornamental flowers; the most favored today are European introductions.

Some agaves are planted along field borders. There is some collection of the juice or agua miel; a little is locally consumed in unfermented condition but most is sold in Mestizo towns. Wild agave buds (never from the domesticated plant) are roasted in pit ovens. In some towns no other wild plants are consumed except in times of acute famine. Elsewhere a variety of wild greens, herbs, mushrooms, and native fruits and berries are collected in season by women. In the Sierra the roots of zacatan grass (*Muhlenbergia macroura*) are gathered by men for sale in Mestizo towns, where it is made into brushes.

Almost every house lot also supports several fruit trees. In the Sierra these are deciduous fruits, the European pear, peach, apricot, apple, and quince, and the native crabapple (tejocote), and cherry (capulín). In warmer locations the Old World fig, citrus (lemons, limes, and oranges), pomegranate, and native fruits such as avocado, chirimoya, guava, and zapote blanco are planted. In still warmer areas are the mamey, zapote prieto, mango, and varieties of banana and plantain. Apples and pears frequently are grafted to the local tejocote. Irrigation may be practiced but otherwise fruit trees receive little care; pruning, for example, is rare or nonexistent. Towns often

735

tend to specialize in a single type of fruit, especially in the Sierra. Besides what growers consume of their own fruit, a considerable amount changes hands within the area and substantial quantities are exported through the external trading system.

Rather recent is a type of intensive commercial market gardening, principally about the shores of Lake Patzcuaro, where irrigation is feasible. Principal plants are chile peppers of several kinds, tomatoes, husk tomatoes, onion, garlic, cabbage, and lettuce. Products go into the Sierra through the regional marketing system as well as into the Mestizo towns. Similar gardening on a smaller scale is carried on in La Cañada and a few other towns in temperate zones. Vegetable production for export is not new, however, and West (1948, p. 47) cites evidence that in the 18th century the once Tarascan towns near Lake Cuitzeo marketed vegetables as far as the Valley of Toluca.

Cultivation is with the plow (fig. 20), except for a few gardening activities. Plows are usually drawn by oxen, but very recently some tractors have appeared. Maize is planted in furrows, back-covered with the plow, and later cultivated once or twice with the plow, followed usually by a hand weeding. Soil for other grain crops such as wheat is plowed and further prepared by harrowing or dragging brush across the surface. Small grains are sown broadcast and harrowed. Harvesting is by hand with the sickle. With very few exceptions fields are cultivated in alternate years; garden plots are cultivated continuously and are usually fertilized. Beans and squash, if grown in any amount, are not planted along with maize but in separate fields. A good many minor crops are planted along field borders in small quantities.

Cattle raising is primarily to provide oxen for draught animals but a few families have small herds in the least unfavorable areas. Even in ordinary years some animals are lost in the dry season, from lack of either water or food. Many of the animals butch-

ered are worn-out draught oxen which have been fattened briefly. A little cheese is made but much more is imported. Milk is not prized and little is produced. When needed, animals are kept in the house lots, where the manure is a valuable fertilizer; at other times they are pastured in the mountains and forests.

Sheep have long been important, but only a few families have flocks. Most sheep are cared for by professional shepherds who may herd the sheep of several owners. Sheep are the principal source of fertilizer in the fields, where they are bedded at night on fallow lands. Landowners frequently pay a small fee for this service.

Hogs are omnipresent in Tarascan towns. Almost every family has at least two or three, sometimes reared on a share basis with the owner. These animals roam the streets scavenging but are fed enough by the owners to ensure their return at night. Some droves of hogs are also pastured in forests or marshy areas. Animals are intensively fattened before butchering. Pork is a popular food, and lard is essential in contemporary Tarascan cooking. Except for special feasts, most large animals are sold to professional butchers who resell the meat.

The Tarascans raise few turkeys but many chickens. Although found in almost every household, most chickens and eggs are sold in Mestizo towns. In the past in the Sierra the price of one egg would buy enough imported beans for a day's ration in a family of five.

Essential to many Tarascan activities are burros. They transport articles on trading expeditions, carry firewood, and bring in the harvests. Horses belong only to a few wealthy persons; mules are rare. Not only do the Tarascans not understand the care of horses and mules but the available fodder and pasturage is unsuited to them. Generally burros, horses, and mules are kept very much as are the horned cattle, but they are not eaten.

Both European and native bees are kept

736

by some families in most settlements. Both wax and honey are prized. Wild honey is also collected. Most bees were killed by the volcanic ash fall from Paricutin Volcano and only slowly returned.

Wild animals are scarce. In the Sierra, where they are most abundant, hunting is primarily a pastime. Deer, peccary, squirrels, rabbits, quail, pigeons, and occasionally armadillos are hunted and eaten. Seasonal duck hunting, mainly on the lakes, is a more serious affair, sometimes undertaken by groups using the spearthrower. Today shotguns are more common. Ducks are eaten locally and also traded.

Fishing (fig. 10) in the past was a major activity for many Tarascans but today is a declining activity. The Nahua name for the area, Mechuacan, meant "land of the fishers" (West, 1948, p. 52). Drainage and desiccation of lakes and marshes has ended fishing in all but Lakes Patzcuaro and Zirahuen and the Balsas and Tepalcatepec rivers, now outside the area of Tarascan speech. The most prized of the original fish in the lakes were viviparous species of the genus *Chirostoma*, one of which is the justly famous pescado blanco of Patzcuaro. Shrimp and frog legs also are taken. About 1930 a black bass from eastern North America was introduced, presumably to restore failing fish resources. Although they now provide excellent sport fishing in Lake Patzcuaro, the bass have hastened the decline of the native fish, as well as being destructive of native fishing gear. Today fish are a major import in the external trading network.

With few exceptions Tarascan communities provide most of their own maize supply, but the greater number receive a significant and even a substantial part of their food supply from elsewhere through trade or purchase. Food patterns are therefore not a simple reflection of subsistence activities.

Tarascan cookery is quite varied, both within a single community and from community to community. Much of the variation, however, is in a few basic dishes.

Maize is the main food, primarily as tortillas, secondarily as the kurunda, a triangular tamale of nixtamal with a little soda. In addition maize is eaten green, in gordos (fried nixtamal cakes), as hominy, in more elaborate tamales, and in a great variety of atoles, or gruels, differing chiefly in the flavoring employed. Hot herbal teas are drunk frequently. Coffee is little used and then mainly as a vehicle for an ounce of alcohol.

Another characteristic Tarascan dish is churípo, consisting of meat (almost always beef) stewed with cabbage, chickpeas, sometimes a few carrots, and strongly flavored with chile and coriander. One or two chunks of meat are served with the vegetables in a bowl of broth. In prosperous villages families eat churípo nearly every day. Either as a substitute or as an addition to the diet, most families will also have dishes featuring fish or cheese.

Beans are a frequent part of the diet but are served more often by families who cannot afford animal proteins. Depending on season, numerous fruits and vegetables are eaten.

Mealtimes normally are about 10 A.M., 2 P.M., and 7 P.M. Poor families have only two meals. The early meal consists of tortillas with a protein dish (meat, fish, eggs, or beans) or greens, varied every few days with atole. Some families have taken over the common Mestizo breakfast of hot boiled milk and hot boiled sweetpotato about 7 A.M., in which case other meals are then moved forward an hour or two.

The noon meal if possible includes churípo and always tortillas, together with supplementary dishes depending on season and wealth. The evening meal is usually the same as the midday meal. Fruit, boiled chayote or squash, and other foods are often eaten as snacks between meals by both adults and children. For ceremonial occasions meals always include tortillas, churípo and kurundas.

The Tarascan diet is potentially a good one, but poverty or bad distribution of

737

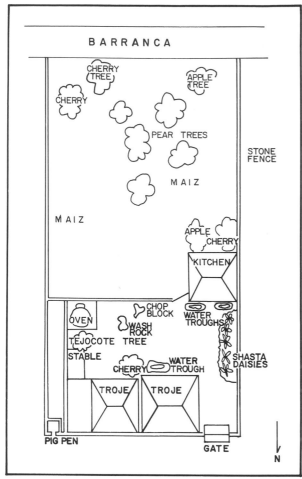

FIG. 11—TYPICAL SIERRA TARASCAN LOT, CHERAN, MICHOACAN. (After Beals, Carrasco, and McCorkle, 1944, fig. 2.)

foods leaves many families inadequately nourished in calories or vitamins or both. Towns preferring white to yellow maize, for example, probably have clinical deficiencies of vitamin A (Beals and Hatcher, 1943).

SETTLEMENT PATTERNS

Typical Tarascan dwellings stand in a fenced or walled lot with a wide gate giving on the street. The gate ordinarily is covered with a small two-shed roof of shakes or tiles resembling the English lych-gate. The largest structure is nearest the street and often mistaken for a house by outside observers; the attic serves for maize storage and the lower room for the house altar and the storage of clothing, equipment and tools, furniture reserved for special occasions, and safekeeping of all kinds. Facing the storehouse across a patio or outdoor work space is the "kitchen" (fig. 11). Here all cooking is done and the family ordinarily eats and sleeps. In addition, a pigpen and usually sheds to shelter burros and other animals or to store fodder stand around the patio. The back part of the lot, which may be of some size, is devoted to gardening, growing of special maize types, and fruit trees.

Wealthy families may have a second storehouse. In the few cases of extended family households each family may have a kitchen and storehouse about a single patio and within the same wall or fence. But the typical lot is the residence of a nuclear family, sometimes extended by the presence of an impoverished or helpless parent or grandparent, unmarried brothers and sisters when the parents are dead, or a newly married son and his wife who customarily remain only until the birth of their first child. One of the basic criteria of good parents is the ability to set up their children in their own residences shortly after marriage. This is common even where parents and children may be closely tied together in their economic activities.

In the centers of larger towns Mestizo-type houses of adobe or stone in adobe mortar prevail. Such construction is more common in the lake region. The house wall in this case is directly on the street and may have windows. Even here the typical Tarascan "kitchen" is often in the rear.

As terrain permits, houses are ranged along streets laid out in a grid pattern centering on a plaza on which face the church and municipal offices (figs. 12–16). This tends to be true of even quite small places, but notable exceptions occur. One is the

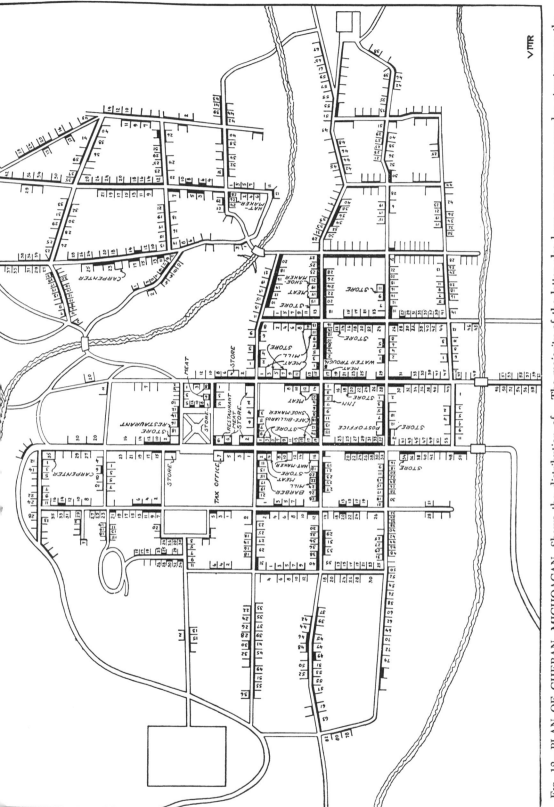

Fig. 12—PLAN OF CHERAN, MICHOACAN. Shows the distribution of the house types and specialists. A fine line bordering the streets indicates vacant property; a medium line indicates the presence of wooden structures without masonry; a heavy line indicates the presence of masonry or adobe structures. The majority of the latter also have one or more wooden structures on the same lot. Location of the majority of the specialized businesses or occupations is shown. The numbers refer to the house numbering system as of 1940. (From Beals, 1946, Map 4.)

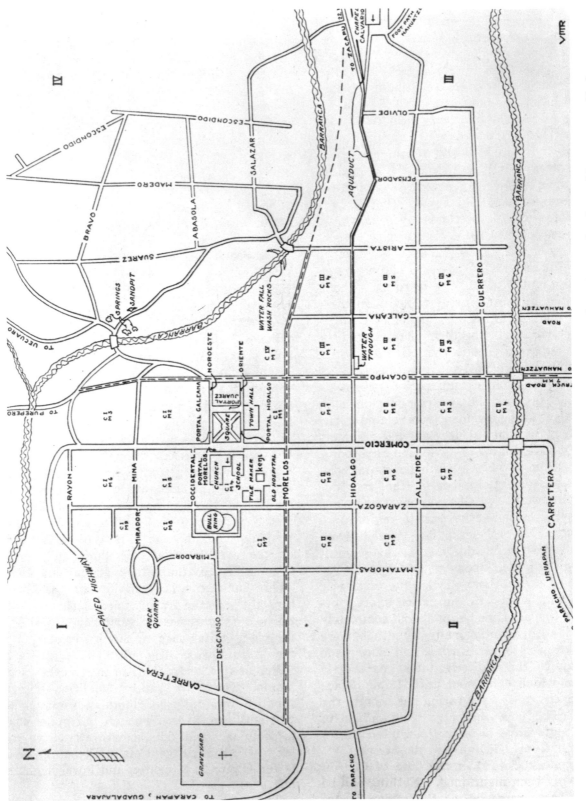

Fig. 13—PLAN OF CHERAN, MICHOACAN. Shows street names and barrio numbers. C, *cuartel* or *barrio*; M, *manzana* or block.

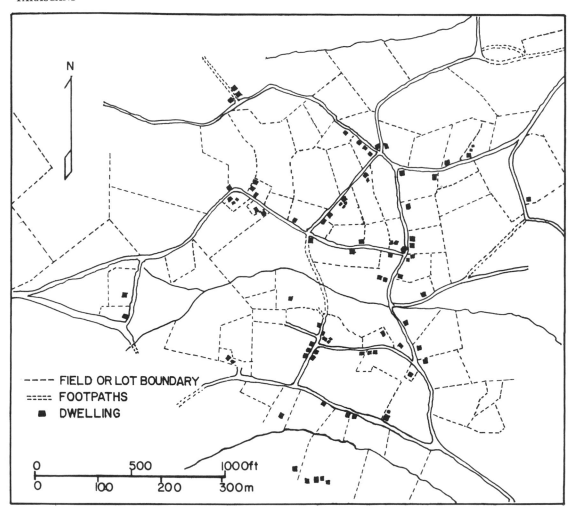

Fɪɢ. 14—PLAN OF URINGUITIRO, 1946. Like most indigenous ranchos of the Sierra, the street pattern is irregular and dwellings are widely spaced. (From West, 1948, Map 15.)

island village of Janitzio in Lake Patzcuaro, the village most visited by tourists, where the terrain prevents a grid-settlement pattern. The towns of the Cañada generally lie along the old road in almost a line-village pattern.

The isolated homestead is almost non-existent among the Tarascans; rancherías or ranchos are rare. The latter often lie on the borders between municipios and are occupied by Mestizos rather than Tarascans. Most of the population lives in villages, to-day organized into municipios with a head village (usually the largest) known as a *cabecera* and smaller villages known as *tenencias.* The cabecera (fig. 18) is sometimes a Mestizo or partially Mestizoized town. An exception is Cheran in the Sierra, perhaps largest of the Tarascan villages, which has no subsidiary towns and only three ranchos.

Officially municipio boundaries are established by the state government and are subject to change. Fissioning of municipios is

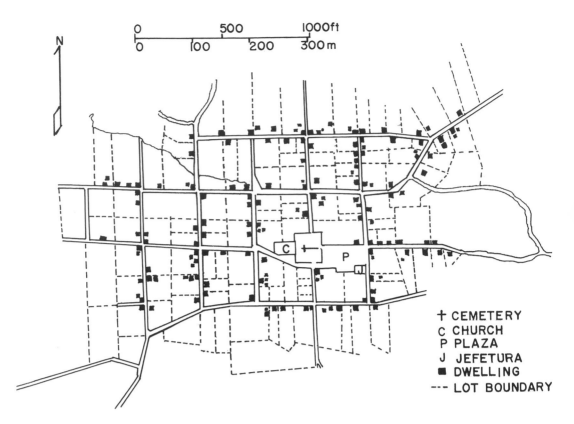

+ CEMETERY
C CHURCH
P PLAZA
J JEFETURA
■ DWELLING
--- LOT BOUNDARY

Fig. 15—PLAN OF AHUIRAN, 1946. The plan is typical of small Sierra towns. Note the scattered dwellings and lot boundaries. (From West, 1948, Map 16.)

C Church
P Plaza
J Jefetura
■ Dwellings

México — Guadalajara Highway

Fig. 16—PLAN OF TIRINDARO, 1946. Representative of compact Tarascan towns, most of which occur in areas bordering the Sierra. (From West, 1948, Map 17.)

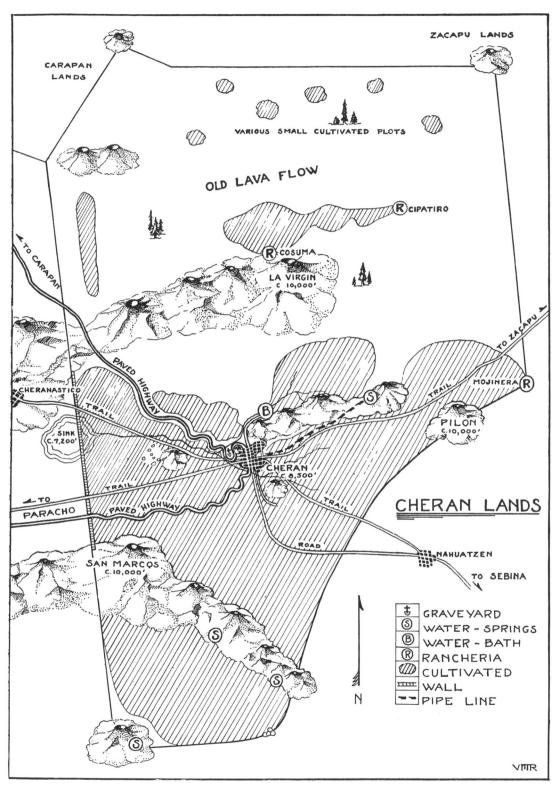

FIG. 17—CHERAN LANDS, SHOWING TOPOGRAPHY, PRINCIPAL CULTIVATED AREAS, AND
VARIOUS CULTURAL FEATURES. (From Beals, 1946, Map 2.)

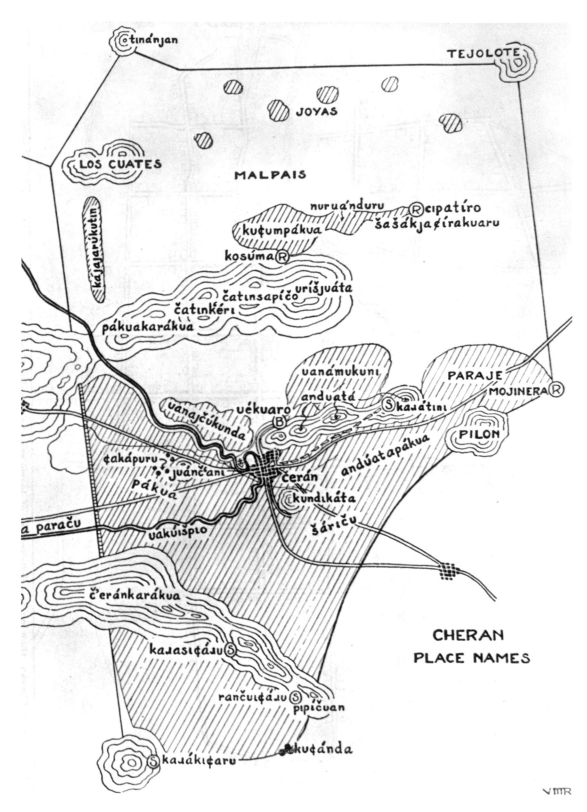

Fig. 18—THE MUNICIPIO OF CHERAN, SHOWING THE MORE IMPORTANT PLACE NAMES.
See fig. 17 for explanation of symbols. (From Beals, 1946, Map 3.)

FIG. 19—TZINTZUNTZAN HUNTING, FISHING, AND WEAVING SCENES. *Top left,* The spear-thrower in use. *Top right,* Weaving a mat. *Bottom left,* Carrying a seine to the canoe. *Bottom right,* Drying bundles of tules. (From Foster, 1948, pl. 9.)

the most common change occurring in the recent past, but there are also examples of relocation of towns and ranchos. The most recent shifts involve resettlement of people from the area devastated by Paricutin Volcano on lands no longer considered Tarascan. Much of the land in present municipios is regarded as communal property, even though permanently cultivated plots may be privately owned in the legal sense. Most communities, however, do not permit land transfers to nonmembers of the community. If anything, this practice has been strengthened in modern times as a protective resistance against Mestizoization. Communities such as Parangaricutiro are examples of what happens when Mestizos are allowed to own land (see figs. 17, 18).

The location of Tarascan settlements of whatever type is related to the accessibility of land or other resources providing the ma-

jor subsistence activities and to the site of springs. Most settlements occur on benches (lake), gentle slopes or benches near extensive cultivated benches (Sierra), or in a few cases on benches on hillslopes; Paracho is the only considerable one in the midst of a flat plain (West, 1948, p. 25). Few communities lie above the 2750-m. contour; the majority are below 2440 m. (West, 1948, Map 1). All Tarascan settlements in Tierra Caliente have disappeared, and only 2 per cent of the population still lives in Tierra Templada.

Tarascan municipios in the Sierra have very definite territories whose location is known, marked, and jealously protected. Disputes over boundaries and illicit use of forest resources are frequent. On the other hand, Tarascan settlements are bound politically with the state government. They also are linked economically in unexpected

745

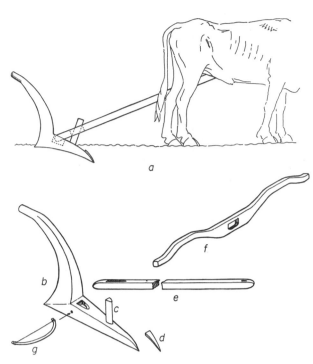

FIG. 20—CHERAN PLOW. *a*, In use, with oxen. *b*, Main frame, made from a single piece of wood. *c*, Peg over which the tongue fits. *d*, Steel plow-share fastened on the point of the main frame. *e*, Tongue which goes over peg (*c*), while the end fits in a sprocket on the main frame. *f*, Yoke; the tongue (*e*) passes through the opening of the yoke and is held by a tapered peg (not shown). *g*, Bow used on the plow in planting to spread the dirt into the already planted furrows; the bow is inserted into the indicated hole. (From Beals, 1946, fig. 3.)

ways both internally and externally through trading relationships and interdependencies.

TECHNOLOGY

Tools

With the exception of the simple digging stick, the round-bladed Tarascan canoe paddle, the distinctive canoe, and the spear-thrower (fig. 19) used for duck hunting on Lake Patzcuaro, Tarascan tools are derived from Spanish prototypes. Another possible exception is the unusual butterfly nets used until recently to catch small fish in the lakes. Almost their only use today is to provide photographs (for a fee) for the tourists on launches between Patzcuaro and Janitzio.

746

Agricultural tools include wooden digging sticks, and spadelike forms. The wooden plow with a metal tip is still the most common type, stirring the soil to some 6 inches (fig. 20). A form of north European moldboard is sometimes attached to the tip; steel moldboard plows from the United States have been supplied in small numbers to some towns. Very recently a few tractors have made their appearance, but oxen provide the main traction for plowing. Metal hoes, spades, sickles, and weeding tools probably derived from the more widespread coa are also employed. Planting and cultivating are done with the plow except for occasional replanting or in fields too rocky or small for plowing. Hand weeding with knife or sickle is common at late stages of maize development.

Many of the metal tools are handmade by Tarascans or nearby Mestizo ironworkers. In wheat-growing areas there are a few power threshing machines but persons with only a little wheat use the hand flail. In the lake region a long-handled wooden scoop is used to lift water by hand for irrigating nearby fields and gardens; it also is probably of European inspiration (fig. 21).

Other metal tools include axes, adzes, and other woodworking implements, generally of local or regional hand manufacture. Three-pronged fish spears and single-barbed duck-hunting spears have metal points (West, 1948, fig. 5). Secondary tools of local manufacture include a primitive woodworking lathe (fig. 22), replaced recently in many places with power-driven lathes where electricity has become available, looms, and ropemaking devices. Of major importance and wide distribution is the modern sewing machine, especially heavy-duty models for the manufacture of hats from palm-leaf braid.

Techniques of Processing and Manufacture

Most processing and manufacturing techniques are simple. The majority are connected with crafts and are discussed below.

FIG. 21—IRRIGATION DEVICE. The pole to which the wooden scoop is attached is approximately 12 feet long. (From West, 1948, fig. 4.)

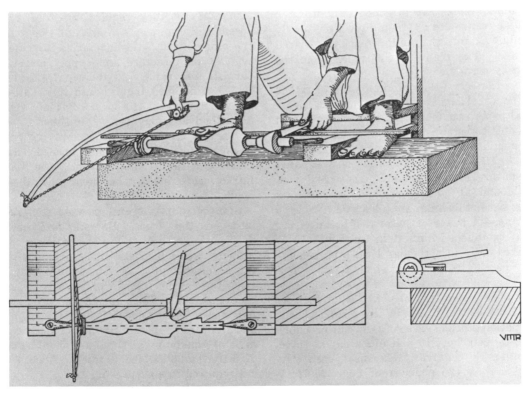

FIG. 22—LATHE DRIVEN BY BOW. A candlestick about 12 in. long is in process of manufacture. The two bottom views show the position of the cutting tool. (From Beals, 1946, fig. 9.)

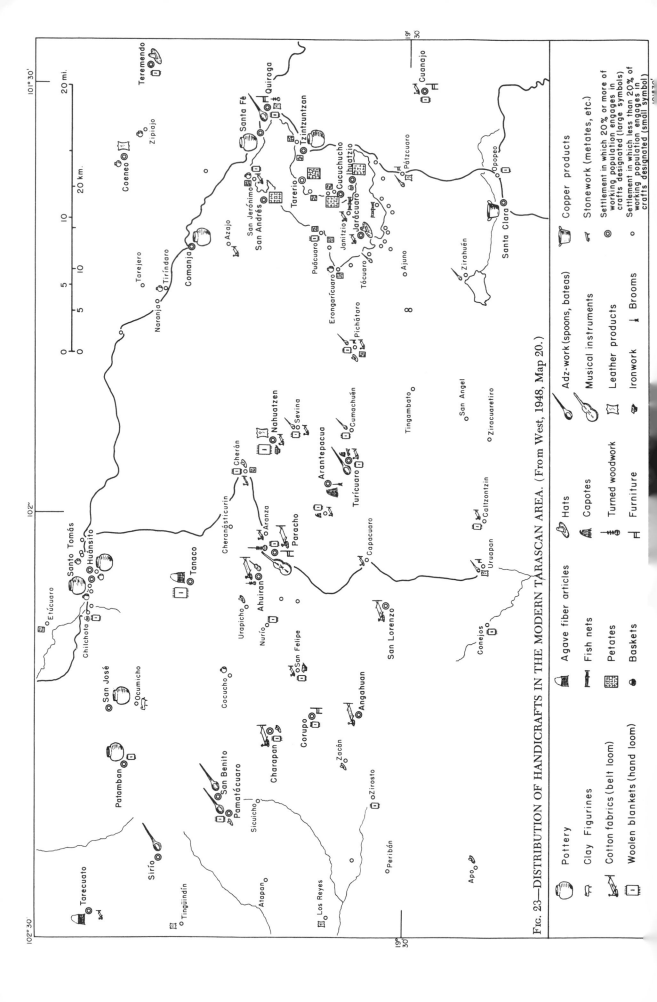

FIG. 23—DISTRIBUTION OF HANDICRAFTS IN THE MODERN TARASCAN AREA. (From West, 1948, Map 20.)

FIG. 24—TZINTZUNTZAN POTTERY MAKING. *a*, Woman making plates while her daughters watch. *b*, Polishing dried pots. *c*, Grinding and mixing glaze. *d*, Women glazing. *e*, Large pots in the kiln for second firing. *f*, Pottery on way to market. (From Foster, 1948, pls. 9, 13.)

Food processing, in addition to cooking methods already mentioned, is related mainly to maize. This is usually boiled with lime (or occasionally oak ashes for special foods) and today is converted to nixtamal at power mills. Green corn is often boiled and dried for storage. Wheat is threshed and sold to flour mills; if flour is used, it is purchased. Fish are sun dried in the lake regions but meat is usually eaten within two or three days of slaughtering animals. (For photographs of various techniques and crafts see Beals, 1946, and West, 1948; for pottery making also see Foster, 1948, and Pozas, 1949).

Crafts

Crafts are numerous among the Taras-

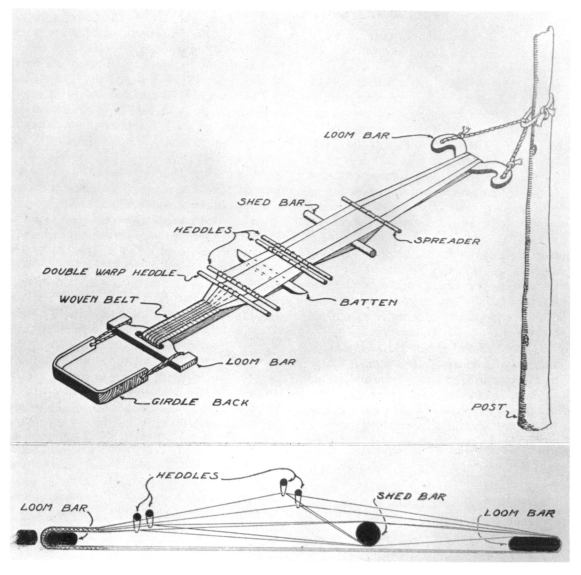

FIG. 25—BELT LOOM. Proportions are distorted to show detail; the actual width of the belt is about 1½ in. The central part of the warp is double. Lower view shows schematically the various sheds created by the shed bar and the four heddles. Length between loom bars is 3 ft. 9 in. (From Beals, 1946, fig. 7.)

cans, who have developed extensive specialization (fig. 23; West, 1948, Table 2 gives distribution of crafts by villages). Wood products, weaving, and pottery making are perhaps the most widespread and important.

The forests are exploited to produce roofing shakes, railroad ties, posts, beams and planks, firewood and some charcoal, turpentine, and pitch pine. Shakes are split with wedges from sections of straight-grained fir

or pine trunks. Beams are squared with the adze; planks are sawed with a two-handled saw. Some commercial sawmill operations provide labor opportunities in the Sierra.

The Tarascans have been noted for woodworking since preconquest times. Today the major center for this craft is the largely Mestizo town of Paracho. Power-driven lathes now are used in some towns, notably Paracho (Kaplan, 1960). Products include

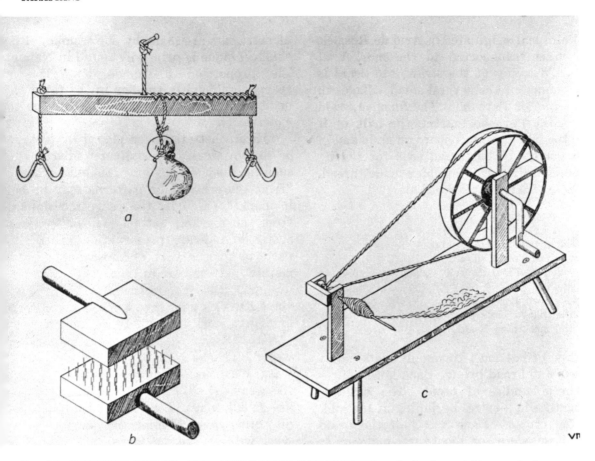

Fig. 26—SPINNING WHEEL AND ASSOCIATED IMPLEMENTS. *a*, Scales for weighing wool: the weight is a 1-pound stone; length of beam, 14½ in. *b*, Carders used to prepare wool for spinning, about 9 by 12 in.; the wires are merely indicated schematically and actually are much more numerous. *c*, Home-made spinning wheel; the wheel is turned with the right hand, the wool fed into the thread with the left hand; the spinner stands to operate the apparatus. (From Beals, 1946, fig. 6.)

furniture (particularly chairs, tables, and chests, often made without metal parts), canoes and water troughs, adzed and carved spoons and bowls of soft woods, and a wide variety of lathe-turned pieces for export including hardwood bowls, vases, candlesticks, chocolate beaters, chessmen, salt and pepper shakers, darning eggs, and toys (fig. 22). Elaborate wood products are the guitars of Paracho, where the industry goes back into colonial times and creates instruments of high musical quality. Violins and bass viols are also made.

Pottery is made in only nine towns, including the mainly Mestizo town of Tzin-tzuntzan (fig. 24). Much of the region, especially the Sierra, lacks suitable clays. Coiling and hand "patching" (attaching flattened pieces of clay to a molded base) are employed, but most pottery is moldmade (see vol. 6, Art. 6, figs. 4,*d*; 5,*a,e*). Domestic pottery is a reddish fabric with a sandy surface texture. Water jars and other forms are often polished or burnished to a glaze-like finish and elaborately painted. Certain communities will use only a special type of water jar. Black or green glazed ware is also produced at a number of towns. Some of the glazed ware carries white stylized animal and floral designs and is widely admired

751

Fig. 27—TARASCAN MEN, MAKING NET (LEFT) AND SPINNING WOOL (RIGHT), JANICHO. (From Starr, 1899a, pl. 22.)

Fig. 28—STREET NEAR THE PLAZA, CHERAN. A stone-and-adobe whitewashed structure is visible near the church. In center is a well-built stone-and-adobe fence capped with straw and shakes; the houses are of wood. (From Beals, Carrasco, and McCorkle, 1944, pl. 3.)

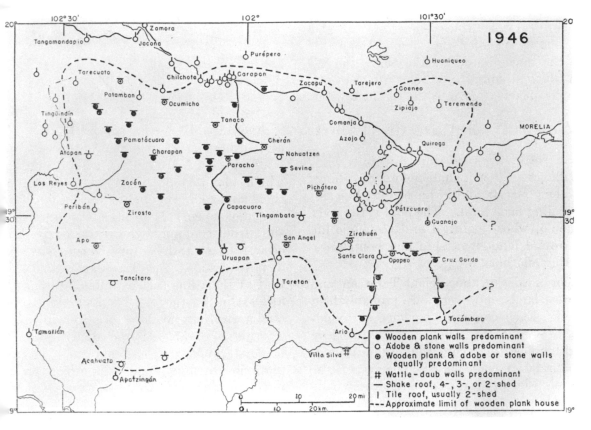

FIG. 29—DISTRIBUTION OF HOUSE TYPES IN THE TARASCAN AREA, 1946. (From West, 1948, Map 18.)

and sold throughout Mexico and even in the United States. Most pottery is fired in kilns. In a few places pottery manufacture is relatively recent. One of the most famous contemporary pottery centers, Santa Fe de la Laguna, began manufacture only in the latter part of the 19th century.

Another fired clay product is roofing tile. Cement tile has recently been introduced in the Sierra. Unfired adobe bricks are made widely. The poor clays of the Sierra give a passable result if mixed with pine needles.

Plain cotton cloth weaving on the belt loom (fig. 25) has been almost entirely displaced by commercial products. Belts for men and women, shawls or rebozos, aprons, tablecloths and napkins are still made of commercially purchased cotton thread. The exceptionally fine dress or wedding rebozos are made only in Mestizoized towns.

Agave fiber is spun with the hand spindle

and woven on the belt loom. It goes into carrying bags, carrying cloths, and sacks. Rope and cord are also produced.

Wool weaving is rapidly declining. Wool is carded, spun with a spinning wheel (fig. 26), and woven on a horizontal European loom with treddles. This loom was introduced possibly in late, even postcolonial, times. Some wool is still woven on the belt loom. The principal product is blankets and serapes. Cloth for women's skirts is still made but has largely been displaced by factory products. Aniline dyes are common but for skirts and dark serapes indigo is still preferred. Openwork woven tablecloths and bedspreads are made on the loom by a few people.

Embroidery and sewing are important. Cross-stitching and embroidering are applied to women's blouses (usually a modified huipil), napkins, and tablecloths. Many

753

Fig. 30—TARASCAN DOMESTIC STRUCTURES. *Upper left,* Simple kitchen with corner posts, Anga-huan. *Upper right,* Elaborate kitchen, Angahuan. *Middle left,* Wooden *troje* with tile roof and adobe support for ridgepole, Ihuatzio, Lake Patzcuaro. *Middle right,* Storehouse, Angahuan. *Lower left,* Large storehouse over gate. *Lower center,* Storehouse with lower part made into a room. *Lower right,* Storehouse, Capacuaro. (From Beals, Carrasco, and McCorkle, 1944, pl. 6.)

of these products are for the tourist trade. Strips of cross-stitch are also made and sold separately, mainly for application at the bottom of cotton petticoats.

Hat making, another declining industry, is found in a number of towns but primarily in the island town of Jaracuaro. Although wheat straw has been employed, most hats are made from braided palm-leaf strips rolled flat and sewed together almost always on the sewing machine. The palm leaf comes from Tierra Caliente. Several villages around Paracho make a large proportion of the braid; palm-leaf and finished braid are always important items at the Paracho market. Hats are marketed mainly in Uruapan and Guanajuato but form an indispensable article of Tarascan male clothing.

In the past tule mat weaving was important but with increasing desiccation, tules (fig. 19) have become scarce. A knife or sharp stone and a wooden mallet are the only tools. Several sizes are made by twilling techniques. Fire fans are also made of tule (see vol. 6, Art. 6, fig. 11). Twilled or wicker baskets of split canes are made in two lake towns. The baskets used in the maize harvest as well as other types come from the now Mestizoized towns of Tingamandapio west of Zamora and Panindicuaro north of Zacapu.

Nets (fig. 27) are made at all fishing villages from purchased cotton thread with a large wooden needle. A few full-time professionals make nets, but in fishing villages men, women, and children may work on nets in spare time. Palm-leaf rain capes, probably of Philippine origin, are made in three Tarascan towns. Braided cords are stretched about a foot apart between pegs driven in the ground. Starting at the bottom, moistened palm-leaf strips are tied to the first cord, half-hitched to the second, and tied back to the first with the loose end hanging down. The process, repeated for each row of cords, creates a thatchlike surface.

Lacquerwork (see vol. 6, Art. 7, figs. 2 and 3) is a famous product of the Tarascan area. In pre-Columbian times lacquer was apparently confined to gourds but in the colonial period it was applied to wood objects, mainly bowls or flat wooden plates and chests. Basic designs appear to have been conventionalized native flowers, but styles have undergone many changes. Japanese visitors in the 17th century may have had some influence; certainly French and especially Russian lacquer left their mark in the Lake Patzcuaro area. In this region wooden bowls also were painted in flamboyant flower designs.

Today both lacquer and painted work are done almost entirely by Mestizos in Uruapan and Quiroga. Much of the material is inferior commercial lacquer rather than the aboriginal type made from an insect (*Coccus axin*) and oil from a salvia.

Tanning and fabricated leather, once important Tarascan products, now are rare. Shoes no longer are made, and most leather *huaraches* (sandals) come from Mestizoized towns. Saddles and riding equipment are made still, mostly at heavily Mestizoized Nahuatzen in the Sierra.

Copper mining no longer is carried on in the Tarascan area. The contemporary copper caldrons, vases, and bowls usually attributed to the Tarascans are made of scrap copper by Mestizo workmen in Santa Clara.

Ironworking still occupies many Tarascan communities. The range of products has declined, and today native ironworking is confined to the manufacture of hoe blades, axes and adzes, woodworking tools and similar objects for local consumption. An occasional part-time worker in gold and silver jewelry may be found.

Houses and Buildings

Storehouses, or trojes (fig. 30) often miscalled houses, and kitchens are of either wooden, stone, and adobe mortar or adobe brick construction. Wooden construction still remains but most wooden structures are of heavy adzed planks notched to inter-

Fig. 31—HOUSE TYPES. *Upper left,* Old log structure, Zacan. *Upper right,* Old wooden *troje,* Tirindaro. *Middle left,* Adobe house, Apo. *Middle right,* Wooden house, Caltzontzin, the refugee pueblo east of Uruapan. These new structures are North American in appearance. *Lower left,* Abandoned adobe two-shed house, San Jeronimo. *Lower right,* Street scene, San Jeronimo. (From West, 1948, pl. 4.)

lock at the corners. Floor and ceiling, also of adzed planks, usually project on the door side of the house to form a veranda. The roof is usually of four sheds formed of pole frameworks, with attached stringers to which shakes are fastened, formerly with tejocote thorns, today with nails. These are the only metal parts used in the house (unless there is a lock), and the separate sheds can be removed as units if the house is moved. Houses are raised about 18–20 inches on a framework of heavy beams resting on stones.

The kitchen (fig. 30) differs from the house in several ways. Almost always the entire floor is of dirt; when it is not, a plank floor covers the area except for a sizable earthen space left for the cooking fire. In larger kitchens the walls are of adzed or sawn planks set vertically and mortised into beams at top and bottom. Roofs are similar to those of the "house." Simpler structures have wall planks running horizontally and perhaps only two roof sheds. Sometimes a section can be raised to provide a smoke vent.

Both types of structures lack windows and have a single door with a mortised frame. The "house" roof has a hatchway into the loft, the principal storage place for maize. Occasionally structures of the house type with two or more rooms are found in Mestizo-influenced towns, but usually, if additional space is needed, another separate house or kitchen is built. A unique aspect of the wooden structures is that with sufficient help from relatives and neighbors the owner can disassemble, move, and reassemble a house in a single day.

Most Sierra Tarascan men have the basic skills and tools necessary to prepare the materials and construct the house and kitchen after a fashion. With few exceptions, however, most men would purchase materials from professional lumbermen and hire a professional carpenter at least to supervise the construction of the house or kitchen. Even a house moving is ordinarily under the supervision of a professional carpenter.

Characteristic of both Mestizo and Tarascan architecture in central Michoacan are wide overhanging eaves (fig. 28). It seems unlikely that this feature is aboriginal, but its distribution appears to coincide approximately with the former limits of Tarascan speech.

In the lake region and the Cañada, adobe brick or stone in adobe mortar construction is almost universal, and is increasingly common in the Sierra. Often houses of the well-to-do will contain two to four rooms, one of which may be a kitchen; others are one-room affairs. In any case windows are much more common. Floors may be dirt but wooden or cement floors are preferred. Masons and carpenters must be employed for constructing this type of house. In both adobe and stone structures, carving may ornament doors, beam ends, and capitals.

Furnishings in the Tarascan troje ordinarily include a table that serves as a house altar. If the owner is a mayordomo of a saint, the altar supporting the saint's image may be quite elaborate and the entire room decorated. Otherwise the altar may consist of religious pictures on the wall with candles and an incense burner on the table, together with valued objects laid down temporarily in a safe place. Other furniture includes wooden armchairs for visitors, tin or wooden trunks for storage, and one or more poles for hanging up clothes. Rarely there may be a bed, reserved for visitors. In adobe houses fronting on main streets a room may have a metal bedstead and otherwise be furnished in Mestizo style. During the day windows are opened on the street, but the room is used only on very special occasions.

The kitchen contains mats for sleeping (rolled up during the day), shelves for storing pottery and other vessels, stools or low chairs, a variety of pottery vessels for cooking and eating, gourds, baskets, brooms and brushes, a metate, and fire fan. In earthen-floored houses fireplaces are usually of six

757

stones placed on the floor or, more rarely, one or two horseshoe-shaped clay ridges. In the lake region the fireplace is more frequently raised on an adobe base as is common in Mestizo houses (Beals, Carrasco, and McCorkle, 1944, pp. 21–24).

The completion of a new house or the moving of an old one are occasions of essentially secular fiestas. Roofing of the new house or moving of the troje or the kitchen are almost the only times when relatives, friends, and neighbors are expected to join in cooperative labor. Feasting, drinking, and dancing accompany house roofing, and the householder and main participants are festooned with tortillas, flowers, and special breads in the shape of animals. There is a street procession with the master builder and his friends and relatives in positions of honor. At other times the house or troje is the scene of mayordomías, weddings, and funerals (Beals, Carrasco, and McCorkle, 1944, pp. 30–31, pl. 8).

Dress and Adornment

Contemporary dress is changing rapidly toward Mestizo standards in the area. Men at work may still wear white cotton *calzones* (a style of trousers) supported by a broad sash, and a cotton shirt or blouse, sometimes colored. A serape is worn or carried against cold and rain, and a straw hat is indispensable. Sandals (huaraches) are worn at work. To a very considerable extent, however, this costume is being replaced with trousers and jacket of blue denim. In addition, more and more men have dark cotton trousers, woolen jacket, felt hat, and shoes for wear into the Mestizo towns. For special events, combinations of these garments may be worn while in the home community. In conservative villages, young men may adorn the straw hat with flowers. Hair is worn short, but long hair is still remembered.

Traditional women's dress (fig. 32) is elaborate and costly. A wide petticoat of white muslin with a strip of embroidery or cross-stitch at the bottom reaches to the

FIG. 32—CHERAN WOMEN'S DRESS. The petticoat is drawn here more visible than usual to indicate the embroidered edge. The apron commonly reaches the bottom of the skirt. The shawl would normally be on the head or about the shoulders. (From Beals, 1946, fig. 8.)

ankles. The material is gathered in many pleats across the back and held tightly with a broad woolen belt. In warm weather or for hard work only the petticoat may be worn, but ordinarily it is covered by a woolen skirt of about the same length. This also is heavily pleated across the back, forming a bunching of material sufficient to provide a seat for an infant held on the back. The skirt is held by one or, for special occasions, several narrow decorated cotton belts wound tightly one on top of another. Sierra skirts are black or indigo; lake-village women sometimes wear red or a reddish plaid. Most women using the old dress bought one such skirt a year, saving the newest one for gala events. An apron is commonly worn over the skirt, often elaborately decorated or brightly colored.

The upper part of the body is covered by a blouse, usually with embroidered or cross-stitched decoration. Blouses vary in elaborateness but many, especially those for everyday wear, approximate the aboriginal huipil and sometimes are open on the sides. The rebozo is almost always worn, as a carrying cloth for goods or infants, a handkerchief, or a towel, as well as for warmth or for protecting the head from the direct sun. Most women possess several of varying qualities for different occasions; the best quality, usually given by the bridegroom's father at marriage, may be considerably more expensive than a common serape. Shoes may be worn for particular needs, but women rarely wear huaraches. Ordinarily they go barefoot.

Women's hair is elaborately combed, dressed with lemon juice and oil, and braided, often with a bit of colored yarn or narrow ribbon. Women may wear men's hats on a long journey but more often they break off a branch with which to shade the head if needed.

Traditional women's dress is fast disappearing in many towns and is approximating Mestizo standards. Ready-made cotton house dresses are much cheaper than the traditional dress, which is often worn only on special occasions.

Children's dress from the earliest age possible copies that of adults (Beals, 1946, pls. 1, 2, 3).

Transportation

Until a few decades ago, many Tarascans still relied solely on the human back (with a carrying strap or cloth across the chest, or a tumpline) for transportation, even on long-distance trading trips. This is still true for short trips to market or to woods and fields, but burros are also used extensively on trading expeditions, to bring firewood or harvested crops to the house, to transport wheat to flour mills or forest products to markets. Horses, mules (except for some long-distance professional traders), or wheeled carts are rare; the last are found principally in La Cañada and other more level areas along the northern margins of Tarascan territory.

With the advent of railroads and later roads, Tarascans turned readily to modern transportation when available. Both trucks and buses are patronized, and a few trucks are owned by Tarascans. Mestizo wholesale buyers for wheat, forest products, and agricultural surpluses became common with the advent of even crude truck trails.

Weights and Measures

Most Tarascan measures are in terms of volume rather than weight or size. Current usage is a mixture of colonial Spanish and the modern metric system. Distances are expressed perhaps most commonly in terms of travel time, but also in leagues, miles, or kilometers. Land is usually measured by the amount of seed sown. West (1948, p. 33) states that 2 liters of maize will plant one hectare; this seems very low. In La Cañada, 5 liters equal one medida and 20 medidas equal one fanega or one *yunta*, the amount of land that can be planted in a season with a single yoke of oxen. In wheat planting 44 liters equal one *carga* or 1 to 1½ yuntas. In the Sierra weights are measured in pounds, kilos, arrobas, and cargas (one muleload); a burro carries ½ carga or 14–18 arrobas. The Spanish *vara* is equated with the meter; and if the term hectare is known, it may be measured in paces rather than meters.

ECONOMY

Division of Labor

Women may help in emergencies such as planting or harvesting, but their participation in major agricultural tasks is rare. Gleaning, however, is done by women and children. The woman is responsible for all household tasks such as food preparation, clothing maintenance, infant and child care, bringing water, aiding in the care of pigs, chickens, or other animals in the household, and caring for flowers and vegetables in the house yard. She does much of the retail selling and buying at markets and, if her husband has no other companions, she will accompany him on long trading trips into the unhealthful lowlands.

Women are active in some handicraft occupations, especially pottery making and textiles. In pottery making (fig. 24) women usually condition the clay, shape or mold and polish the products, and prepare the glaze if one is used. Men normally provide the raw materials. Men do much of the painting; setting up the kiln and firing are usually cooperative.

Women help with net making and repair in the lake area, plait palm leaves for hats, do some of the weaving and most of the embroidering and cross-stitching. On the other hand, women rarely if ever weave blankets or serapes made on the broadloom and apparently never make hats. They do share machine sewing of clothing with men. The occasional Tarascan lacquerworkers in the Sierra are women, as are some of the Mestizo producers at Uruapan. The finest work in recent times is produced by Mestizo men. Women do not participate in wood-working or forest exploitation. A few bake bread for sale and make paper flowers. In the main, however, women have little part in the productive activities of the Tarascan economy.

Men build the houses, provide firewood, store and look after farm products, and do most of the work connected with larger animals. They do virtually all agricultural work, work connected with forest exploitation, herding, hunting, fishing, and virtually all craft production except in textiles and pottery. Men do the major trading and run the stores in the few instances where these are Tarascan rather than Mestizo in ownership.

Children, according to their sex, begin to aid their parents at an early age. Almost as soon as girls can accompany their mothers to the fountain, they have their own small water jar. At a little older level, boys may have their own tumpline to carry home a stick or two of firewood.

Specialization

The only Tarascans who do not farm are those who own no land and can neither rent nor buy it. All farmers hope to grow at least enough maize for household requirements; beyond this, specialization in farming depends on soil, climate, knowledge, and demand. In the Sierra some men specialize in forest exploitation or animal herding; in the lake region, in fishing, mostly as supplementary occupations to farming. Others devote themselves to seasonal trading. The greatest individual specialization is in craft activities; a person engaging in one craft or nonfarming occupation rarely undertakes another.

The most marked specialization is not by individuals but by villages. Although more than one craft may be found in a village, usually one or two predominate. Thus Jaracuaro is the major hat-making center, Janitzio emphasizes fishing (as do some other lake villages), Paracho woodworking and

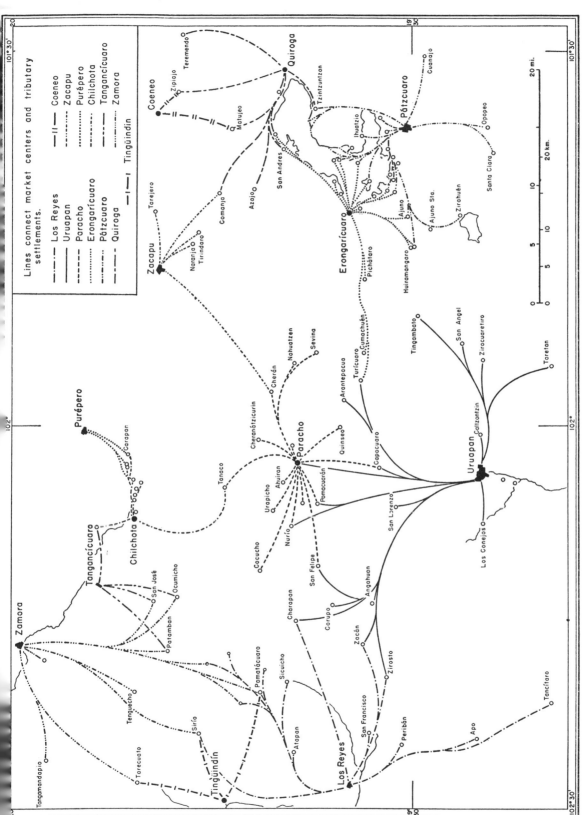

Fig. 33—DISTRIBUTION OF MARKETS AND THEIR LOCAL TRADING TERRITORY IN THE MODERN TARASCAN AREA. Black circles and town outlines represent markets. Many non-Tarascan towns tributary to the main markets are not indicated. (From West, 1948, Map 21.)

FIG. 34—THE PATZCUARO MARKET. *Top*, Canoe arriving from Janitzio. *Bottom*, Fruit stands. (From Foster, 1948, pl. 10.)

weaving, Nahuatzen embroidery and forestry. West (1948, pp. 56–71) discusses this subject in detail (fig. 23). His Table 2 shows historical changes in it. Village specialization accounts for much of the market and trading activities, both internal and external.

Property and Land Tenure

Most property in regular use is individually owned except for lands in modern ejidos. In some sense household equipment and tools may be viewed as family property but in cases of separation the individual leaving the household would normally take with him or her the appropriate implements of frequent use. Another exception is major property acquired after marriage; such property belongs jointly to husband and wife and ultimately to the children, among whom it will be divided.

Property often considered as communally owned includes forest lands and fields cleared for temporary cultivation on mountain slopes. Even privately owned plots in large areas of permanent cultivation retain a trace of communal interest; after the harvest dates, set by municipal officials, such lands are open to public grazing of animals.

In theory sons and daughters share equally in inheritance, although in fact sons often receive a larger share. Thus house lots and gardens, houses (which may be owned separately from the land), large equipment, animals and farm lands may be owned either by wife or by husband, unless acquired after marriage, with independent rights of disposal. In some quite prosperous families most of the property is owned by the wife, even though the husband may do all the farming. The income of the family from farming, regardless of land ownership, or from crafts and supplementary occupations normally is viewed as belonging to the family, and major expenditures or sales of property usually are not undertaken without family discussion. In most instances the wife has charge of family funds. In the rather rare cases of extended families maintaining joint residence, sometimes all income is pooled even to the extent that funds for purchases of clothing or food are drawn from the extended family purse.

Production and Consumption Units

In almost all activities the nuclear family is the common unit of production. In a few cases the unit is an extended family; in others, such as long-distance trading enterprises or forestry, two or more men may form a loose association or even a partnership, the latter perhaps more common between brothers. Fishing and duck hunting in the lake region also call for cooperative efforts. In the main, however, if additional labor is needed for productive enterprises, it is hired on a wage basis.

Trade and Markets

The trade and marketing system is intimately related to the system of craft specialization, differences in agricultural production, and the demand among Tarascans for products, not only from the modern industrial world but even more for such food items as salt, fish, cheese, and tropical fruits. The internal exchange of produce takes place mainly through regional markets, mostly located in Mestizo towns such as Uruapan, Los Reyes, and Tinguindin to the south and west; Paracho in the Sierra; Zamora, Tangancicuaro, Chilchota, Purepero, Zacapu, and Coeneo to the north; and Quiroga, Erongaricuaro, and Patzcuaro in the lake region. The location of the principal markets and the main towns related to each one is shown in figure 33. Lesser markets are held in some of the Indian towns.

Most market activity (fig. 34) takes place on Sunday, although Patzcuaro has an important market on Friday as well. In addition, most Tarascan towns have large markets during major religious fiestas, especially those of the patron saints. These are so

FIG. 35—TARASCAN AREA. *Top,* View looking northwest across Tzintzuntzan and Lake Patzcuaro from the *yácatas. Lower left,* Tarascan girls. *Lower right,* Mestizo types. (From Foster, 1948, pl. 4.)

arranged that many Mestizo traders have a regular circuit of fiesta markets. In addition, Patamban has a special market for the sale of its pottery to traveling vendors. Even a religious pilgrimage undertaken as a vow often is also a major trading enterprise.

Women predominate in the activities of the regular markets, the majority selling fruits, vegetables, and sometimes other produce or handicrafts. Forest products, grains, herbs, prepared foods, raw materials such as palm leaves, semifinished products such as palm-leaf braids for hats, are among other items of Tarascan origin appearing in markets. In addition, markets have vendors, usually Mestizos, of factory products such as hardware, cloth, religious objects such as pictures, medals, and rosaries (especially at religious festivals). Although articles of equivalent value may be exchanged, all pricing is in monetary terms.

Trading over longer distances is in the hands of men. Most mule transport is managed by Mestizos; Tarascans tend to use burros or to carry goods on their backs. Much of the long-distance trading involves the exchange of highland and lowland products. Goods are assembled from highland sources as far away as the pottery markets of Guanajuato and Jalisco. Locally grown deciduous fruits, herbs, craft specialties such as woodwork and fine pottery are important. The return loads include dried fish, dried beef, cheese, and tropical fruits from Guerrero, and chile peppers from Colima. The longest trips go as far as San Geronimo on the coast of Guerrero, and an occasional trader reaches Acapulco. The usual goal, however, is Petatlan, approximately a six-week round trip.

Undoubtedly the opening of roads has greatly modified the patterns described, but no recent studies are known. If the early effects have continued, the *arrieros*, both Mestizo and Tarascan, must be rapidly vanishing or have changed to the use of trucks and buses.

Most Tarascan towns have at least one small store. The majority of these are operated by Mestizos. They carry a limited stock of basic necessities, factory-made cloth, matches, soft drinks, and a few processed or tinned luxury foods. Storekeeping has low status among Tarascans, but often the stores are good places for visitors to get preliminary information and to meet local residents, especially if the municipal offices happen to be closed.

Labor Export

During harvest seasons a great many Tarascans work for wages both in their own villages and in neighboring communities. Men who hire labor to help in their own harvests may also hire out as harvest workers. Other labor opportunities on highway construction, railway maintenance, or in Mestizo enterprises in nearby areas are sought by many who need supplementary money. Others hire out as sheep herders. Those who must live mainly on wage labor are pitied and of low status.

Many Tarascans migrated to the United States during the unsettled period of the revolution and the cristero wars, and many did not return. Some also have become *braceros* or contract laborers in more recent times; the number may be substantial but exact data are unavailable. Those who save their earnings in the United States often have bought land. Many also have brought back plants and seeds to try out.

Wealth and Its Uses

The most valued wealth is in land. Silver is prized but it does not produce. There is much talk of the rich and the poor, but few persons are identified as "rich." A man who harvests 50 or more cargas of maize is defined as wealthy; however, there is great secretiveness about the amount of land owned and the amount of grain harvested. Government tax records generally include only a fraction of the land owned.

The first claim on wealth seems to be

more adequate food, followed by better clothing. People wealthy by Tarascan standards apparently do not make any display in their housing. The most pretentious houses often are owned by persons known to be "comfortable" but not wealthy. After necessities are met, the major expenditure of wealth seems to be in the support of religious festivals and in weddings. These differ widely in elaborateness and cost but are the only occasions for public display of wealth. The primary measure of a "good" man, nevertheless, is his ability to provide each of his children with a house and enough land to be independent farmers when they marry.

SOCIAL ORGANIZATION
Family and Kinship

The basic kinship unit is the nuclear family with occasional augmentation of unmarried brothers or sisters or a dependent impoverished elderly person. After marriage the young couple normally live in the home of the bridegroom until the birth of the first child, at which time they usually and certainly ideally should move into their own residence. This is true even though the husband may continue to work with his father, cultivating family lands cooperatively. Not infrequently, the parents give lands to their children after marriage except for the youngest son. The latter, frequently in his own house but sometimes in his father's, continues to work with his father in farming the remaining lands and inherits the residue of the parents' estate. In such cases, the son gradually assumes direction of the economic activities.

Occasional extended families are those where parents and one or more sons live in a single compound and carry on all economic activities jointly. Usually each son has his own kitchen and often a house or troje. The parents continue to hold all their lands, which are farmed cooperatively. Such enterprises usually if not always break up when the father dies even though an elder son may actually have directed the economic activities for many years. Lands and other property are divided equally among the nuclear families, sometimes including any married daughters living away. Perhaps more frequently, though, the latter will have received lands from the parents after marriage. In all arrangements older siblings have a responsibility to aid the marriage and economic independence of any children unmarried at the time of the parents' death.

Despite the ideal of equal inheritance by all children regardless of sex, the system is difficult to carry out. Disagreements over inheritance are the most frequent source of conflict and may continue for years.

Once a nuclear family has been established, few obligations to kinsfolk exist. In theory siblings should, and sometimes do, aid one another. The main occasions for formal responsibilities are in house moving (where wooden houses exist) or in the roofing ceremonies marking completion of a new house. Kin must also attend religious festivals, marriages, and funerals; not to do so is taken as a public announcement of hostility. This applies to the most distant of kin. If relations between kin are good, money, food, liquor, or musicians may be contributed, and women will help in food preparation.

A special relation exists between nephew and uncle: the latter has an important (and costly) role in elaborate weddings. This relationship is expressed by the optional extension of the term *papá* to some uncles, either paternal or maternal. This is the only deviation from the Spanish kinship terminology in normal use. Some Tarascan terms survive, but most people do not know them. Kinship terms are often used for non-kin to indicate either respect or affection. Where kinship is believed to exist, even though genealogical connections are forgotten, kin terms appropriate to relative ages and sexes should be used.

The compadrazgo or ritual kinship is very elaborate. The most important relationships are with the godparents of baptism, confirmation, and marriage. The godparents of baptism and marriage are fed and given gifts of food when they assume their roles. They also undertake special obligations; they usually give annual presents and are responsible for funeral costs of their godchildren or for rearing them if they are orphans. Their permission is formally sought for the marriage of their godchildren, and they are honored at the wedding when their responsibilities terminate. The godparents of marriage are lifelong counselors of the newly married couple. Between compadres (that is, between godparents and the parents of children) the relationships are essentially those of siblings but often with even closer respect and friendship relations.

Two other types of compadres exist. At weddings all close senior relatives of the bride and groom go through a household ceremony making them compadres. They henceforth normally address each other as "compadre" or "comadre." For reasons of friendship or in the belief it will be beneficial to the health of an ailing child individuals may be asked to become a compadre or godparent of the crown. This may involve a ceremony in church in which the priest places a crown successively on each person, repeating a formula for the occasion. In some places this is done before the image of one of the saints kept in private houses by a mayordomo, who substitutes for the priest. These types of compadrazgo carry primarily the obligation to observe special respect relationships and to address one another as compadre or comadre.

The establishment of a new nuclear family is a complex affair. There is a fairly frequent custom of "kidnapping" the bride where parental opposition is expected, but most marriages involve elaborate forms of petitioning the bride's family, of betrothal parties, and an elaborate wedding ceremonial (in addition to observing the civil registry and the church rituals). Betrothal parties and weddings are the major opportunities for ostentatious display of wealth and social position. Ceremonial exchange of gifts according to elaborate rules takes place. Clothing, one of the principal gift items, is usually of a special type not made well enough to be worn; such clothing circulates through many hands. At weddings extended street processions are designed to display the gifts and the number of participants. The latter is evidence of the size of the kinship group and of the number of compadres, as well as of the number of friends and neighbors willing to lend their presence. The betrothal and wedding procedures are so complex that a professional marriage "manager" is employed.

Functions of the actual and fictitious kin group are few at the formal level but are important. Attendance at weddings, mayordomías, house roofing or moving, and funerals is obligatory. On such occasions contacts are renewed with rarely seen relatives and with the compadres, neighbors, and friends of the host. Closer relatives and compadres also contribute labor, food, liquor, music, or money. Failure to meet the obligations of these special events is an open declaration of hostility.

Local and Territorial Units

Existing territorial units are officially designated as *ranchos* (all with less than 100 inhabitants) and *pueblos* (from 200 inhabitants up) grouped together in *municipios* in which one pueblo is designated the *cabecera*. There are a few isolated homesteads or temporary lumber camps. Municipios have official boundaries, but pueblos and smaller units do not (West, 1948, pp. 18–20, lists all settlements of Tarascan speech).

Larger pueblos may be divided into *cuarteles* (quarters) and these in turn in *manzanas* (blocks). These divisions are primarily for administrative purposes, but cuarteles have some recognition in ceremonial organization. The geographical aspects of municipios are dealt with in the section on settlement patterns.

The historical origins of Tarascan municipios have not been studied. Tradition suggests they represent aboriginal communities or amalgamations of such communities (although present settlements are not necessarily on aboriginal sites). Certainly it is presumptive to assume that they are purely artificial Spanish or Mexican creations even though their organizational structure and unwieldy size today suggest this conclusion.

Tarascan municipios certainly exceed the size of most local groups defined in anthropological literature as communities. This is true especially of cabeceras of multisettlement municipios, although *tenencias* often fall within classic community-size limits. The Tarascan municipios nevertheless possess interesting devices to meet the problem of size.

The most essential and organized community functions are carried out almost exclusively by male heads of households. The number of persons with whom face-to-face contacts are desirable is hence reduced to less than one-fifth of the total population. Even in a large single settlement municipio such as Cheran, a competent town official knows the name and residence of virtually every household head in the community. In addition, the system of cuartel or tenencia officers and block chiefs establishes a network of communications of a personal character.

Further reinforcement of the community is given by kinship (above) and ceremonial structures (Ceremonial Organization). Neither is community-wide, but involves overlapping networks of relationships which do blanket the local unit. Women and children are thus placed with respect to spouse and father. Household heads, if unknown, can soon be identified. A man is someone's relative or compadre or he may have given a particular mayordomía or have been an officer in a fiesta. Thus any stranger can quickly be placed within the social structure and some of his relationships with others readily established.

Political Organization

Tarascan municipios are politically organized in secular fashion with little of the intertwined political-ceremonial organization of most Indian groups in Middle America. The central governing body is the *ayuntamiento* of five elected members and five elected alternates or *suplentes*. Usually each member and his suplente are elected from a specific cuartel or barrio or other subdivision of the municipio. The office of mayor or *presidente municipal* rotates each year among the cuarteles or other subdivisions and is filled by the member of the ayuntamiento for the district. The only other elected official is a judge or *alcalde* elected at large.

Officials appointed by the ayuntamiento usually include a treasurer, secretary, *síndico* or supervisor of public works (mainly concerned with community labor), and a varied group of paid minor officials such as police (actually messengers and general factotums) and forest guards. The presidente municipal further appoints heads for the tenencias or for cuarteles, and in large communities at least appoints block chiefs or captains. The presidente may also appoint commissions to carry out special functions, usually involving the collection of a special head tax or assessment from heads of families. The most common and recurring commissions are those connected with community fiestas (see Rituals).

Only such appointed functionaries as police, forest guards, and the town secretary receive salaries from the municipio. The treasurer is paid a percentage of collections; the judge or alcalde receives fines and fees for executing legal papers. The presidente municipal tries small cases himself and can levy fines up to a small fixed amount; this he retains as his only financial perquisite.

Town income comes principally from fees for registering cattle brands, license fees for businesses, and taxes remitted by state and federal governments. Real estate taxes are collected by the federal government, which maintains tax offices in many towns; there is widespread evasion through under-declaring land areas or not registering them at all. Other direct taxes include assessments on forest products exported from the municipio. When taxes are insufficient, special assessments may be collected by a commission to finance specific public works. More common, however, are labor levies, principally to clear boundary trails and to improve trails and bridges.

The presidente carries out general administration with the advice of other ayuntamiento members, with whom frequent meetings are held. The presidente through the secretary represents town interests with outside government agencies, state and federal. These may include police, judiciary, highway, forestry, fishing, school, telecommunications, and rural electrification officials. Election returns also must be certified to the state government. The presidente calls town meetings to nominate candidates for local offices and to consider any other grave or unusual problem. For many purposes he communicates with the community through cuartel or tenencia chiefs and block captains or utilizes the police for communications with specific individuals.

The alcalde hears certain minor cases as judge but his main function is investigating more serious charges, deciding if a case exists, and, if one does, preparing the evidence and necessary papers to submit to the nearest appropriate court. The treasurer's and síndico's functions are the obvious ones. The town secretary is very important in relations with the outside world; his literacy and ability must be considerable, and he is the only official not always a townsman. Often his original appointment has been recommended by some high governmental official, and the secretary often has informal and more or less concealed political functions. An adroit man who can satisfy both his patron and the townspeople may wield considerable influence.

Cuartel or tenencia chiefs are agents of the presidente. They carry out instructions of the presidente or transmit them to block captains and advise the presidente of problems needing his action. Block captains transmit instructions to the heads of families but also have other important functions. They decide who must give labor service or see that all turn out or pay for substitutes when there is a general call. They may be used for special purposes; for example, the 1940 census data were collected by block captains after meetings and training sessions with census bureau representatives. Finally, block chiefs determine who shall serve in the *ronda*.

The *ronda* is the true police force. A man from each block must serve for a two- or three-week period, usually two or three times a year. Only town officials, schoolteachers, and aged persons, usually of some public distinction, are exempt. The ronda is formed into subgroups, usually one per cuartel, and patrol the community at night. The ronda may also be called upon to gather evidence when a crime occurs or to apprehend a known criminal.

Despite the importance of town political government, few people show interest in elections if all goes well; if things do not go well, they may take more direct and violent action. But attendance at town meetings to nominate candidates is small, and few cast ballots in elections. Election returns hence are frequently rigged by the ayuntamiento and secretary, in the best instances, to ensure the carrying out of majority opinion. Returns for state and federal elections usually show a 100 per cent vote for the candidates with majority support.

RELIGION

Tarascan religion is a form of folk Catholicism, that is to say, a locally modified variant of 16th- and 17th-century Catholicism as interpreted and transmitted by the missionary orders. It is important to observe that, in contrast with many other Indian groups, the local modifications of the Tarascans include no identifiable aboriginal elements within the formal ritual and belief structure. Some belief in or memory of aboriginal supernaturals appears to survive in myths and tales but witchcraft, although widespread, is of purely European origin, except for a few elements, such as the role of owls, which have both European and native counterparts.

Tarascans today are not all believers or may be inactive or indifferent, especially among men. Nevertheless, even unbelievers generally support the rather secularized community religious festivals. Important variations between towns exist. Some towns in postrevolutionary times have been strongly affected first by *cristero* and later by *sinarquista* movements. In many towns conflict exists between supporters of the local folk religion with its system of fiestas and supporters of those priests who are attempting to eliminate the mayordomía system and sponsoring the more modern and more closely controlled religious sodalities.

Despite church objections to the fiesta system, the Tarascan versions are much more orthodox than among some Indian groups. Particularly the lay reader or *maestro* achieved no importance among the Tarascans, perhaps partly because of their accessible location and the absence of such a sharp break historically between the termination of the missions and the advent of secular clergy. Catholic supernaturals nevertheless have been reinterpreted extensively and many modifications introduced into the belief system with respect to the characteristics, powers, and interrelations of God, Mary, Jesus, the Saints, and the Devil. The Devil, in some of his manifestations, possibly is the most important supernatural for many Tarascans. (Tarascan religion and the general problem of folk religion are excellently presented by Carrasco, 1952b.)

Rituals

Tarascan rituals fall into the following well-defined categories.

(1) Church rituals. These are rituals conducted by the priest in accordance with current church practice and hence need no description. The most important ritual, the Mass, is performed in relation to the cult of the saints with its fiestas and mayordomías, however much the local priest may be opposed to the folk-religious activities. Such Masses are paid for as are special Masses for any other purpose such as a wedding.

(2) Rituals accompanying fiestas and mayordomías, of several types:

(a) Community fiestas (see vol. 6, Art. 16, fig. 8). Examples are fiestas of the patron saint and Corpus. These fiestas are large, prolonged, and very secularized. The fiesta of the patron saint and sometimes other community fiestas are usually accompanied by a large 7- or 10-day market. Administration of these fiestas is by the ayuntamiento or town council.

Community fiestas, in addition to the celebration of Mass or Masses and the holding of a market, usually involve hiring one or more bands (most Tarascan municipios support a band but a band never performs in community fiestas of its own municipio), use of elaborate fireworks setpieces, and usually some special features. Fiestas of patron saints, for example, usually are accompanied by two or more days of bull riding. Corpus may involve special processions of animals and displays of occupational activities, and sometimes a mock market of goods and products in miniature. Food is also provided for musicians and special functionaries, and relatives and friends of those responsible. (For Danza de los Viejitos, see vol. 6, Art. 9, fig. 7.)

Many outsiders participate in the community fiesta, drawn either as purchasers

770

or vendors in the market or to have a good time. At a large fiesta there are numerous vendors of agricultural, handicraft, and machine products. In addition there are traveling gamblers, barbers, cooks with food stands, liquor vendors, and prostitutes.

(b) Fiestas or mayordomías of the church. Despite the classification, these fiestas are administered by a special body, usually known as *cabildo,* not under the control of the church. Saints "belong" to the cabildo which selects mayordomos to serve as custodians of each saint's image. Mayordomos carry out the traditional household fiesta, organize and support the dance group associated with some saints, and pay for a Mass. Meals are served to all comers at the mayordomo's house on the day of the fiesta.

(c) Fiestas of occupational groups. The custody of some saints is in the hands of special occupational groups such as the *arrieros* and honey gatherers. The only difference from the church fiestas is that the mayordomos are almost always chosen from among the members of the occupational group, and the general administration (selecting the mayordomo each year and supervising his performance) is usually by the past mayordomos.

(d) Private fiestas. Some mayordomías were initiated by a group of men who shared interest in a particular saint. Initially they purchased a suitable image, clothing, and other accouterments and served successively as mayordomos. The organizers and past mayordomos act as the administrative group. The ritual patterns themselves show no differences from other mayordomías.

(3) Public secular rituals. These include ritual aspects of house-roofing or house-moving fiestas and weddings. Less certainly to be included here are ritual meals given godparents of children, funerals, and the Day of the Dead. Funeral observances are extremely simple as a rule, but may involve priestly functions and church services. More elaborate are observances of the Day of the Dead, although there is great variation from town to town. Preparations, such as cleaning weeds from the cemetery, usually are a community function organized by the presidente municipal and carried out by young men, often organized in work groups by cuarteles or other municipio divisions. The care of individual graves, decorations of flowers, food brought to the graves (but eaten by the mourners and their friends), burning of candles, and paying for prayers by priests or *rezadores* (professional "prayers," perhaps the only vestige of the lay reader) are the responsibility of individual families.

Ceremonial Organization

Contemporary ceremonial organization parallels the classification of rituals. Quite probably the Tarascan towns once possessed a combined political-ceremonial organization as in most other colonial Indian communities of Middle America. The name of one important ceremonial organization, the *cabildo,* strongly suggests this, although today its functions are purely ceremonial. Equally, some surviving aspects of the cabildo organization suggest that the organization of hospitals and other innovations by Don Vasco de Quiroga gave the political-ceremonial organization of Tarascan towns in colonial times distinctive features.

Church organization, where a complete break has occurred with the cabildo, is conventional. Sacristans, acolytes, and altar societies are dominated by the resident priest and possess no distinctive functions.

Community festivals are carried out by the political organization through special commissions (see Rituals). A further word may be said on the latter. For a large fiesta several commissions are named from among men of some substance. In Cheran, for the festival of the patron saint, a commission is named for each cuartel. Two commissions have responsibility for hiring bands, one for employing a fireworks maker, and a fourth to pay for Masses. These functions rotate by barrio annually. The commissions decide on the size of the assessment to be levied on heads of families—usually at two levels depending on economic status—and undertakes its collection. In this they may call on the presidente to exercise police powers and throw resisters into jail. Any deficit must be made up by members of the commission who also have other expenses such as feeding band members or the fireworks maker, providing the latter with timbers and poles for set-pieces, etc. In addition, family heads are commissioned by the presidente to sponsor dancers, others reconstruct the bull ring or provide bulls for bull riding. The members of the principal rancho are expected to provide a *chirimía* band.

In its best-preserved form, the cabildo organization includes several types of officers and functions. Most interesting and unusual is the *kengi* appointed annually by the cabildo. The kengi lives during his year in office in the hospital or a substitute building, collects contributions of wheat and corn for support of the priest (theoretically these contributions are tithes), stores and cares for the grains in church warehouses, and sells or otherwise disposes of them at the direction of the priest. A special rather elaborate ceremony marks the end of a term of office and the induction of a new kengi. Curiously, the office carries little social prestige although spiritual rewards are high.

Associated with the kengi and also appointed by the cabildo is the *colector*, who serves one year as an assistant (*prioste*) before holding office for a year. (The titles of these offices may vary somewhat from town to town.) The colector functions very much as a sacristan, aiding the priest and supervising the condition of images and altars. Many of the altar cloths and decorations are provided by the cabildo, which regards them as cabildo rather than church property. In at least one case of a feud between cabildo and priest, the cabildo stripped the church of its decorations, claiming them as cabildo property. At the conclusion of his two years of service, the colector becomes a *principal* and a member of the cabildo.

The cabildo itself hence is a self-perpetuating organization. Its major function is the allocation of the saints belonging to it among competing applicants for mayordomías. Usually there are many applicants who make extensive gifts to the cabildo (its major source of income). Charges of bribery and favoritism are common, especially when factionalism is strong, but there is little evidence that cabildo members benefit personally in any significant way although they are well supplied with aguardiente and food.

Organizations for occupational and private mayordomías are sufficiently dealt with under Rituals. No other ritual activities are formally organized.

RECREATION

The major recreations of Tarascan adults are visiting, talking and gossiping, the various religious fiestas and mayordomías, and secular fiestas such as marriages. For women major opportunities for gossip are at the water fountain and cornmill, although close relatives and compadres may visit in the home. Men usually meet and talk in the street, plaza, or stores. More recently the *cantina* and in some towns pool halls are centers, especially for younger men.

For all ages and sexes the greatest recreational events are community fiestas. These are times of gaiety, indulgence, and the spending of hoarded savings for both necessities and luxuries. (Tarascans are fascinated by miniature objects, and most households have a collection to which members constantly add new items.) Drinking and dancing by both sexes is a common part of both public and private ceremonies. Bull riding always draws large crowds, and young men practice in the hills for weeks before a fiesta. Men and often whole families also visit fiestas in other towns.

Young men spend evenings in the streets talking and joking, or perhaps visit a poolroom if one exists. A few recent sports such as basketball evoke limited interest. Families who have visited the United States may have brought back phonographs which are played for family and friends. Radio is still not too common, and music is its special appeal. Local bands are critically evaluated. Many bandmasters attempt the composition of *sones* or tunes in regional style; a few get into regional or even national *mariachi* repertories.

Children's recreations are limited. Girls mostly accompany their mothers and begin token water carrying and maize grinding almost as soon as they can walk to the fountain. The few opportunities for girls to play together generally involve playing house. Boys in general have more freedom to roam the streets and fields. They play a number of games such as marbles, apparently all of recent introduction. (For hopscotch and stick-dice, see vol. 6, Art. 10, figs. 3, 13.) At a somewhat later age than girls, they too begin token participation in adult activities and accompany fathers to woods and fields.

REFERENCES

Aguirre Beltrán, 1952
Alcarez, 1930
Alvarado, J., 1939
Anderson, 1946
Barlow, 1948
Barragán and González Bonilla, 1940
Basauri, 1928b
Beals, 1946
—— and Carrasco, 1944
——, ——, and McCorkle, 1944
—— and Hatcher, 1943
Bourke, 1893
Brand, 1943, 1944, 1951
Carrasco, 1952b
Castillo, 1945
Cook and Simpson, 1948
CREFAL, 1959
Foster, 1946, 1948, 1960b, 1961
Friedrich, 1957, 1958
Gómez Robleda, 1943
Inst. Investigaciones Sociales, 1957
Kaplan, 1951, 1960
Kirchhoff, 1956

León, F., 1939
León, N., 1887a, 1887b, 1889a, 1889b, 1902b, 1906, 1934
León M. and Contreras, 1944
Lumholtz, 1902
Medioni, 1952
Mendieta y Núñez, 1940
Mendizábal, 1939
Pozas A., 1949
Relación de Michoacán, 1869, 1875, 1903, 1956
Rendón, 1947, 1950
Ricard, 1933
Rubín de la Borbolla and Beals, 1940
Sáenz, 1936
Stanislawski, 1947, 1950
Starr, F., 1899a
Storm, 1945
Swadesh, 1940, 1960
Toor, 1925
West, 1948
Zavala, 1937, 1941
Zuno, 1952

SECTION V: NORTHWEST MEXICO

36. Northwest Mexico: Introduction

EDWARD H. SPICER

Northwest Mexico is a unity neither geographically nor culturally. At the time of the arrival of Europeans there were evident two sharply distinct types of Indian culture. These appeared to be neither variants of the same general type resulting from necessities of ecological adaptation nor representatives of stages of growth in a single line of cultural development.[1] It is nevertheless true that the very great majority of Indians shared in one of the two types and that this could consequently be regarded as the dominant culture of the region. From Nayarit in the south to Arizona in the north speakers of Uto-Aztecan languages exhibited varieties of this type, and they were dominant both in the high mountains and in the desert lowlands. In the extreme western part of the region another culture type appeared; this was the way of life of the relatively very few speakers of Hokan languages.

Northwest Mexico comprises three distinct physiographic provinces (Tamayo, 1960). The eastern part of the region, the Sierra Madre Occidental, is a highland characterized by temperate climate and rugged topography. The western edge of the Sierra Madre is deeply dissected by the canyons of rivers draining westward into the Gulf of California (see vol. 1, Art. 2, fig. 12). At this jagged margin the Sierra gives way sharply to a lowland coastal area, a considerable part of which is known as the Sonoran Desert. This is hot country, comprising a subtropical southern part and a northern arid part characterized by highly distinctive desert vegetation, such as the giant cactuses. Across the Gulf of California to the west is the peninsula of Baja California, which in many respects resem-

[1] For general views concerning the limits of the cultural area and its external relations, see Kroeber, 1939; Beals, 1943b; Kirchhoff, 1954; and Underhill, 1954. I have followed Beals' delimitation with reference to the southern boundary rather than Kirchhoff's. The northern boundary should be thought of as extending as far as the valley of the Gila River. There was no essential difference between the Upper Pima inhabiting what is now Arizona from those inhabiting what is now Sonora. It is only in very recent times that profoundly different acculturative influences have affected the Upper Pima living in the United States as compared with those in Mexico. The great majority of Sonoran Upper Pima have migrated into the United States since 1900.

777

bles the mainland desert; the peninsula, however, lacks a vital feature of the latter, namely, large rivers with dependable water supply.

These three areas—temperate highland, hot lowland, and desert peninsula—offered sharply different problems in adaptation for human groups. The highland was supplied with sufficient rainfall for agriculture without irrigation, but topographically it hardly offered opportunity for much growth in density of population without irrigated farming. It was an area of great seasonal range in temperature, a condition which led to migrations from higher areas in summertime to the bottoms of canyons in winter. It was well supplied with game, ranging from deer to turkey and rabbits. It was a habitat which, under conditions of primitive agriculture, lent itself to small-size settlements and widely scattered population. Much of the highland was extremely rugged, giving rise to conditions which could be expected to result in isolation of the inhabitants from one another and consequent cultural diversification. The fact remains, however, that there was a cultural and linguistic similarity throughout the whole highland area, suggesting a recency of settlement.

In contrast, the desert lowland between the Sierra Madre and the Gulf of California consisted of vast stretches of territory quite uninhabitable because of lack of water. The rainfall was heavily concentrated during July and August with only very light and uncertain winter rains. In most parts the rainfall averaged between 40 and 80 cm. annually, but in many areas it was less than 40 cm. Nevertheless, there was abundant and dependable water in certain limited areas as a result of the large rivers which drained the highland and at intervals cut across the whole desert lowland. There were nine such major rivers—Santiago, Piaxtla, San Lorenzo, Culiacan, Sinaloa, Fuerte, Mayo, Yaqui, and Sonora. The population of the lowland was concentrated

along the valley bottoms. The annual floods became the basis of agriculture which supported numerous settlements. In addition to the agricultural opportunities there was an abundance of wild food resources. Besides deer and small game, there were the edible fruits of numerous cactuses, the beans of mesquite trees, agave plants, and many other seed- and fruit-bearing plants. Besides, the coast provided fish and shellfish in abundance. The lowland was an area with potentialities for large concentrations of population, even without irrigation techniques, potentialities which were beginning to be realized at the time of the entry of the Spaniards.

The peninsula had none of the possibilities for population development offered by the other two areas. Similar to the driest parts of the coastal lowland, it was even more arid with annual rainfall rarely attaining 40 cm. even in highest altitudes. Except in the extreme north bordering the Colorado River there was insufficient water for agriculture. The greater part of the peninsula provided no water other than springs dependent on uncertain and always scant rainfall. It was true, however, that there were fairly good wild food resources in the form of cactus fruits, agaves, and mesquite beans as on the mainland.

Most of the people of northwest Mexico at the time of the arrival of the Spaniards spoke languages of the Uto-Aztecan stock.[2]

[2] Swadesh (1959b) has proposed the term Yutonawan for this stock. Mason (1940) used Utaztecan, whereas Kroeber (1934), following earlier scholars such as Sapir, employed Uto-Aztecan. Although using the older term for designating the stock, we shall in other matters of terminology use Mason's 1940 classification, since it is the most systematically developed. It should be emphasized that the classification of Uto-Aztecan languages is by no means settled and that there are other widely used schemes. The most important of these is the language map compiled by Mendizábal in 1937, amplified and developed by him and Jiménez Moreno in 1943, and subsequently further modified in collaboration with Arana Osnaya (Noriega and Cook de Leonard, 1959). For the development of the linguistic classification of northwest Mexican

The exceptions were the inhabitants of the peninsula of Lower California and those of the Sonoran coast who came to be called Seri by the Spaniards. The peninsular people and the Seri, insofar as we know their affiliation, spoke languages of the Hokan stock (Mason, 1940; Swadesh, 1959b).

From the southern margins of the region under consideration in Nayarit north to the valley of the Gila River in what is now southern Arizona, an extent of more than 1500 km., the languages used at the time of the arrival of the Spaniards belonged to the Uto-Aztecan stock. This included all the inhabitants of the highland and the great majority of the lowland people. All three of the southern families of the Uto-Aztecan stock were represented, namely, Taracahitian, Piman, and the Coran subfamily of Aztecoidan (Mason, 1940, pp. 80–81). The Aztecoidan representatives were confined to the southern part of the region and included the Cora and Huichol languages of the Coran subfamily. The Coran languages were the most closely related to those of the Nahuatlan subfamily, such as Mexicano, of any of the Uto-Aztecan languages. There were possibly three dialects of Cora; the dialect differentiation of Huichol is uncertain. To the north of this relatively narrowly distributed subfamily were the two widely extended families of Piman and Taracahitian.

In terms of numbers of speakers, Taracahitian was the most important of the language families of northwest Mexico (Sauer, 1935, p. 5). It included at least three subfamilies: Tarahumaran, Cahitan, Opatan, and a questionable fourth. Cahitan embraced the greatest number of speakers.

languages, the reader should consult Orozco y Berra, 1864; Thomas and Swanton, 1911; Sauer, 1934; Kroeber, 1934; Mason (with Whorf), 1936; Mason, 1940; F. Johnson, 1940; Jiménez Moreno, 1944; Swadesh, 1959a, 1959b; and Noriega and Cook de Leonard, 1959. For discussion of relationships among Uto-Aztecan languages based on lexicostatistical data, see Romney, 1957, and Hale, 1958.

It may have included as many as 16 different languages, but the full language status of these is doubtful, most of them not having been adequately recorded. The Cahitan-speakers were concentrated in the desert lowland areas of what is now Sinaloa and southern Sonora, but at least two Cahitan languages were spoken by highland dwellers in western Durango—Acaxee and Xixime. The major lowland Cahitan groups were Tahue in Sinaloa, Tepahue at the edge of the highland farther north, Cahita in the lowland of northern Sinaloa and southern Sonora, and Guasave along the gulf coast from the mouth of the Sinaloa to the mouth of the Fuerte rivers. None of these language groups is well known except Cahita, the languages of the others having become extinct before adequate recording.

Mason's listing (1940, p. 81) of the languages comprising the Cahitan subfamily is as follows. Cahita included five dialects: Yaqui, Mayo, Tehueco, Cinaloa, and Zuaque. The Tepahue group included four languages: Tepahue, Macoyahui, Conicari, and Baciroa, with no identified dialects. Tahue included five languages with no dialects differentiated: Tahue, Comanito, Mocorito, Tubar, and Zoe. Guasave comprised four dialects: Comopori, Ahome, Vacoregue, and Achire. Acaxee was composed of two dialects possibly and Xixime of three. A seventh group, Ocoroni, may have consisted of three languages: Ocoroni, Huite, and Nio.

The considerable differentiation within the Cahitan subfamily indicated by this listing is hardly consistent with what is known from either the early Spanish records or our knowledge of surviving groups of Cahitan-speakers. The large number of names attached by the Spaniards to the groups suggests local group designations rather than real language differentiation; and the modern known representatives of Cahitan—Yaqui and Mayo—are mutually intelligible. Moreover, the Jesuit missionary who made the one existing adequate description of Cahita in the 17th century was able to distinguish only three possible dialects (Buelna, 1890, p. 5). Missionaries working in the Cahita area seemed able to move easily from northern Sinaloa to the Yaqui River without serious language difficulty (Pérez de Ribas, 1645, *passim*). Kroeber (1934) has called attention to the difficulties of solving the problems of language differentiation and affiliation in northwest Mexico in view of the unavailability of records of the languages for modern studies.

The Tarahumaran subfamily exhibited a greater homogeneity than Cahitan. Forms of Tarahumaran were spoken over a large area of the highland in what is now southwestern Chihuahua. Mason (1940) records no dialectical differentiation among Tarahumaran-speakers and lists only one language: Tarahumara. This seems very likely a misinterpretation of the records. The early missionaries spoke of local variation in Tarahumara and listed a number of probable dialects, usually: Guazapar, Tubar, Jova, Varogio, Pachera, and Juhine. Chinipa was probably a locality name for Varogio-speakers. Modern studies of Varogio (also spelled Warihio, Varohio) suggest that it is closer to Tarahumara than Mason indicates (Kroeber, 1934, p. 13). Mason lists Jova as Opatan and Varohio, Chinipa, Guasapar, and Temori as possibly Cahitan. The wide extent of Tarahumara-speakers and likelihood of isolation of groups in the Tarahumara area make it plausible to believe in dialectic variation, but the problem requires more careful research (cf. Basauri, 1929, p. 77).

The third subfamily of Taracahitian is Opatan, which was primarily the language of the Indians of the northern, central, and eastern part of what is modern Sonora. Speakers of Opatan occupied the greater part of the drainage of the Sonora River and the upper drainage of the Yaqui River. Although spoken by considerably more people than Tarahumaran (Sauer, 1935, p. 5),

there seems to have been less linguistic diversification. Mason lists as distinct languages of Opatan only two: Opata and Eudeve. He also lists two dialects of Opata, namely, Batuc and Nacosura and two variants (?) of Eudeve: Heve and Dohema. That there were two major variants of Opatan, a southern which may have been called Eudeve and a northern, or Teguima, seems probable (J. B. Johnson, 1950, pp. 8–9; Lombardo, 1702).

The third Uto-Aztecan family of northwest Mexico was Piman. Piman-speakers extended throughout the whole length of northwestern Mexico from Jalisco in the south to the Gila River in the north. There was, moreover, a remarkable similarity in all the varieties of the family, suggesting a recency of migration and lack of time for differentiation as a result of their wide separation from one another. Mason (1940) identifies only two major languages: Piman and Tepehuan. Piman was spoken chiefly in the lowland, in southern and western Sonora and southern Arizona, and exhibited (according to Mason) six dialects: Papago, Piato, Himeri constituting the Upper Pima variety and Nebome, Ure, and Cocomacague constituting the Lower Pima variety extending into the highland of southeastern Sonora. The other major division, Tepehuan, was the language of highland people exclusively; Mason distinguishes three dialects: Northern Tepehuan in Chihuahua and Durango, Southern Tepehuan in Durango and Jalisco, and Tepecan in Jalisco. The peculiar distribution of the Piman subfamily, embracing people of both the highland and the lowland and extending in sinuous fashion for 1500 km. north and south, constitutes one of the more interesting problems of northwest Mexican ethnology (Kroeber, 1934, p. 3). Another facet of this problem is the fact that Piman is the most divergent from the other southern Uto-Aztecan families; that is, Taracahitian and Aztecoidan are much more similar to each other than Piman is to either of them.

780

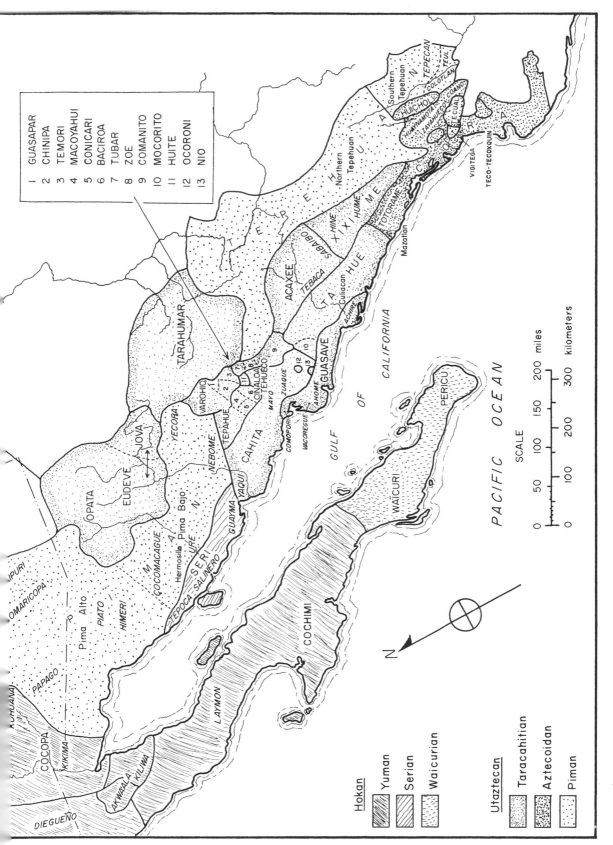

Fig. 1—THE ABORIGINAL DISTRIBUTION OF TRIBES IN NORTHWEST MEXICO. (Adapted from F. Johnson, 1940.)

A relatively small number of people in northwest Mexico spoke languages of another stock—Hokan. The peninsula was sparsely populated; among the inhabitants were several groups in the north who spoke dialects of the Yuman family of Hokan (Mason, 1940, p. 78). There were two subfamilies: Cocopa and Cochimi. Dialects of Cocopa, possibly numbering six, were spoken in the vicinity of the Colorado River delta in the extreme northwestern part of Sonora and northern Baja California; these included Cocopa, Kikima, Kiliwa, and Paipai. Immediately to the south in Baja California were speakers of the imperfectly known subfamily of Cochimi (Baegert, 1952, pp. 94–104), no speakers of which have survived to the present.

Across the gulf on the Sonora coast from the southernmost of the Cochimi were the groups to whom the Spaniards assigned the name Seri. Their language shows some relationship to the Yuman languages, but is classified by Mason as belonging to a different substock of Hokan from the Yuman languages. The nature and number of dialects of Seri is not known, although Mason lists some four band names as dialect groups (1940, p. 78).

The existence of other groups on the peninsula is known, but their linguistic affiliation is unlikely to be determined. These were the Waicuri south of the Cochimi group and the Pericu at the tip of the peninsula.

The linguistic distributions, the relatively close relationships between most of the Uto-Aztecan languages of the region, and the apparent relative lack of dialectic variation point to a recency of settlement of the Uto-Aztecans in the region or to a fluidity of movement in the period immediately prior to the coming of the Spaniards. The relative homogeneity of cultural type among Uto-Aztecans also points in this direction. The precise nature of movements remains to be determined, but a hypothesis of migrations and shifts in tribal locations in the 1400's and 1500's seems a good working approach to the cultural history of the region.[3] The locations of major groups, however, became relatively stabilized during the 1600's. The immediate effect of Spanish domination was stabilization of tribal territories accompanied by concentrations of populations locally around missions, mines, or haciendas and, usually, a greater or less degree of depopulation. Extensive migrations did not take place again until after a century or more of Spanish domination, as Spanish–Apache warfare moved to a climax during the 1700's and various groups such as the Opata and Sobaipuri were dislocated.

A major influence over the whole region flowing from Spanish contact was the activity of the Jesuit missionaries. The Jesuits made contact with every Indian group in northwest Mexico and sooner or later established mission communities among all but the Yuman groups in the vicinity of the Colorado River delta (Decorme, 1941). The Jesuit influences may thus be regarded as the common denominator of Spanish contact. The influences from Spanish mining communities affected Indians differentially depending on how close they were to the mines. Some Indians, such as the Huichol and the Tepehuan of Durango, the Tarahumara of Chihuahua, the Mayo of southern Sonora, and the Opata and Lower Pima of eastern Sonora, were profoundly affected by forced labor and the living conditions of the mining communities because of the location of important mines in their territory. On the other hand, the mines had little effect on many Cahitan-speaking people such as the Yaqui, or the Seri, or the northernmost Pima. Similarly Spanish influence emanating from colonists during

[3] There are no general culture histories dealing with the region as a whole. Of some use in piecing together various local developments and suggesting over-all trends in Indian–White relations and cultural change are: Bancroft, 1884; Decorme, 1941; Mendizábal, 1946a; Ezell, 1955; and Spicer, 1961.

the colonial period affected Indian cultures variously according to whether their land was desirable for grazing or agriculture and whether or not the encomienda system was instituted in their territory. The lowland people of southern and central Sinaloa were obliterated by the 1700's as a result of the operation of the encomienda system, but elsewhere the system was not instituted.

On the other hand, the Jesuit program was a powerful influence for innovation on all the Indians of the region. Every Jesuit mission was an agricultural establishment as well as a religious center. Each was also a source of ideas for government and community organization. Acceptance in some degree of new sources of subsistence such as livestock and crops, new work disciplines, forms of political organization, as well as religious concepts and rituals characterized the response of all those groups among whom Jesuit mission communities were established. Although by no means were all the tribes affected in precisely the same way, similarities in the postconquest cultures from the Cora to the Opata are to be explained as a result of common mission influences. This influence continued for most northwest Indians over a period of nearly two centuries, from 1592 when the Jesuits took over northwest Mexico until 1767 when they were expelled. Subsequent missionary influences were relatively minor, as for example the Franciscan influences on Cahitans or the Dominican on Yumans where those orders for a short time replaced the Jesuits.

Another major factor in cultural change emanated from success or failure in military resistance to Spanish domination. Most of the tribes engaged in some sort of military revolt during the period of Spanish dominance. The Tepehuan revolt of 1616, the periodic Tarahumara revolts during the 1600's, the Yaqui–Mayo revolt of 1740, the Seri revolt of 1748, the Upper Pima revolts of 1695 and 1751 each set in motion trains of events which profoundly affected Indian–

Spanish relations. They resulted either in intensifying Indian solidarity against Spaniards, as in the case of Tarahumara, Yaqui, and Seri, or in the breakdown of Indian organization and the acceleration of assimilation, as among Cahitans of Sinaloa. By the time of the War for Independence Spanish military domination had been generally accepted by the Indians, but in many instances the peace was an uneasy one. As Apache raids from the north, begun in 1684, intensified in Sonora and Chihuahua, it became possible for Indians—such as the Yaqui, Mayo, Opata, and Lower Pima—to conceive of their independence from Mexico.

The collapse of Spanish power during the last half of the 1700's resulted in a breakdown of organized programs, both ecclesiastical and secular, for changing Indian life. The weakness of the Mexican state and national governments for 50 years after their inauguration made new programs impossible. Moreover, a somewhat ineffective application of force by the Mexican government in most instances intensified Indian hostility. The general result was the rise of conditions of isolation which enabled most of the Indian groups to integrate the Spanish innovations of the earlier phases deeply into their local cultures. Emergent Spanish–Indian cultures, which combined European and native traditions in a variety of ways, took form. The extent to which the new cultures were Spanish or Indian in content depended heavily on the intensity of Jesuit contact. Near one extreme were the Seri of the Sonora coast who showed perhaps the least Spanish influence; after an initial period during which some Seri lived in Jesuit missions for 40 years or more, no effective mission control had been maintained over them. At the other extreme were the Opata who had experienced a century and a half of peaceful and intensive contacts in Jesuit mission communities; the Opata culture which emerged by the late 1800's was heavily Spanish in content, even in terms per-

783

haps of some of its major orientations. Somewhere between these extremes ranged the other still identifiable Indian cultures of northwest Mexico.

A tentative arrangement of the major Indian cultures with reference to the extent of their Spanish-Mexican content toward the end of the 19th century might be as follows, beginning at the most Hispanicized end of the continuum: Opata, Tepehuan, Mayo, Yaqui, Cora, Upper Pima, Lower Pima, Huichol, Tarahumara, Seri, Cocopa. This classification should be recognized as highly tentative. The systematic comparative analysis necessary for a sound classification has not yet been carried out, although the descriptive data are now available (see references listed at the end of this article).

After the 1910 Revolution a new and important phase in Indian cultural development got under way. New programs of directed change took form in the 1920's, but were not systematically applied until the time of the Cárdenas administration beginning about 1939. A federal Department of Indian Affairs was established which approached problems of Indian adjustment largely through formal education in boarding schools and aid to Indians in legal matters. Yaqui (Fabila, 1940), Seri, and Tarahumara were somewhat affected among northwest Mexican Indians. Later, in 1948, an additional federal-directed program was inaugurated with the creation of the National Indian Institute, which adopted a many-sided approach including special types of Indian leadership training and community organization along with formal education. A major focus of the Institute work was on economic resource development and the stimulation of producers' cooperatives. Centers were established among Tarahumara (Plancarte, 1954), Huichol, and Cora, and a fishing cooperative set up among Seri.

Our knowledge of the nature of Indian population in northwest Mexico is uncertain. Different results in reporting popula-

tion arise as a result of different definitions of "Indian." There is no very certain way of evaluating the early estimates of population by missionaries and others who made the first contacts (See Sauer, 1935). There are nevertheless some fairly generally accepted figures for the Indians of the northwest, based chiefly on annual reports of the working Jesuit missionaries. Sauer (1935, p. 5) estimates the population of northwest tribes, exclusive of Cora, Huichol, Tepehuan, and Tarahumara, as about 540,000. Early estimates of Tarahumara population indicate that it may have been in the neighborhood of 18,000. Basauri (1940c, 3: 356) reports Tepehuan population at time of contact as about 25,000. The Huichol and Cora may have numbered 10,000. The population of the peninsula just before 1767 was 12,000 (Baegert, 1952, p. 54), but this represented a decline from earlier estimates of 40,000–50,000 (Aschmann, 1959, p. 148). Sauer's estimates may be somewhat high, especially for the Opata, but that the total aboriginal population was of the order of a half-million seems reasonable. It may be noted that the most populous of the physiographic provinces of the region was the lowland of Sonora and Sinaloa with perhaps nearly four times the population of the highland province. The peninsula, as we might expect given the technological condition of the people and the natural resources, was relatively very sparsely populated.

An interesting question in the history of northwest Mexico is the nature of Indian population change during the four centuries of contact. There were wholesale extinctions, including the reported disappearance of groups such as the 70,000 Tahue, the 100,000 lowland Cora-speaking Totorame, and the 90,000 barranca- and highland-dwelling Cahitans (Sauer, 1935; Mason, 1940). Despite these early instances of depopulation and more recent absorptions of Indians (Hinton, 1959), the 1940 census reported for the north Mexican states of Sonora, Chihuahua, Baja California, Sinaloa, Nayarit, Chihuahua, and Durango, a population of 542,994 characterized by the "Indian-Colonial" level of living standard. This is a figure of the order of the estimate above for the time of contact (Sexto Censo de 1940, Mexico, 1943). However, as a measure of surviving persons identifying themselves as Indians the "index of Indian-Colonial culture" is of questionable value, even though in Mexico the index is frequently interpreted as indicating "surviving Indian traits" (León-Portilla, 1959). A better measure of persisting Indian identification is undoubtedly language. If the numbers of persons speaking Indian languages are considered, there is indication of a sharp decline in Indian population in the region. For 1950 the census reported only 63,278 speakers of Indian languages over the age of five in the states mentioned above (Caso and Parra, 1950), a decline of 6,699 under 1940. This, however, is not wholly satisfactory as a measure. For example, one of the most numerous groups in the northwest in 1950 were the Yaqui, but owing to extensive migration outside their tribal territory beginning in the 1880's and earlier there were almost no monolinguals among them in 1950 and hundreds spoke only Spanish. Yet their way of life and their identification was as Indians. In short, no measures have yet been devised which can be used to tell us clearly what the change in "Indian" population has been.

In general nevertheless we may say that persons who identify themselves as Indian appear to have declined in numbers in extreme fashion in Baja California, in Sinaloa, and perhaps in Nayarit. In Sonora the decline has been less marked and there are indications that Indian population has increased in Chihuahua. We are, however, everywhere in past and present dealing with approximate and not strictly comparable figures.

The trend in population change for some of the groups which became stabilized in their tribal territories during the colonial period is nevertheless pretty well established. Thus there seems little doubt that the Tarahumara population has approximately doubled; in mid-1700 it was about 18,000; in 1950 between 40,000 and 50,000 (Plancarte, 1954). Cora-speaking people declined from a probable 150,000 to about 3,000 in 1950. Yaqui declined from 30,000 or 35,000 (Pérez de Ribas, 1645) at the time of first contact to a probable 15,000 in 1940 (Spicer, 1947). Mayo increased from 25,000 in the early 1600's (Pérez de Ribas, 1645) to 31,000 in 1950 (Séptimo Censo de 1950, Mexico, 1953). Seri declined from 5000 to 200 (Griffen, 1959). Such figures emphasize the wide variety in contact conditions.

The cultural relations of the Indians of northwest Mexico are by no means easy to determine, because of the almost complete obliteration of pre-Spanish patterns in many instances and the fusion of aboriginal and introduced patterns in others. There are two major time levels for which we have usable information: (1) accounts of the early explorers and of the Jesuit missionaries which describe various aspects of Indian cultures and provide us with something of a base line; (2) recent accounts, most important of which are those of travelers of the late 19th century and ethnographers of the 20th century.

Two distinct types of culture existed in the region: the gathering-hunting culture of the peninsular Yumans and Seri and the agricultural culture participated in by all the Uto-Aztecan-speakers. Such a classification requires justification as there is admittedly a wide variety of cultural content as between Huichol, for example, and Upper Pima.[4]

[4] For useful compilations of culture-trait lists and discussion of cultural relations based on trait distributions, see: Beals' classic study (1932a) of the comparative ethnology of northern Mexico before 1750; Kroeber's interesting analysis (1931, pp. 39–51) of the cultural relations of Seri, Yuma, and Pima; Bennett and Zingg's attempt (1935, pp. 355–

The chronological relations of the two cultural types in the region remain a problem concerning which there is only speculative solution. Zingg (1939) has considered the development of the Uto-Aztecan type from early Basket Maker culture in the region, which seems likely, but requires much more archaeological evidence for confirmation. It has also been speculated that Seri culture is intrusive on the mainland, in the sense that it was brought by migrants from the peninsula. There is no question about a profound difference between Seri culture and language from any groups now neighboring them, but enclavement seems just as possible as intrusion. Archaeological relations are as yet too imperfectly studied, but Seri chronological placement will probably turn out to be an aspect of the general problem of the Sonoran coastal cultures, such as the Guasave. Other chronological matters are equally obscure. As pointed out above, the distribution of the Pima suggests relatively recent movement, but no clear evidence has been presented to indicate which direction movement may have taken. Were the Pima highland people who migrated northward into the desert lowland or did originally lowland people move up into the highland? The former is suggested, but of course inconclusively, by Papago traditions of northwestward expansion into their present locations. Moreover the Lower Pima seem to have been under pressure in their location in southern Sonora as indicated by the ready migration of hundreds at the suggestion of Cabeza de Vaca and by Yaqui traditions. Were Lower Pima under pressure as a result of Opata expansion southward, Yaqui expansion northeastward, or of Piman expansion southward into Opata and Yaqui territory? The last seems

the least likely, but there is no balance of evidence for either of the other two. Tribal relations in Sonora, Sinaloa, and Chihuahua at the time of Spanish arrival require a great deal more archaeological and ethnographic work for full understanding.

The dominant culture was a life way strongly rooted in agricultural production. None of the Uto-Aztecan-speakers appears to have been a marginal agricultural group despite even very unfavorable conditions for farming, such as those of the Papago of the extreme desert area between the gulf and the San Miguel and Santa Cruz river valleys. The raising of corn, beans and teparis, and varieties of squash and pumpkins was well established. These cultivated crops were of basic importance, regardless of the extent to which wild foods were utilized. In areas of uncertainty of rainfall, as in the northern lowland, and where only one crop a year was possible, as throughout the highland, there was heavy reliance on hunting and more especially wild-food gathering. Among some groups such as Upper Pima (Castetter and Bell, 1942, p. 57) wild foods constituted as much as 80 per cent of the food supply, but nevertheless seasonal movement, settlement patterns, and other important aspects of life were focused by the interest in agriculture.

The differences between the two varieties of Uto-Aztecan culture can be explained to a large extent in terms of the influences of contrasting habitat on common subsistence patterns. In the highland, agricultural activity was limited. Highland Cora, Huichol, highland Pima (Tepehuan), Tarahumara, and highland Cahitans (Acaxee and Xixime) were dry farmers, entirely dependent on summer rainfall. Conditions were not especially difficult, but subsistence required constant effort, and the economy was not one of abundance. In the lowlands natural conditions varied widely. Some Upper Pima (those who came to be called Papago) of the most arid north were hard-working dry farmers who devised check dams and other

94 and table) to place the Tarahumara culture in a wider context; and Underhill's trait list summary (1954) for the United States Southwest in its relation to northwest Mexico. Basauri (1940c), vols. 1 and 3, are also useful for descriptive summaries of the cultures of northwest Mexican Indians.

forms of water conservation; similar intensive methods, including irrigation ditches, characterized the Opata of central Sonora. The vast majority of the lowland Uto-Aztecans, however, practiced river-flood farming, which required no extensive artificial works. The lower reaches of the major rivers, from the Santiago to the Gila, constituted sometimes very extensive flood plains where, at least from the Yaqui River southward, it was possible to raise two crops a year. The lowland peoples in addition had available large supplies of edible wild foods in the form of mesquite beans, edible seeds such as amaranth, and the fruits of a great variety of cactus ranging from prickly pear (*Opuntia*) to giant forms such as pitahaya and saguaro. The lowland subsistence pattern was one which involved abundance of both wild and cultivated food in the limited areas of the river bottomlands and offered great potentialities for increase in population density.

The effects of contact with Spaniards on these economies were hardly revolutionary. Wheat made possible a winter crop in the Upper Pima agricultural cycle, and other new crops added some variety to the by no means monotonous Indian diet. However, the native crops remained the staples. Spanish improvements in agricultural technology had important potentialities for Indian agriculture and in some places these were realized for a short period. Irrigation techniques were promptly introduced in both highland and lowland, but in the highland improved land tended to be taken over by colonists and in the lowland became a source of conflict between ecclesiastical and secular authorities. There was no program for general development of Indian agriculture except that carried on by the Jesuits, and it was the growth of the controlled economy of the Jesuit mission communities which led usually to Indian dispossession of good farmland.

The major effect of Spanish contact on Indian economy in the northwest was to diversify the existing small-scale subsistence farming with the addition of livestock. Sheep and cattle were introduced immediately by the Jesuits, who spent much time instructing Indians in the care of the animals. By the end of the Spanish period livestock were solidly established as sources of both wool and meat. Undoubtedly this turned the Indian economies in the direction of lesser reliance on wild foods. Nevertheless there was very little change in the scale or the efficiency of Indian agriculture throughout the colonial period. Systematic attempts to increase its efficiency and to integrate it into the Mexican national economy did not begin until the 1930's.

The general pattern of the Uto-Aztecan settlements was described by the Spaniards as *ranchería*. They meant by this a type which fell between the compact pueblo, or village, and the roving band. The ranchería of northwest Mexico was a loose cluster of houses which sometimes moved its location seasonally and was not necessarily to be found in the same place from one year to another. The houses were never built contiguously, but rather, even in the areas of greatest population density, as among lowland Cahitans, always at some distance from one another and often surrounded by fences of cane. In highland areas the distance between household units might be a half-mile or more. In general the houses of the lowland rancherías were a little less widely dispersed than those of the highlands. In the highlands, as among Tarahumara and Huichol, a ranchería was rarely larger than 200–300 persons. In the lowlands, although rancherías of 300 were usual, there were also some of 1000 inhabitants.

The settlement pattern of the highland Uto-Aztecans was less affected by Jesuit mission influences than that of the lowlands. Yet the Jesuits apparently succeeded in introducing a new level of organization among highland peoples. This was represented in the pueblo, which consisted of several rancherías within a given locality who recognized the same set of ceremonio-political officials introduced by the Spaniards. This local unit of associated rancherías may not have been entirely new with Spanish contact, but the Jesuit introduction of church buildings certainly gave focus and definition to any pre-existing unit larger than the ranchería.

In the lowland, while Jesuit influence did not transform completely the settlement patterns of all groups, there was a shift affecting the great majority. This consisted of an increase in both size and compactness of settlements. The characteristic development was that which took place along the lower Fuerte, Mayo, and Yaqui rivers, where after 1600 mission communities were established. Rancherías of a few hundred inhabitants each were consolidated into towns of 2000 or 3000 each. Occasionally Indians adopted the Spanish form of close living in contiguous houses, but more often they maintained their separate household pattern, although building somewhat more closely together than before the missions.

In terms of technology and material culture the Uto-Aztecans were very similar. The most notable areal specializations were in house type, which included dome-shaped, grass-covered structures in the northern lowland; oval mud-and-stone houses with peaked grass-thatched roofs in the southern highland and central and southern lowland; rectangular houses in the central lowland covered with heavy, twilled cane mats, as well as other types. All the Uto-Aztecans made coiled basketry, pottery, twilled mats, and wove cotton. The arts were variously developed in detail, but existed in basically the same form throughout the region. There was an absence of tailored clothing; men's wear consisted of breechclout and cloak for cold weather or special occasion, women's wear of knee-length skirt. In general, the Indian crafts were stimulated and developed, especially weaving, as a result of Spanish contact, and weaving in the highland continued as an important art into the latest phase of contact. On the other hand, all crafts in the lowland were steadily replaced.

Men hunted and did most of the farmwork, but women assisted in the farming and did most of the wild-food gathering. The division of labor in agricultural activity was not sharp until the introduction of livestock when men became the herders. There were probably no full-time specialists until after the arrival of the Spaniards. Land tenure was generally based on use right of family units, but in the denser Cahitan settlements and other lowland groups there was community assignment of land. Trade was confined to simple developments in luxury items such as parrot feathers, shells, and colored stones. There was regular trade throughout the area in these products, but there were no markets in the form of permanent or recurrently utilized sites for barter. There was no indication of money or an equivalent and no suggestion of important forms of wealth display or accumulation or social stratification based on wealth possession. The Upper Pima were characterized by an interesting form of hiring out their labor to neighboring people as a means of tiding over bad drouth years in their arid country.

Bilateral forms of kinship organization obtained among all the Uto-Aztecans. The kinship terminology was bifurcate collateral with Hawaiian cousin terminology. Except for the Upper Pima, who had strong tendencies toward the development of patrilineal extended families and who possessed a unique patrilineal system of descent names, none of the Uto-Aztecans exhibited any forms of unilineal descent. The largest kinship units were extended families, and there was generally no unilineal structure involved in these (Beals, 1932b). Ranchería exogamy occurred but was not universal. There was no consistent or important difference between highland and lowland kinship patterns.

Until the arrival of the Jesuits there were

no organized social units larger than the ranchería communities. Rancherías were generally composite, that is, composed of unrelated households. A sense of territorial boundary was usually strong between rancherías, particularly those located on the flood plains of the large rivers. An elder or group of elders acted as peacetime authority, meeting regularly with the adult males to discuss the welfare of the community. Emphasis in leadership was on age and achievement in supernatural relations. There were separate war leaders who exercised authority only in time of war.

The ranchería unit was autonomous. None of the Uto-Aztecans maintained peacetime tribal organization. There was, however, among both highland and lowland Cahitans strong wartime tribal organization. It included in its authority all the rancherías of a given dialect group, such as Yaqui or Tehueco, and operated to defend well-marked territory.

Spanish contact, despite an initial sharper definition of tribal boundaries, did not result in the growth of any new tribal-wide political organization uniting the rancherías of a tribe or dialect group. It did, however, generally result in the consolidation of rancherías into larger local groups than before. Although apparent throughout the Uto-Aztecans, it was far more marked among lowland Cahitans. Combinations of Indian and Spanish forms of ritual kinship groups and ceremonial sodalities, together with the introduced village-government structure, united groups of rancherías into unusually cohesive local groups of several thousand persons. It was these products of the "reduction" program of the Spaniards which became the most effective vehicles of resistance in most of the revolts against Spanish and, later, Mexican domination. This form of town organization persisted among all the groups, where it was introduced from Cora to Upper Pima on into the 20th century.

Variation in emphasis of ceremonial interest and in detail of ritual was very great among Uto-Aztecans, but there was nevertheless a framework of religious concept which was common to all. The cosmology included conceptions of stages in creation and a universal flood, a view of life as involved in an opposition between supernaturals controlling wet and dry seasons, a belief in serpents associated with springs and other sources of water which were the source of supernatural power, a dominant male and a dominant female supernatural probably connected with heavenly bodies, and the attachment of high ritual value to the deer and to flowers. These features of the cosmological beliefs were not developed in the same way or given the same significance for all the tribes; major variants may be seen as distinguishing Pima from the other Uto-Aztecans rather than as distinguishing highland from lowland cultures (Underhill, 1948).

Other common religious elements consisted in prophesying shamans who could diagnose disease, foresee future events, and control the weather, and whose power was a result of dreams which came unsought. Such shamans were important leaders and practiced their ritual often in accompaniment with groups of men and women singers and in connection with all-night dances. It was they who prescribed the ritual for a variety of cures, including sucking rituals and the making of ground paintings. The latter were especially important for the cure of diseases caused by unsatisfactory relations between human beings and animals.

Important in the ceremonies of all the Uto-Aztecans was the drinking of intoxicating drinks made from corn, cactus fruit, or other ferments. A cult of war was widespread, exhibiting greatest intensity among Cahitans. It included ceremonial cannibalism, a scalp pole dance, and various forms of victory dance. Material objects which were the focus of ceremonies seem most often to have been made for temporary use and destroyed after the

789

ceremony, rather than as permanent representations of supernaturals. In the highland, peyote was a sacred material and figured in shamanistic and group ceremonials.

The organization of ceremony has been obscured by contact influences emanating from the Jesuits, but there is much evidence for ceremonial sodalities with formal initiation, a hierarchy of officers, special forms of recruiting, the employment of masks, and perhaps secret ritual (Beals, 1945a, pp. 202–07). Both men and women participated in such organizations.

Spanish contact resulted in general not in any breakdown of the ceremonial systems but rather in their reinforcement. The native cosmologies were enriched by the inclusion of new supernaturals, especially the Virgin of Guadalupe and Jesus, but also a number of Catholic saints. The Christian flood myth reinforced belief in the native one. The Catholic system of godparents was fused with the Indian ceremonial sponsor system. Catholic religious sisterhoods and brotherhoods were combined with the native ceremonial sodalities. In general, the Jesuit-introduced concepts and rituals together with the Spanish church and town governmental systems were integrated in varying degrees with the Indian socioceremonial life (Bennett and Zingg, 1935, pp. 296–335; Zingg, 1938, pp. 1–67; Spicer, 1954b, pp. 55–94). The resulting fusion gave rise to unusually tightly integrated folk cultures.

The other major cultural type discernible in the region was represented by the Seri of the Sonora coast and probably the Cochimi and other less well known peninsular people like the Waicuri. It was much simpler and characterized by far less variation than the agricultural ranchería type (Kroeber, 1931). Subsistence activities were

fishing, hunting, and gathering. Subsistence was derived from fish, shellfish, sea turtle, cactus fruits and flowers, deer and small game, seeds of seaweed, and several kinds of edible roots. The technology was simple but included bow and arrow, coiled basketry, and apparently pottery (for at least the Sonora coastal people). Textile weaving was absent. Houses were made of ocotilla frames, tunnel shaped and brush covered. Men and women went naked but paid much attention to painting their faces.

The social organization consisted of small bands of not more than 40 or 50 individuals. The bands moved about within recognized territorial boundaries. Kinship was bilateral, characterized by important avoidance relations between individuals and their parents-in-law and a variety of gift exchange obligations. The unit of exogamy is not known. There were no larger units than the bands, several of which spoke the same dialect. Some were maritime and some were inland. No formal leader of a band was recognized, although elders were respected.

Shamanism was important. Shamans' power came through dreams and visions, and could be used for a variety of purposes. Small fetishes were employed as protective objects.

The effects of contact on this culture pattern were of two kinds. On the one hand the peninsular people who were brought under the mission system became extinct within 250 years. The Seri, on the other hand, escaped intensive mission influence through various circumstances and continued for 400 years as marginal people. Their population steadily declined; they adopted clothing and fishing equipment but continued into the middle of the 20th century with only minor alterations in their social and religious life.

REFERENCES

Aschmann, 1959
Baegert, 1952
Bancroft, 1884
Basauri, 1929, 1940c
Beals, 1932a, 1932b, 1943b, 1945a
Bennett and Zingg, 1935
Buelna, 1890
Caso and Parra, 1950
Castetter and Bell, 1942
Decorme, 1941
Ezell, 1955
Fabila, 1940
Griffen, 1959
Hale, 1958
Hinton, 1959
Jiménez Moreno, 1944
Johnson, F., 1940
Johnson, J. B., 1950
Kirchhoff, 1954

Kroeber, 1931, 1934, 1939
León-Portilla, 1959
Lombardo, 1702
Mason, 1936, 1940
Mendizábal, 1946a
Mexico, 1943, 1953
Noriega and Cook de Leonard, 1959
Orozco y Berra, 1864
Pérez de Ribas, 1645
Plancarte, 1954
Romney, 1957
Sauer, 1934, 1935
Spicer, 1947, 1954b, 1961
Swadesh, 1959a, 1959b
Tamayo, 1960
Thomas and Swanton, 1911
Underhill, 1948, 1954
Zingg, 1938, 1939

37. The Huichol and Cora

JOSEPH E. GRIMES and
THOMAS B. HINTON

Huichol (*wii-záari-taari*) and Cora (*náayariite*) are two related but distinct tribes that live in the Sierra Madre Occidental mountains of the states of Jalisco and Nayarit, Mexico.[1] They have proved more resistant to acculturative pressures than have most Mexican groups. They appear to be more similar in their cultures to other northwestern Mexican peoples than to those central Mexicans who are their nearest indigenous neighbors to the south and southeast. Most descriptive work to date has specialized in material culture, religion, or linguistics, and no comprehensive picture of either group is available.[2]

Figure 1 shows the location of both tribes. From east to west, significant geographical features are (1) the Sierra de Bolaños, eastern boundary of the Huichol; (2) the Camotlan canyon, with the Huichol community centers Tuxpan and San Sebastian Teponahuaxtla; (3) the Chapalagana canyon, high on the sides of which are the Huichol centers Santa Catarina and San Andres Cohamiata; (4) the Huajimic canyon, with the Huichol center Guadalupe

Ocotan; (5) the Jesus Maria canyon, with the Cora centers Jesus Maria and San Francisco; (6) the Sierra del Nayar mountain

[1] Huichol phonemes are stops p, t, c (ts), k, q (kʷ), fricative z (voiced or voiceless depending on locality, sometimes trilled, always retroflex), flap r (retroflex), nasals m, n, semivowels w, y, laryngeals ʔ (glottal catch), h (devoiced homorganic vocoid), vowels i, e, a, u (range [uᵛ] to [oˆ]), ʌ (high back unrounded), tones high ('), low (unmarked), open juncture (−). Cora has a similar inventory; Cora s corresponds to Huichol z and has a similar retroflex quality. Cora also has l and č (tš) as distinct phonemic units, and o and u are probably distinct due to influence of Spanish loans. In syllable structure Cora has both nuclear and onset ʔ and h, whereas Huichol has them only in the onset. The status of Cora prosody is still doubtful; (') in Cora forms is tentatively interpreted as a stress accent, and an open juncture, though audible, is not recorded. There is probably a dental series t, n, s, r in Cora in contrast with the alveolar series, and labiovelar pʷ, mʷ in contrast with the labials. Italicized forms in this article are Spanish unless specified otherwise, or unless (as in the case of proper names) the context is clear otherwise.

[2] The senior author has done linguistic and some ethnographic research among the Huichol since 1952, and has made brief field trips to the Cora. The junior author spent a year in 1959–60 doing intensive ethnographic field work among the Cora.

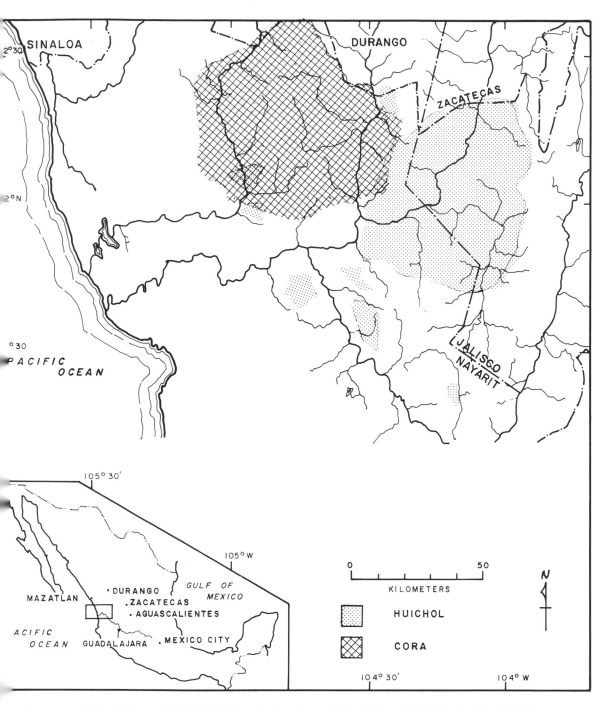

Fɪɢ. 1—GEOGRAPHIC DISTRIBUTION OF HUICHOL AND CORA, SHOWING STATE NAMES

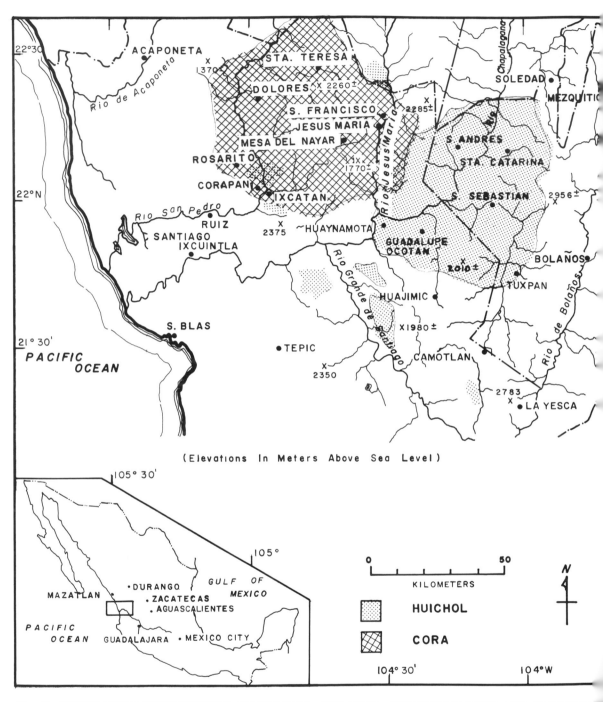

(Elevations In Meters Above Sea Level)

HUICHOL

CORA

0   50

KILOMETERS

N

Fɪɢ. 2—GEOGRAPHIC DISTRIBUTION OF HUICHOL AND CORA, SHOWING TOWNS AND ELEVATIO

mass, with the Cora centers Mesa del Nayar, Santa Teresa, and Dolores; (7) the piedmont of the Sierra Madre Occidental mountain system, with the Cora centers San Juan Corapan, San Pedro Ixcatan de los Presidios, and Rosarito; (9) the Rio Santiago or Lerma and the Rio San Pedro; (10) the Nayarit coastal plain.

Nuño de Guzmán's expedition in 1531 was the first European contact for the area. During the two centuries following, considerable intercourse took place between the Cora and surrounding Hispanicized groups, from which came many Spanish elements including European domestic plants and animals. It was not until 1722, however, that Spanish troops penetrated the Sierra del Nayar and reduced the Cora. At that time the Jesuits concentrated the Cora in their present centers, while the Franciscans established missions in the three northern Huichol centers. The land titles of those three centers date from the same period. Modern Cora culture took form in the 18th century, and has since proved resistant to change. In the mid-1800's Guadalupe split from San Andres, Tuxpan from San Sebastian, each taking the southern part of the parent territory, with intercommunity friction resulting. In the 1860's many Cora and a few Huichol fought with the insurgent Lozada. After the Mexican Revolution the entire mountain area adhered to the Villista faction led by General Buelna. The Cora were won over by the victorious Carranzista group; but no such effort was made in the southern sector, and the Huichol fled to the coast or to Cora communities to escape the military action against Buelna. This scattering led to increased bilingualism and to the establishment of numerous Huichol ranches outside the parent communities. In the late 1920's and early 1930's the Cora fought first for, then against, the "Cristeros," who protested against the government's rigorous policy regarding ecclesiastical organizations; another wave of Huichol scattered to be out of the way of the fighting.

The two languages are a little more distantly related than are Spanish and Italian; next in genetic closeness comes Nahuatl in the Uto-Aztecan family.

Fabila (1959) estimates a total population of 7,043 Huichol: Tuxpan 950, San Sebastian 950, Santa Catarina 1,113, San Andres 1,250, Guadalupe 1,100, and outlying ranches 1,680. Around 80 Mestizos, mostly cattle raisers, live in the Huichol communities. The 1960 federal census lists 4,700 Cora in the Municipio del Nayar; there are probably 7,000 in the tribe as a whole. Jesus Maria and Mesa del Nayar have 1,500–1,800 inhabitants; San Francisco and Ixcatan have only around 300. Mestizo ranchers live in the Jesus Maria canyon and along the western margin, especially in Ixcatan, but are nearly absent in the sierra.

The Jesuit José de Ortega (1754) gives a brief but excellent sketch of the 18th-century Cora. Lumholtz' expedition of 1895–96 is the main ethnographic source (1900, 1902, 1904) for both groups. His observations are accurate for material culture, but his conclusions about society and religion are premature and sketchy. Preuss's trip to Jesus Maria in 1906 resulted in a volume of texts (1912) and several articles on Cora religion and language. Much of his work was unfortunately destroyed during World War II before publication. Preuss believed that Cora and Huichol myths and religious practices contain elements of ancient Mexican origin, and interpreted his findings accordingly. Zingg (1938) made atomistic but fairly accurate observations on the Huichol, but his interpretations are doctrinaire. Klineberg (1934) studied Huichol social psychology briefly. Beals, Redfield, and Tax (1943) and Underhill (1948) point out similarities of both groups to the American Southwest. Weitlaner (1945) and Monzón (1945a) interviewed a Cora in Mexico City and published on kinship and

795

FIG. 3—HUICHOL FAMILY CAMPING UNDER TEMPORARY SHELTER BY THE CHAPALA-GANA RIVER, NAYARIT. They came down from the village of Las Huasimas to seek shrimp and berries. (Photographed by Donald Cordry, 1937.)

social organization. Hinton (1961, 1964) studied Cora social structure in depth. Grimes and Grimes (1962) described Huichol kinship terminology, and Grimes (1961) described the Huichol economic system. Vogt (1955) sketched the acculturation of both groups and compiled a com-

prehensive bibliography. Fabila (1959) gives plausible population estimates for the Huichol, but proposes an action program without sufficiently examining attitudes that could well render such a program impracticable. The McMahons (1959, 1967) have done descriptive work on the Cora language, and McIntosh (1945, 1954 [with Grimes]) and Grimes (1955, 1959, 1960, 1964) on Huichol.

SUBSISTENCE SYSTEMS AND FOOD PATTERNS

Seasonal maize agriculture provides most of the food. Able men of each household clear brush from steep hillsides in the spring, burn off the cuttings (and frequently the surrounding mountainsides) in April or May, and till the few level plots available with a plow without moldboard. Entire households work together to plant plowed fields and hillside plots with a dibble stick after the first rains in mid-June, weed once in late July, sometimes again in late August, harvest in November after the plants dry, shell and store in December. Beans, squash, and cucumbers are also grown in the plots. Plots run around 3000 sq. m. per adult and less per child in the household. Some families cultivate orchards and small gardens, watering by hand during the dry season. Minor crops include grain amaranth, sesame (Cora), chile, tobacco, sugarcane, sweetpotatoes, watermelon, banana, mango, and, in the mountains at Santa Teresa, peaches and apples.

Most families keep one or more cows and consume milk and cheese during the rainy season. Cattle sold to Mestizo buyers are a chief source of cash. The Huichol sacrifice bulls, but otherwise neither group consumes much meat. Some sheep are raised for wool. Pack and barnyard animals are common. Deer, peccary, and iguana are hunted; fish and crustaceans are caught. Agave hearts, *nopal* pads and fruit, *pitahaya* fruit, plums, wild greens, seed pods, tubers, mesquite and *guamúchil* pods, and gourds are gathered. Cora households tend to have more food and animals than Huichol households.

Meals are taken by 9 A.M. and again by 5 P.M.; some families eat three times daily. At a meal an adult eats between eight and 12 14-cm. tortillas. When available, beans, squash, chile, tomato, beef, venison, fish,

cheese, fruit, and wild greens supplement the tortillas. The Cora take no beverages with meals; the Huichol may drink coffee, cinnamon tea, or corn gruel. The Huichol eat salt at meals unless under a vow; at ceremonies saltless tamales, maize dough or parched corn balls, maize beer, or soup of venison, fish, beef, or bean are served. Maize is prepared as tortillas, tamales, roasting ears, gruel, or parched; the Cora tend to use parched corn only for offerings, whereas the Huichol also eat it and salted hardtack tortillas on trips. Beans and squash are boiled; boiled beans are fried in locally produced lard; meat and squash are cut into strips for sun drying or are baked in an earth oven.

SETTLEMENT PATTERNS

Houses generally have one room with 9–15 sq. m. floor space. Most are rectangular; a few Huichol houses are round or hexagonal. They are made of stone, adobe, poles, or wattle, depending on the climate and on the materials available, and are thatched with palm leaves or grass. A rock-and-mud fire table, either built up solid from the ground or laid over a raised pole frame, has walls built up at one end to hold the tortilla griddle and pots over the fire, and has a space at the other end for a grinding stone and dough tray. The Huichol generally use a bed of bamboo poles laid on the floor, over trestles, or on a permanent pole frame. Otherwise, both groups sleep on the floor on mats or hides, occasionally on beds of rawhide strips. Furniture is limited to a stool or two; shamans and Huichol elders may own a ceremonial chair with a backrest. Some houses contain two rooms, each at least 8 m. square, with a partition that divides sleeping quarters from cooking space. Fabila reports some Huichol houses of three 4-by-4-m. rooms. Additional buildings include maize cribs on stilts and with thatched roofs (used seasonally for sleeping), ranch oratories and community tem-

797

Fɪɢ. 4—HUICHOL MAIZE CRIB ON STILTS, IN USE AS SLEEPING QUARTERS, EL AIRE, NAYARIT. (Photographed by Donald Cordry, 1938.)

ples (Huichol), and official buildings. Fabila gives ground plans representative of the last three types.

The Huichol prefer to be outdoors. Maize and beans are usually cooked outside; only grinding, eating, and sleeping are more likely to be done indoors. Each house has a swept yard where most household activities take place.

Each household has a house, usually a maize crib, sometimes a cooking arbor, animal corral, or (Huichol) oratory. From one to 12 related households in a loose cluster near a spring constitute a ranch. Each ranch is named and is also identified (Huichol) by the elder's name. Ranches are rarely closer than 15 minutes' walk from each other, and may be as much as two days' walk from the community center. Some households have wet and dry season ranches; many change residence every two or three years, though elders of ranches within the Huichol communities tend not to move. Households move to be near current maize plots, to be near relatives, or to escape stressful social situations.

Communities are divided by natural and traditional boundaries, which are often in dispute. Communities are political and ceremonial centers for their affiliated households. Each community has a building for business and some ceremonies. In each center there is a church, but in San Sebastian and Santa Catarina the building is used as a Huichol temple. Cora centers have separate jails and schools as well. Each Huichol center except Guadalupe has a temple; several prominent ranches also have temples. In addition to community buildings, there are private dwellings occupied by their owners and relatives during ceremonies and by officials whose presence in the center is required during their tenure of office. Most members of the community, however, spend the greater part of their time on ranches some distance from the center.

Jesus Maria is divided into four *barrios*. Membership is inherited patrilineally and classifies individuals for eligibility to politico-religious offices (Monzón, 1945a). At present many families have houses in barrios other than their own, but it is claimed that this was not so formerly. Barrios have no significance as far as ranch location is concerned. They appear to be limited to Jesus Maria.

About a fifth of the Huichol live outside their communities. The outlying ranches were formed after the Mexican Revolution and now provide a refuge from political or social stress within the communities. Outlying ranches retain community affiliations, and their elders are consulted on important community decisions. Intercommunity marriages are sufficiently numerous that most Huichol have a few relatives in every community. Visits lasting from one day to several months on relatives' ranches are common. On the other hand, few Cora live outside their communities, although in the last several decades drouth has driven some from the mountain communities toward the west, where they have set up ranches and intermarried with people from the western communities. They return home for fiestas and to discharge ceremonial obligations. Intercommunity marriages are common only in the west, and intervillage visiting is rare.

Mestizos live near community centers. In Jesus Maria Mestizos are limited to only one of the barrios, even though the community is also the seat of the Municipio del Nayar.

TECHNOLOGY

Agricultural tools include a short curved machete and a long heavy one, axe, wooden plow with or without steel point, dibble stick with or without steel point, a piece of steel or bone to harvest maize, picking baskets, *ixtle* sacks for transporting produce, sharpening stones, and corncob disks for shelling maize. In building, steel bars are used for digging; a sharpened bamboo with perforated eye serves as a needle to pass tying strips through thatch; for adobe there are gourds in cord slings to carry water, a hoop with cord net to carry mud, and a frame for shaping bricks.

In food preparation there is a clay pot or galvanized bucket for cooking maize in water with lime, a stirring stick, legless trough metate (Cora), conventional legged metate (both groups), muller, mortar and pestle for chile, tortilla griddle, cast iron hand grinder for maize, copper vessel for rendering lard, basket for straining it, clayware or enamelware for frying and boiling, enamelware plates and spoons, dippers made from gourds cut sagittally, water gourds and galvanized water buckets, gourd balances for weighing. Cora women make heavy unpainted pottery bowls and cooking pots, using a joint of cane to shape and

799

smooth the vessel. A generation ago Huichol women also made pots; now only a few make griddles. Large narrow-mouthed or covered water jars bought from Mestizos have replaced large gourds for water storage. Small gourds serve as canteens.

The Huichol produce alcohol by fermenting sprouted maize in large gourds and by fermenting an agave mash in cowhide bags hung from a pole frame, then distilling it in a clay pot covered with a copper vessel of cold water under which is suspended a small clay receiver.

Cordage is twisted by hand, spun on a 30-cm. spindle with wooden whorl, or made into two-strand cord on a whirler. Four-strand rope is made on a frame that rotates four wooden cranks simultaneously at one end while a single crank at the other unites the strands. Backstrap looms are used with simple, weft float, warp float, and double-cloth techniques to give geometric and stylized life forms. Woolen and cotton shoulder bags and *ixtle* carrying bags with straps are the principal products. The Huichol also weave sashes (see vol. 6, Art. 8, fig. 18) and decorative bands; the Cora make woolen blankets on the backstrap loom. Huichol women use three types of cross stitch in embroidery and three running stitches. Cora women are on the average slightly less proficient than Huichol women though they participate in the same over-all textile technology. Fibers of ixtle, cotton, and wool are processed for spinning; bark and rawhide are used untwisted or braided. Most cotton and wool is imported already spun and dyed, but dark natural wool, wild indigo dye, or commercial dyes are used. Muslin and calico are imported; some clothes are bought ready made, especially by men. Lumholtz' publications give a detailed picture of Huichol crafts and a fair idea of Cora crafts, many products of which are indistinguishable from their Huichol counterparts.

Fishing is done with hooks, square-knotted hand nets of cotton string, wooden

tipped spears (Cora), poison of three kinds (Huichol), or with the bare hands (Huichol). Hunting is now almost exclusively by rifle; the Huichol rarely use the traditional net deer snare. Animal gear is of the kind encountered throughout northwestern Mexico, though the Huichol do not use the sidesaddle.

Conventionalized ceremonial objects are made of reed, bamboo, gourd, cotton wool, wool yarn, cotton thread, muslin, cotton cloth, cardboard, feathers, beeswax, beads, or coins; they are painted with natural or imported pigments mixed with a glue binder taken from the juice of a wild orchid. Prayer arrows are decorated with designs symbolic of the deities to whom the prayers are directed, and may have miniature representations of the things desired attached to them. Diamond-shaped figures to prevent the entry of a departed spirit by an unwanted path and to decorate the hats of children participating in ceremonies, rectangular figures to represent the outward appearance or "face" of deities (the last two of which Lumholtz erroneously interprets as "shields") are made of sticks and yarn. Decorated gourd bowls carry specific requests to the deities they symbolize. The Huichol do some rough stone sculpture to produce images of deities and symbolic stone tablets.

Typical Huichol men's dress appears in figure 7. Lumholtz' descriptions still serve except that wool shirts and head nets are now archaic. Some men wear embroidered shirts, sashes, small embroidered bags hung below the sash, more than one decorated shoulder bag, cape, bead earrings, and decorated palm hat for everyday wear, but most vary the elaborateness of their costume according to the occasion. Special adornments include necklaces of large beads, mirrors and Catholic medals hung around the neck, beadwork rings and wristbands, woven bands worn over the sash or around the wrist, macaw and hawk feathers on the hat, and, for those who have made the peyote pilgrimage, tails of gray squirrel on the hat. Huichol women wear calf- to ankle-length skirts and high-necked, three-quarter-length sleeved blouses that reach the skirt top, and a *quechquemitl* that is usually worn on the head, sometimes over the blouse. Women's clothes are made of print material or of embroidered unbleached muslin. Both sexes wear bead ornaments, paint the face, usually with red pigment mixed with lard or honey, and decorate their clothing with flowers. Many men and a few women wear rural Mestizo dress part of the time. (Most articles sold to tourists as "Cora" are actually Huichol.)

Cora dress, with shirt and *calzones* of unbleached muslin for men and a long skirt and blouse similar to those worn by the Huichol for women, resembles that of rural Mestizos of two generations ago. Men of Santa Teresa and Dolores tie a large bordered kerchief over the calzones so that it hangs in back like a triangular kilt. In the west some men wear conventional trousers. Men wear locally or commercially made braided palm hats; women cover their heads with a *rebozo*. Men carry a small woven or embroidered shoulder bag for a pocket. Loincloths worn by adult men within the last 35 years at Jesus Maria have disappeared; children still wear them sometimes. Woven sashes like those the Huichol wear have also disappeared. Old men occasionally wear a long deerskin apron that hangs from neck to knees. Both sexes use cowhide sandals, some with rubber-tire soles. Blankets are carried in cold weather.

Most eastern Huichol men braid their hair or let it hang loose. The western Huichol wear a bowl-shaped cut or a European short cut; Cora men wear their hair short. Women of both tribes wear their hair loose or in a single braid down the back.

Huichol characteristically travel on foot. Donkeys, horses, and mules are principally pack animals, used secondarily for riding. Whole families walk to the coast, carrying grinding stones and cooking utensils on their backs, and returning with loads of supplies as well. The Cora travel more by animal than the Huichol, but also carry goods on foot. No motor transportation enters the area, but all Huichol centers and Jesus Maria have airstrips, and a few Indians use air service.

Linear measures are (1) finger width, (2) outstretched thumb tip to outstretched middle finger tip, (3) nose to tip of middle finger of outstretched arm, (4) double arm span, (5) day's journey. Lengths are compared by means of a knotted rope or a notched bamboo. Land area is measured by the number of measures of maize seed that could be planted on it. Dry volume is in seed measures or in hectoliter sacks. Liquid volume is in liters or in 20-liter cans. Weight is in kilograms, 11.5-kg. *arrobas* (for lard), or in hectoliter sacks of maize.

Within a household men produce and store food and women prepare it; men care for range animals and women for barnyard animals; men build buildings and women care for what is in them; men procure fibers and cloth and women fashion clothing from them. Men do not weave, embroider, or prepare ground maize (though they may operate the metal grinder and parch maize); otherwise a fair amount of overlap in sex-assigned tasks is permitted when circumstances make a temporary shift desirable. Children begin chores at around five years of age. All members of the household help in all phases of agriculture except cutting and burning brush and plowing.

All Huichol and Cora are basically farmers. A few Cora are employed as schoolteachers by the state or national governments, but these also farm. Certain Huichol are outstanding in activities in which nearly all participate in a general way, such as violin playing among men and textile work among women. Chanting and the fabrication of pottery, stools, and chairs among the Huichol, and rope twisting, wicker basket making, tanning, and tile and adobe making among the Cora, are undertaken by

801

specialists at their convenience. These do not, however, support themselves exclusively by their specialty, but exercise it when convenient and as a favor to the consumer, with no attempt at volume production. Better-known shamans get considerable income from fees; some shamans appear to seek a profit but most do not.

Land is communal and cannot be bought or sold; an individual has use rights to a field as long as he works it, after which it reverts to the community. The right of inheritance of orchards is recognized. Dwellings, livestock, and movable goods are privately owned by both men and women. Outsiders may rent community land, but the Indians view these arrangements with misgivings.

The Huichol household is the basic unit of production and consumption. Several households may cooperate in some phases of agriculture, and frequently cooperate in the expense of a ceremony. Religious officials cooperate to produce what is consumed at community-wide ceremonies. A community base for production is seen only in fence building and construction or maintenance of ceremonial structures. In ceremonies the households giving the ceremony join with visiting kin as consumers. The entire community is the consuming unit only in the community-wide ceremonies.

The Cora production and consumption unit is the nuclear family. Relatives or cogodfathers assist each other on a small scale, and a man may recruit his neighbors to help weed or harvest in return for money, food, or gleanings. Occasionally a field is worked on shares with the harvest divided according to work performed. Each community plants a large plot, the produce of which feeds participants in ceremonies. Work on it is done by members of the community at large under the foremanship of community officers. The workers are fed at community expense. Top officials accompany the crews to fast and pray for the venture.

Middle American markets are absent.

Maize is purchased on the buyer's initiative, usually at the seller's ranch. Other exchange is also carried out on a personal basis. The marginal agricultural system precludes much income from potential cash crops such as surplus maize or (Cora) sesame seed. For articles not manufactured locally the Huichol travel to Mestizo centers; the Cora either go outside or buy from small Mestizo-owned stores in the area. Groups of Mestizos make trips in to peddle goods or to buy cattle. Huichol travelers buy things to sell at home, but make little profit from them. A money value pegged to Tepic prices can be stated for anything, and little barter occurs.

In December Huichol go to the maize harvests of Tepic and the coast in order to earn money. In March and April entire families, and occasional Cora individuals or families, go to the coast to work from a few days up to two months in maize and tobacco. With the money they earn they purchase maize to piece out their own usually inadequate supply (sometimes depleted soon after the harvest by sale to get quick cash), and also purchase manufactured articles. Some Huichol work for pay for Mestizos in the tribal area on a long-term basis paid in lump sums; they also work for daily wages for Mestizos and for Huichol who are not close kin. A few Cora and fewer Huichol have been to the United States as *braceros*. Quite a number of men have gone to Tepic, Guadalajara, and Mexico City on official business. Very few Huichol and Cora live in Tepic or other towns.

Wealth is stored by hoarding in the house or burying, or by investment in livestock. The Huichol disapprove display of wealth in diet or clothing; a person who eats or dresses too well (except at ceremonies) risks loss of support from the gods. Fruit orchards and village houses are Cora signs of wealth also. A Huichol with more than two cows is taxed at a higher rate when levies are made for community expenditures. A Cora with more than 50 cows is considered rich; the wealthiest have up to 300, but the "rich" are few. Most Huichol lack foresight and squander their money, though a few (Klineberg, 1934) are prosperous in cattle. In contrast, the Cora do not spend money freely, and have a reputation for miserliness and inhospitability. The Huichol beg in Mestizo towns, whereas the Cora do not, and look critically on the Huichol for this trait.

Politico-religious officers must sustain part of the expenses of community-wide ceremonies and must pass on a respectable amount to their successors. This outlay tends to prevent any appreciable accumulation of personal wealth and for the majority represents a sacrifice.

SOCIAL ORGANIZATION

Kinship terminology is Hawaiian; Huichol further distinguishes lineal kin one generation from ego. Cora cousin terminology is reckoned by *seniority*, the relative ages of the siblings from whom a cousin pair descended, not the relative ages of the cousins themselves.

Table 1 compares kinship terminologies. Abbreviations are: Br(other), Si(ster), Sb (sibling); Fa(ther), Mo(ther), Pa(rent); So(n), Da(ughter), Ch(ild); Hu(sband), Wi(fe), Sp(ouse). Gen±1, consanguineal relative one generation removed from ego in either direction, Ø zero, + ascending only, − descending only. O(lder), Y(ounger), M(ale), F(emale), st(eprelative), / or, — reciprocal with. Terms are customarily possessed in both languages; here possessives are omitted. Examples: *Gen+1M* "any male consanguineal of the first ascending generation from ego"; *GenØCh* "child of any consanguineal of ego's own generation."

Nuclear families together with recently acquired sons-in-law, grandchildren with or without their parents, or widowed parents of adults form households, which are basic units. The Huichol "elder" is the dominant

household head of a ranch, and speaks for the ranch in community deliberations.

Huichol marriages are contracted within the bilateral kindred composed of all known kin, preferably between close kin. Cora marriages with relatives in paternal and maternal lines, or with relatives who have the same surnames, are prohibited. First-cousin marriages are common among Huichol, rare and disapproved among Cora.

The Huichol groom joins the bride's father's household until he can erect his own house on the same ranch and plant his own maize. He remains there for a few years; after that, his household may move to ranches of relatives of either side. As a child grows up he keeps constant company with siblings and parents; in addition, on whatever ranch he lives, he has around him consanguineals of his parents' generation and their families, and is usually spoiled by the elder. His wife will come from one of the ranch-wide play groups of his childhood. Around 5 per cent of Huichol households and a few Cora households are polygynous; sororal polygyny is preferred. A few Huichol have up to five wives. Husbands initiate divorce for sterility, either partner for cruelty. Fathers and elders sometimes take back women when they are dissatisfied with a match already made.

For the Cora, residence after marriage depends on convenience and economic considerations; virilocality predominates slightly. There are few Cora–Huichol or Indian–Mestizo unions.

Ritual kinship is contracted at baptism, at the rare Catholic marriage ceremonies and confirmations, at sale of cattle (Huichol), and at a ceremony in which children are initiated into the drinking of *mescal* (Cora). Close kin are preferred as co-godparents. The Cora forbid marriage between godchildren and members of their *padrinos'* families (Weitlaner, 1945).

Huichol ranches are political units, acting through their elders; Cora ranches are less formalized. Huichol elders and past *gober-*

TABLE 1—KINSHIP

HUICHOL (WESTERN)	CORA (JESUS MARIA)[3]
ʔiwáa GenØ	ʔiwaáraʔa Sb/relative
maaci OGenØM	háʔa OBr/Gen+1(O than Pa)So
kuuríi OGenØF	kúʔu OSi/Gen+1(O than Pa)Da
muuta YGenØM	huú YSb/Gen+1(Y than Pa)Ch
miita YGenØF	
tárú, ʔázi YGenØ	
kémáaci Fa(EgoM)	táhta Gen+1M
qéeci Fa(EgoF)	
yáu (eastern), páapa Fa	
káʌ-wáari stFa	
warúuci, máama Mo	náana Gen+1F
téiwáari stMo	
niwé Ch/GenØCh	yáuh Ch/GenØCh(EgoF)
	péʔeri Ch(EgoM)
niwe-wári stCh	
tátáaci Gen+1M(not Fa)	naú Gen+1M—GenØSo/Gen+2So—
	Gen+1ChSo/stFa (all EgoM)
téi Gen+1F(not Mo)/	tí Gen+1F/Gen+2FDa/stMo
Gen+1F(eastern)	
maa-cúri GenØCh(EgoM)	taá Gen+1M(EgoF)—GenØDa(EgoM)
niwe-cíe GenØCh(EgoF)	
teu-kári Gen±2	yaasú Gen+2M/Gen−2(EgoM)
mii-tári Gen+2M(EgoF)/	
Gen−2F(EgoM)	
tewaríi Gen±2M(EgoM)	
maʔʌʌ Gen−2(EgoF)	yaáqa Gen+2F/Gen−2(EgoF)
qʌʌci Gen+2F	
keicarí-wáame, kʌcau-ríza,	tuʔurú Gen±3
tuuru, tee-zúuri, turúuza,	waákʌsaʔa Gen±4
teu-ríza, mʌtʌzí, tuu-cíi	
Gen±3 and beyond, all interchangeable	
kʌná Hu	kʌʌn Hu
ʔʌyá Wi	ʔʌh Wi
kémá SiHu(EgoM)/WiBr	yáʔubeʔe SiHu/SpBr/PaSbDaHu
ʔiwarúu BrWi(EgoF)/HuSi	hʌíʔita BrWi/SpSi/PaSbSoWi/
qée WiSi/HuBr/SiHu(EgoF)/	WiBrWi
BrWi(EgoM)	
yee-turízá ex-qée; link	
dead; Ego already married	
múune WiFa/DaHu	múʔun SpPa—ChSp/SpPaSb—SbChSp
warʌkáʌ WiMo	
muʔee HuPa/SoWi	
muunéwári WistPa/stDaHu	
muʔee-wáari HustPa/stSoWi	
neʌ-kíi PaSiHu/WiSiHu/WiSbCh	
wizí PaBrWi/HuBrWi/HuSbCh	
cáʔiizi ChSpPa	
zeerái SpPaPa/ChChSp	

nadores, and Cora *principales,* reach decisions for the community by consensus and express them through officers they elect by consensus or, among the Huichol, sometimes by lot. The list of officers for each community varies; most Huichol communities have a descending hierarchy that includes *gobernador, alcalde, capitán, alguacil, sargento, secretario,* and *topiles.* Each incumbent has to find his own successor when officers are changed every one to five years; and inasmuch as the financial responsibilities of office are heavy, successors are hard to find. Jesus Maria, as representative of Cora communities, has *gobernador, teniente, alcalde, centuriones, tenanche mayor, primer mayordomo, mayordomo grande,* two *jueces, fiscales* who act as bell-ringers, *alguaciles,* and as helpers to the gobernador, eight *justicias* or *ministros* under the alcalde, and one *topil.* The Cora

gobernador has simultaneous civil and religious functions; in the latter he is assisted by the *bástaᵓa* (Cora "old man"; fig. 3) and the tenanche mayor, who in turn directs the mayordomos. There are two mayordomos for each principal saint. Each mayordomo is assisted by a tenanche; *pasoniles* coordinate the work of some tenanche groups. In effect, Cora civil and religious organization is integrated; the Huichol religious hierarchy, on the other hand, is largely independent of and coordinate in rank with the civil. In it, each principal saint or temple is under the care of a mayordomo, who is assisted by a *tepuu-tári,* a *prioste, tenanches* (always female), ceremonial clowns, and *topiles.* Independent of the politico-religious offices, the Cora have ceremonial and dance groups; the principales name people for life to the danzantes, *maromeros, moros* (fig. 8), musicians, drummers, *pachitas* singers; they name people for five-year periods to the *judíos* and *fariseos* of Holy Week, *malinches* (who must be and remain virgins for the period), and *viejos de la danza* (one each for the danzantes, maromeros, and moros). The Huichol use *judíos* to pursue the image of the Virgin in re-enactment of a magic flight motif on Good Friday, but the group is not a formal one.

One of the Indian authorities from each community is recognized as *juez auxiliar* of the municipio in which the community is located, and another as *representante* in land questions. Except for homicide, the communities are judicially autonomous. In the Municipio del Nayar the Cora are a majority, and the presidente municipal is nearly always a Cora; otherwise, there is little Indian participation in state or national government. There are federal rural schools in the Cora centers but not in the Huichol. Federal agencies such as public health and census are not well accepted. The Summer Institute of Linguistics has begun pilot literacy campaigns in both in-

---

[3] The Mesa del Nayar kinship terms (McMahon, personal communication) differ sufficiently from the Jesus Maria terms to be worth including here. Note especially the honorific system, the additional terms for vertically distant consanguineals, and the step-relative terms. Forms preceded by H are honorific. They are used principally for lineal kin in ascending generations, or for close kin when no lineals are denoted.

táata Gen+1M, yáᵓu Gen+1M slightly more respectful, táatasaᵓa stFa, yáᵓupʷasaᵓa stFa. náana Gen+1F, náanasaᵓa stMo. nauú H. nauusí Gen+1M(not Fa)/Gen+1FHu/GenØSo, téi Gen+1F (not Mo)/Gen+1MWi, taá H taátabiᵓi GenØDa/Gen+1(Y than Pa)M(EgoF). yáuh Ch/GenØCh, péᵓeri So(EgoM), yáuhsaᵓa stCh. haáciᵓi OBr/Gen+1(O than Pa)So, kuucíᵓi OSi/Gen+1 (O than Pa)Da, huú YSb/Gen+1(Y than Pa)Ch, háᵓa WiOBr/Gen+1(O than Pa)So/GenØFHu (no plural, applied to Morning Star), kúᵓu WiOSi/Gen+1(O than Pa)Da (no plural). yaasú H yaasúuriᵓi Gen−2/Gen+2M/WiPaFa, yéᵓeqa H yeéqariᵓi G+2F/WiPaMo. tuᵓurúh H tu-urúuciᵓi Gen±3, mʷátʌᴧ Gen±4, waákʌsaᵓa Gen±5, tʌᵓʌsqá Gen±6, mʷeéyuᵓu Gen±7. kʌ̸ʌn Hu, ᵓʌ̸h Wi, yáᵓubeᵓe WiBr/SiHu/GenØFHu, hʌíta WiSi/BrWi/ Gen+1(Y than Pa)SoWi/GenØMWi, múᵓun SpPa/ChSp.

Huichol kinship terminology is uniform throughout the region except for the few instances noted in the table.

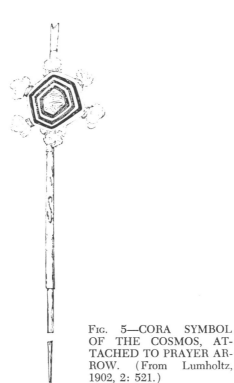

FIG. 5—CORA SYMBOL OF THE COSMOS, AT-TACHED TO PRAYER AR-ROW. (From Lumholtz, 1902, 2: 521.)

digenous languages, and the government's Instituto Nacional Indigenista has begun an action program for the entire area.

RELIGION AND WORLD VIEW

Religion remains basically indigenous, with an overlay of 18th-century Catholicism that includes baptism, saints, and the ritual calendar. Cora and some Huichol equate saints with native deities whose function remains the assurance of rain, health, and material welfare; most Huichol add the saints to the native list of a hundred or so deities without equating them.

Verbal prayers, prayer arrows, stick-and-yarn symbolic offerings, cotton, gourd bowls, yarn-and-bead pictures (Lumholtz, 1900), and food and drink offerings help the laity communicate with the gods. Shamans (see vol. 6, Art. 20, fig. 4) also communicate through chants and prayers and by shaking hawk plumes. The Cora take

offerings to caves and cliffs throughout their country (see vol. 6, Art. 20, fig. 2); Huichol shrines (see vol. 6, Art. 20, fig. 1) range from the Pacific to the state of San Luis Potosi, with the most important ones located in a declivity below Santa Catarina. Both groups share a cave shrine at Mesa del Nayar. Such Huichol rituals are largely of household or ranch scale—resorted to in crises of sickness and impending crop failure—and only occasionally of community scale. The Cora ceremonies, however, with the exception of curing rites, are community affairs supervised by officials "for all of us, for all the Cora, for all people in the world." Nothing reminiscent of the central Mexican calendric systems has come to light; dates or lunar phases are neither obligatory, auspicious, nor inauspicious for ceremonies.

Catholic community ceremonies are organized by community officials. The Huichol keep Ash Wednesday (not necessarily on that day, however), Holy Week, and the community patron saint's day. The Cora of Jesus Maria keep New Year's, *Pachitas* (the two and a half weeks preceding Ash Wednesday), Holy Week, Ascension, *Jueves de Corpus*, San Antonio, Santiago, Santa Ana, Assumption, San Miguel, Rosary, All Saints', Guadalupe, and Christmas.

The Cora give three all-night *mitotes* as community functions in connection with the maize cycle; ranches also hold mitotes. The Huichol hold their maize ceremonies principally on ranches, only occasionally by communities: Green Maize, Squash (in which children are featured participants; fig. 6; see also vol. 6, Art. 9, fig. 7), Roasting Ears (when purple maize is offered to the sun), Parched Corn (when peyote observances are concluded, fig. 7) and Seed Maize. Ceremonies to bring rain, cure sickness, neutralize sorcery, or celebrate the peyote pilgrimage are held as needed. Neglecting ceremonies may bring individual, family, or community disaster because the

Fɪɢ. 6—HUICHOL GROUP AT SQUASH CEREMONY, LA MESA, NAYARIT. Typical nuclear family sleeping hut in background. At left, a miniature ceremonial chair holding a piece of rock crystal wrapped in cloth and tied to a prayer arrow, which represents a deceased ancestor. Deer horns on the chair represent *Káuyúu-maari*, the messenger to the other deities. Clay incense burners and green squash are placed as offerings. Two of the women hold Squash Ceremony yarn figures that represent five-year-old children. The children carry gourd rattles. (Photographed by Donald Cordry.)

a

b

Fig. 7—HUICHOL RITUAL. Shaman invites the deities, including the Virgin of Guadalupe, to the sacrifice and branding of cattle during the Parched Corn ceremony.

deities feel personal neglect and send misfortune as a reminder to the offender. The Cora tend to emphasize community disaster, the Huichol individual disaster. (For Huichol *híi-kúri* (peyote) dance scenes recorded by Lumholtz, see vol. 6, Art. 9, fig. 8, 9.)

Myths, usually chanted by the shaman, account for origins and for the placement and function of the deities. Chants last up to three nights, and despite their repetitious style, contain a considerable amount of detail. Animal stories account for the physical characteristics of fauna and highlight

808

Fig. 8—CORA RITUALS. *a*, Officials ("old men") pray to Morning Star deity for success of a community field. *b*, Danzantes (on foot) and *moros* (mounted) in a procession on the day of San Miguel. (Photographed by Joseph E. Grimes.)

social sore spots. In one Cora series San Pedro replaces the coyote as trickster.

Illness is sent by deities who feel they have been neglected, by dead relatives who want the company of the living, by neglect of the customs, by sorcery, or by natural causes. The shaman makes diagnosis by dreaming, ingestion of peyote, or by chanting and receiving through his chant communication from the deities. Initial treatment is by blowing smoke, brushing with hawk plumes, and sucking small objects from the affected part. Complete treatment includes a ceremonial pilgrimage with offerings at the place where the offended deity resides. Some individuals have considerable knowl-

edge of medicinal herbs; they are not necessarily shamans.

Sorcery is practiced by shamans. Other shamans can either dream the sorcerer's identity, in which case he is in danger of revenge, or they can perform ceremonies to neutralize the spell.

Deities are classified under kinship terms. Those in each group share common attributes. Table 2 gives a comparison in extremely broad terms of the terminological and functional divisions of the pantheons; only the principal deities are mentioned. It is probable that no Huichol, even a shaman, knows all the deities held by the tribe as a whole.

809

TABLE 2—DEITIES

HUICHOL	CORA
"Grandfathers": sun deity (prominent in west), fire deity (prominent in east), both under earth.	"Father," *Tayáʔu*: equated with Dios, Jesu-cristo, sun, and fire. Under earth.
"Aunts": 4 principal rain deities who live in caves below Santa Catarina, sea god, others. Symbolized as snakes.	"Aunt" or "Mother," *Tatí*: fertility of earth. Lives in west, sends rains from Pacific. Her bowl carried in *mitotes*. Equated with Virgins of Rosario and Candelaria.
"Elder Brothers": gods of maize, deer, peyote. Reside in peyote area of San Luis Potosi. Symbolized as deer. *Káuyúu-maari*, one of them, is trickster, messenger to other deities, equated with death god and Devil. Morning Star cult not as central as in Cora.	"Elder Brother Star": Morning Star (fig. 8,*a*) or San Miguel (fig. 8,*b*). Culture hero, protector, monster slayer. (*Tayáʔu*, *Tatí*, and Elder Brother are the principal deities in Jesús María.) "Devil": important in witchcraft.
"Grandmothers": earth and general fertility. Moon insignificant.	"Grandfather sun, grandmother moon": fertility.
"Great-grandparents": miscellaneous deities.	*téqaʔaci*: spirits of ancient times, now personified in rocks and hills, especially around *mitote* sites. Control rain clouds.
	bustaani: bones of "gigantic ancestors."

Five is the thematic and ceremonially significant number for both groups. The Huichol face east and speak to the gods at south, north, east, west, and center, sometimes up and down as well. Cora turn east, west, north, south, and center, sometimes up and down.

AESTHETIC AND RECREATIONAL PATTERNS

Contemporary Cora art is limited to the manufacture of shoulder bags and a few religious items. On the other hand, Huichol art is as prolific as it was in Lumholtz' day.

Huichol music includes songs and chants. Songs are made up by individuals, accompanied on violin and guitar of native manufacture (fig. 9). They are used for individual and group dancing during ceremonies, for enlivening nonceremonial gatherings, and for individual enjoyment. Chants communicate with the gods; shamans chant, accompanied by two assistants chosen for the occasion, who take up refrains. Shamans sometimes accompany themselves on a vertical log drum with deerskin head (fig. 6;

vol. 6, Art. 20, fig. 4). There are a few lullabies. Songs, chants, and lullabies are in Huichol. Mestizo-style instrumental groups play rural Mestizo hit tunes for pay at some ceremonies.

Cora music is confined to ceremonial occasions. Musicians play violins, guitars, and a large drum for church fiestas and *tarimas*. In the tarima one to three of either sex dance on a boxlike platform made from a large pine trunk; some solo dances on the tarima include knife juggling. Dancing that is partly social, partly ritual, takes place in the pachitas and mitotes. Shamans' chants and the mitote songs are in Cora. Pachitas songs are in Cora or a mixture of Cora, Spanish, possibly Nahuatl, and nonsense words.

Though both groups are reserved around outsiders, among themselves much joking, laughing, and (Cora) tussling takes place. Conversation is the main form of recreation. Games are rare.

Seniority is respected, though the Huichol laugh at the senile. Greetings are casual.

Fig. 9—HUICHOL MEN PLAYING VIOLIN AND GUITAR DURING A LULL IN THE FESTIVITIES
(Photographed by Joseph E. Grimes.)

Marriageable Huichol girls show patterned modesty behavior around unmarried adolescents.

Huichol communities send parties each winter to the sacred peyote region in San Luis Potosi. Peyote is used to induce dreams, to keep awake during ceremonies and long trips, and as medicine. The Cora purchase it from the Huichol and use it similarly, but without the cult that surrounds the pilgrimage to procure it. Other hallucinogens such as mushrooms are not used.

The Huichol use maize beer and locally distilled cactus spirit. Both groups buy raw alcohol and tequila. Intoxication not associated with ceremonies is rare; the Cora, however, use little alcohol at the mitote.

Community ceremonies are the sole occasion when most members of the community have direct contact with each other. At smaller ceremonies the participants are mainly from the same ranch or from ranches between which interaction is high. While the main fiesta participants carry out their roles, the rest chat, observe, drink, dance, hold illicit affairs (at the risk of discovery and revenge), quarrel (most Huichol bring their animosities into the open only under influence of alcohol), or sleep.

LIFE CYCLE AND PERSONALITY DEVELOPMENT

In delivery the mother bears down on a rope hung in the corner of the house. The husband is usually present, also sometimes a woman who knows how to give help (though not a professional midwife); others may watch. A Huichol elder or shaman five days later dreams an Indian name, either related to the agricultural stage when the child was born or to a deity interested in the child, or chosen simply as a name. The child is first carried from the house on the fifth day, and Cora grandparents ask *Tayáʔu's* blessing. At Catholic baptism a Spanish name is given and ritual relationships are formed; the Cora give only Spanish names. The Huichol sometimes take the newborn child to the caves of various deities to sprinkle him with holy water and present him formally to them.

Children are usually weaned around two years of age, but may suckle longer. The Huichol carry babies on the hip, the Cora in a rebozo slung from the shoulder across the back. The Huichol begin bladder training before eight months, bowel training when the child walks, but do not treat the child harshly when he fails. Children are punished by withdrawal of parental love for a brief period, and sometimes by spanking or beating. Learning is informal, but ceremonial attendance and participation, trips with parents, and participation alongside adults in household labor make the adolescent culturally self-sufficient. Lumholtz mentions Cora puberty rites; these have disappeared in Jesus Maria and perhaps elsewhere. Cora children, however, are initiated into the use of intoxicants by a religious ceremony.

Marriage is arranged by the parents on the initiative of the boy's father, who makes up to five formal requests before he gets a definite answer. The Huichol marry between 13 and 15 years of age, the Cora at 12 to 18 for girls and 15 to 24 for boys. The pair (who among the Huichol may not know they are to be married until the ceremony begins) are exhorted by their parents, and frequently (Huichol) by the oldest male relative who can attend; they then (Huichol) break a tortilla symbolically and each eats a half. The Huichol couple is then put to bed; sometimes their clothes are taken from them to prevent escape. Even after several weeks the groom may run away, usually by that time to escape his mother-in-law's domination, for he is largely under her direction during the first year of marriage. The Cora used to make elaborate marriage feasts.

Death is followed by interment in the community graveyard or in a convenient location on the ranch. The Cora place the body with head to the west. Cave burial (Lumholtz, 1902) is no longer used. After five days both groups hold a ceremony to get rid of the spirit. The Huichol put diamond-shaped yarn-and-stick ceremonial objects at all entrances but one to the ranch where the shaman is chanting (which may not be the one where the death occurred), then through his chant summon the spirit with *Káuyúu-maarí's* aid to the ceremony. On the way back from the spirits' dancing ground just west of Ruiz, Nayarit, the spirit is cleansed in five successively hotter pools of water and made to eat rotten fruit and drink stagnant water for his misdeeds; namely, sexual intercourse of any kind, murder, and robbery. At the ceremony the shaman gives the spirit offerings and announces its disposition of its property, then dismisses it with the choice of returning to Ruiz or accompanying the sun. Remembering the five pools on the Ruiz road, spirits reportedly usually choose the sun.

The Cora shaman calls the spirit, which has stayed around the house since death, then sends it off amidst the prayers and farewells of the family. The shaman cleanses the house with holy water and a prayer stick. Tamales are left on a table for the deceased's journey. His soul goes to a round hill covered with caves far to the northwest. There the dead dwell and dance like the living. Mestizo and evil Cora souls go to *infierno* beneath the ground or under the sea.

ANNUAL CYCLE

Details of the agricultural and ritual cycles are given under those sections. From June to September everyone is busy in agriculture; ceremonies are brief and infrequent, directed chiefly toward immediate needs of rain and crop protection. From September on, when the crop is safer, ceremonies become more elaborate. After the harvest in October or November there is plenty of food for the dry season ceremonies and the Huichol peyote ceremonies. Because of the seasonal agriculture, the chief occupation during the dry season is care of livestock, planning and giving of ceremonies, and pilgrimages.

REFERENCES

Beals, Redfield, and Tax, 1943
Fabila, 1959
Grimes, 1955, 1959, 1960, 1961, 1964
—— and Grimes, 1962
Hinton, 1961, 1964
Klineberg, 1934
Lumholtz, 1900, 1902, 1904
McIntosh, 1945
—— and Grimes, 1954
McMahon, 1967
—— and McMahon, 1959
Monzón, 1945a
Ortega, 1754
Preuss, 1912
Underhill, 1948
Vogt, 1955
Weitlaner, 1945
Zingg, 1938

38. The Southern Tepehuan and Tepecano

CARROLL L. RILEY

ITHIN THE LARGER PIMAN STOCK the Southern Tepehuan and the Tepecano form a linguistic unit. These two groups have only dialectic difference, their language varying considerably from that of the Northern Tepehuan (Mason, 1952, p. 38). Of the several suggestions for the origin of the name Tepehuan, Mason (1952, p. 39) feels it is most probably Nahuan and contains the root *tepe(tl)* "mountain." Tepecano is probably a variant of the word Tepehuan. Good summaries of the rather limited published material on Tepehuan and Tepecano can be found in Mason (1952, 1959). My work, which covers several field trips between 1958 and 1962, is largely unpublished.[1]

At present most of the Southern Tepehuan live in the mountainous country in extreme southern Durango state, south of the town of Mezquital at altitudes ranging from 1200 m. to over 2000 m. (fig. 1). A second, smaller group lives in the municipality of Pueblo Nuevo to the west, and a third near Huajicori in Nayarit. Population estimates give about 3000 Tepehuan, two-thirds of whom live in the Mezquital area

(Cerda Silva, 1943, p. 546). Major Tepehuan villages include Santa Maria Ocotan, Xoconoxtle, and Lajas. The Southern Tepehuan area has shrunk considerably since the beginning of Spanish conquest. When Ibarra entered the Durango area in the mid-16th century the Southern Tepehuan extended far north and west of their present-day terrain. There may have been, even then, a break between the Southern and Northern Tepehuan, isolating the two groups and allowing the marked language difference to develop, but early Spanish sources do not clearly differentiate between the Northern and Southern Tepehuan. It is tempting to believe that at conquest times the two groups were closer culturally than they are today and perhaps were linked by a series of intermediate dialects which have now disappeared.

Most of the missionary effort of late 16th- and early 17th-century Durango went to the Northern Tepehuan, but mission stations

[1] This Tepehuan work has been supported largely by research grants from the U.S. Public Health Service (NIH) and the Graduate Research Council of the Southern Illinois University.

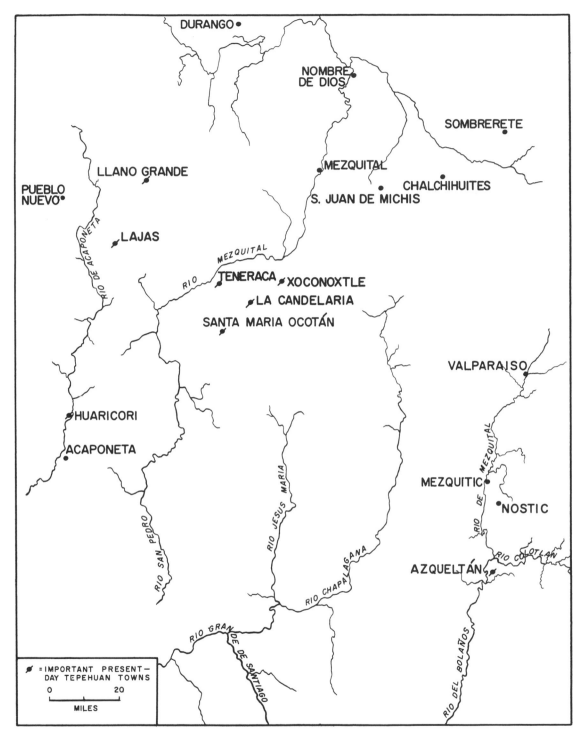

Fig. 1—SOUTHERN TEPEHUAN AND TEPECANO

also were founded at Mezquital 90 km. south of Durango and at Agua Zarca some 50–60 km. farther south. In 1616 the Tepehuan rose in a savage rebellion; Durango itself was threatened by nearby Tepehuan villagers, and there was action at Canatlan north of Durango and in Mezquital to the south. After the rebellion, the Southern Tepehuan continued to give periodic trouble, especially around Mezquital, where they raided Spanish ranches and farms. Eventually in the late 17th and 18th centuries the Tepehuan withdrew to the southern Durango sierras.

The Tepecano are quite isolated from other Tepehuan groups though they consider themselves to be Tepehuan. The remnants of the Tepecano today live in the small town of Azquelatan (variously, El Castan) in the Bolaños canyon. At one time this group extended over a much larger territory; the Franciscan missions of Colotlan, Nostic, and Chimaltitlan were probably in their area (Mason, 1913, pp. 344–45). Even in recent times they may have extended farther up and down the Bolaños, for as late as 1960 inhabitants of the town of Nostic just south of Mezquitic spoke of having "Tepecanito" grandparents. The Tepecano probably represent a southern offshoot of the Southern Tepehuan that in pre-Spanish times penetrated the warm valley of the Bolaños. They perhaps became cut off from the Tepehuan because of Huichol expansion eastward or because of the relocating of Indian groups in early Spanish times. It is possible that the expansion of the Tepecano into the Bolaños was part of a general realignment that accompanied the breakup of the Mesoamerican Chalchihuites culture around 1350 B.C. At that time there may have been an expansion of the simple hill culture Loma San Gabriel; I feel that on present evidence the historic Tepehuan and Tepecano may be descended from the Loma San Gabriel people (Riley and Winters, 1963, p. 184).

The present-day Tepecano are almost completely acculturated—even the language is dying out—but their culture as reported by Hrdlička (1903) and Mason (1913, 1918) seems generally similar to that of the Southern Tepehuan. Here we shall tentatively regard them as a highly acculturated branch of the Southern Tepehuan.

SUBSISTENCE

The Southern Tepehuan are farming and herding people who live in scattered homesteads in the mountains or in mountain valleys. The normal diet of the Tepehuan is corn, made into tortillas or, less commonly, atole, and beans. A considerable amount of cheese is eaten especially in summer and fall. Goat meat, considered a luxury, is served as *caldo* or broth. Beef is reserved for fiestas or funerals and wild game (deer and squirrel) for the *mitotes*. Oranges, bananas, and peaches grown at semitropical Xoconoxtle are eaten in season and found at both Catholic and native festivals.

There is very little urban specialization; in the relatively acculturated village of Xoconoxtle some two or three women sell soft drinks and a few canned goods brought laboriously across the mountains on burroback. One woman also sells locally distilled mescal. Villages farther back in the mountains lack even the rudimentary "stores" and depend on Mexican traders for supplies.

Settlement Patterns

The Tepehuan "towns" are nothing more than government centers with rectangular flat- or gable-roofed adobe church, government building, jail, communal cook- and guesthouse, and sometimes a deserted schoolroom. There is normally a scattering of family dwellings within a mile or so of the town center. Some of these are temporary, their inhabitants spending much of the year in the country, but others are inhabited the year round by families that have cornfields or orchards in the vicinity. The typical Tepehuan house (fig. 2) is a

Fɪɢ. 2—SOUTHERN TEPEHUAN HOUSE, XOCONOXTLE

rectangular one-room structure (average 4 by 3 m.) with walls of stone or adobe (or both) built up approximately 2 m. Four posts, one at each corner of the house, support a gabled roof covered with zacate grass thatch. The earthen floors are gradually hollowed out by repeated wetting-down and sweeping, thus making a pit house. Occasionally, pit houses are made deliberately, the floor being cut down a third- to a half-meter as part of the original construction of the house.

Tepehuan houses generally rest on a prepared earth platform 10–20 m. across. These platforms are kept very clean; on them the younger children play in relative freedom from the dangerous scorpions that inhabit the area. Normally there are two houses on each platform: one serves as cookhouse, the other as sleeping quarters for the family.

Although the prevalent settlement pattern is the *ranchería,* the Tepehuan feel considerable loyalty to their particular village. The dividing line between towns is

normally some natural feature such as a barranca or river. Cross-cutting the village organization, however, is that of the *apellido* group, containing individuals with the same last name. Each village normally has three or four major apellidos but, as far as is known, no apellido is confined to a particular village. Apellido groups are always distinguished by Spanish surnames (i.e. Flores, Galván, Reyes), and possibly the modern Indians have discarded the secret Tepehuan names reported by Lumholtz (1902, 1: 462).

TECHNOLOGY

The agricultural tools and riding and pack equipment used by Southern Tepehuan and Tepecano are essentially those of the north Mexican villager except for an iron-bitted coa employed in the more distant Tepehuan towns. Transportation is entirely by foot or horse, and loads are carried by pack burro. Some of the implements, for example the mano and metate, are pre-Spanish but have

817

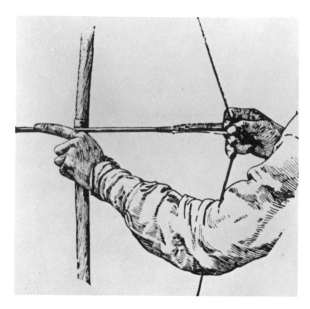

FIG. 3—SOUTHERN PIMA ARROW RELEASE. (From Lumholtz, 1902, 1: 128.)

FIG. 4—YOUNG SOUTHERN PIMA. (From Lumholtz, 1902, 1: 123.)

818

been widely adopted in non-Indian Mexico. One piece of equipment, the bow and arrow (fig. 3) is not shared with Mexicans; this is used ceremonially, and arrows also become prayer arrows. For weights and measures, metric terms or older Spanish ones (e.g., vara) are normally used.

The dress of male Tepehuan (fig. 4) is a two-piece white cotton suit with loose trousers and a shirt that falls over the trouser waist. Women wear full dresses of colored cotton cloth (often red) with skirts that fall to the ankle or below. These garments are homemade by women of the family from cotton cloth purchased in the Mexican towns or from traders. Neither sex normally wears underwear. In winter a thick wool blanket is draped loosely over the body. These blankets are not woven locally but are purchased from Mexicans or from the Huichol or the Cora.

The Tepecano seem to have abandoned "Indian" dress and to wear ordinary Mexican clothing: for the men, jeans or trousers and work shirts; for the women, short cotton dresses. In Xoconoxtle, a village that maintains contact with the outside world, this standard Mexican dress is often worn by men though not by women. In the more distant Tepehuan villages cowhide sandals are worn. In Tepecano country, and to a large degree in Xoconoxtle, the more efficient Mexican huaraches of tire rubber are preferred.

ECONOMY

Among the Tepehuan, men do the heavy agricultural work, especially plowing. They also herd cattle and goats, hunt, and go on trading expeditions. Women look after the house, cook, care for children, and help in the harvest. It is common for a woman to help her husband milk and tend the cows; quite small children often act as herdsman for cattle and goats.

There is a certain amount of part-time specialization. Some men spend a great deal of their time trading, and certain women are in demand as seamstresses. Several political offices are filled each year, giving every able-bodied man in the village a good chance eventually to serve in the village government. There is one very important specialist: the curandero or shaman who, as a youth, trains for five years (five is a Tepehuan sacred number) under the direction of an older shaman. The training involves retreats, ideally one month per year, in which the boy (or girl) retires to a secluded spot and lives on saltless tortillas and water, giving up his time to prayer and meditation. Other training involves learning the long ritual prayers that accompany curing ceremonies.

Property in land and houses belongs to the family and normally descends from father to son. The right to establish a house in a particular favored place (near a stream, for instance) resides by custom with a given family. Sons often build near their father's residence and share grazing and farming lands. Personal property—clothing, tools, jewelry—belongs to a particular individual and can be sold or given away at will. There is a certain amount of trade; the Tepehuan make trips to Mexican markets for cloth, legged metates, and metal utensils and tools. In turn they sell livestock, fruit, corn, pita (fibers of the maguay), and mescal. Transactions may be either cash or barter.

SOCIAL ORGANIZATION

The Southern Tepehuan normally live either in biological or patrilineal extended families. Until recently it was a practice for the boy to spend five months at his wife's father's home working for her relatives. After this the young couple moved in with the husband's family or established their own home.

Tepehuan life is greatly influenced by the territorial villages on the one hand and the apellido group on the other. The village functions as a political unit and there is a series of officers elected yearly; the *goberna-dor, segundo, tercero, aguicil(es)*, the *fiscal*, and the *topil*. These specific officers, of course, were introduced by the Spanish though conceivably they had counterparts in pre-Spanish days. They deal with the everyday life of the village, direct community projects, arrange the church festivals, and handle dealings with outsiders. There is also a separate, religious official called the *jefe del patio*, who directs the first-fruits ceremonies in the fall, before which the fresh corn may not be eaten, and also directs the village mitotes.

The apellido groups appear to be the remnants of nonlocalized patrilineal clans. A check of church archives in Mezquital gives no examples of inter-apellido marriage even when the individuals are from different villages. The leader of each apellido, always an old man and probably a shaman, is also called the jefe del patio and he directs the apellido mitotes. Both villages and apellidos are also supposed to have a female jefe del patio to control women's affairs. At one time the religious leader or leaders may have been of paramount importance; the early Spanish sources suggest that the Tepehuan were originally shaman controlled.

RELIGION AND WORLD VIEW

The present religion of the Tepehuan is an involved mixture of Catholic and native elements. Important figures include Dios Padre (sometimes identified with the sun), Jesus Nazareno (identified with the moon), Madre Maria (who has several helpers including the Virgin of Guadalupe), the Morning Star and a culture hero, Ixcaitiung ([gu] iš kai tyioŋ [the] ruling man) (Riley and Hobgood, 1959, pp. 355–56; Gámiz, 1948, pp. 68–69 ff.).

This latter figure has certain Quetzalcoatl aspects especially in his fall from purity by fornication and drunkenness, his repurification (by dancing the first mitote), and his final long journey (to heaven).

The religious leaders are also curers (*cu-*

819

FIG. 5—SHAMAN IN CURING CEREMONY, XOCONOXTLE, SOUTHERN TEPEHUAN

randeros) and are basically sucking shamans, who may be of either sex but are ordinarily male (fig. 5). Like the Pima, they tend to specialize but any given shaman may treat several kinds of disease. Treatment is normally in a five-day ceremony and the shaman prays, chants long stereotyped *oraciones* (probably the *perdones* of the Tepecano), uses massage, and blows smoke from a pipe over his patient's body. Shamans may refer patients to another practitioner but there does not seem to be a special diagnostician. One element in curing is a ritual confession by the patient. Other members of the patient's family may sit with him or her and receive the benefits of

820

the curing ceremony. Occasionally a special mitote may be held for curing purposes, and sick people also use the regular mitotes to focus on themselves the atmosphere of blessedness prevalent at mitotes.

The mitotes are five-day fertility or thanksgiving ceremonies in which there is fasting and extensive prayers. The night of the fifth day is given over to ritual dancing; on the following sunrise the participants break their fast, eating from a variety of foods heaped on an altar placed to the east of the dance platform. At the apellido mitotes only bearers of the particular family name attend this daybreak climax ceremony. Their mates, male or female, remain behind at the mitote campground. These attend mitotes only as visitors, for marriage does not change the apellido status of either sex.

AESTHETIC AND RECREATIONAL PATTERNS

The Southern Tepehuan probably have lost much of their aboriginal arts. Pottery is still made but with little interest in decoration, and weaving has virtually disappeared. There is at present no painting of designs or pictures on houses. The making of clay pipes that strongly resemble those of late pre-Spanish Chalchihuites is still practiced by certain curanderos. There are two kinds of music: the fiesta music, which is essentially Mexican, and mitote music played with a musical bow and a three-hole end flute of *carrizo* reed. Drinking of mescal is very common at the fiestas although drinking is forbidden at mitotes. Peyote is not used at present by the Southern Tepehuan but has been reported for the Tepecano (Mason, 1913).

The fiestas are held at Easter, Guadalupe Day (December 12th), Christmas, and on village saints' days. They are largely village Mexican in nature with dancing of matachines. One other festival is celebrated by drinking of mescal but is essentially non-Christian. This is the elote (green corn) first-fruits festival held around the first of

October and directed by the jefe del patio.

LIFE CYCLE

Tepehuan children are normally delivered by midwives though a shaman may also be called in. Two sets of padrinos are chosen: one baptizes the child on the day of birth and gives it a Christian name; the other set, five days after birth, buries the afterbirth and over it plants a mescal or some other long-lived plant. The child is nursed for a year or so but is gradually given caldo, soft meat, and tortillas. There is no formal schooling in any Southern Tepehuan village at present though a few families at Xoconoxtle (and probably also among the Tepecano) arrange to have their children go to Mexican schools. Boys are taken with fathers or older brothers from the age of five or six and learn man's duties. Girls similarly learn from mothers or sisters. From the age of seven or eight boys join men at the mitotes and sit in a circle separate from women, girls, and small children.

Marriage generally takes place before either sex is 20, and great store is set on virginity in unmarried girls. Marriages are arranged by the parents of the couple; the boy's parents visit the family of the girl for five nights and on the fifth night their offer is accepted or rejected. Technically the boy and girl have nothing to do with the marriage but (at least at present) they probably initiate the proceedings.

At death a Tepehuan is buried in the village cemetery, which is kept small because a large plot of cemetery land "becomes hungry." Traditionally the ceremonies over the dead last for five days with a shaman in attendance to guard against the soul's return to the body. The night of the fourth day the "name" padrinos are made drunk on mescal; on the fifth day the body is buried, sometimes with bread to feed the spirit on his journey to the other world.

ANNUAL CYCLE

The Tepehuan yearly cycle is, of course,

FIG. 6—SMALL CROSSES, PLACED IN LOG IN FRONT OF SOUTHERN PIMA HOUSE. (From Lumholtz, 1902, 1: 128.)

tied up closely with the planting and harvesting seasons. This part of Mexico is an area of summer rains which begin about the time the maize is planted. In the spring there is a mitote to promote the growing of crops and after harvest another thanksgiving mitote. A third mitote is often held in January or February to bless and supernaturally reinforce the village during the dry cold winter months. Families may gather at the villages for a time after crops are gathered in the fall but normally spend the winters in rancherías looking after cattle and goats. In early fall there is plenty to eat and large numbers of people gather at the villages. This is the time of the elote festival; in fact, the fall is probably the most important ceremonial season for the Southern Tepehuan.

REFERENCES

Basauri, 1940c
Beals, 1932a
Cardoso, 1948
Cerda Silva, 1943
Gámiz, 1948
Hackett, 1923–37
Hrdlička, 1903
Lumholtz, 1902
Mason, J. A., 1912, 1913, 1918, 1948, 1952, 1959
Pérez de Ribas, 1944
Riley and Hobgood, 1959
—— and Winters, 1963
Rouaix, Decorme, and Saravia, 1952

39. The Northern Tepehuan

ELMAN R. SERVICE

NORTHERN TEPEHUAN INDIANS number between 3000 and 4000, scattered over a large remote area deep in the Sierra Madre Occidental of southwestern Chihuahua (fig. 1). The most immediate neighbors are the large tribe of Tarahumara on the northern side.

The close linguistic affiliation of the Northern with the Southern Tepehuan Indians suggests that at one time there was a close connection, if not identity, between the two groups. The Southern Tepehuan today have a closer resemblance to Tepecano and Cora-Huichol than to the Northern Tepehuan. The latter, who live over 350 km. to the north, have no knowledge of their southern relatives, nor does there seem to have been any contact between the two within recorded history.

The habitat of the Northern Tepehuan is a spectacularly rugged highland varying from 1900 to 3000 m. in altitude. Access to this sparsely settled, unexploited woodland is made very difficult because of the tremendous gorges (*barrancas*). There are no

trucking routes into any part of it, which accounts for the untouched appearance of the region compared to the more heavily exploited habitat of the neighboring Tarahumara, many parts of which are reached by truck and wagon trails.

The major event in the postconquest history of the Northern Tepehuan was the coming of the Jesuits in 1708 (Alegre, 1841). The Indians were collected into small "convent towns," of which a centrally located one, Baburi (now Baborigame) became, and remains today, the residence of the official tribal head. In 1767 the Jesuits were expelled from the New World, and the Northern Tepehuan were left undisturbed for nearly 100 years.

In 1860 a Mexican named Ponciano Falomir settled at Baborigame and brought a few Mestizo peons to work a small mine and to herd cattle. With this small-scale hacienda, the present Mestizo community of about 150 people began. Small, short-lived mining enterprises were established elsewhere in Tepehuan territory, and tiny

822

Fig. 1—NORTHERN TEPEHUAN AREA, CHIHUAHUA

Mestizo communities here and there in fertile valleys became enclaved within the Indian community.

The first ethnological investigations of the Northern Tepehuan were those of Lumholtz, who left brief notes of observations (1891, 1902) made during his travels in the Sierra between 1892 and 1897. J. Alden Mason (n.d., 1948) has recorded language texts and taken a few ethnological notes. Burton Bascom, of the Summer Institute of Linguistics, has been working on the Northern Tepehuan language for a number of years. I visited the Sierra in the summers of 1952 and 1955 and made a more intensive study of the Baborigame vicinity in the fall and winter of 1957–58. Attention is called also to information in Aldama (1945), Basauri (1929), Beals (1932a), Ocampo (1950), and Warwick (n.d.).

SUBSISTENCE SYSTEMS AND FOOD PATTERNS

The Northern Tepehuan maintain small-scale subsistence gardens supplemented by chickens and occasionally turkeys, a few goats, pigs, and a cow or two, and in exceptional cases small herds of scrub cattle. Burros are common, mules less so, and horses rare.

The nearly universal crops are maize, beans, and squash. Wheat, barley, oats, potatoes, and peas are known and sometimes planted.

Considerable use is made of undomesticated resources. The "head" (heart) of the wild maguey is cooked and a crude alcoholic distillate called *lechuguilla* is made from the fermented mash. The *nopal* and *tuna* cactus fruits and a gigantic pink mushroom are seasonal delicacies. A great variety of leaves, seeds, and roots are gathered for medicinal use and for food spices. Best known are the leaves of the mountain laurel, orégano, and a kind of anise.

Of animals hunted or trapped for food the deer and turkey are most valued. Squirrels, rabbits, opossum, and raccoon are used in about this order of decreasing frequency.

Food habits and menus are standardly of the sierra type. Most of the rural Mexican dishes are liked, and tortillas, tamales, boiled beans, and stews are common. Other dishes are of the type considered "Indian." Pinole and atole are the most frequent maize dishes. Meat of any kind is usually rare or expensive, as are eggs, milk, and cheese. Beef is the most highly prized meat, and the most significant festivals, which feature sacrifices of bulls, are notable for the gorging that occurs.

The Indians cannot afford coffee, tea, or chocolate, but value them highly. Salt and sugar must also be purchased, hence the Indians often do without them. Alcoholic drinks are very highly prized, and drunkenness is not considered at all reprehensible even when women or small children succumb. The homemade *tesgüino* is the usual form in which alcohol is taken.

SETTLEMENT PATTERNS

The Indians live scattered in only vague residential agglomerations. The named villages in the territory are the closely agglomerated adobe houses of Mestizos. There are six named political regions (*gobernancias*) in the Northern Tepehuan territory. Baborigame is the best known, being the seat of Indian government and having as well the largest Mestizo town (150) and the most Indians in the vicinity (about 800). The six major regions are distant from each other, making social relations among them unimportant, infrequent, and indefinable. Commerce between these areas is largely carried on by Mestizos.

Within each gobernancia the largest subdivision is a moiety, the people of *arriba* (up-[stream]) and those of *abajo* (down-[stream]). These are largely, but not strictly, neighborhoods and maintain their identity in competitive games and in a ceremonial and political division of labor. They have no function in determining marriages nor is membership thought of in terms of descent. There is a tendency for the moieties to be *de facto* patrilineal because men more frequently inherit land from their fathers and stay in the neighborhood than do women.

TECHNOLOGY

Most of the tools of rural Mexico—shovels, axes, hammers, the iron-tipped wooden plow, guns, traps, looms, and so on—are known and to a limited extent used by the Indians. The more purely "Indian" tools are seen as makeshifts to be used in the absence of "good" tools; that is, poverty rather than custom determines the difference between Mestizo and Indian technology. Thus, an occasional Indian has an old rifle or shotgun but others can afford only a bow and arrow. Homemade pottery jars, pots, plates, gourd cups and dippers, and wooden spoons are used only by those families who cannot buy, or have failed to steal, the much-appreciated metal utensils.

Only a few items are made that are specialized enough to be called crafts. The manufacture of the tiny violins, taught by the Jesuits long ago to the sierra people, is perhaps the most notable. Some men also are somewhat specialized in making bows and arrows, but this is a relatively simple craft, for the bow is not backed or laminated. A few families work at hat making. Women weave blankets (the *poncho* is not used) and *fajas* (sash-belts) on a horizontal loom.

Houses are usually of only one room made of logs or rough planks and shakes. Roofs are gabled at a low pitch from a center beam, with roofing shakes held in place by stones. A sort of interior ceiling of poles makes a storage place for grain in the gabled area. Household furnishings are simple. Boulders, stumps, a log, more rarely a low bench, serve as seats. People sleep on the floor on a reed *petate* or goatskins. Cooking is done on an open fire on the floor.

Dress and adornment are somewhat variable, but the great majority use the cheap undyed muslin which is made into the traditional *calzones* and *camisas* found in other areas of Indian Mexico. Perhaps more peculiar to the sierra is the *cotense,* a square white piece of cloth folded into a triangle and knotted low on the hips with the triangle at the rear, like a sort of "buttocks-kerchief." A wool *faja* is wound higher on the waist. A gay bandana neckerchief, usually red, is also worn. The straw hat and tire-soled *huaraches* complete the standard costume.

Woman's dress consists of a skirt of colorful calico reaching to just below the middle of the calf. Two or three low horizontal ruffles on the skirt are usual. A long-sleeved, loose-waisted blouse is made of muslin, with several vertical tucks in the back. A colored bandana (again, usually a red print) is worn on the head, knotted under the chin. The Mexican *rebozo* is not worn.

ECONOMY

The household division of labor by sex and age resembles that of the Mestizos but employs women in rather more varied tasks. Woman's work includes the expectable household chores and child care, but also the making of tesgüino, weaving and pottery making, the milking of cows or goats, and helping in the maize harvest. Rather unexpected is the amount of labor by women in herding domestic animals, which is probably a consequence of their individual inheritance and ownership of some of the animals (see below).

Men do most of the heavy outdoor work such as plowing and planting, axe work and carpentry. Hat making is usually man's work, though not strictly so, as is basket weaving and rope braiding.

Household property is not jointly held by the married couple. Even a flock of chickens may be divided up in complex ways, some belonging to the wife, others to the husband, and sometimes even some to particular children. Each owner enters into economic relations of trade, barter, or reciprocity with others on an individual basis.

825

Inheritance of land is expectably patrilineal, with inheritance by daughters when expedient or necessary. The result is a normal patrilaterally extended family occupying a neighborhood, but in recent years the land-tenure pattern has been modified by ejido laws. The ejido of 16,000 hectares pertains to the whole community of Baborigame, Indians and Mestizos alike. Anyone can petition to clear an unused plot, of which he retains possession so long as he cultivates it. The most fertile land thus can pertain to a family line because it could be used for a long enough time. Most of the plots, however, need a long fallowing interval sooner or later, and finally someone may claim it who is not related to the original family. The consequence is a frequent disjunction between residence and genealogical relationship.

Production and consumption units are the households, modified by exchanges of labor and produce between households. Typical of the labor exchange is the house-building and harvesting parties. They always end in a tesgüino debauch. The beer is not pay for the labor, as it is sometimes interpreted, but merely the convivial aspect of it; the "pay" is the later reciprocal return of the labor. The conception of the "sanctity" of private property is weak; articles are sometimes taken without permission and often, when an owner of something is stingy about its use, it is frankly stolen. Pre-emption of this sort is so common that Mestizos consider Indians to be congenital thieves. And they are very clever and resourceful at stealing; the point is that to them theft does not seem so reprehensible as does the retention of something that another person needs. Yet the society is not communistic; all property pertains to individuals and the people are very acquisitive. Generosity in giving, however, is valued, too, and the ideal state would seem to be the one in which all families have their own property but in equal amounts.

Purely commercial relations between the Indians themselves are almost nonexistent. Between Indians and Mestizos commerce is frequent but extremely petty and subsistence-oriented. The Indians rarely hold any money; it intermediates between production and consumption sometimes but not for more than a very brief interval. "Wealth" is not money. It is the bounty of a good family, good friends, and the security of health, fertile land, and animals. Animals, being the most "liquid" of these resources, are the most frequent measure of prosperity.

SOCIAL ORGANIZATION

Marriage customs are unspecific. The only restriction is that first cousins should not marry. Marriages are not arranged by the families, and the widespread Mexican Indian custom of "robbing" is typical. The boy takes his bride to his father's home to wait for the girl's family to get over their (real or feigned) anger. They may live there up to a year or so, after which a separate house is built and some of the father's land bestowed on the son. This is the ideal patrilocal pattern, but it is frequently altered by acquisition of land elsewhere from the ejido or from the girl's parents. The marriage is consensual—there is neither church nor civil marriage among the Indians—and it is a fragile alliance. It is common for the first-born child to be adopted by the boy's parents, but this is not universally done.

All children are baptized in the church, hence there must be *padrinos* of the baptism for each child, but there are no others inasmuch as confirmation and church weddings are not practiced. *Compadres* are frequently close relatives, often siblings. Only very rarely are Mestizos and Indians compadres, yet the word is a common term of informal address between members of the two groups.

The pattern of kinship terminology is highly "descriptive" in that all four grandparents are distinguished, mother's sister and brother and father's sister and brother are all distinct from each other and from mother and father and further categorized by younger-older criteria. In ego's generation, however, cousins and siblings are undistinguished and there is no cross-parallel nor sexual dichotomy. "Elder brother," however, has a special term of respect in address. Children are not characterized as younger or older in terminology, and the sexes are distinguished only by an infix. Grandchildren-grandparents' terms are self-reciprocal as are nephew-niece with uncle-aunt. Descriptive terms are used for affinals except in ego's generation, where brother-in-law and sister-in-law are the same word. In no case do terms vary with the sex of the speaker. Terms of address are frequently distinct from those of reference. Personal names are Spanish and freely used in address.

The politico-religious organization exists alongside the political organization of the Mestizo community and is allowed to adjudicate most of the problems and crimes involving Indians. Each of the six *gobernancias* has a gobernador and assistant elected for a two-year period, changing moieties each term. A formal meeting of the gobernadores takes place January 6 each year in Baborigame and at other times when some problem arises which involves the whole tribe. Each gobernador is supposed to represent the wishes of his own district.

Over the whole tribe stands the *capitán-general*, appointed for an indefinite term by the gobernadores. The capitán-general has one assistant and seven *justicias* appointed by him along with one *capitán*, a *sargento*, and several *soldados*. The major function of capitán-general and his aides is to maintain order and to judge crimes. Punishment is by public whippings (done by someone of the moiety opposite to that of the criminal) at a post erected in the *convento*, a spacious walled enclosure adjacent to the church in Baborigame.

The gobernadores and the capitán-general also appoint certain officials who have only ceremonial duties. Each gobernador appoints five *fiesteros* for his own district for a one-year term. Their duties are the upkeep of the church and to provide beef, tesgüino, and *matachines* dancers at the fiesta of August 15 (Virgen Santísima). The capitán-general appoints four *fiscales* in each region for an indefinite term. Most of their duties take place in Holy Week, when they take care of the images, see that the church and convento are swept, and so on. The seven justicias are in charge of the fiesta of January 6, for which they provide bulls and tesgüino. Other minor ceremonial officials are eight *cabos*, who have various duties during Holy Week.

RELIGION AND WORLD VIEW

Much of the religion of the Indians is a folk-like Catholicism remaining from the time of the Jesuits and modified somewhat by later contacts with Mestizos. In this summary the more peculiarly local and "Indian" variants will be emphasized.

The Creator is called *Diušüroga* (literally "God our Father"). One of God's helpers is *Ku'kúduli*, the Deer God, custodian or guardian of deer; *Úgai* is another god or spirit manifesting itself as a light in the sky when someone dies; *Ku'kúvuli* is a mountain god or spirit which also, as in Spanish mythology, takes the form of an owl when it announces a death; and *Avadli'kidʌ* is a spirit who makes winds.

Rituals are mostly Christian in origin, with emphasis on signs of the cross and on incantations involving the phrase "Nombre de Dios." Most of the lore is old-Spanish, including such usual items as the influence of the phases of the moon, the hot-cold dichotomy in food and illness, evil-eye, *susto*, Tuesday and Friday as unlucky days, and herbal love potions. Folktales are of the widespread rural Mexican style and subjects.

Rural Mexican remedies are in use, and the typical beliefs about the causes of illness are held. Curing in the form of shamanism, however, seems to have a strong aboriginal basis, mixed with certain Mexican elements. The shaman is a diagnostician, hence he may be used to discover lost objects and clear up mysteries other than the causes of illness. He is called *bajadios* (who "brings God down"). The petitioner and his family assemble in a house and make offerings of tesgüino to God. The shaman then in total darkness chants and rattles his gourd to lure God to the roof of the house. Finally he ascends a ladder to the storage place under the roof, whence the people hear confused mutterings as he and God converse. After the seance the bajadios sleeps and God's message comes to him in a dream. Ordinarily illness is revealed to have been caused by a particular person, and in some cases death by illness has been treated as homicide and the person accused by the bajadios is taken to the capitán-general and publicly whipped.

Aesthetic and Recreational Patterns

Music is the old-Spanish *matachines* tunes. The violin, gourd rattle, and reed whistle are the instruments, in contrast to Mestizo music which features guitars. There is no dance other than the standard matachines. There is no drama except those elements included in the religious fiestas.

The typical game is *correr la bola,* just as among the Tarahumara. In a woman's version of ball-running two small hoops of twisted grass are thrown ahead with sticks about 1 m. long. Otherwise it is exactly like ball-running.

The formal social gatherings are on the ceremonial occasions. The most important of these take place during Holy Week, particularly Thursday through Sunday. The liberal use of tesgüino and ball-running are local additions to the folk-Catholic processions and dramas. January 6 is the next most important fiesta, marked by sacrifice of bulls, tesgüino drinking, and matachines dances. The fiesta of San Francisco, celebrated on October 24 to coincide with the completion of the harvest, is the other important ceremonial day. Beef, tesgüino, and matachines dances are the focus of the entertainment.

Life Crisis Rites

Pregnancy is accompanied by few taboos. The only fear of "marking" the child is that a lunar eclipse will cause deformation.

Delivery is made in a kneeling or squatting position with the husband clasping the mother under the arms from behind. Heat is applied to the mother's stomach after delivery. The umbilical cord and afterbirth are buried deeply because of a great fear that dogs will eat them. The baby is washed immediately and given the breast as soon as possible. The mother observes the old-Catholic *dieta* which taboos "cold" foods and bathing for 40 days. The second-born of twins is killed.

Puberty is not ritually celebrated. Unceremonialized marriage takes place in the middle teens for girls and in the early 20's for boys.

Illness and death are attributed to spirits and witchcraft. The dead are usually buried in the church cemetery. It is believed that the soul remains around his house for one month and goes away when a fiesta of farewell is held for him, during which his best clothes, food, and tesgüino are laid out for his journey. The house is abandoned because after this period there is fear of the soul's malevolence should it return. Four months after the death another fiesta is held and another one year later. The souls go to the sky, but there is no clear conception of the nature of the afterworld.

REFERENCES

Aldama, 1945
Alegre, 1841
Basauri, 1929
Beals, 1932a
Lumholtz, 1891, 1902
Mason, J. A., n.d., 1948
Ocampo, 1950
Warwick, n.d.

40. The Yaqui and Mayo

EDWARD H. SPICER

By the 1930's the Yaqui and Mayo were reported to be the only surviving members of the Cahitan subfamily of the Taracahitian family of the Uto-Aztecan stock (Beals, 1945a, pp. 1–3). Taracahitian had been the largest linguistic family in northwest Mexico at the time of Spanish contact, and Cahitan was the largest subfamily. Sauer (1935, p. 5) concluded that there were at least 115,000 Cahitans and that Yaqui and Mayo constituted 60,000 of these.

The Yaqui were widely dispersed throughout Sonora with heavy concentration in the aboriginal homeland along the lower reaches of the Yaqui River in southern Sonora. They were also living in southern Arizona, in California, and elsewhere in the western United States. A conservative estimate of Yaqui population for Sonora and Arizona in the 1940's was about 15,000 (Spicer, 1947). Mayo were not so widely scattered; they lived along the lower courses of three major rivers of northwest Mexico, the Fuerte in northern Sinaloa and the Mayo and the Yaqui in southern Sonora. There were reported to be more than 30,000 Mayo (Caso and Parra, 1950, p. 70) in 1950.

The language of the Yaqui and Mayo was named Cahita by the Jesuit missionaries in the 17th century (Buelna, 1890). This was a misnomer, like many names applied by the Spaniards. In the language of the Indians the word meant "nothing" and may have been used as a reply to Spaniards who asked the name of the language on first contact, indicating that the Indians did not understand what was being asked. Yaqui, Mayo, and Tehueco were reported by the first missionary to describe them as being dialects of a single language (Buelna, 1890, pp. 5–6); Yaqui was the dialect of the Yaqui River area, Mayo of the Mayo River area, and Tehueco one of several of the Fuerte area. Numerous other groups of Cahitan-speakers were named in the early accounts, but no descriptions of the other languages were made. It is not known how closely the Cahitan languages were related or the degree of differentiation into dialects. The evidence available points to a considerable homogeneity (cf. Beals, 1943a, pp. 1–2).

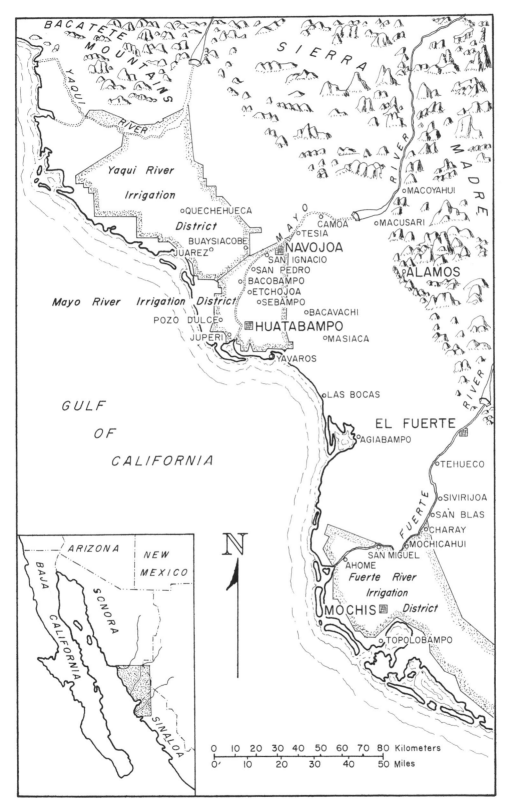

FIG. 1—MAJOR PLACES OF MAYO SETTLEMENT.
(Adapted from map by Patrick Gallagher in Erasmus, 1961.)

In the 1900's there were only dialect differences between the languages spoken by people who called themselves Yaqui and Mayo. There were far more monolinguals among Mayo than among Yaqui. In 1950 nearly 7000 Mayo over the age of five, or between one-fourth and one-fifth of the total, were reported to be monolingual (Caso and Parra, 1950, p. 70). For Yaqui there were reported fewer than 300 monolinguals over the age of five years (*ibid*, p. 70). This condition reflected the history of the two groups. The Yaqui after 1886 were forcibly dispersed by the Mexican government to all parts of Sonora, to the Valle Nacional in Oaxaca, and to Yucatan. Many fled the deportation program to the United States and took up residence there. These circumstances led not to the loss of the Yaqui language, which was preserved wherever family groups clustered, but to the learning of Spanish or English as a second language on the part of all Yaquis. Although some Mayo were caught up in the deportation program for Yaqui, the great majority remained in the vicinity of the Mayo River or moved south to the Fuerte River area in Sinaloa. No clear determination has been made as to the origins of the several thousand persons now living on the Fuerte River who call themselves Mayo (Beals, 1945a, p. 3; Gill, 1957, pp. 99–131).

Although closely linked throughout their known history, the historical experience of the Yaqui and Mayo has been very different and probably accounts in large part for the observed cultural differences between the two groups in the 20th century. Engaged in periodic warfare with one another before Spaniards entered the area, the Mayo sought immediate alliance with the Spaniards whereas the Yaqui resisted conquest. The Yaqui fought and defeated Spanish soldiers in 1533 and again in 1609–10; they were in fact not conquered during this early phase and ultimately asked for Jesuit missionaries, who came in 1617 unaccom-

panied by soldiers. Both Mayo and Yaqui underwent more than 125 years of peaceful contact with Jesuit missionaries following 1617.

In 1740 a revolt broke out in the Mayo country. Fighting was bitter, involved both Mayo and Yaqui, and led to the reported killing of 5000 Yaqui in the final battle.

A few years after the War for Mexican Independence a vigorous Yaqui leader named Juan Banderas organized a successful revolt against the new state of Occidente. The revolt was organized chiefly by the Yaqui and two Opata leaders. Opata, Lower Pima, and Mayo all joined with Yaqui; Mayo leaders were prominent in the fighting. The Indians in their coalition were successful in driving most Mexicans out of their territory for a year or more. In 1832, however, Banderas was captured and executed, and the movement for Indian independence from Mexico lost impetus except among Yaqui and Mayo (Zuñiga, 1835; Paso y Troncoso, 1905, pp. 50–51).

The 19th century was a period of smouldering resistance to domination by Mexicans on the part of Yaqui and Mayo. They fought on various sides in the struggle for power between *caudillos*. Indian–Mexican hostility culminated in fighting in the late 1870's and 1880's. Under the leadership primarily of a Yaqui, Juan Maria Leyva (Cajeme), Mayo and Yaqui organized over a period of years to fight for the expulsion of all Mexicans from their territories. A series of battles in the early 1880's led to the capture of major Mayo leaders and their execution and finally to the complete disintegration of any fighting force in the Mayo country. Yaqui continued to fight under the leadership of Cajeme, who had had extensive experience in the Mexican army during the wars against the French. In 1886 the Yaqui were severely defeated, and in 1887 Cajeme was captured and executed (Corral, 1887).

After the defeats, as the Mexicans occupied the two areas with troops and sought to pacify the Indians by offering security through work on haciendas in the Mayo country and the giving of parcels of land on the Yaqui River, the tribal reactions were quite different. In the mountains north of their river the Yaqui maintained a guerrilla force, which continued to fight, with occasional intervals of peace, on into the early 1900's. The clearly defined objective of expulsion of Mexicans from their territory and independent local government seemed always present in the minds of the succession of Yaqui leaders (Hernández, 1902, p. 142). Yaqui military resistance was never fully broken despite an organized campaign of deportation on the part of the Mexican government which ended only with the overthrow of the Díaz regime in the 1910 Revolution.

The Mayo, on the other hand, ceased all military resistance after the defeats of the early 1880's. Large numbers accepted work as peons on the numerous haciendas. In 1890 a prophet movement appeared among them (Troncoso, 1905, pp. 181–84) which affected all Mayo, but to which Yaqui paid no attention. A young woman who became known as Saint Teresa reported supernatural knowledge of a coming flood which would destroy all Mexicans and leave only Indians alive. Numerous young men and women began to preach the new doctrine and the way to be saved.

The Yaqui never ceased their uncompromising resistance to domination. Guerrilla bands fought until 1918 in various parts of southern Sonora, supported in part by food and funds relayed to them from Yaqui scattered over Sonora working on the haciendas.

Even in the 1950's Yaqui–Mexican relations remained explosive, and Sonora newspapers were accustomed to print headlines presaging "Yaqui revolts" whenever difficulties of any kind developed. On the other hand, Mayo had been subdued long enough so that Mexican school textbooks described them as an inherently peaceful people in contrast with Yaqui. Their communities were for the most part infiltrated by Mexicans, and local government was out of their hands as an ethnic group. A Mayo, Román Yucupicio, became governor of Sonora in the 1930's.

Ethnographic knowledge of Yaqui and Mayo culture in post-Spanish times begins with information collected in the 1880's. The climax of the Yaqui–Mexican wars came in 1886. The conflict stimulated much interest in the Indians. Ramón Corral as a high state official interviewed the Yaqui leader, Cajeme, before his execution and became interested in the Indians; he gathered material for a short biography of Cajeme and wrote sketches of the history and ethnography of several Sonoran tribes, including the Yaqui and Mayo (Corral, 1887). Bancroft, the United States historian, about the same time published his extensive *Native Races of the Pacific States* (1883–89). It was Fortunato Hernández who began more comprehensive firsthand studies of the Indians of Sonora. He was a medical doctor living in Hermosillo, educated in the tradition of the *científicos* of the Díaz period; his volume on *Las Razas Indígenas de Sonora* (1902) was stimulated by a need to understand the Yaqui resistance, which appeared entirely irrational to Mexicans. The volume was a compilation of data on language, history, and ethnography from many sources and inaugurated scientific ethnography in Sonora. Systematic study in the tradition of modern ethnology began with the work of Ralph Beals (1932a, 1943a, 1945a), whose orientation toward historical reconstruction by interpretation of trait distributions led to understanding of the place of Yaqui–Mayo culture in North American ethnography. Holden, Erasmus, and I have offered further contributions. My studies have been oriented toward the description of functioning communities rather than historical reconstruction and toward the delineation of processes of cultural change (Spicer, 1940, 1943, 1954a, 1954b, 1961).

Yaqui ethnography is probably better known than Mayo. Our knowledge of Mayo culture is based heavily on the general survey made by Beals in the early 1930's (Beals, 1945a) and on studies by Erasmus consisting of the community study of Tenia in the 1940's (Erasmus, 1948) and subsequent intensive economic and structural studies of various Mayo communities in the 1950's (Erasmus, 1961). Our knowledge of Yaqui ethnography is based on Beals' early survey (1945a); on my two studies of an Arizona and a Sonora community (1940, 1954b), which were made in the 1930's and 1940's respectively; on Holden's observations of particular aspects of culture in Torim (1936); and on intensive studies of Easter ceremonies (Painter and others, 1955; Painter, 1960) and other aspects of ritual in Arizona (Wilder, 1941). The cultures are perhaps better known than any other cultures of northwest Mexico.

Contemporary study of Yaqui and Mayo culture reveals two very different phases in the development of what was essentially the same cultural type 100 years ago. Beals has made a sensitive comparison of modern Yaqui and Mayo culture. He regards the difference in general configuration as pre-Spanish in origin. Although tending to see psychological factors as important determinants, Beals regards the problem as unsolved (1945a, pp. 211–15). I view the differences as resulting from historical factors which have been operative chiefly over the past 80 years but with roots in the Spanish contact situation somewhat farther back (Spicer, 1961; 1954b, pp. 207–08). Essentially my view is that the characteristics of Yaqui culture which Beals well sums up as "nationalism" are primarily a result of very strong integration of the Jesuit-created towns under conditions of comparative isolation during the first 150 years of Spanish contact. This town organization developed even tighter integration under pressure of Mexican attempts at domination which were unsuccessful until the 1880's. Success-

ful Yaqui efforts for independence, from the 1820's until the 1880's, stimulated solidarity of Yaqui vis-à-vis Mexicans and brought about strong organization of town government, church institutions, and military sodalities. Until 1887 these tightly organized communities were going concerns governing strictly the lives of all Yaqui who lived in them. During this time a vigorous folk culture integrated at the level of the town came into existence. Since that time this culture continued to exist despite the temporary breakup of the communities after 1887 and later infiltration by Mexicans. Mayo towns were never quite so tightly organized as Yaqui because of Spanish interference from the 1680's on, partly as a result of reduced population and partly because of Spanish and Mexican colonization in the heart of the Mayo country on both the Fuerte and Mayo rivers. Mayo were not able to achieve quite the solidarity of the Yaqui towns during the 19th century for similar reasons, and their breakup was more complete in the latter part of the 19th century. Thus, according to this interpretation of history, Yaqui culture of the mid-20th century was a revival of what had been an unusually tightly integrated system of folk culture, whereas Mayo culture was a disintegrating system of what had never achieved quite so tight an integration. The forces of disintegration which had struck Mayo culture with great intensity during the defeats of the 1870's and 1880's did not begin to have similar effects on Yaqui culture until perhaps the 1940's. In this interpretation, the Mayo turn to Messianism as early as 1890 and their continuing interest in magical nativistic religion to the present is consistent with the cultural processes operative in Mayo communities. Similarly the Yaqui devotion to practical politics and military means of maintaining their identity is consistent with their experience.

The Yaqui culture of the 1930's and 1940's about which we know a good deal had developed its dominant patterns by the late 1800's. These patterns differed more in intensity from Mayo patterns than in fundamental type. We shall attempt to describe Yaqui culture as a system of common understandings and then indicate the differences of Mayo culture and the variations in the two as a result of recent influences from the dominant Mexican culture. The general type of Yaqui–Mayo culture was that of a sacred folk culture organized at the level of the autonomous town, or village community, of 2000–4000 inhabitants (Steward, 1955, pp. 52–56; Redfield, 1953, p. 47).

The unit of Yaqui society was the small community devoted to subsistence farming. Yaqui had farmed the river bottoms of the Yaqui River for an unknown period before the arrival of the Spaniards. They raised corn, beans, squash, and probably cotton. They also cultivated amaranth. Their farming techniques were simple. They relied on the annual overflow of the river, on the heavy rainfall of summer, and to some extent on the lighter rainfall of the winter months. They were able to raise two crops a year without building any extensive irrigation works, and it is doubtful that they employed ditches in their farming except for temporary channels to distribute the flood water more conveniently when the annual overflows arrived. Jesuit missionaries reinforced Yaqui farming by the introduction of livestock, which became important before the end of the 1600's, and by the introduction of new crops, particularly wheat and watermelons. Yaqui produced a surplus which was used by the Jesuits in extending their mission system northward and to Baja California. This system of two-crop farming supplemented by livestock, particularly cattle and sheep, was continued by Yaqui through the 19th century and was taken up again after 1920 when the disturbances following the 1910 Revolution ended. In addition they supplemented farming with a wide variety of wild foods, the most notable being mesquite beans of which

Fig. 2—POTAM VIEWS. 1, Yaqui house, showing storage of corn and pumpkins on roof. (Photographed by Tad Nichols.) 2, The Potam church, viewed from the Guardia. Guardia cross in right foreground. (From Spicer, 1954b, pl. 2.)

meal was made, many different cactus fruits, and oysters and clams of the coastal region of their territory. Deer and large tree-dwelling wood rats were abundant and extensively hunted, and some Yaqui fished successfully. In general Yaqui lived in a habitat of abundant food. The chief difficulties were not uncertainty of water supply but rather excessive floods which occasionally wiped out fields completely. Consequently we find little ceremonial interest in weather control and in fact no focus in religion on subsistence activities, with the exception of maintaining good relations with the supernaturals who controlled the deer.

The technology was simple but basically that of farmers the world over. They made pottery which was of paddle-and-anvil construction and probably rarely decorated. They wove cotton cloth on horizontal belt looms (for Mayo, see vol. 6, Art. 8, figs. 3, 6), and probably also made fiber textiles. One of their major craft interests was in making basketry (for Mayo, see vol. 6, Art. 6, fig. 9,*a*), particularly mats. For mats they employed the abundant native cane, which was split, hammered flat, and woven into large twilled forms which were used for house coverings and for sleeping mats. Pottery and loom weaving were almost lost arts by the end of the 19th century, possibly as a result of the disturbed conditions of life on the Yaqui River resulting from warfare with Mexicans. Yaqui early adopted Spanish forms of clothing, including cotton trousers and twilled palmetto hats for men and embroidered shirtwaists and ankle-length skirts for women. Their need for cotton clothing was a basis for development of trade with Mexicans during the 19th century and continued to be so during the 20th century. They made extensive use of a single-thong, leather-sole sandal as late as the 1950's. House types (fig. 2) were similar to those of rural Mexicans, consisting of flat-roofed rectangular forms made either of adobe bricks or, more commonly, of cane and mud wattle, with dirt-covered roofs. There was little distinctive in Yaqui material culture by the 1930's from that of rural Mexicans of the Sonoran region. Their food patterns were also closely similar, consisting of wheat- or corn-flour tortillas, pozole, atole, tamales, beans, meat and chile, and other common Mexican foods. It was only in connection with ceremonial paraphernalia that any really distinctive material culture patterns were to be found by the 20th century.

The Yaqui subsistence-farming economy was supplemented by trade with Mexicans. Yaqui had never developed a market system of their own before the coming of the

Spaniards and apparently did not do so during the period of mission communities. During the 19th century individual Yaqui engaged in trade with the growing Mexican towns of Sonora, such as Guaymas, transporting corn, beans, mats, and parakeets by burro which they exchanged for cloth, metal goods, coffee, and sugar in the Mexican markets. By the 1930's trade was carried on almost entirely within the Yaqui communities through Mexican storekeepers who maintained residence there. There was also considerable supplementation of farming with wage work on Mexican ranches and in mines in Sonora. Money was generally used and had been since Jesuit times.

Yaqui settlement pattern was that established under Jesuit influence before the middle of the 1600's. The whole length of the lower 60 miles of the Yaqui River flood plain was divided into territorial units called "pueblos," or towns. There were eight of these (fig. 3), the Jesuits having concentrated Yaqui, who were living in scattered rancherías, around eight churches evenly spaced over the length of the lower river area where most Yaqui rancherías were located. Each town had jurisdiction over all the people living within the demarcated territory surrounding a church. The boundaries between the town territories were marked at intervals with groups of three large wooden crosses 7 or 8 feet high. In the 1940's, although Yaqui still thought in terms of the eight towns, they were no longer located as they had been in Jesuit times or even in the 19th century. The water of the Yaqui River no longer flowed to the gulf past all the eight town sites established by the Jesuits. Large amounts of water had been diverted to irrigate tracts south of the Yaqui River where Mexicans and North Americans had settled and where a large city, Ciudad Obregon, was developing. This had left the old sites of the three western-most town centers without water—Belem, Huirivis, and Rahum. Belem territory was so completely waterless that there were no

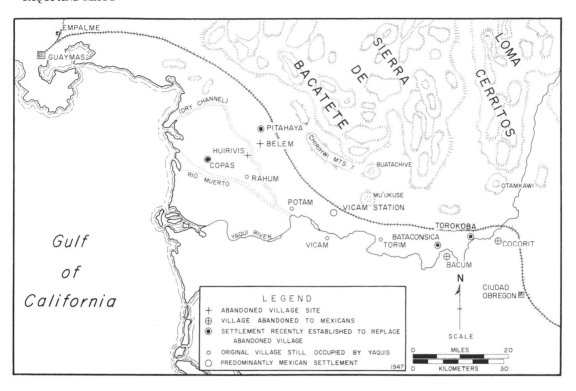

Fig. 3—THE EIGHT PUEBLOS, 1947. (From Spicer, 1954b, fig. 3.)

people living there. (It should be said that in 1960 Belem was again occupied by families whose support was by wage work in neighboring Guaymas and Ciudad Obregon.) There was a little water for domestic supply at one point in Huirivis territory, where a few families were struggling to re-build the old town, while the majority of persons from that territory lived in the town of Potam. Somewhat more water was available for farming as well as domestic use in the territory of Rahum; here the old town site had been reoccupied and the people were struggling to continue. The only towns of the former eight which did not have to make such desperate efforts to exist were the three central ones—Potam, Vicam, and Torim. Two eastern ones—Cocorit and Bacum—had been settled by Mexicans, who had taken over the town government. The people of one of these, Bacum, had moved across the river and were attempting to re-

build their old institutions at a site called Bataconsica. Thus the pattern of the compact town, developed in the Jesuit period, was a strongly held ideal which Yaqui were trying to re-create.

The internal form of the town centers constituted a mixed pattern. Each was lived in by Mexicans as well as Yaqui. Mexican storekeepers, military personnel, and school-teachers lived in adobe houses built contiguously and flush with streets laid out on a grid pattern. Small sections of each of the towns took this form, and some Yaqui built and lived in the same style of houses. The larger part of each town consisted of separate households laid out irregularly. The usual Yaqui household consisted of one or two rooms, either detached or adjacent, with somewhere near an open ramada for cooking with a fireplace of mud raised a couple of feet from the ground, and perhaps other ramadas for lounging and for

837

sleeping in hot weather. It was usually surrounded by a woven cane fence 6 or 7 feet high.

The town as a social unit was a product of Jesuit organization using Spanish conceptions of government. It was also a product, but in lesser part, of Indian ideas and traditions. The conditions under which the two traditions had combined were, first, 150 years of peaceful interaction between Jesuit missionaries in small numbers and some 30,000 Yaqui and, second, a century of conflict between Yaqui and Mexicans. The first set of conditions had resulted in a well-knit, self-consistent integration of governmental traditions; the second set of conditions had intensified Yaqui interest in their relative autonomy experienced during the Jesuit period, in their collective land management system, and in their mixed Catholic-aboriginal religious system. The town, under stress of warfare in the 19th century, had become a highly organized, sharply focused social unit.

The town did not allow of a permanent tribal organization. Yet it was long-standing tradition with Yaqui to organize as a total tribe to protect their tribal territory. This was the case at the time of first Spanish contact and it continued to be for the next four centuries. However, even during the 19th-century wars with the Mexicans in which the Yaqui towns were constantly working closely together, no real tribal organization emerged. Once a battle or series of battles was over, each town asserted its autonomy again; only during wartime was there an organization in which any town recognized a leadership above its own governors. In the 1930's the Mexican army of occupation in the Yaqui country sought to create a tribal organization as a means of communicating with the town governors, and to some extent a go-between organization developed, but the Yaqui conception remained rooted in the autonomy of the towns. Again President Cárdenas in 1939 acted as though a unified tribe existed when he issued a de-

cree setting aside a portion of the old tribal area as exclusively under Yaqui ownership. However, on into the 1950's no real working tribal organization recognized by the town governments came into existence. In 1958 a federal government-sponsored plebiscite was held for the purpose of determining whether Yaqui wished to continue the colonial town type of organization or set up a municipality structure articulated with the state of Sonora. Yaqui voted overwhelmingly for the continuance of the old town-governor system. Thus the unit of government remained essentially what it had been since the days of the Jesuits, and the articulation of this with the state of Sonora and the nation of Mexico remained undefined. Yaqui were deeply resistant to the growth of a new level of integration involving them formally in the nation by which they had been dominated.

The town was an organization in which five realms of authority were integrated. These realms, or *ya'uram*, were the civil, the church, the military, the fiesta, and the customs authorities. Each had its officers in hierarchical arrangement. The civil authority derived from the Spanish governor system and consisted of five governors elected annually, together with assistants; they managed land assignments, presided at trials, coordinated the activities of all five authorities, and controlled relations with other Yaqui towns and with Mexicans. The church was a complex organization with a governor, a hierarchy of *maestros* in charge of all church-centered ceremony, and two ceremonial organizations for men and two for women. Both the regular round of ceremonies following the Catholic calendar and crisis rites from baptism to funerals were organized and managed by this hierarchy. The military society consisted of a sodality of officers with Spanish military titles dedicated to the Virgin of Guadalupe; their functions besides organizing war parties in time of war were as guards of the governors and as important performers in most ceremonies. The fiesta authority had responsibility for the annual ceremony to the town saint and for carrying out funerals; it was a self-perpetuating group of dual functionaries known as the Moors and the Christians. The customs authority was ritually the dominant authority, assuming absolute control of the whole town once each year during Holy Week; it consisted of two men's sodalities dedicated to the service of Jesus and to Christ the Child with highly important duties during the winter ceremonial season.

This organization with a roster of some 60 distinct offices met at least once a week on Sundays throughout the year. Its meetings were open to all Yaqui of a town; in the meetings special speaking privileges were given to older men who had held office in the civil authority at some time during their lives. Procedure, under the chairmanship of the first governor, was democratic, all townsmen being permitted to speak, but there was no vote and no majority rule; the basic theory of procedure was that unanimous agreement could be reached as a result of open discussion of issues.

The Yaqui kinship system was bilateral. The terminology was bifurcate collateral with Hawaiian cousin terminology. The household showed no clear tendency toward any one form of composition. Marriage was ambilocal or neolocal. The usual household consisted of several nuclear families, related sometimes through the male line, sometimes through the female line, but also often including families related only through ritual kinship. Men sometimes had two or more mates, but there was a strict proscription against repeating the marriage ceremony, so that often a man might have undergone marriage with only one of the women of his household, often with none. The Catholic prohibition against divorce was accepted, but the changing of mates was very common with no accompanying ceremony. Within a household no tradition of male or of female dominance was apparent. The

oldest person, providing he or she was competent, was usually the ultimate authority, but ordinarily decisions were group matters.

The cooperation of households in economic and ceremonial matters was highly developed through the operation of a ritual kinship system which was a combination of the Catholic godparent system and a native kind of ceremonial sponsorship, the precise structure of which is not known. The Yaqui ritual kinship system was an elaborate one, evidently stimulated by the European introduction and also probably elaborated as a result of the forced breakup of real genealogical kin groups during the period of deportation. The basic obligation was that of caring for a person at death, an obligation which originated in the ritual sponsoring of a person at baptism, confirmation in the church, marriage, or entrance in any of the ceremonial sodalities. The number of sponsors or godparents that one might have was unlimited, because sponsoring for one of the customs sodalities could be repeated indefinitely. It was thought necessary to have three pairs of sponsors or ritual kin, because the death ritual required six persons. All sponsors of the same person were coparents, *kompalem*, to one another as they were to the parents of the person sponsored. There was thus a complicated network of relationships created by the ritual kinship system which operated to knit many otherwise unrelated households into cooperating units. Much of the vast obligation in ceremony was met through this system, which supplemented the kinship obligations in a very important way.

Yaqui religion was inextricably intertwined with the town organization, and an important function of the ritual consisted in the constant redefinition and sanctioning of the autonomous town orientation in Yaqui culture. The religion may be described in terms of a number of recurrent activities oriented to the honoring of certain supernatural beings. There were five such sets of activities: (1) devotions to Jesus managed and carried out by the two men's sodalities of the customs authority which took place from January to May; (2) devotions to the Virgin Mary, also called Our Mother by Yaqui, managed by the church and with a prominent part played by the men's sodality called the matachines; (3) devotions to the spirits of the dead which went on weekly and monthly throughout the year but which reached a climax annually in the celebration of the Days of the Dead in November; (4) devotions to the Virgin of Guadalupe which also were a regular feature of ceremony throughout the year but which came to a focus on the Day of Guadalupe in December; and (5) annual devotions to the patron saint of the town, which varied from town to town depending on the patron but most of which occurred in the summer months. There was a strong sense of contrasting season in ceremony; the dry months of winter and spring were the period of the dominance of Jesus and the forbidding and disciplining men's organizations which served him especially. The summer months of rain, river overflow, and ripening wild and cultivated foods were the period of the presence of Our Mother and her brightly costumed devotees, the matachín dancers.

The cult of Jesus had been deeply integrated into Yaqui life since Jesuit times. The two men's sodalities responsible for the ceremonies of Lent and Holy Week each year were composed of members dedicated by lifetime vow to their service. They assumed control of the town during their ceremonial season and strictly enforced attendance at ceremonies and taboos on work and sexual intercourse during Holy Week. Their organization showed many features in common with Western Pueblo ceremonial sodalities, but there were also similarities in their costume, particularly their masks, to the devil-clowns of 16th-century European religious drama. The Lenten ceremonies were complex dramatizations of events in the life of Christ, which Yaqui mythology now represented as having taken place in the Yaqui country. The sacredness of the land in the face of the threat of Mexican encroachment had been reinforced in this way and by the combination of the Christian and the native Cahitan flood myths (Spicer, 1945; Giddings, 1959).

The cult of the Virgin Mary was also of great importance. She was identified with various forms of the cross and with the Yaqui traditional female supernatural called Our Mother. The beginning of the rainy season in late June and early July was heralded with household fiestas dedicated to the Virgin and participated in by the matachín dance organizations of the various towns. Matachines traversed the whole length of the Yaqui country, going to dance wherever they were asked. The beginning of the rainy season was climaxed in a celebration of the Virgin of the Road, at which the matachines of all the eight towns danced together in one great and colorful ceremony.

The cult of the dead was ever present in Yaqui devotions, each family keeping a book in which the names of the ancestral dead were written down and which was placed on the altar, ideally, at every ceremony as a means of honoring the ancestors. Burial grounds, concentrated around the churches of each town, were the scene of family gatherings at least one night a month throughout the year and also of formal offering of services by church functionaries in the presence of the family members once a year on the Catholic ceremonial days of All Saints and All Souls.

The Virgin of Guadalupe was the patroness of the military organization of the town, all officers being dedicated to her for life. Her image was carried by the top ranking captains in every Sunday service and on other ceremonial occasions. A dance called the Coyote dance, but not representative of that animal, was performed by the mem-

bers of the military sodality on many ceremonial occasions, together with their ritual
saluting of the sun.

The annual fiesta honoring the patron of
the town or of the church varied in detail
from town to town, each having its distinctive features, such as a rooster pull at
Vicam, but there was a general pattern
common to all. Managed by fiesteros who
were part of the town governmental system and who chose their own successors
each year, it was a complex event in the
form of competing fiestas. One fiesta was
sponsored by the fiesteros called Christians
who were denoted by blue headdresses and
the other by the red fiesteros who were
called Moors. Games and nonsacred dances
were a part of the activities as well as
feasting. The climax was a ritual battle
between the Moors and the Christians and
a final bacchanalia in the church.

Quite apart from the church-sponsored
activities were the dances and activities of
the pascola (fig. 4) and deer dancers. They
were separate in that they were removed
from the sacred context, but physically their
dances were combined with many church
ceremonies and particularly with those
which centered at private households. The
pascola dancers performed as a result of
dreamed vision rather than ritual vow to a
supernatural and derived their knowledge
from animals of the "woods" rather than
Christian supernaturals. Together with the
deer dancer, they perpetuated through their
dances, music, pantomime drama, and
storytelling much art and knowledge which
had not originated in the European tradition.

Yaqui ceremonialism was demanding on
the individuals who participated in it and
these constituted many persons in every
community. Ceremonies were frequent. Interest in ceremonies was high. It was clear
that the ceremonial system was a major,
perhaps the major, orientation of Yaqui. It
was a system which bore little relation to

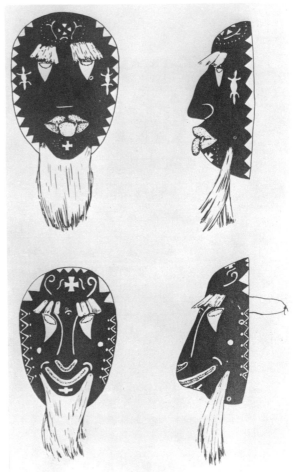

FIG. 4—TWO TYPES OF PASCOLA MASK.
(From Spicer, 1954b, fig. 7.)

subsistence and the problems of making a
living. A major focus was the maintenance
of Yaqui territorial integrity and the autonomous town system and the stimulation of
solidarity among Yaqui. The cement of the
whole system was the dedication of individuals by vow to serve the supernaturals for
life or for shorter terms as singers, dancers,
soldiers, or in other offices. The vow was an
insurance against the recurrence of illness.
It should be recognized, therefore, that a
second major focus of this religious system
was curing and the maintenance of good

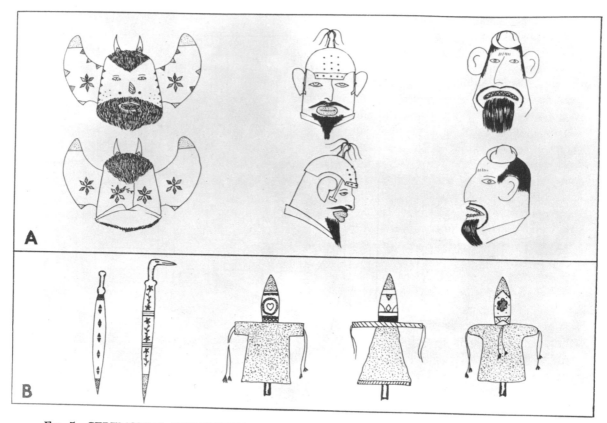

Fig. 5—CEREMONIAL PARAPHERNALIA. *A*, Helmet masks of Chapayeka, 1942. *B*, Paraphernalia of the Judas Society. (From Spicer, 1954b, fig. 9.)

health. The group ceremonials shared this function with the activities of individual practitioners of herbal and magical curing. In every village there were several *hitebim*, or curers, some of whom through dreams gained power to ward off illness caused by witches.

Although most of the external forms were Spanish in origin, the fundamental orientation of Catholic Christianity, namely, salvation of the individual soul and the objective of heaven had not been incorporated into the ceremonial system. The objective was rather the perpetuation of the "Eight Pueblos" and their exclusive possession by Yaqui.

Yaqui art was subsumed in Yaqui ceremonialism. The major emphasis was on dance and music. Dance was exclusively reserved for men, and there were no purely social forms of dance. There were, however, both sacred and secular forms. Dance steps were chiefly Indian in tradition; choreography, as in the matachín dances, European. Both native and European musical traditions were important, and guitars, violins, and harps were used as well as native flutes and drums. What little decorative art existed was related to ceremonial paraphernalia (figs. 4, 5)—both geometric and realistic elements on masks, the lance heads of the member of the men's sodality representing Pontius Pilate, and on a few other ritual objects. Pottery was not decorated, and weaving had died out. Storytelling had become formalized in the activities of the pascolas, who specialized in the art of fiction, particularly the humorous story. Poetry was alive both in the form of the traditional deer songs and in popular songs composed to Mexican music by young men.

This sketch of Yaqui culture may serve as a basis for considering the modern ethnography of Cahitans in general. It is based also entirely on observations and investigations made in towns on the Yaqui River in 1939, 1941–42, 1947, 1956, and 1958 (Spicer, 1954b).

Beals' account (1945a) of Mayo and Yaqui culture in the 1930's indicates that there were only minor differences in detail as between Yaqui and Mayo culture traits. Such details as that matachín dancers may be either girls or boys among Mayo and are always male among Yaqui, or that houseyard crosses are commonly carved and decorated and may be 7 or 8 feet tall among Mayo whereas they are uniformly plain and rarely more than 4 feet tall among Yaqui are interesting and indicative of differences in the acculturation processes as they have operated among the two peoples. There are many other such differences in ritual, the elements of material culture, and minor belief. Study of these will no doubt shed light on the processes of cultural variation, but nevertheless they are only details. The two cultures had a common origin and shared a large body of culture elements.

But there were differences of considerable importance between modern Yaqui and Mayo culture. Beals found in 1932 that the political organization—that is, the town governmental system—had broken down among Mayo (Beals, 1945a, pp. 83–90). The civil authority was known only from memory, and apparently this was true also of the military authority. There remained in curtailed form the church organization, the customs authority, and the fiesteros. It appears that Mayo communities did not have continuity through the 19th and 20th centuries as Mayo-managed towns. This was in contrast with the situation on the Yaqui River, where although towns were disrupted in the 1880's and brought under Mexican control, most Yaqui town organizations came back into operation at the latest by the 1920's. Mayo communities in the 1930's and later were of two general kinds: on the one hand, there were areas of Mexican towns, such as in Navojoa, Echojoa, Los Mochis, and others, in which Mayo were concentrated. On the other hand, there were newly settled villages, such as Tenia, away from the river (Erasmus, 1948) where Mayo went after release from hacienda service following the 1910 Revolution.

In the urban segments the Indians were living under the domination of Mexicans in the larger community. It was to be expected that the civil and military organization would disintegrate under these circumstances. It is more surprising that there should have been no revival of town government in the newly settled communities, but this seems to have been the case and may be attributed to cultural loss as a result of infiltration of Mayo communities in the 19th century and cultural disintegration experienced as peons on the haciendas. We may assume that the culture-bearing unit among Mayo had ceased to be the colonial type of town and had become the family or friendship group within the unstructured urban segments of the Sonora and Sinaloa Mexican towns. There is no question, however, that ceremonial activity of the same type and organized along the same lines as the Yaqui went on in these segments (Beals, 1945a) and this continued to be the case through the 1950's. Easter ceremonies of the same general type, for example, continued to be given at places such as San Miguel on the Fuerte River and at Masiaca.

Mayo ceremonialism was the persistent element of the culture. It was, moreover, continuing to develop, as indicated in the

843

rise of a new religious cult in 1957 near Ahome on the Fuerte River (Erasmus, 1961). This had its origin in the vision of a young man who claimed to have seen God and received instructions for the giving of a modified type of fiesta. The prescribed ceremonies utilized all the old forms, including matachín and pascola dancers, but combined in new ways and in a ritual context which gave greater separation from the church organization. This cult, which embodied so many elements of older Cahita tradition, spread rapidly among Mayo and had been accepted by a few Yaqui by 1960. It was indicative of the continuing strength of Indian tradition outside the context of the old town complex.

Yaqui lived not only in the old or relocated towns of the Yaqui River valley but also in the cities of Sonora and Arizona. They had established settlements of several hundred on the outskirts of Ciudad Obregon, Empalme, Guaymas, and Hermosillo, and were to be found in smaller groups almost everywhere in the state. In the Sonora cities, much the same process had taken place that had characterized the Mayo, but there was less cultural loss and more vigorous organization. Each of the urban segments, or barrios, continued to give annually an Easter ceremony (Barker, 1957) managed by the men's sodalities as the climax of a ceremonial year which included the whole round of personal crisis rites—weddings, confirmations of various kinds, and funerals. A ceremonial organization was maintained, while civil and military organization had disappeared or shrunk to include only a "governor" who acted as a go-between with officials and other non-Yaqui. In economic life the urban Yaqui of Sonora were completely absorbed into the lower levels of the wage system.

Conditions were much the same in the Arizona Yaqui communities. It appeared, however, that there was more retention of cultural content but in a more atomistic context of social life. Whereas church organization tended to remain intact in the Sonoran urban segments, in Arizona this was not always true. Even in the settlement with greatest internal solidarity (Spicer, 1940) images were owned by individual families and the office of church governor had disappeared along with the civil and military offices. It should be said, however, that the military organization had persisted in Arizona until the 1940's. Other aspects of ceremonialism were different in detail but not in general plan, and it was clear that this was the persistent feature of the old folk culture under new conditions of participation in a wage economy.

There was a strong sense of identity as Yaqui in both the Sonora and Arizona communities and this was related to a coherent conception of their own history, which was fostered in formal sermons and in contacts with the river towns. Interest in the "Eight Pueblos" and in the traditions of fighting for their defense gave a basis for ethnic distinction and pride in their past.

REFERENCES

Bancroft, 1883–89
Barker, 1957
Beals, 1932a, 1943a, 1945a
Buelna, 1890
Caso and Parra, 1950
Corral, 1887
Erasmus, 1948, 1955, 1961
Fabila, 1940
Gámez, 1955
Giddings, 1959
Gill, 1957
Hernández, 1902

Holden and others, 1936
Kurath and Spicer, 1947
Painter, 1960
———, Savala, and Alvárez, 1955
Paso y Troncoso, 1905
Pérez de Ribas, 1645
Redfield, 1953
Sauer, 1935
Spicer, 1940, 1943, 1945, 1947, 1954a, 1954b, 1961
Steward, 1955
Wilder, 1941
Zuñiga, 1835

41. The Tarahumara

JACOB FRIED

THE TARAHUMARA are a Uto–Aztecan-speaking tribe inhabiting the mountainous southwestern corner of the state of Chihuahua (figs. 1–3). They call themselves *rarámuri*, meaning runners-on-foot. Their culture is of the basic *ranchería* pattern, linking them to the Cora–Huichol–Tepecano group to the south, the Sonoran–Sinaloan group to the west, and the Pima–Papago group to the north.

Three subcultural groups are readily discernible: mountain dwellers (*pagótame*), canyon dwellers (*poblanos*), and pagans (*gentiles*). The first two show marked Spanish–Mexican influences in their culture and contrast mainly in adaptation to their ecological settings. The canyon dwellers, who represent 10–12 per cent of the Tarahumara population, have had more stable contacts with Mestizos, and are more acculturated than the sierran group. The pagans, who live in nearly inaccessible and desolate areas, are even more staunchly conservative of the aboriginal life-way.

GEOGRAPHY

The sierra in southwestern Chihuahua takes the form of a high broken plateau. Deep gorges and lesser canyons abound; the terrain is covered by forests of pine and oak. There are few extensive level tracts of land suitable for large-scale agriculture, and the soils are thin and poor. The climate is generally cool and stimulating in the mountains; the deeper gorges are markedly warmer. There is a summer rainy season.

HISTORY OF MAJOR POSTCONTACT EVENTS

Jesuit missionaries visited the Tarahumara as early as 1608, but did not establish the first permanent mission until 1639. By 1648 six *pueblos* (church-centered communities) were in existence. From 1645 to 1690 native resistance to Christianization and pueblo-centralization caused considerable bloodshed.

Rich silver and gold mines were discovered in southern Chihuahua in the early 17th century, and with extraordinary rapidity the Spaniards located numerous mining regions deep in Tarahumara country. Ensuing clashes between miners and Indians led to urgent attempts by army and civil officials to pacify the natives. Thus, along

846

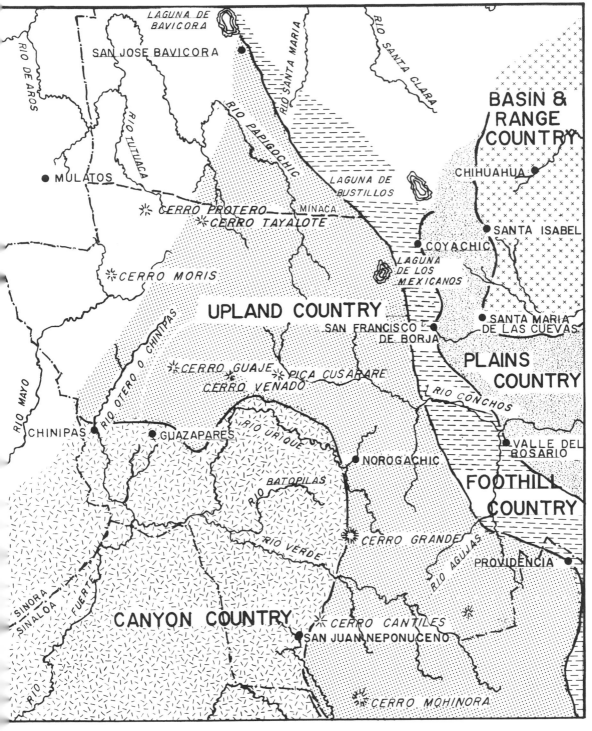

Fig. 2—THE TARAHUMAR COUNTRY. Heavy solid line: Early 17th-century boundaries. Heavy broken line: Boundaries after westward expansion of the Tarahumara in the 17th and 18th centuries. Light broken line: Territory occupied by peoples with distinct cultural affiliation with the Tarahumara. Dates are those of the earliest references to the Tarahumara west of the early 17th-century boundary. (Adapted from Pennington, 1963, Map 1.)

FIG. 3—THE TARAHUMAR COUNTRY. Boundary as of 1959 outlined. Hard surface road from Cuauhtemoc to Chihuahua and southeastward. (Adapted from Pennington, 1963, Map 2.)

849

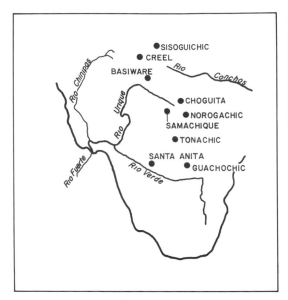

Fig. 4—PUEBLOS STUDIED BY THE AUTHOR

Fig. 5—YOKING OXEN, NOROGACHIC PUEBLO

with the religious authorities, civil authorities tried to impose a more manageable political order on the dispersed Tarahumara by setting up special native "governors" and "captains" (police).

The expulsion of the Jesuits in 1767 removed one immediate source of acculturative pressure. From 1800 to 1825 Apache raidings reached a crescendo of violence and terror. Pancho Villa's Mexican raiders roved the region in 1917 spreading disorder and disease.

Though Catholic missionary efforts were renewed and Mexico passed through the revolutionary period of political and land reforms in the first two decades of the 20th century, the basic integrity of Tarahumara culture was not seriously threatened. Renewed efforts by the federal government to ameliorate harsh economic conditions, raise educational standards, and politically integrate the dispersed local groups, begun in the 1930's and continuing into the present, have so far produced only modest successes. (See Plancarte, 1954, pp. 81–96, for details on the work of the Instituto Nacional Indigenista in planning culture change.)

Mining and lumbering activities since the early 1940's seem to exert strong attractions only on those Tarahumara already closely associated with established Mestizo centers. Today, the Tarahumara remain one of the least acculturated tribes in the Americas.

POPULATION

Population can be only roughly estimated for this mobile, highly dispersed tribe at somewhere between 40,000 and 50,000.

HISTORY OF ETHNOLOGICAL INVESTIGATIONS AND MAJOR SOURCES

Modern ethnological investigations began with Lumholtz (1902), who very thoroughly traveled throughout the Tarahumara country in the early 1890's. In 1925–26 Basauri (1929) carried out three short field trips and published a brief, highly condensed general monograph. The most detailed ethnographic account available, one based on intensive field investigation lasting over nine months (1930–31), is that of Bennett and Zingg (1935). Plancarte (1954) has produced a well-balanced summary of the culture, together with an assessment of culture-change problems, based on over six years of residence among the Tarahumara. The results of my eight months in the field in 1950–51 studying social control have been recorded (1952, 1953). Many of the ethnographic data in this article were obtained during this field trip. Passin's account (1943) of kinship organization is the most comprehensive available.

Interpersonal relations and outstanding characteristics of Tarahumara personality were described by me (1961) and by Passin (1942). An assessment of value orientations was attempted by Zingg (1942).

The best sources of ethnological information concerning the early contact and Jesuit periods are Alegre (1841) and Treutlein (1949). The latter is a particularly good source on the founding of mission centers and the struggle against aboriginal culture patterns. Champion (1955) described culture contact and acculturation since 1890.

Despite the classic work of Bennett and Zingg, much more needs to be known about regional variation of culture. The *gentiles* especially deserve intensive study.

SUBSISTENCE SYSTEMS AND FOOD PATTERNS

The Tarahumara are primarily agriculturalists, the basis of their diet being corn, beans, squash, and potatoes. Goats, sheep, cattle, and dogs are important domesticated animals; the goat is the commonest. Pigs and chickens are kept only by the more acculturated Indians. Fruit is grown almost solely for sale to Mexicans. Cattle are prestige animals, but by no means all families own them; indeed, some families possess no stock at all, a sign of poverty by Tarahumara standards.

Because the terrain is neither rich nor available in broad open spaces a family usually grows the crops in two, three, or even more individual small pockets of soil, often separated by several kilometers. Animal dung, when available, is the universal fertilizer.

FIG. 6—TARAHUMARA FISHING WITH BLANKETS, RIO FUERTE. (From Lumholtz, 1902, 1: 405.)

FIG. 7—PLANTING CORN, BASIWARE PUEBLO

FIG. 8—WOMAN WEAVING BLANKET, GUA-CHOCHIC PUEBLO

Corn in the form of *pinole* or *isquiate* (parched ground cornflour in water) is by far the commonest food; beans, squash, and several wild greens follow in importance. Wheat and potatoes are minor. *Tesgüino* (corn beer) is a very important food. It is taken in great quantities during the frequent fiestas and work parties (*tesgüinadas*) that are the basic social and economic events of community life (fig. 24). Goat, sheep, and cattle meat are eaten usually only on ceremonial occasions or work fiestas, but no such event would be complete without meat and corn beer. Tobacco is grown and passionately enjoyed in cigarette form.

Hunting of deer, wild turkey, squirrels, rabbits, and field mice, and fishing (using vegetable-root poisons) are of secondary economic importance. Lumholtz (1902, 1: 405) illustrates Tarahumara fishing with blankets (fig. 6).

Fields are first cleared and fertilized, and then fenced off to keep out both domesticated and wild animals. They are then tilled by a yoke of oxen dragging a wooden plow (fig. 5). A digging stick is used in planting, a hoe in cultivating and weeding (fig. 7). Corn and squash are grown in the same field, beans in separate upland clearings.

Dried corn is prepared for eating by being first toasted, then ground to a flour on a metate. Meat, beans, and greens are boiled.

The typical Tarahumara meal is one of pinole or isquiate, with boiled beans or wild greens if available. The pattern of eating is one of extreme variability, ranging from whole household participation to individual taking of snacks whenever hungry. In general, eating, like all other activities of life, follows no compulsive, inflexible routine.

SETTLEMENT PATTERNS

The basic settlement pattern is the *ranchería,* a scattered grouping of families living in relative proximity. A ranchería is made up of household clusters, each consisting of a single-roomed log house and one or two log grain-storage cabins, and a small flat clearing or *patio* for dancing, feasting, or working. These are scattered along a small valley with a stream or arroyo close by. Large rancherías may have as many as 15 or 20 houses, but the more usual number is five or six.

The component households of a ranchería, as well as the members of a single household, are highly mobile in space and time. Families must tend their several agricultural plots, scattered over many kilometers all during summer and early fall, and in winter many households move with their herds to sheltered canyon sites. But wherever the most valuable parcel of land is located, there a more substantial house and storage cabin are constructed; this is the "home" ranchería.

The ranchería is a most important local group. There are lines of social and economic interchange between members of a ranchería, but these are not of a sustained or continuous nature. (See section on Social Organization below.)

SEASONAL MOBILITY PATTERNS AND SOCIAL GROUPINGS

Seasonal mobility is a major feature of Tarahumara life. In winter, those who have animals and land, and houses or caves in the deeper canyons, retire to these protected habitations. But not all families are winter migrants and cave dwellers. Many remain in the high sierras, because they have neither land nor animals to be protected; some, however, move to caves still higher in the mountains where they can be closer to a good wood supply. Thus, the social groupings of households change with the seasons. Those who move to canyon caves or houses have a new set of neighbors. In some cases, members of different pueblos may move closer together. These winter groupings are broken when, with the advent of spring, families move back to the sierras. Now they have other neighbors in different rancherías where they own land, and the personnel of fiesta and work parties varies.

FIG. 9—TARAHUMAR ARROW RELEASE. (From Lumholtz, 1902, 1: 262.)

TECHNOLOGY

Tools

The most important tools are steel axes, iron knives, hoes, chisels, crowbars, and an iron key for striking sparks. These, and needles for sewing clothing, are secured by occasional trade with Mestizos.

Techniques of Processing and Manufacture

The most plentiful raw material is wood. Large trees, once felled, are split by axe and oak wedges to make boards, beams, roofing, and fencing.

Blankets are woven by women from sheep's wool on a simple horizontal loom (fig. 8). Goat and cow hides, prepared for

853

a

FIG. 10—TYPICAL SIERRA HOUSE AND GRAIN STORAGE STRUCTURE, SANTA ANITA PUEBLO

FIG. 11—TARAHUMAR DWELLINGS. *a*, Stone and wood, typical of headwater region of the Rio Fuerte and Rio Conchos. *b*, *Canoas* leaned against a ridgepole supported by two forked branches. (From Pennington, 1963, pls. 32, 33.)

b

trade with Mestizos, are crudely tanned with animal brains or oak bark.

The basic household utensils consist of a stone metate, various sizes of clay pots (*comales*) for toasting, boiling, and storing foods; clay dishes; gourds split in half for dippers and water carriers; long wooden spoons; twilled baskets of single or double weave of various sizes for storage.

The cane flute and single-faced drum (sheepskin over a split wood round frame) are ancient Indian instruments, but the violin and guitar are also manufactured by the Tarahumara, copying Spanish designs faithfully. The weaving of colorful wool sashes

and narrow hair ribbons represents the highest aesthetic efforts of these people.

Bows and arrows (fig. 9) are still being made. A variety of traps for small game—squirrels and rats—are commonly seen about a house.

The plow is made from a conveniently shaped tree with a branch projecting at the right angle, fitted with a steel or stone point.

Houses

The typical sierra house is rectangular, with a gabled roof made of grooved overlapping single logs or shingles. Front and

854

Fig. 12—GRAIN STORAGE STRUCTURE, SANTA ANITA PUEBLO

Fig. 13—STONE STORAGE STRUCTURE NEAR NARARACHIC. (From Pennington, 1963, pl. 7.)

back of the structure are closed by leaning boards upright against the frame; these are removed and replaced as entrance or exit is required (fig. 10). The use of doors and latches is not common in isolated sections. Stone (fig. 11,*a*) and adobe houses are found in the canyons.

The fireplace often consists of no more than a simple arrangement on the hard-packed earth floor. In some cases a stone and mud chimney collects and conducts the smoke to the roof. In the summer a simple brush shelter can be built on the far end of the patio for cooking or working purposes.

The grain bins are more carefully constructed than the residences, with walls, floors, and ceiling made of nicely fitted planks, held together by careful notching of the ends (fig. 12). The corn-drying structure, erected near the cornfield, is somewhat smaller and simpler, being made of rougher log or hewn boards.

Household furnishings are extremely simple. Mats of twilled fibers and a few goat skins, together with the rough wool blanket, make up the usual bedding. Storage is on the ground in baskets or crude wooden chests, or up along the edges of walls where they join the roof beams. Chairs and tables are not used. Outside, simple feeding troughs of grooved logs, animal pens, and corrals are usually found.

Fig. 14—TARAHUMAR MEN. (From Lumholtz, 1902, 1: 149.)

Dress and Ornament

The typical male attire (fig. 14) consists of a diaper-like breechclout held in place by a colorful woven sash, a cotton broad-sleeved blouse of colonial Spanish type, a plain white cloth headband to keep the hair in place, and, in colder or wet weather, a heavy woolen fringed blanket. Cowhide-soled sandals are worn, though barefooted-ness is very common. As a survival of Jesuit influence, nearly all men wear a simple rosary of Job's-tears with a cross pendant. A small leather wallet, to hold money, to-bacco, matches, or a knife, completes the costume.

The women's dress (fig. 15) consists of from one to five loose cotton skirts, depend-ing on the season, held in place by a some-what wider woven sash than that used by men. They wear either a shirt similar in cut

Fig. 15—TARAHUMAR WOMAN. (From Lumholtz, 1902, 1: 150.)

to the man's or a simple poncho-like gar-ment made of a single piece of material. Footgear is the same as the men's. The hair is also held in place by a headcloth or, less commonly today, by a narrow, artistically decorated woven ribbon. A shawl serves to carry children, firewood, grain, wild greens, or fruit. Strings of beads made of seeds or colored glass are worn by all women as well as the rosary and cross. Hair is combed and cleaned with pine-wood combs.

Transportation

The Tarahumara are proud foot-runners, who ordinarily disdain the beasts of burden, the burro or horse. The typical carrying device is a sturdy blanket carried over the shoulder, or the cloth shawl of the woman. Heavy weights, like logs, are balanced on the shoulders. Burros are used in the Mestizo manner for heavy transport, and many Tarahumara who engage in trade own them.

Weights and Measures

Every Tarahumara owns a box for reckoning grain. It measures 7.5 by 7.5 by 3.4 inches and holds half a decaliter. The meter of cloth and the Mexican *peso,* as standards of value, and the single day of work as a unit of time, are used in dealing with Mestizos. Informally, a gourdful of liquid or an ordinary-sized eating dish serve as crude approximations of quantity. Otherwise, Tarahumara estimate weight by hefting or by size, trusting to their practiced eye.

ECONOMY

Division of Labor

The primary economic unit of Tarahumara society is the nuclear family. Because of the simple composition of this unit, and the variety of tasks carried out daily, the patterns of work division are inherently flexible. Though it is the ideal pattern that agriculture is men's work, care of the house and children and certain domestic manufactures, women's work, and herding a task for children, such a division of labor is subject to much variation in practice. On occasion, men may cook or wash clothes, even sew or make reed baskets. Herding is in fact done not only by women and children but also by men. Similarly, some women are quite skillful in the use of axe or hoe. Thus, despite the ideal pattern, various *situational* factors influence task performance: e.g. lack of children, disruption of harmony due to interpersonal disputes, mobility in the annual cycle which separates family members,

inefficiency of a spouse at a task, and personal preferences for certain type of activities (some men *like* to weave or herd, for example).

Specialization and Trade

Technology and economic organization are too simple to support occupational classes. Basic activities can be accomplished by the members of a single household (with occasional help of neighbors or relatives) using very simple tools. The normal man can, with some assistance, build his own house, storage bins, fences and corrals, make his own plows, digging sticks, axe and hoe handles. His wife (ideally) can manufacture clay dishes and pots, weave blankets, and sew all the family's clothing.

However, this does not mean that every household necessarily produces all its own artifacts. Actually, the Tarahumara get an important segment of their material culture from Mexicans: axe and hoe heads, needles, knives and cloth. Salt is another such necessity. From trade with Indians living in the hot canyons, they obtain vegetables, medicinal plants, gourds, plant fibers, reeds, and special wood.

Not all women, in fact, produce all the blankets, pots, mats, or baskets they use. Sometimes raw materials or skill or both may be lacking. Especially good pots, blankets, or baskets, produced in certain pueblos noted for their superior abilities, are acquired through trade or barter. This is a modest sort of ranchería or geographical specialization. However, this does not invalidate the essential self-sufficiency of the individual household.

Property

Individual ownership of all forms of property is a cornerstone of the culture. There is never any doubt (if there is, it leads to a dispute before native officials) as to who owns a given artifact, blanket, pot, animal, parcel of land, or fruit tree, or what happens to these in case of divorce, death, sale, or loan. A person who fails to respect individual ownership, even within the nuclear family, either by use without permission or by theft, is subject to strong punitive action by native officials.

In marriage there may be joint *use* of each partner's property, but, as divorce cases show, the property reverts to its original owner, and all property accumulated by joint efforts is carefully and fairly divided between them by the native officials.

Property (land, animals) is inherited separately from each parent, and upon their death it is to be divided equally among all the children. A widowed spouse in theory receives nothing, but in every case recorded a widow (but not a widower) inherits some of her husband's property, for accepted economic reasons. Property of a deceased unmarried person is divided among his siblings or close relatives.

However, in keeping with the sense of fairness so strong among the Tarahumara, native officials often make special arrangements to punish a spouse guilty of bad behavior or to award property to the more needy partner. Clearly, these officials operate on the principle that any division of property must secure the individuals from want, wherever practicable.

Production and Consumption Units

Though the primary economic unit is the nuclear family, it is not a completely self-enclosed social or economic unit. The households of a ranchería are linked by mutual work fiestas (*tesgüinadas*). The work party permits a household to recruit additional labor for certain heavy or sustained types of work where large numbers of workers can effectively be employed simultaneously, such as clearing fields, plowing, weeding, building houses, corrals, and fences.

Trade with Mestizos

Trade with, and at times even economic dependence on, the Mestizo has been a feature of Tarahumara life for hundreds of

years. Certain basic necessities of life—axes, hoes, needles, thread, salt, cloth—are secured by trade. In periods of drought and poverty, when relatives or neighbors cannot help, the Mestizos are sources of food and money. Thus, the Indians go among Mestizos, hiring themselves out as occasional agricultural workers or herders in order to overcome periods of economic or interpersonal stress, and Mestizos travel among Indians in order, through trade for corn, wheat, fruit, hides, blankets, and animals, to supplement their often meager resources. Despite a basic hostility and mutual contempt, Indians and Mestizos often find they need each other.

Trade contacts take the form of a rather formal personal relationship between a Mestizo and his Indian trading partner. Such a partner is called *noráwa*. Only a known Mestizo could transact business with the wary, suspicious Tarahumara. Trade between Indians of the canyons and the sierras also follows this noráwa pattern, for the Tarahumara are equally shy of Indian strangers.

Labor Export

As the Tarahumara are not always self-sufficient, they may have to work for a "rich" Indian (one with considerable landholdings and herds of animals) or a Mestizo. In addition, miners have for centuries employed Tarahumara as beasts of burden, runners and messengers, and as transport workers.

Wealth and Its Use

Tarahumara society is essentially egalitarian; personal freedom and independence are jealously guarded possessions of everyone. Prestige, in the ideal pattern, is given to those whose *behavior* merits high regard. A wealthy man may well be respected, but this would not be based solely on his wealth in land, animals, and especially cattle. The Tarahumara do not display wealth either in their dress, possessions, or housing. Indeed, the rich often attempt to hide evidence of wealth for fear of being asked for loans of food or oxen, or being called upon to donate animals for religious sacrifices. Despite ideal norms that stress generosity and mutual economic assistance, the Tarahumara are not an open-handed people, and social pressures are at times needed to coax individuals to meet social or religious obligations.

Participation in certain religious fiestas requires the participants to buy expensive costumes, or donate goats or cows for sacrifice. Not all persons selected to fill important ceremonial offices are pleased with their nomination and some seek to avoid the expenditure of resources and time. A clash between personal values and group-centered ones frequently occurs.

Social Organization
Family and Kinship

The Tarahumara family is of the nuclear type: father, mother, and unmarried children form the core of a household. Marriage is usually monogamous, but isolated instances of polygynous and even polyandrous households are to be found. In first marriages, temporary matrilocal residence is the preferred pattern, but both patrilocal and neolocal types are possible depending on economic or personal factors. Marriage rules are not clearly formulated. Close cousin marriages are usually avoided; most couples are members of the same pueblo. Trial marriages are still common. If after a year or so the partners are satisfied, they are then formally married by native officials, and in that case, marriages are more likely to be stable. Thus, aboriginal patterns (polygyny and trial marriage) are still conserved alongside the Catholic Spanish-imposed marital patterns.

In a discussion of family and kinship *behavior* (not structure) it is necessary to point out the marked variability and flexibility of all institutions as a general cultural

characteristic. Ideal norms, as verbally expressed by informants, are usually "preferred" rather than "compulsory" ones; alternative patterns exist to permit different responses to the variety of special conditions—high spacial mobility, divorce, death, poverty of resources, and physical isolation.

In its formal structure Tarahumara kinship terminology shows a perfectly bilateral arrangement with such refinements as differentiating between older and younger siblings and names for third and fourth generations above ego.

Formally, one may expect the closest cooperation, aid, and companionship from ego's own generation. This can stretch beyond siblings to cousins and second cousins, reckoned bilaterally. However, in actual behavior, the Tarahumara react to all persons, kin or non-kin, alike in terms of personal feelings of friendliness or antagonism, so cousins or siblings can be either friends or deadly enemies.

The generation immediately above or below ego assumes importance likewise to the degree that actual contacts are rewarding between members of these age strata, but usually siblings of both mother and father are the kinsmen to whom the child typically develops closest ties. These are, in fact, persons most often visited and who most often give economic aid, or care for children. Grandparent-grandchild relations conform to these mentioned for parents' siblings. Where contacts are intense, as in temporary matrilocal residence, close ties are formed.

As for affinal relations, depending on residence patterns and personal preferences, there can be close or distant social and economic ties. Siblings-in-law of the same sex often have strong bonds of mutual aid and friendliness.

A joking relation between siblings-in-law is usually expressed during tesgüinadas and takes the form of teasing, good-natured wrestling, and humorous insults; between siblings-in-law of opposite sex, the sexual teasing is even more pronounced. Grand-

859

parents also tease children in public in this manner.

There are no avoidance practices. *Compadrazgo* (ritual kinship) among the Christianized Tarahumara is recognized, but seems to be limited to baptism rites, and hardly seems functional in any other context.

Local and Territorial Units

Though the isolation of the Tarahumara family unit is one of the outstanding characteristics of the culture, it is of course a relative matter. The ranchería is the local grouping of the greatest significance because it is between the few households of a ranchería that most frequent face-to-face contacts that influence social and economic life of largely independent and self-sufficient households occur. Neighboring houses are occasionally linked by mutual work-aid patterns and combined religio-economic fiestas as well as kinship ties (see sections on Religion and Fiestas below). Ranchería members most often lend food, care for children, or borrow oxen from each other. Such mutual assistance is actually most common between relatives, especially when persons who reside close by are on friendly terms; otherwise, convenience and proximity can outweigh kinship as selective factors.

The Tarahumara do not form a politically cohesive group. There are still no effective tribal leaders, councils or special associations that succeed in unifying the scattered independent, isolated component groups, despite the earnest attempt in 1938 to create a cohesive political organization through convening a congress of all the Tarahumara leaders (*gobernadores*).

The pueblo is the basic territorial and highest political unit of the society. Each pueblo's boundaries enclose an area of some 15 miles in radius. Each pueblo has a religio-administrative center composed of a church and, usually, a courthouse-jail (*comunidad*) which serves as a gathering place. Members of the dispersed rancherías convene here to participate in religious festivals, bring grievances and disputes for adjudication, attend footraces, and, informally, to meet friends, to arrange various affairs, and to gossip.

Pueblo affairs are controlled and directed by a body of native officials, some of whom are elected directly by vote of all adult members, others, appointed by the elected officials (see section on Political Organization below).

Interpueblo contacts are fostered by (1) trading relationships (noráwa), (2) attendance of tesgüinadas, (3) seasonal mobility patterns, (4) pueblo exogamy and matrilocal residence, (5) interpueblo footraces, and (6) fiesta attendance.

Political and Religious Organization

The modern Tarahumara culture displays a remarkably transparent coexistence of Spanish-Christian socio-cultural patterns with aboriginal Indian ones. At the pueblo level, the Spanish-Christian oganization predominates, and at the ranchería level, the Indian.

At the pueblo level, modern native officials have maintained a striking identity in name and function, actual behavior, and ideology to their prototypes, chosen and trained by the Jesuit missionaries of the 17th century to carry on the internal administration of their missions. Although the numbers and names of native officials show local variations, the gross pattern is the same; namely, a *gobernador* (siríame) and his assistants, called by such terms as *mayor, capitán, teniente, fiscal,* and *soldado* (fig. 16).

The duties of the gobernador combine religious and secular elements. He organizes the elaborate Christian church fiestas: fixes the dates, designates the persons to contribute food and animals, and the dance leaders. Of equal importance is his function as chief judge and informal adjudicator of in-

Fig. 16—NATIVE OFFICIALS, HOLY WEEK CHURCH FIESTA, CHOGUITA PUEBLO

Fig. 17—NATIVE OFFICIALS ADJUDICATING A DISPUTE, SAMACHIQUE PUEBLO

ner and interfamily disputes. By means of stereotyped oratory, he delivers at all public affairs admonitory sermons that actually are summaries of the ideal norms of the society, specifying in detail what is right and proper and what is wrong and punishable. The adjudication of disputes over land, animals, inheritance, or property division, as well as punishing crimes, is a formal procedure, with the gobernador and his chosen officials serving as judges, each solemnly holding a special staff of office, a symbol of power and authority (fig. 17).

The *mayor* promotes and arranges marriages, specializes in the affairs of children, and settles domestic difficulties of marriage partners. Like the gobernador, he has the power to intervene if he deems it necessary. In general, he operates by warnings, admonitory talks to lazy, ill-tempered, uncooperative or neglectful spouses, or disobedient children.

In theory, corporal punishment is an exclusive right of the native officials; public whipping is the severest form of punishment. The sermons delivered to correct offenders represent a shaming type of punishment.

At the ranchería level, the non-Christian religio-magical practitioner and the pueblo officials are actually not in conflict, but maintain compartmentalized as well as cooperative relations. The two systems, in fact, carry out similar and overlapping religious and social control functions. Pueblo officials mediate between man and the supernatural world in its Christianized guise, and the church fiesta is the ceremonial vehicle. The native practitioners are priest-doctors who mediate between man and the supernatural world of souls of the dead, animal "beings," mythical water-serpents, *rusíwari* and *disagíki* (invisible malignant beings), and witches and sorcerers. The ranchería fiesta is the ceremonial vehicle of the priest-doctor. Dancing, the drinking of tesgüino, and food offerings are the basic elements of the complex (fig. 18).

861

Fig. 18—FOOD OFFERINGS ON ALTAR, RAN-CHERÍA CURING FIESTA, NOROGACHIC PUEBLO

Fig. 19—"MONARCO," LEADER OF MATA-CHÍN DANCERS, SANTA ANITA PUEBLO

Both systems of religion are used to insure health of man and his animals, good crops, and fine weather (see section on Sickness and Curing).

In terms of social control, fear of sorcery and retaliation by witchcraft in conflict situations both causes and prevents overt conflict.

Relation of Pueblos to Local and Federal Government

The connection between the official machinery of federal, local, and municipal government and the isolated autonomous pueblos is a most tenuous one, except in the most acculturated zones. Plancarte (1954, pp. 35–37) gives an account of political relations and history of attempts to establish closer ties.

RELIGION AND WORLD VIEW
Basic Religious Concepts and Ritual

Tarahumara religion is both a compartmentalization and a blending of two traditions: Spanish Catholicism and aboriginal

Uto-Aztecan. One is based on the native official-church/fiesta-pueblo setting; the other on the shaman-ranchería fiesta–local group setting. The Christian elements, however, are heavily overlaid with aboriginal culture elements of dance, costume, and ritual technique; and despite the fact that the Catholic ceremonial calendar of events is adhered to, the resultant ceremonies are syncretic. The native fiestas, on the other hand, are clearly Indian. The symbolic entities here include the souls of the dead (who are greatly feared and given rich ceremonial recognition), animal entities associated with the dead (the owl with male, the fox with female, and a bird with children's souls; see Section on Folklore below). References to sun and moon deities may also be noted at times. The ritual importance of the rain dance (the *dutúburi*), the sacrifice of animals, the corn beer offerings, and flute and drum music, together with Dionysian abandon in drinking and sexual behavior are Indian in form, spirit, and function.

862

Catholic religious elements include: a vocabulary of terms such as Jesus, Mary, God, hell, sin, and the names of some saints; universal use of a rosary and crucifix; the manner of making the sign of the cross; and an abbreviated church service led by a *maestro*. The church fiesta dances are carried out by a set of dancers called *matachines*, supported by *chapeones*, and led by a head dancer, the *monarco* (all Spanish terms) (fig. 19).

The ordinary Tarahumara knows little or nothing of Christian theology, except what he learns through the sermons of the *gobernador*, who pronounces obviously Jesuit-inspired principles of ideal social conduct, laced with stereotyped references to Jesus, Mary, and the Devil.

The concept of an important god-figure, called Onorúame or Tata Dioshi (dios, in Spanish), contains a mixture of Christian and Indian ideas. While he is said to look like a handsome bearded man, he has a particular liking for corn beer, white oxen, and goats, and occasionally visits humans to request sacrifices and fiestas. The association of Onorúame with Jesus is strengthened by the common use of the crucifix by priest-doctors in their curing rituals. Mary is identified, somewhat vaguely, with a female deity (the moon?), a counterpart to Onorúame.

The Christian devil is an important figure and is occasionally associated with Chamúku, an aboriginal evil being who lives in a whirlpool or a deep cave and who steals souls, causing illness and strife.

The deep intertwining of Catholic and Indian concepts is manifested in the patio arrangements for the curing fiestas. The main altar with its three crosses and offerings to Onorúame has its aboriginal counterpart in a smaller altar, erected opposite it, which is for the souls of the dead. A third, tiny altar for the owl and fox spirits is also included.

Major church fiestas are celebrated on the following dates: Guadalupe (December 12), Noche Buena (December 25), Pascua Reyes

Fig. 20—CHANTER OFFICIATING AT FIELD CURING FIESTA, SANTA ANITA PUEBLO

(January 6), Holy Week, Easter, and Candelaria (February 2).

Ranchería fiestas are of various kinds: curing ceremonies for the health of animals, men, and crops; for rain; for good weather; first-fruit fiestas (green corn) and harvest ceremonies; and a series of fiestas for the dead (fig. 20).

Folklore

Aboriginal religious beliefs center about the concept of the soul (especially soul-loss as a cause of illness in man and animals), certain malignant spirit entities (*disagíki, rusíwari*—tiny, birdlike beings), a water serpent, *korimáka* (a devil-like being), souls of the dead, and witchcraft and sorcery.

The wind is personified as a good being, the whirlwind as an evil one. Whirlpool-beings are evil, fat, and piglike, and can cause disease (seize souls). The rainbow is sent by evil underground beings; a shooting star is a sorcerer flying to seize souls. Owls, snakes, certain birds, toads, lizards, and other animals are feared in connection with

863

native concepts of disease. There is a rich body of animal tales and others related to the mythological past.

Sickness and Curing

Souls of the recent dead, contact with malignant beings and animals, and even ordinary persons (in dreams) can cause illness in both man and beast. Thus, disease and its causes are related to the native religious belief system. Doctors (*owirúame*) are therefore also priests. Curing ceremonies (see vol. 6, Art. 20, fig. 8) involve the whole elaborate fiesta pattern with its sacrifices, offerings, drinking, singing, and dancing. Some owirúame practice curing by extracting maggots or bits of wood or stone from ailing parts. At times simple herb remedies are prescribed. A few peyote shamans still exist who cure by ritual eating of peyote. Sorcerers (*sukurúame*) are greatly feared and respected (see vol. 6, Art. 20, fig. 7), for they cause illness by seizing souls in dreams (*sepawúmera*, 'to eat the soul') and only they can effectively combat other sorcerers.

Cosmogony and Cosmology

The blendings and blurrings of Catholic and pagan beliefs make it difficult to lift out Tarahumara theological concepts; they are not systematized or well understood. In general, God (Onorúame) made the world and regulates it. At first the sun was too close to the earth, burning and scorching it, but six mythical beings danced the *dutúburi* and so moved the sun back. Men and animals were made from clay. A heaven and a hell exist. The dead journey slowly after death toward heaven if they have been "good." Heaven is apparently much like this earth.

AESTHETIC AND RECREATIONAL PATTERNS
Arts and Crafts

The aesthetic and artistic aspects of Tarahumara life are not highly developed or organized. The only notable exception is in the field of the religious ceremonial, where heavy acculturation is prominent.

The culture is practical and materialistic in orientation, and the considerable leisure at times available is not often used by Tarahumara to pursue aesthetic values. They prefer to sleep, hunt, fish, or advance practical matters by making hoe or ax handles, hide rope, or split logs. Not least, they are quite capable of doing nothing, all by themselves, for hours at a stretch.

Painting and sculpture are almost entirely lacking; they appear only in the occasional crude carving seen on wooden crosses, and in the painting of the body on ceremonial occasions. Pots, containers, spoons, houses, and other items of material culture are of simple, functional character.

Aboriginal design elements found in body painting (zigzag and dots) and in pottery, blankets, head ribbons, and sashes (geometric, repetitive motifs) are obviously those of the general ranchería Uto-Aztecan tradition.

Music and Dance

Music shows the existence of two traditions, Indian and Spanish, but the Indian is still clearly aboriginal while the Spanish has been subtly Indianized. In the ranchería setting, the flute and drum, the deer-hoof rattle, and the wood hand-rattle accompany the chanting, which is made up of short repetitive phrases. In the church fiestas, the violin and guitar accompany the dancers. However, the Tarahumara are not averse to mixing the two modes. In larger ranchería fiestas, before and during the Catholic ceremonial fiestas, the dancers and musicians can practice and perform alongside their aboriginal counterparts (dancing *dutúburi*). Similarly, during the church fiestas the aboriginal dancers and their musical accompanists perform.

The dance (see vol. 6, Art. 9, fig. 10) is the most complicated, elaborate, and organized of Tarahumara activities. In church

FIG. 21—BOYS PRACTICING FOR HOLY WEEK CEREMONIES, CHOGUITA PUEBLO

FIG. 22—MAN, DRESSED AS A WOMAN, TEASING WOMEN AT A FUNERAL FIESTA, NOROGACHIC PUEBLO

fiestas various troops of dancers elaborately dressed in fantastic Spanish-Indian folk costume (*matachines*) are organized and sponsored by *chapeones*. These dances are simplified versions of old Spanish folk dances. Lines of dancers execute simple parade maneuvers, circling and turning according to the directions of the leader (*monarco*). Another important group of dancers, *pascoleros*, wearing deer-hoof rattles and metal-rattle belts, lead dance groups of men and boys whose bodies during Easter fiestas are elaborately painted (fig. 21).

The most important aboriginal dance is the dutúburi, which is danced in the patio before an altar in ranchería fiestas. The leader is a *chanter*, who uses a rattle and hums repetitive short phrases. The men attending the fiesta dance in single line to the left of the chanter and move back and forth a few steps from the altar. The women meanwhile line up in a single file on the right-hand side of the chanter and move horizontally across the patio, executing a simple step and holding hands.

Humor and Games

The following remarks are derived principally from the context of the tesgüinada. Here the humor is overwhelmingly sexual in content. Brothers- and sisters-in-law tease each other by making lewd remarks, wrestling, and touching of sexual parts, and making loud requests for sexual intercourse. The wearing of women's costume and comical imitation of female behavior by men, and, obversely, women imitating men drinking and dancing cause much mirth (fig. 22). Humorous jests about another's sexual inadequacy, or inability to run well, excite much witty repartee. Anyone tripping, slurring speech, or flatulating evokes amused comment. Some of the situations joked about have failure as a theme; for example, a gobernador making a serious speech makes an accidental pun, or a man goes out to fish and comes back empty-handed.

The Tarahumara take great pride in their prowess as foot-runners, and consequently races (see vol. 6, Art. 10, fig. 2) are the

FIG. 23—A TARAHUMAR CALL. (From Lumholtz, 1902, 1: 160.)

most exciting, competitive of sports. Large interpueblo races are matters of great importance and require considerable preparation. Races can also be informally arranged among participants of a tesgüinada.

Races are run along a marked course, usually up and down a river valley, range from 2 to 12 miles in extent, and last from a few hours to a full day and night. The race (*dalahípu*) is run between competitive teams of men who must kick a wooden ball along the course the required number of laps. Betting is keen and wagers include almost anything of value—beads, cloth, blankets, or animals. The women's footrace (*dowérami*) is like the men's except for a wooden hoop and stick instead of a ball.

The running down of deer and chase of squirrels can be considered as sports.

Cuatro (*dihibapa*) is a game similar to quoits. It is played by casting small disks of rounded stones or potsherds into shallow holes spaced from 20 to 100 feet apart. Another simple game is throwing sticks (*kuhubála*). Each player casts a 2-foot oak stick at a goal stick, attempting to come as close as possible to it. *Quince* is a parchesi-like game played with four marked sticks and two pebbles as counters. The idea is to move the pebbles along a rectangular course to a goal. The sticks are thrown to indicate the number of moves to make. *Tábatci* is a dicelike game played with a single bone counter with points counted according to the side it falls upon in the cast (see vol. 6, Art. 10, fig. 14). *Palillo* is a man's game much like lacrosse. It is a stick-and-ball game, played on an unmarked field, with almost no rules or restrictions. The object is to bat the ball into the air where it can be caught by hand. (For other games, see vol. 6, Art. 10, figs. 6–8).

Patterns of Etiquette

As the basic pattern of Tarahumara life is one of simplicity and isolation, easy, relaxed, graceful manners are not a feature of interpersonal relations. Visiting patterns are quite formalized. It is impolite to enter a house directly on making a visit; one either sits down near the house and waits to be recognized (fig. 23), or shouts out a salutation in warning of his presence. The host invariably offers a visitor some food, usually pinole. In social gatherings, one personally salutes each guest separately with an abbreviated handshake, and murmurs *kwíra* (Dios cuida). Corn beer is always politely offered and politely refused before final acceptance. One always offers to share food with others present, and this is never refused. In the acceptance of food or favors from others, thanks (*matétera ba*) are always given.

It is considered impolite to stop, or notice, a person and ask where he is going or what his mission is. Persons traveling avoid contact with strangers. It is not considered proper to remain long at a visit, or appear to want to spend the night in another's home; this is a basic violation of privacy.

Native officials, shamans, and chanters are very respectfully and formally greeted, deferred to, and served separately in gatherings.

Narcotics and Stimulants

Peyote (*hículi*), a cactus, the dried top of which is eaten, contains hallucinogenic properties. It was used at one time in a special curing ritual and in sorcery by feared shamans, but this practice has largely disappeared (see Bennett and Zingg, 1935, pp. 291–95).

Tobacco is highly prized and enjoyed. It is smoked in cigarette form, wrapped in cornhusks. No Tarahumara fiesta or tesgüinada is complete without tobacco. The smoking is not ritually formalized in gesture or procedure. Ordinary tobacco is grown in a garden; wild varieties are also occasionally used.

The drinking of corn beer (*tesgüino*) to the point of profound inebriation is an outstanding recreational pattern of the Tarahumara, and is the very core of the fiesta and the tesgüinada. The serving of tesgüino to guests is a formal matter, accompanied first by polite refusals, then acceptance. The host must see to it that there is enough corn beer for continuous distribution lasting many hours (fig. 24). The beer is always blessed by chanters and used ritually as part of the sacrifice, which also includes various foods. Like tobacco, it has sacred properties and is used in curing man, animals and crops.

Fiesta Patterns

The various kinds of religious fiestas, church and ranchería types, and the work tesgüinada, have been described above; here only the social and recreational aspects are reviewed. These ceremonial and work

Fig. 24—DONOR OF A TESGÜINADA BEGINNING FIRST FORMAL DISTRIBUTION OF CORN BEER TO WOMEN, CHOGUITA PUEBLO

occasions, together with the Sunday pueblo reunions, are the essential integrating mechanisms for the otherwise dispersed, independent Tarahumara.

Fiestas and tesgüinadas permit a spontaneity, gaiety, and abandon otherwise quite lacking in the life of these reserved people. The shyness and fear of outsiders, as well as members of the opposite sex, is weakened, then broken by heavy drinking. Jokes, gossip, teasing, and actual physical contact are intensely enjoyed; outside the permissive fiesta setting they are rigidly excluded. Young people meet and form liaisons and thereby gain sexual experience. Prestige is sought by some individuals, who prove their prowess as runners, dancers, or as donors of important ceremonials.

LIFE CYCLE AND PERSONALITY DEVELOPMENT

When pregnant, women carry on their usual tasks until the last possible moment. In

867

many cases as her time nears, the woman will go alone to some secluded part of the mountains, there prepare a bed of grass, and, with the limb of a tree as support, give birth in a crouched position. Sometimes a female relative or even her husband will accompany her. The umbilical cord is cut with a stone knife and the afterbirth buried in a hole. The child is then washed and wrapped in cotton cloth. Infanticide is practiced for a variety of reasons, psychological as well as economic.

When a male child is three days old, or a female four days, a shaman performs a special ceremony to safeguard the health of the child and parents. The ceremony is repeated three times for boys and four times for girls, at intervals of two or three weeks. Then the child is baptized and named. The institution of godparent seems more a formal than functional one.

The child is breast fed freely at intervals determined by the child's hunger, for periods up to three years. A mother is not embarrassed to breast feed her infant before others. Usually after six months the child is also fed corn gruel; after a year, cooked meat is included in the diet. The infant is constantly kept in close bodily contact with the mother. It sleeps in her arms at night. After two months the child is carried on the mother's back in a square of cotton cloth or blanket. At two years the child is permitted a great deal of freedom to rove about the house with little bodily restriction. The father often plays or cares for the child if the mother is occupied.

Bowel and bladder training is informal and not a focus of tension, unless a child reaches the fourth year and is still incontinent. Until the age of six, the treatment of boys and girls is very similar, except that girls are always fully clothed and boys may run about nude in warm weather. Sleeping habits are extremely irregular even for the very young; children are permitted to stay awake until they fall asleep of their own accord. However, after the age of five or

six many children may experience partial or even total parental neglect when tesgüinada attendance, work in distant fields, and herding activities disperse older family members. Young children very soon learn to prepare food, cook, or forage for food. A strong training in independence begins here.

Children as soon as possible are made responsible for care of property, animals, and land. A condition of potential independence from direct parental supervision is reached at an early age—from seven to ten years—by many children, both in the psychological sense of feeling independent and in the physical ability to be so.

The games of children after the age of five or six reflect the adult division of labor. Girls' play consists of keeping house, preparing food, and caring for their corncob dolls. Boys play at yoking oxen, plowing, making tiny houses and corrales, hunting, fishing, hiking, and throwing stones and sticks. Gangs of boys are occasionally formed, but by no means all boys have such an experience; isolation and heavy responsibilities interfere. As soon as a child is old enough to assist the parents in any practical task, it does so.

Between the ages of 12 and 15 is the average period of transition from childhood to young adulthood; for girls it is somewhat earlier.

Punishment, ideally, is never corporal. Stereotyped admonitions are supposed to correct behavior. Only native officials are permitted to whip those guilty of serious delinquencies such as loss of property, theft, fighting or continual disobedience (fig. 25).

Girls are taught to be modest in dress and never expose their body after the age of six or seven. Even after marriage, the woman never undresses before her husband and she engages in sexual intercourse clothed. Girls become markedly shy and even fearful of men and boys at this time. This basic shyness continues as a feature of the female aspect when in the company of a male.

She never looks directly at a man, but gazes to one side. Strong overt and covert attitudes of both parents teach the girl to avoid potential sexual experiences. Their severe reserve breaks down finally during the tesgüinadas under the influence of corn beer. Sexual matters are not discussed outside the tesgüinada setting, and are usually avoided. Girls may not even be warned of the onset of menstruation, which then causes them much anxiety and confusion. Menstrual taboos seem absent. Active sexual participation begins for boys with full tesgüinada participation, which itself signifies attainment of adult status, for to attend is to work and thus fully to participate in an adult role. One is now clearly marriageable. Masturbation is commonly practiced by boys and is not considered harmful, though it is the subject of an occasional humorous sally. Adult activities are already covered above.

In old age the independent, proud Tarahumara attempt to care for themselves as long as possible, maintaining a separate household apart from their married children. Even the handicapped and the ill may insist on living alone; their sons or daughters come to visit them with gifts of food or clothing.

Burial of the dead was formerly in caves, but the more Christianized are buried in cemeteries. The newly dead are greatly feared, for they are believed to hover nearby, and until they are helped along on their long journey to heaven by a cycle of funeral fiestas (three for men and four for women), the habitation and its contents, the immediate family and animals, and all those in contact with the corpse, must be purified and protected by ritual curing.

Tarahumara temperament, male and female, is characterized by a strong ego-centered, independent, and individualized orientation. They are sensitive to any form of rebuke. Their primary defense in conflict situations is withdrawal in some form, social or emotional. They are particularly

Fig. 25—GOBERNADOR DELIVERING CORRECTIVE ADVICE TO CHILDREN, BASIWARE PUEBLO

sensitive to being taken advantage of, and demand redress for any wrong felt. Individual-centered values often override family- or group-centered obligations.

Annual Cycle

The following schedule holds for rancherías located near canyons.

January: Early in the month wheat is sown. Men are engaged in making fences and corrals; women card wool and make blankets. At this time the majority of the families, those with goats and sheep, are living in their canyon caves or houses. Men ascend to the sierras to hunt deer, squirrels, and rabbits.

February: By late February preparations are made in the fields in the sierras for the sowing of corn. Families now make numerous trips during the week from canyon to sierra sites. Wood is cut all through the winter in preparation for use in the construction of houses, storage, bins and fences.

869

March: In the beginning of March many families are still living in the barrancas, but most work is done in the sierras. The ground is fertilized and plowed with oxen. It is a time for work tesgüinadas, combining religious elements with practical help. The fencing-off of fields is done by cooperative labor. Corn-storage bins and houses are constructed. In late March the families have all moved to their sierra rancherías.

April: Early in April men and boys follow plowmen, planting corn seeds in the furrows, using digging sticks. Various tesgüinadas and curing fiestas are held. All animals have now been taken to the sierras. Men still hunt and fish; women make blankets, baskets, and pots.

May–June: Early in May the planting of corn is completed. There is little or no hunting, but some fishing. The fruit trees in the canyons begin to produce, and orchard owners descend to gather fruit. Wild vegetable products are now available in abundance.

July–August: The planting of a bean crop in upland fields occurs in July. Tesgüinadas accompany the plowing and, later, weeding in bean fields, as well as the hoeing and weeding of corn.

September: This is the best month for hunting deer, which are now fat. Two to four men often cooperate in running down deer. House repairing is common. The first green corn is gathered, and first-fruit ceremonies held. Fodder for animals is collected from the fields.

October: The mature corn and beans are now intensively harvested. Tesgüinadas are very frequent. Hunting and fishing are still favored activities of men. Wild vegetables are still abundant. Sheep are now shorn.

November–December: In November preparations for the major church ceremonials of December and January begin; ceremonial officials are nominated, and dancers and musicians practice. Animals are moved to their winter canyon quarters again. Much wood cutting is done. A limited number of families plant wheat in mid-December.

REFERENCES

Alegre, 1841
Basauri, 1929
Bennett and Zingg, 1935
Champion, 1955
Fried, 1952, 1953, 1961
Lumholtz, 1902
Passin, 1942, 1943
Pennington, 1963
Plancarte, 1954
Treutlein, 1949
Zingg, 1942

42. Contemporary Ethnography of Baja California, Mexico

ROGER C. OWEN

OVER THE ENTIRE PENINSULA of Baja California, Mexico, no single well-integrated aboriginal culture now exists. South of the 30th parallel there are no Indians whatsoever excepting small groups of Yaqui introduced from Sonora (Hohenthal, 1951, p. 3; Cook, 1937; Aschmann, 1959). Between the 30th parallel and the international border, however, there are survivors of four, possibly five, aboriginal groups each characterized by a different dialect and different self-name: Cocopa, Tipai, Paipai, Kiliwa and, possibly, Koʔaɫ.[1] All these are members of the Yuman branch of the Hokan family; all the dialects are mutually unintelligible or nearly

so; and Kiliwa appears to be the most divergent.

The Cocopa, until recently resident on the Colorado River delta, have been moving to San Luis, Sonora. As there are only one or two families left around El Mayor, Baja California, this article will not be further concerned with them (cf. Gifford, 1933; W. H. Kelly, 1942, 1944, 1949).

The other four groups inhabit the central highlands of the northern part of the peninsula (Hinton and Owen, 1957). The Kiliwa, southernmost of the groups (about 50 in number), are scattered in and around the Arroyo Leon area on the northern slope of the Sierra San Pedro Martir (Meigs, 1939) (fig. 2,*a*). They are presently selling their lands to Mexican ranchers; many of the Indians are now working on Mexican ranches and some are taking up residence with the Paipai. The principal Paipai settlement is around the former Dominican Mission, Santa Catalina Virgen y Martir (Meigs, 1935), where approximately 150 individuals

---

[1] Tipai have been called Mexican Diegueno, Eastern Diegueno, and Southern Diegueno; "Tipai" is what they usually call themselves. The Paipai were originally labeled "Akwa 'ala" (Gifford and Lowie, 1928); Paipai represents their 'self-name.' Linguistic analysis suggests that Koʔaɫ is a southern variant of Tipai (J. Joel, personal communication); social analysis suggests that a group by this name has distinct aboriginal ethnic identity.

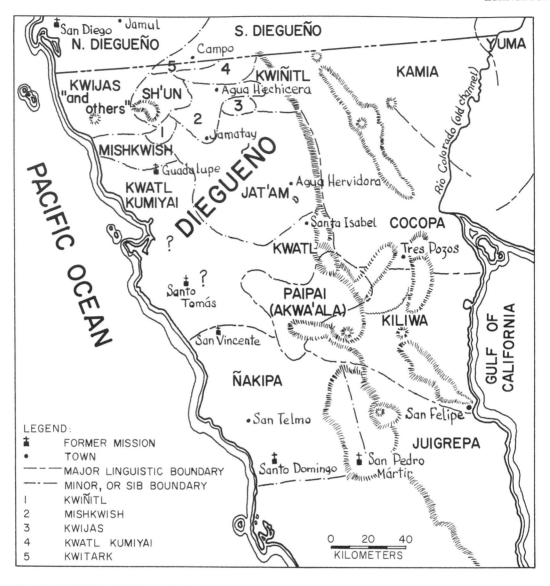

FIG. 1—NATIVE GROUPS IN NORTHERN BAJA CALIFORNIA. (As reported by Meigs, 1939.)

now live (fig. 2,*b*). Another settlement of Paipai, with many resident Kiliwa, is in the western end of the Trinidad Valle at a ranchería named San Isidoro (approximately 50 people). Resident also at Santa Catarina, as the former mission is now called, are about 30 Koꞌał, thoroughly intermarried with the Paipai. The Tipai, the northernmost of the groups, are scattered in the

mountains between Santa Catarina and the international border; a major settlement is at La Huerta de los Indios (approximately 75 individuals). There are not over 500 Indians in Baja California.

All these populations are in mountainous areas: the Kiliwa in the Sierra San Pedro Martir; the other three in the Sierra Juarez. Settlements are found in interior valleys

a

b

Fig. 2—SETTLEMENTS IN BAJA CALIFORNIA. *a*, Kiliwa household at Rancho Los Quatros on the north flank of the Sierra San Pedro Martir. *b*, Houses and fields, Santa Catarina.

Fig. 3—A KILIWA FAMILY. The man on the right is well over 6 feet tall.

from 2500 to 4500 feet. These valleys are the result of erosion on the basic granite of the sierras (Shor and Roberts, 1956; Allen, Silver, and Stehli, 1960). The entire region is desert with either Upper or Lower Sonoran vegetation, depending on elevation; the crests of the mountains are covered by pine forests. Rainfall is scant and unreliable; strong winds are frequent. Owing to low rainfall and very early frosts the area is poorly suited to agriculture; absence of grasses and desirable fodder makes it marginal for cattle.

The Indians were first intensively contacted by Europeans with the establishment of a chain of Dominican missions in the last years of the 18th century (Meigs, 1935; Engelhardt, 1929; Martínez, 1956). The missionaries were driven out in the middle of the 19th century, and the Indians apparently retired to mountain canyons. They were regarded as dangerous to travelers in the early part of the 19th century (Thwaites, 1905, p. 207) and were still considered camp thieves in 1906 (North, 1908, 1910), but little is really known of them during this period. They played a minor role in an American invasion attempt in 1910 (Aldrete, 1958, pp. 52, 74; Martínez, 1958, p. 11; Owen, 1963a).

Meigs (1939) has written a reliable but brief report on the Kiliwa; Philip Drucker (1941) has compiled a culture-element distribution for the Paipai (Akwa 'ala) and the Tipai; and Hohenthal (1951, 1960) has done work on the Kiliwa, Paipai, and the Tipai. An earlier paper is confused (Gifford and Lowie, 1928). An excellent attempt to

874

Fig. 4—SHELLING CORN, SANTA CATARINA, BAJA CALIFORNIA. The granitic boulder serves as one house wall.

reconstruct aboriginal linguistic distributions has been made (Massey, 1949); and a few popular descriptions have been written (cf. Henderson, 1952a, 1952b). Anyone contemplating work in Baja California should be aware of an extensive bibliography published by Barrett (1957) and an excellent travel guide by Gerhard and Gulick (1958). During 1958–59, the University of California at Los Angeles carried out an intensive research program in ethnology, archaeology, linguistics, and physical anthropology at Santa Catarina, Baja California, under the direction of J. B. Birdsell.

All the Indians participate in either small-scale farming, ranching, wage labor, or some combination of these. Some Indians

work as cowboys at Mexican ranches; some work as goat or sheep herders; many families go to Mexicali in the winter to pick cotton. With few exceptions, all are extremely poor. Small additions to both income and diet are made by hunting (deer and rabbits) and by collecting wild foods (acorns, pine nuts, cactus fruits, berries, seeds). Deer and pine nuts are usually sold. Basic dietary staples include large, thin wheat tortillas and frijoles, sometimes supplemented by greens, wild foods, and (rarely) by meat, usually rabbit. The diet, on the whole, is monotonous and nutritionally deficient (Owen, 1962).

Most of the Indians live on "reserves," land not legally theirs by federal act (Ho-

Fɪɢ. 5—PAIPAI POTTER AT WORK, SANTA CATARINA, BAJA CALIFORNIA

henthal, 1951, p. 31) but sometimes protected for them by local Mexican civil officials. Santa Catarina is the largest of these (approximately 200 sq. km.); most of the others have only a few acres. When not occupied by Indians, these reserves are often taken over by Mexicans. On the larger reserves household units are widely scattered; the smaller sites often consist of only one. Households are composed of usually two or more wattle-and-daub *jacales,* each of only one room; the house walls are of willow branches, the roofs thatched with yucca. Many Indians are now building houses of adobe bricks.

Most of the Paipai know most or all of the Kiliwa personally; they also know most, if not all, of the Tipai. Kiliwa and Tipai, on the other hand, are often strangers. Santa Catarina is frequently a common meeting ground for members of all the groups.

Most technological skills stem from the European farming and cattle complex; there is a strong American "cowboy culture" influence on the Indians. Native pottery (paddle and anvil; fig. 5) and agave-fiber netting are still made and used. Most of the knowledge concerning use of wild foods still exists; some older men know how to make war clubs, rabbit sticks, bows and arrows, and other such items (Michelsen, 1967). They are now made only for tourists.[2]

Individual ownership of land prevails though the land is not supposed to be either

[2] Approximately 200 items were collected and deposited in the Museum of Man, San Diego, California; a smaller collection is at the Department of Anthropology, University of California, Los Angeles.

876

sold or bequeathed to non-Indians. Land lying fallow may be used by any Indian.

All the Indians participate to some degree in the cash economy in that most staple items (wheat, flour, shortening, beans, coffee, sugar) must be purchased either from small Indian-owned stores on the reserves or from traveling salesmen (*fiuqueros*). Cash comes into the economy through sale of cattle, wage work, sale of harvested crops, and miscellaneous sources.

There are remnants of approximately 10 named, patrilocal bands in the area. Residence is ideally patrilocal though more frequently bilocal; marriage takes the form of serial monogamy usually without ceremony. Inheritance is bilateral for property and possessions, patrilineal for names. Exogamy is extended, ideally, to all known bilateral relatives. Each dialect group has a slightly different system of kinship terms but all are basically Yuman in type. *Compadrazgo* exists, stemming from baptism, but no lasting bonds are established by it. Each reserve has a headman (fig. 6), called "general" on the larger ones, who is usually elected; he ordinarily has little or no power except when representing his own kin group. The primary function of these individuals is to serve as a point of articulation with the outside world—primarily with Mexican officials and tourists. Indians have voted in federal and local elections and regard themselves as Mexican citizens, despite the fact that they contrast themselves with "Mexicans."

Religion is non-Catholic and centers around witchcraft, ghosts, and curing. Formerly there were curing shamans who sometimes obtained their power through the use of Jimson weed; now the Indians rely on Mexican spiritualists for determination and curing of supernaturally caused illness. Illness is also treated through a large herbal (Owen, 1963b). Commemorative fiestas for the dead are sometimes held among the Tipai; the deceased are no long-

FIG. 6—JUAN ARVALLO, FORMER "GENERAL" OF SANTA CATARINA, ADDRESSING THE ASSEMBLED MEMBERS OF THE RESERVE

er cremated but buried, although their personal possessions and the houses in which they lived are usually destroyed. Important days in the Catholic calendar are sometimes occasions for social dances, and graves are decorated on All Souls' Day. No other religious ceremonies exist. Protestant missionaries are now active in the area, with some success.

Gambling (playing cards) is the most common amusement; dances and horse-races are held on occasion. Dances take the form of either aboriginal line-dances accom-

FIG. 7—SINGERS AND DANCERS, SANTA CATARINA. The Tipai man with the large gourd rattle is the last native singer in Baja California; he learned to sing among the Mohave of the Colorado River, at the turn of the 19th century. He is accompanied by two Paipai. (Photographed by Michelsen.)

panied by a singer with a gourd rattle or are ranchero-style with a guitar. The last native singer (fig. 7) is now 80 years of age (Michelsen and Owen, 1967).

Everyone who can buy them smokes cigarettes, but drinking (tequila) is disesteemed and fairly rare; no narcotics are used and no alcoholic beverages are made.

Adults are inhibited and suspicious, and intensive interaction among them is usually confined to the immediate family. Fighting often results when men are drinking but only rarely results in serious injury. Youths, all of whom learn their native languages before Spanish, become independent in their early teens; girls are often married at 15. Hostilities between adults of different kin groups are frequent and often of long standing; such hostilities sometimes take the form of accusations of witchcraft. Competitive relationships between families are common; group cohesion, beyond the immediate kin group, is slight. Though schools are to be found on the larger reserves, they often have no teachers; less than 10 per cent of the Indians are literate to any degree, though most of the adults are fluent in Spanish.

These Indians still exist as population clusters because they have faced no pressure for their land from Mexicans. Such pressure is now growing.

REFERENCES

Aldrete, 1958
Allen, Silver, and Stehli, 1960
Aschmann, 1959
Barrett, 1957
Cook, S. F., 1937
Drucker, P., 1941
Engelhardt, 1929
Gerhard and Gulick, 1958
Gifford, E. W., 1933
——— and Lowie, 1928
Henderson, 1952a, 1952b
Hinton and Owen, 1957

Hohenthal, 1951, 1960
Kelly, W. H., 1942, 1944, 1949
Martínez, 1956, 1958
Massey, 1949
Meigs, 1935, 1939
Michelsen, 1967
——— and Owen, 1967
North, 1908, 1910
Owen, 1960a, 1960b, 1962, 1963a, 1963b, 1965
Pattie, 1905
Shor and Roberts, 1956
Thwaites, 1905

43. Remnant Tribes of Sonora: Opata, Pima, Papago, and Seri

THOMAS B. HINTON

Survivors of these northwest Mexican groups are distributed as shown in figure 1. Pima Bajo speech survives in the Sierra Madre and among a few families at Onabas on the lower Yaqui River. A few identifiable Pima descendants live around Ures in the Sonora valley. Opata and the related Joba languages have become extinct within the last 30 years. However, the inhabitants of the villages of Tepupa, Terapa, and Ponida, and individual families in some of the former Opata towns, are still considered Indians although culturally there is little to distinguish them from non-Indians (Hinton, 1959; Johnson, 1950; Owen, 1959). The Sonora Papago are extensions of five of the dialect groups of the Arizona Papago and are nearly identical in culture to their relatives north of the border.[1]

The Seri survive as a single community composed of the amalgamated remnants of several former Serian groups. The semi-permanent fish camp of Desemboque, Sonora, is their principal settlement with several smaller camps occupied seasonally.

Pima and Papago belong to the Piman, and Opata and Joba to the Tara-cahitan branches of Uto-Aztecan; and the Seri language has been classified with Hokan-Coahuiltecan (Mason, 1940).

Habitat ranges from the oak- and pine-covered mesas of the mountain Pima, through the well-watered river valleys of the Opata and the desert basins of the Papago, to the almost rainless coastal desert of the Seri.

The Opata and Pima Bajo were concentrated into missions in the 17th century, and the Upper Pima groups, who later became the southern Papago, in the next century. Except for a brief revolt of the Pima and Papago in 1752, these tribes, and especially the Opata, readily accepted Spanish patterns. All underwent considerable pressure

[1] I am indebted to David Brugge, William King, and Edward Moser for information drawn from their knowledge of the Pima Bajo, Papago, and Seri, respectively.

Fig. 1—MAP OF SONORA, SHOWING LOCATION OF PIMA BAJO, OPATA, PAPAGO, AND SERI INDIANS IN 1960

from the Apache—a factor which may have been important in their acculturation. Since mission days a continuing gradual assimilation into the general population of Sonora has been taking place.

The Seri were brought under mission influence for a brief period in the 18th century. The attempt was unsuccessful and they returned to their old nomadic life on the Gulf coast, leading an independent existence well into the 20th century.

No population figures can be given for the linguistically extinct and much Mestizoized Opata and Joba. An estimate of 4000 would include all those in the area who retain some degree of Indian identification (Hinton, 1959). There are an estimated 1400–1500 Pima Bajo: 1000 in the Maicoba–Yepachic area, 200–300 in the area of Dolores, Chihuahua, 120 in the Onabas group (*ibid.*). There are about 300 Papago living in Sonora, and as many more who are natives of Mexico now residing in Arizona. The Seri number slightly over 300.

The Opata were visited by Bandelier (1890) and Hrdlička (1904a), who published notes on the group. J. B. Johnson (1950) followed a visit to the area with a valuable paper reconstrucing Opata culture from ethnohistory. Owen in 1955 studied Opata descendants in a Sonora village (Owen, 1959); in the same year I surveyed assimilation among Opata, Joba, and Pima Bajo (Hinton, 1959).

Lumholtz passed through the Pima Bajo area in the 1890's and commented on the Indians (1902). Brugge visited these people in the 1950's and has published some observations on the Pima (Mason and Brugge, 1958). No major field work has been attempted. Lumholtz made an extended trip to the Sonora Papago area in 1907 and recorded (1912) distribution and still existing customs. The Papago, in which the Sonora group is included, have been adequately described by Underhill (1939, 1946), Joseph, Spicer, and Chesky (1949), Nolasco (1965), and others.

McGee visited the Seri in 1894–95 for a short time, but his report (1898) does not give a complete or an accurate picture of the Seri. Kroeber spent six days with the group in 1930 and made some comparisons with surrounding peoples (1931). Griffen worked at Desemboque for several weeks in 1955 and has written an excellent summary of modern Seri culture (1959). Linguistic studies have been carried on by the Mosers of the Summer Institute of Linguistics. A comprehensive Seri ethnography is still needed.

SUBSISTENCE SYSTEMS AND FOOD PATTERNS

Opata, Pima, and Papago are subsistence farmers, some of whom own a few cattle. Wage labor is now a major source of income in all these groups, and a steady shift in this direction continues. Food patterns for these agricultural Indians are of conventional north Mexican types.

The Seri since about 1930 have been engaged in independent commercial fishing; the product is sold for cash to buyers who truck it to the urban market. Now subsidiary, but still important, is the taking of game, sea turtle, and shellfish, and the gathering of wild plant products. Seri diet consists of fish and wild foods heavily supplemented by coffee, sugar, white flour, and other commercial items.

SETTLEMENT PATTERNS

Settlement patterns of the Opata and Onabas Pima are not distinct from those of other rural Sonorans. The Pima of the Sierra Madre live in scattered ranches and come to Maicoba, Yepachic, or Yecora to trade or to attend to religious needs. Mexican Papago may live in small rancherías or even in the towns in the area. In the Pozo Verde area near the border some seasonal movement to flood-farm fields still occurs. Houses in these three groups are variations of the conventional Mexican ranch types of adobe or wattle-and-daub dwellings. Some mountain Pima utilize caves.

881

Fig. 2—SERI WOMAN OF PUNTA CHUECA, SONORA, WITH BASKET AND SHELL NECKLACES. (Photographed by Donald Cordry, 1963.)

At Desemboque Seri live in single-family dwellings immediately adjacent to the beach. Here the house type is a wattle-and-daub *jacal* (hut) similar to that of poorer Mestizos. At intervals during the year groups composed of several families move to temporary fishing or gathering camps along the coast. Here dwellings are the traditional brush windbreaks.

TECHNOLOGY

Opata, Pima, and Papago technology closely follows that of non-Indians. Among the Seri, fishermen employ a plank dory propelled by a sail or an outboard motor; chief fishing gear is hook and line with explosives used to secure bait. Sea turtles are taken at night with a harpoon and lantern.

Pottery is made by Papago women by the paddle-and-anvil method; Opata and Pima use coil and scrape techniques (Owen, 1957). Pottery is now seldom made by the Seri. Twilled baskets and hats are woven by Opata (fig. 4) and Pima women (Brugge, 1956). The weaving takes place in a semisubterranean hut known as a *huki*, which is supposed to keep the palm-weaving material moist. Seri basketry (see vol. 6, Art. 6, figs. 9, 13) is the coil type (fig. 5). The Seri manufacture other items, such as pelican-skin blankets and shell necklaces, which, like much of their basketry, are disposed of to travelers.

The dress of Opata, Pima, and Papago is wholly that of the rural Mexican. Long hair is worn by men only among the Seri, where it hangs loose or is braided. Seri men with long hair wear a kilt of colored cloth over their otherwise conventional trousers. Seri women wear a distinctive, long-sleeved, full-length dress. Face painting (figs. 5, 6) is still employed, largely by females.

ECONOMY

Seasonal labor in the new agricultural areas of western Sonora is well established among Pima and Opata. Pima also work in lumber

FIG. 3—SERI BLIND WOMAN, PUNTA CHUECA, SONORA. (Photographed by Donald Cordry, 1963.)

883

FIG. 4—OPATA WOMEN SEATED IN FRONT OF A SEMI-SUBTERRANEAN
HUT (*HUKI*) USED WHILE WEAVING PALM LEAF, TEPUPA, SONORA

FIG. 5—SERI BASKET MAKER, DESEMBOQUE,
SONORA. Note face paint. (Photographed by Roger
C. Owen.)

Fɪɢ. 6—SERI INDIAN GIRLS WITH PAINTED FACES, PUNTA CHUECA, SONORA.
(Photographed by Donald Cordry, 1963.)

FIG. 7—SERI INDIANS AT PUNTA CHUECA, SONORA. (Photographed by Donald Cordry, 1963.)

mills in the sierra. Basic economic orientation of the Mexican Papago is toward wage work in Arizona. Agriculture in all these groups is becoming increasingly more marginal.

Among the Pima groups and the Papago, ejidos have been organized to protect remaining landholdings. Possession of such land rights tends to inhibit the complete dispersal of the Indian communities.

Consumption patterns are the same as those of non-Indians except among the Seri, where a system of kinship rights and obligations enters into the distribution of wealth (Griffen, 1959; E. Moser, personal communication).

SOCIAL ORGANIZATION

Opata family and kinship usages are completely Hispanicized. Those of the Pima Bajo are not well known but are apparently highly acculturated (Mason and Brugge, 1958). Papago family structure is patrilineal with both sibs and moieties present, and kinship terminology is Yuman (Underhill, 1939). It is believed that this system is somewhat more poorly preserved in Sonora than in Arizona. For a detailed account the reader is referred to Underhill (1939).

Seri retain native usages, and kinship appears to be the chief factor integrating the modern community. Terminology is Yuman and marriage is monogamous, with initial residence being patrilocal although this may shift later (Griffen, 1959; Moser, personal communication). Marriage is arranged by parents and is accompanied by an extended period in which a bride price of goods amounting to several hundred pesos in value is turned over to the family of the bride. Joking and avoidance relationships and gift-giving obligations are present among certain relatives. No unilateral kin groups occur (Griffen, 1959). Separate political organization survives nowhere except for remnants of village organization at the Papago rancherías of Pozo Verde, San Francisquito, and Quito-vac (W. King, personal communication). All the Indian groups are served by state or federal rural schools.

RELIGION

All groups but the Seri are nominal Catholics. Strictly native forms are no longer remembered among the Opata and Joba, but remnants of native practice are evident in Holy Week observations, which are roughly parallel, but much more secular and less formal, to those of the Yaqui (J. B. Johnson, 1950; Owen, 1958). Pima and Papago preserve some non-Christian forms; shamanism, sorcery, mythology, and at least one ceremony survive. The latter is the *viikita* or Papago harvest fiesta which is held at Quitovac, Sonora, in the late summer. Both Sonora and Arizona Papago of the Huhuwas dialect group participate (Underhill, 1946; King, personal communication).

Seri religion remains non-Christian and is not well known. Shamanism, however, is prominent, and myth cycles occur. The only ceremony which still takes place is a four-day observance performed for girls at the onset of puberty (Griffen, 1959; Hinton, 1955).

AESTHETIC AND RECREATIONAL PATTERNS

Fiesta and recreation follow general north Mexican patterns except among the Seri. Fiestas consist of visits to the church, processions, drinking, and social dancing. The Easter Passion play takes place in the Opata area; in some places the *matachin* dance occurs.

Among the Seri, a *pascola* dances on a board at the girl's puberty rites to the accompaniment of a singer who uses a tin can as a rattle. Native games are still played by the Seri and possibly by the Papago.

Distilled mescal is favored as an intoxicant by all groups. Tesgüino (corn beer) is made by mountain Pima.

LIFE CYCLE

Opata and Joba life cycles and socialization are conventional Mexican; that of the Pima is not known. Papago forms are discussed in detail by Joseph, Spicer, and Chesky (1949). The Seri retain native patterns in which rites of passage are still important. In at least two of these, those of puberty and death, a system of ceremonial sponsorship known as *amák* comes into play (Griffen, 1959).

ANNUAL CYCLE

The annual cycle of the Catholic farming groups follows the agricultural round and Catholic fiesta calendar. The day of San Francisco (October 4) is the most important religious holiday among the Papago and Pima Bajo, and most attend fiestas held at Magdalena and Maicoba on this date. For the Opata, Holy Week is the principal observance of the year. The Seri do not celebrate Catholic holidays.

REFERENCES

Bandelier, 1890
Brugge, 1956
Griffen, 1959
Hinton, 1955, 1959
Hrdlička, 1904a
Johnson, J. B., 1950
Joseph, Spicer, and Chesky, 1949
Kroeber, 1931
Lumholtz, 1902, 1912
McGee, 1898
Mason, 1940
—— and Brugge, 1958
Nolasco, 1965
Owen, 1957, 1958, 1959
Underhill, 1939, 1946

REFERENCES

Acosta, J. de
1590 Historia natural y moral de las Indias. Seville. (Other eds. 1880, 1940.)
Adams, R. M.
1961 Changing patterns of territorial organization in the central highlands of Chiapas, Mexico. *Amer. Antiquity,* 26: 341–60.
Adams, R. N.
1956 La ladinoización en Guatemala. *In* Arriola, 1956, pp. 213–44.
1957 [comp.] Political changes in Guatemalan communities. *Tulane Univ., Middle Amer. Research Inst.,* Pub. 24.
1960 Exploración de la madera en el municipio de Totonicapan. *Bol. Inst. Indig. Nac.,* vol. 2. Guatemala.
Adán, E.
1922 La organización actual de los zapotecos. *An. Mus. Nac. Arqueol. Hist. Etnog.,* 1:53–64.
Agüero, C. de
1893 Vocabulario castellano-zapoteco. Sec. Fomento. Mexico.
Aguilar, F. de
1579 Historia de la Nueva España. *An. Mus. Nac. Mex.,* ep. 1–7, pp. 3–25 (1903). (Another ed. 1954.)
Aguirre Beltrán, G.
1950 Pobladores del Papaloapan. MS.
1952 Problemas de la población indígena de la cuenca del Tepalcatepec. *Inst. Nac. Indig.,* Mem. 3. Mexico.
1953 Formas de gobierno indígena. *Cultura Mex.,* Pub. 5.
1958 Cuijla: esbozo etnográfico de un pueblo negro. Fondo de Cultura Económica. Mexico.
—— AND R. Pozas A.
1954 Instituciones indígenas en el México actual. *In* Caso, 1954, pp. 171–269.
Aladro Azueta, F.
1944 Informe sobre la exploración sanitaria del municipio de Tlacotepec, Puebla. Mexico.
Alba, C. H.
1949 Las industrias zapotecas. *In* Mendieta y Núñez, 1949, pp. 493–600.

—— AND J. Cristerna
1949 La agricultura entre los zapotecos. *Ibid.,* pp. 449–89.
Alcarez, A.
1930 Las canacuas. *Mex. Folkways,* 6: 117–28.
Aldama, F. R.
1945 Geografía del estado de Chihuahua. Chihuahua.
Aldrete, E.
1958 Baja California heroica: episodios de la invasión filibustera-magonista de 1911 por el Sr. Enrique Aldrete, testigo presencial. Mexico.
Alegre, F. J.
1841 Historia de la compañía de Jesús en Nueva España al tiempo de su expulsión. C. M. de Bustamente, ed. 3 vols. Mexico.
Alexandre, M.
1890 Cartilla huasteca con su gramática, diccionario y varias reglas para aprender el idioma. Mexico.
Allen, C. R., L. T. Silver, and F. G. Stehli
1960 Agua Blanca fault: a major transverse structure of northern Baja California, Mexico. *Bull. Geol. Soc. Amer.,* 71: 457–82.
Alva Ixtlilxochitl, F. de
1891 Obras históricas. 2 vols. Mexico.
Alvarado, J.
1939 Hipótesis sobre la cerámica tarasca. *Rev. Artes Plásticas,* no. 2. Mexico.
Alvarado, P. de
1838 Lettres à Fernand Cortés. *In* Ternaux Compans, Recueil de pièces relatives à la conquête du Mexique, pp. 107–50. Paris.
Alvarado Tezozomoc, H.
1949 Crónica mexicayotl. Mexico.
Amram, D. W., Jr.
1937 Eastern Chiapas, Mexico. *Amer. Geog. Rev.,* vol. 27, no. 1.
1948 Eastern Chiapas revisited. *Ibid.,* vol. 38, no. 1.
Ancona, E.
1878 Historia de Yucatan desde la época más remota hasta nuestros días. Merida.

1889 *Idem,* 2d ed. Barcelona.

ANDERSON, E.
1946 Report on maize from Cheran. *In* Beals, 1946, pp. 219–23.

ANGHIERA, P. M. D'
1912 De orbo novo, the eight decades of Peter Martyr d'Anghiera. *Tr.* from Latin with notes and introduction by F. A. McNutt. 2 vols. New York and London.

ANGULO, J. DE
1925a The linguistic tangle of Oaxaca. *Language,* 1: 96–102.
1925b Kinship terms in some languages of southern Mexico. *Amer. Anthr.,* 27: 103–07.
1926 Tone patterns and verb forms in a dialect of Zapotek. *Language,* 2: 238–50.

—— AND L. S. FREELAND
1925 The Chontal language (dialect of Tequisistlan). *Anthropos,* 20: 1032–52.
1933 The Zapotekan linguistic group. *Int. Jour. Amer. Ling.,* 8: 1–38, 111–30.

ANONYMOUS
1900 Zapoteken, grosser Eingeborenenstamm in Mexiko. *Handworterbuch der Zoologie, Anthropologie, und Ethnologie,* 8: 657–58. Breslau.
1948 Primer congreso de la juventud zapoteca. *Bol. Indig.,* 8: 274–76.

ARANA OSNAYA, E.
1959 Afinidades lingüísticas del Cuitlateco. *Proc. 33d Int. Cong. Amer.,* 2: 560–72.

AREIZAGA MILLAN, M.
1945 Estudio sanitario del municipio de Teziutlan, Puebla. Mexico.

ARREAGA, A.
1946 Los Pocomames orientales: su frontera lingüística. *Bol. Inst. Indig. Nac. Guatemala,* 1 (2–3): 47–52.

ARRIAGA CERVANTES, E.
1944 Exploración sanitaria de Tlatlauqui, Puebla. Mexico.

ARRIOLA, J. L., ed.
1956 Integración social en Guatemala. *Seminario de Integración Social Guatemalteca,* Pub. 3. Guatemala.

ASCHMANN, H.
1959 The central desert of Baja California: demography and ecology. *Ibero-Amer.,* no. 42.

AUGUR, H.
1929 Blindness among Mexican Indians. *Science,* 70: xiv.

1954 Zapotec. New York.

AULIE, E., AND W. AULIE
1953 Terminos de parentesco en Chol. *Mem. Cong. Cien. Mex., Cien. Sociales,* 12: 151–58.

BACA, F. M.
1897 Estudio craneométrico zapoteca. *Proc. 11th Int. Cong. Amer.,* pp. 237–64.

BAEGERT, J. J. (S.J.)
1773 Nachrichten von der Amerikanischen Halbinsel Californien, mit einen zweifachen Anhang falscher Nachrichten. Mannheim. Tr. by C. Rau, An account of the aboriginal inhabitants of the California peninsula. *Smithsonian Inst.,* ann. rept., 1863, pp. 352–69; 1864, pp. 378–99.
1952 Observations in Lower California. Tr. from German with introduction and notes by M. M. Brandenburg and C. L. Baumann. Univ. California Press.

BAER, P., AND M. BAER
1949 Notes on Lacandon marriage. *SW. Jour. Anthr.,* 5: 101–06.

BALSALOBRE, G. DE
1892 Tratado de las idolatrías, supersticiones, dioses, ritos, hechicerías y otras costumbres gentílicas de las razas aborigines de México. *An. Mus. Nac. Mex.,* vol. 6.

BANCROFT, H. H.
1882–89 The native races of the Pacific states of North America. 5 vols. (Zapotec, 1: 615–83.)

BANDELIER, A.
1877 On the art of war and mode of warfare of the ancient Mexicans. *Peabody Mus., Harvard Univ.,* 10th ann. rept., 2: 95–161.
1878 On the distribution and tenure of lands and the customs with respect to inheritance among the ancient Mexicans. *Ibid.,* 11th ann. rept., 2: 385–448.
1879 On the social organization and mode of government of the ancient Mexicans. *Ibid.,* 12th ann. rept., 2: 557–699.
1890 Final report of investigations among the Indians of southwestern United States, Part 1. *Papers Archaeol. Inst. Amer., Amer. Ser.,* vol. 3.
1892 Final report of investigations among the Indians of southwestern United States, Part 2. *Ibid.,* vol. 4.

BARKER, G. C.
1957 The Yaqui Easter ceremony at Hermosillo. *Western Folklore*, 16: 256–62.

BARLOW, R.
1944 A western extension of Zapotec. *Tlalocan*, 1: 267–68, 359–61.
1945 Dos relaciones de Cuilapa. *Ibid.*, 2: 18–28.
1948 La prensa tarasca de Paracho, Michoacan, 1939–40. *Int. Jour. Amer. Ling.*, 14: 49–52.

BARNARD, J. G.
1852 The Isthmus of Tehuantepec, being the results of a survey for a railroad to connect the Atlantic and Pacific oceans. New York.

BAROCO, J. V.
1959 Map of the Tzeltal-Tzotzil area of Chiapas. *In* McQuown, 1959.

BARRAGÁN, R., AND L. A. GONZÁLEZ BONILLA
1940 Vida actual de los tarascos. Mexico.

BARREDA, N. DE LA
1730 Doctrina cristiana en lengua chinanteca . . . México. Facsimile ed. *Mus. Nac. Antr., Ser. Cien.*, 6. *Papeles de la Chinantla*, 2. Introductory material by H. F. Cline (see Cline, 1961b.) Mexico.

BARRERA GONZÁLEZ, M.
1949 Informe sanitario y problemas médico-sociales del pueblo de Tepoztlan, Morelos. Mexico.

BARRERA VÁSQUEZ, A., AND S. RENDÓN, trs. and eds.
1948 El libro de los libros de Chilam Balam. Fondo de Cultura Económica. Mexico.

BARRETT, E. C.
1957 Baja California. [Bibliography.] Los Angeles.

BARRIOS, M.
1949 Textos de Hueyapan, Morelos. *Tlalocan*, 3: 53–75.

BASAURI, C.
1928a La situación social actual de la población indígena de México. *Pub. Sec. Educación Pública*, vol. 16, no. 8. Mexico.
1928b Los tarascos de la Cañada de Chilchota. *In* his 1928a.
1929 Monografía de los tarahumaras. Mexico.
1940a Familia "zoque-mixeana": mixes. *In* his 1940c, 3: 403–32.
1940b Familia "zoque-mixeana": zoques. *In* his 1940c, 3: 387–402.
1940c La población indígena de México. 3 vols. Mexico.
1940d Tribu: chinantecas, h-me, wan-mi. *In* his 1940c, 2: 545–68.
1940e Los indios triques de Oaxaca. *In* his 1940c, 2: 427–63.

BATRES, L.
1889 Antropología mexicana: clasificación del tipo étnico de las tribus zapotecas y acolhua. *In* Memoria que el Secretario de Justicia Baranda presenta al Congreso de la Unión, pp. 257–62. Mexico.

BAUER-THOMA, W.
1916 Unter den Zapoteken und Mixes des Staates Oaxaca der Republik Mexiko: ethnographischen Studien. *Baessler Archiv*, 5: 75–97.

BEALS, R. L.
1932a The comparative ethnology of northern Mexico before 1750. *Ibero-Amer.*, no. 2.
1932b Unilateral organizations in Mexico. *Amer. Anthr.*, 34: 467–75.
1935 Two mountain Zapotec tales from Oaxaca, Mexico. *Jour. Amer. Folklore*, 48: 189–90.
1936 Problems in the study of Mixe marriage customs. *In* Essays in anthropology, pp. 7–13.
1941 The western Mixe of Oaxaca. *Amer. Indig.*, 2: 45–50.
1943a The aboriginal culture of the Cáhita Indians. *Ibero-Amer.*, no. 19.
1943b Northern Mexico and the southwest. *In* El Norte de Mexico, pp. 191–99.
1945a The contemporary culture of the Cáhita Indians. *Smithsonian Inst., Bur. Amer. Ethnol.*, Bull. 142.
1945b Ethnology of the western Mixe. *Univ. California Pub. Amer. Archaeol. Ethnol.*, 42: 1–176.
1946 Cheran: a sierra Tarascan village. *Smithsonian Inst., Inst. Social Anthr.*, Pub. 2.
1951 The history of acculturation in Mexico. *In* Homenaje Caso, pp. 73–82.

—— AND P. CARRASCO
1944 Games of the mountain Tarascans. *Amer. Anthr.*, 46: 516–22.

——, ——, AND T. MCCORKLE
1944 Houses and house use of the sierra Tarascans. *Smithsonian Inst., Inst. Social Anthr.*, Pub. 1.

—— AND E. P. HATCHER
1943 The diet of a sierra Tarascan community. *Amer. Indig.*, 3: 295–304.

——, R. REDFIELD, AND S. TAX
1943 Anthropological research problems with reference to the contemporary peoples of Mexico and Guatemala. *Amer. Anthr.*, 45: 1–22.

BEAUMONT, P.
1855–56 Crónica de Michoacán, año de 1825. 2 vols. Morelia.
1932 Crónica de Michoacán (1565). *Archivo General de la Nación*, Pubs. 17, 18, 19. Mexico.

BECERRA, M. E.
1924 Breve noticia sobre la lengua e indios tsoques. *Mem. Soc. Cien. Antonio Alzate*, 43: 147–52.
1933 El antiguo calendario chiapaneco: estudio comparativo entre este y los calendarios precoloniales maya, quiche, y nahua. Mexico.

BECERRA COBOS, J. DE LA L.
1944 Informe general sobre la exploración sanitaria del municipio de Amozoc de Mota, Puebla. Mexico.

BEEKMAN, J.
1956 The effect of education in an Indian village. *In* Estudios antropológicos, pp. 261–64.

BELMAR, F.
1890 Cartilla del idioma zapoteco-serrano. Oaxaca.
1892 Códice Dehesa. Homenaje a Cristobal Colón. Antigüedades mexicanas, publicadas por la junta colombina de México en el cuarto centenario del descubrimiento de América. Secretaria de Fomento. Mexico.
1897 Ensayo sobre la lengua trique. Lenguas indígenas del estado de Oaxaca. Oaxaca.
1898 Disertación sobre las lenguas zapoteca, chinanteca, mixe y trike, y comparación con zoke y el mixteco. MS in Newberry Library, Chicago.
1899 Idiomas indígenas del estado de Oaxaca: el Chocho. Oaxaca.
1900 Estudio de el chontal. Oaxaca.
1901 Los chochos: estudio lingüístico. Oaxaca.
1902a Estudio del idioma ayook. Oaxaca.
1902b El cuicateco. Oaxaca.
1905a Lenguas indígenas de México. Familia mixteco-zapoteca y sus relaciones con el otomí. Familia zoque-mixe, chontal, huave y mexicano. Mexico.
1905b La familia mixteco-zapoteca en relación con la otomí. Mexico.
1905c Indian tribes of the state of Oaxaca and their languages. *Proc. 13th Int. Cong. Amer.*, pp. 193–202.
1921 Glotología indígena mexicana. Mexico.

BENÍTEZ P., A.
1943 Informe general sobre la exploración sanitaria de Tlaquiltenango, Morelos. Mexico.

BENNETT, W. C., AND R. M. ZINGG
1935 The Tarahumara: an Indian tribe of northern Mexico. Univ. Chicago Press.

BERENDT, C. H.
1869 An analytic alphabet for the Mexican and Central American languages. New York.
1870 Apuntes sobre la lengua chaneabal, con un vocabulario. Reproduction in Peabody Mus., Harvard Univ.
1873 Die Indianer des Isthmus von Tehuantepec. *Verhandlungen der Berliner Gesellschaft für Anthropologie, Ethnologie und Urgeschicht*, 5: 146–53.
1876 Remarks on the centers of ancient civilization in Central America and their geographical distribution. *Bull. Amer. Geog. Soc.*, 8 (2): 5–15.

BERLIN, H.
1951 The calendar of the Tzotzil Indians. *In* Tax, 1951, pp. 155–61.
1957a Las antiguas creencias en San Miguel Sola, Oaxaca, Mexico. *Hamburgischen Museum für Völkerkunde*, no. 4.
1957b A survey of the Sola region in Oaxaca. *Ethnos*, 16: 1–17.

BERNAL, I.
1962 Bibliografía de arqueología y etnografía: Mesoamérica y norte de México, 1514–1960. *Inst. Nac. Antr. Hist.*, Mem. 7.

BEVAN, B.
1938 The Chinantec and their habitat. (The Chinantec: report on the central and southeastern Chinantec region, vol. 1.) *Inst. Panamer. Geog. Hist.*, Pub. 24. Mexico.

BIART, L.
1885 Les Aztèques: histoire, moeurs, coutumes. Paris.

BILLIG, O., J. GILLIN, AND W. DAVIDSON
1947–48 Aspects of personality and culture in a Guatemalan community. *Jour. Personality*, 16: 153–87, 326–68.

REFERENCES

Blom, F.
1954 Ossuaries, cremation and secondary burials among the Maya of Chiapas, Mexico. *Jour. Soc. Amer. Paris*, 43: 123–35.

—— and G. Duby
1955–57 La selva lacandona: andanzas arqueológicas. 2 vols. Editorial Cultura. Mexico.

—— and O. LaFarge
1926–27 Tribes and temples. 2 vols. *Tulane Univ., Middle Amer. Research Inst.*, Pub. 1.

Boas, F.
1962 Anthropology and modern life.

Bonilla R., L.
1948 Exploración sanitaria y práctica de la reacción de Mantoux en Tianguistengo, Hidalgo. Mexico.

Borah, W.
1960 Sources and possibilities for the reconstruction of the demographic process of the Mixteca Alta, 1519–1895. *Rev. Mex. Estud. Antr.*, 16: 159–71.

Boturini, L.
1745 Idea de nueva historia general de la América septentrional. Madrid.
1933 *Idem*, 2d ed. Paris.

Bourke, J. G.
1893 Primitive distillation among the Tarascos. *Amer. Anthr.*, 6: 65–69.

Brand, D. D.
1943 Primitive and modern economy of the Rio Balsas, Guerrero and Michoacan. *Proc. 8th Amer. Sci. Cong.*, 9: 225–31.
1944 An historical sketch of geography and anthropology in the Tarascan region. *New Mexico Anthr.*, 6/7: 37–108.
1951 Quiroga: a Mexican municipio. *Smithsonian Inst., Inst. Social Anthr.*, Pub. 11.

Brasseur de Bourbourg, C. E.
1857 Histoire de nations civilisées du Mexique et de l'Amérique Centrale. Paris.
1861 Popul Vuh: le livre sacré et les mythes de l'antiquité américaine, avec les livres héroiques et historiques des Quichés. Paris.
1864 Relation des choses de Yucatan de Diego de Landa . . . accompagné de documents divers historiques et chronologiques. Paris.

1865 Mixtèques, Zapotèques, Mijes, Wabi, Chontales, et Chinantecas, etc., dans l'état d'Oaxaca. *Archives Comm. Sci. Mexique*, 1: 123–25.
1868 Quatre lettres sur Mexique. Paris.

Briggs, E.
1961 Mitla Zapotec grammar. Inst. Ling. Verano and Centro Invest. Antr. Mexico. Mexico.

Bright, W.
1955 A bibliography of the Hokan-Coahuiltecan languages. *Int. Jour. Amer. Ling.*, 21: 276–85.

Brinton, D. G.
1882 The Maya chronicles. *Library Aboriginal Amer. Lit.*, no. 1. Philadelphia.
1885 The annals of the Cakchiquels. *Ibid.*, no. 6. Philadelphia.
1890a Ancient Nahuatl poetry. *Ibid.*, no. 7. Philadelphia.
1890b Rig-Veda Americanus. Philadelphia.
1891 The American race. New York.
1892 Chontales and Populucas: a contribution to Mexican ethnography. *Proc. 8th Int. Cong. Amer.*, pp. 556–64.
1894 Nagualism: a study in native folklore and history. Philadelphia.

Bruce S., R.
1965 Jerarquía maya entre los dioses lacandones. *An. Inst. Nac. Antr. Hist.*, 18: 99–108.

Brugge, D. M.
1956 Pima bajo basketry. *Kiva*, vol. 22, no. 1.

Buelna, E.
1890 Arte de la lengua cáhita por un padre de la compañía de Jesús. Mexico.

Bunzel, R.
1940 The role of alcoholism in two Central American cultures. *Psychiatry*, 3: 361–87.
1952 Chichicastenango. *Amer. Ethnol. Soc.*, Pub. 22.
1959 Chichicastenango and Chamula. *In* R. G. McCarthy, ed., Drinking and intoxication: selected readings in social attitudes and controls, pp. 73–86. Pub. Division Yale Center of Alcohol Studies. New Haven.
1960 El papel del alcoholismo en dos culturas centroamericanas. *Bol. Inst. Indig. Nac.*, 3: 27–81. Mexico.

BURGOA, F. DE
1674 Geográfica descripción de la parte septentrional del polo ártico de la América, y nueva iglesia de las Indias occidentales. Mexico.
1934 *Idem. Archivo General de la Nación*, Pubs. 25, 26.

BUSIERRE, M. T.
1863 L'empire Mexicain: histoire des Toltèques, des Chichamèques, des Aztèques et de la conquête Espagnole. Paris.

CABRERA, A. J.
1876 La huaxteca potosina: ligeros apuntes sobre este país. San Luis Potosi.

CALDERÓN, E.
1908 Estudios lingüísticos. I: Las lenguas (sinca) de Yupiltepeque y del barrio norte de Chiquimulilla en Guatemala. II: Las lenguas de Oluta, Sayula, Texistepec en el Istmo de Tehuantepec en México. Guatemala.

CALNEK, E. E.
1959 Distribution and location of the Tzeltal and Tzotzil pueblos of the highlands of Chiapas from earliest time to the present. *In* McQuown, 1959.
1962 Highland Chiapas before the Spanish conquest. Doctoral dissertation, Univ. Chicago.

CANCIAN, FRANCESCA M.
1964 Interaction patterns in Zinacanteco families. *Amer. Sociol. Rev.*, 29: 540–50.
1965 The effect of patrilocal households on nuclear family interaction in Zinacantan. *Estud. Cultura Maya*, 5: 299–315.

CANCIAN, FRANK
1963 Informant error and native prestige ranking in Zinacantan. *Amer. Anthr.*, 65: 1068–75.
1964 Some aspects of the social and religious organization of a Maya society. *Proc. 35th Int. Cong. Amer.*, 1: 335–43.
1965a Economics and prestige in a Maya community: a study of the religious cargo system in Zinacantan. Stanford Univ. Press.
1965b Efectos de los programas económicos del gobierno mexicano en las tierras altas mayas de Zinacantan. *Estud. Cultura Maya*, 5: 281–97.

CANGAS Y QUIÑONES, S. DE
1928 Descripción de la villa del Espíritu Santo. *Rev. Mex. Estud. Hist.*, 2 (app.): 176–91.

CANTELLANO ALVARADO, L.
1949 Exploración sanitaria del municipio de Hueytamalco, Puebla, y sus principales problemas médicos. Mexico.

CARDOSO, J.
1948 Sangre de los tepehuanes. Mexico.

CARLO, A. M., ed.
1951 Historia de las Indias. Vols. 1–3. Mexico.

CARMICHAEL, J. H.
1959 Balsalobre on idolatry in Oaxaca. *Bol. Estud. Oaxaqueños*, Sept. 1, pp. 1–13.

CARRASCO PIZANA, P.
1945 Quetzalcoatl, dios de Coatepec de los costales, Guerrero. *Tlalocan*, 2:89–90.
1950 Los otomíes, cultura e historia prehispánicas de los pueblos mesoamericanos de hable otomiana. *Inst. Hist.*, Pub. 15. Mexico.
1951a Las culturas indígenas de Oaxaca, México. *Amer. Indig.*, 2: 99–114.
1951b Una cuenta ritual entre los zapotecas del sur. *In* Homenaje Caso, pp. 91–100.
1952a El sol y la luna: versión mixe. *Tlalocan*, 3: 168–69.
1952b Tarascan folk religion. *Tulane Univ., Middle Amer. Research Inst.*, Pub. 17.
1960 Pagan rituals and beliefs among the Chontal Indians of Oaxaca, Mexico. *Univ. California Pub., Anthr. Records*, vol. 20, no. 3.
1961a The civil-religious hierarchy in Mesoamerican communities: pre-Spanish background and colonial development. *Amer. Anthr.*, 63: 483–97.
1961b Un mito y una ceremonia entre los chatinos de Oaxaca. *In* Homenaje Townsend, pp. 43–48.
1963 Las tierras de dos indios nobles de Tepeaca en el siglo XVI. *Tlalocan*, 4: 97–119.
1966 Documentos sobre el rango de tecuhtli entre los nahuas tramontanos. *Tlalocan*, 5: 133–60.

——, W. MILLER, AND R. J. WEITLANER
1959 El calendario mixe. *El Mex. Antiguo*, 9: 153–72.

CARRASCO PUENTE, R.
1948 Bibliografía del Isthmus de Tehuantepec. Sec. Relaciones Exteriores. Mexico.

CARRERA STAMPA, M.
1954 Los gremios mexicanos: la organización gremial en la Nueva España, 1521–1861. Mexico.

CARRILLO Y ANCONA, D. C.
1881 Historia antigua de Yucatan. Merida.

CARRILLO GONZÁLEZ, M.
1950 Exposición de las condiciones sanitarias prevalentes en el municipio de San Sebastian Zinacatepec, Puebla. Mexico.

CASO, A.
1941 Culturas mixtecas y zapotecas. Bib. del Maestro, "El Nacional." Mexico.
1954 [ed.] Métodos y resultados de la política indigenista en México. Inst. Nac. Indig., Mem. 6. Mexico.
1962 The Mixtec and Zapotec cultures. Bol. Estud. Oaxaqueños.

—— AND M. G. PARRA
1950 Densidad de la población de habla indígena en la República Mexicana. Inst. Nac. Indig., Mem. 1. Mexico.

CASTELLANOS FERNÁNDEZ, H.
1950 Informe médico sanitario del municipio de Xochitlan Romero Rubio, Puebla, y el problema del bocio coloide. Mexico.

CASTETTER, E. F., AND W. H. BELL
1942 Pima and Papago Indian agriculture. Univ. New Mexico, School Interamer. Affairs, Interamer. Ser., Studies 1.

CASTILLO, I. M. DEL
1945 La alfabetización en lenguas indígenas: el proyecto tarasco. Amer. Indig., 5: 139–51.

CASTILLO SÁNCHEZ, N.
1944 Informe general sobre la exploración sanitaria del municipio de San Jose Mihuatlan, distrito de Tehuacan, estado de Puebla. Mexico.

CASTILLO TEJERA, N.
1961 Conquista y colonización de Chiapas. In Los Mayas del sur, pp. 207–20.

CAZORLA VERA, E.
1935 Las problemas de la región zapoteca. Neza, 1(4): 1, 5.
1937 La numeración zapoteca. Ibid., 3 (2): 53–56.

CEPEDA DE LA GARZA, R.
1944 Informe general sobre la exploración sanitaria de Villa de Xochitepec, cabecera del municipio de Xochitepec, estado de Morelos. Mexico.

CERDA SILVA, R. DE LA
1940a Los mixes. Rev. Mex. Sociol., 2: 63–113.
1940b Los zoque. Ibid., 2: 61–69.
1941 Los huave. Ibid., 3: 81–111.
1942 Los cuicatecos. Ibid., 4: 99–127.
1943 Los tepehuanes. Ibid., 5: 541–67.
1957a [ed.] Etnografía de México: síntesis monográfica. Inst. Invest. Soc., Univ. Nac. Autónoma Mex.
1957b Los mexicanos. In his 1957a.
1957c Los tzotziles. In his 1957a, pp. 535–52.
1957d Los choles. In his 1957a.
1957e Los triquis. In his 1957a, pp. 339–50.

CERVANTES Y C., R.
1945 Un casamiento en Zoogocho. Anuario Soc. Mex. Folklore, vol. 3.

CHAMPION, R.
1955 Acculturation among the Tarahumara of northwestern Mexico since 1890. Trans. New York Acad. Sci., 17: 560–66.

CHARENCEY, H. DE
1879 Vocabulaire Francaise-Nagranda. Rev. Ling. et Philol. Comparée, 12: 334–37.

CHARNAY, C. J. D.
1863 Le Mexique: souvenirs et impressions de voyage, 1851–1861. Paris.
1887a The ancient cities of the New World, being travels and explorations in Mexico and Central America, 1857–1882. New York.
1887b Ma dernière expédition au Yucatan, 1886. Tour du Monde, 53: 273–320.

CHAVERO, A.
1887 Historia de la conquista. In D. V. R. Palacio, ed., México a través de los siglos, vol. 1. Mexico.

CHAVES, G. DE
1865 Relación de la provincia de Meztitlan. Col. Doc. Ineditos, 4: 530–55.

CHÁVEZ OROZCO, L.
1943 Las instituciones democráticas de los indígenas mexicanos en la época colonial. Inst. Indig. Interamer. Mexico.

CHÁVEZ TORRES, R.
1947 Exploración sanitaria de Zochitepec, estado de Morelos. Mexico.

CHIMALPAHIN QUAUTLEHUANITZIN, F. DE
1889 Annales de Domingo Francisco de San Antón Muñon Chimalpahin Quauhtlehuanitzin. Sixième et septième relations (1258–1612). R. Siméon, tr. and ed. Bib. Ling. Amer., vol. 12. Paris.

CHRISTENSEN, B.
1953a Los otomíes del estado de Puebla. *In* Huastecos, Totonacos, pp. 259–68.
1953b La pesca entre los otomíes de San Pablito, Puebla. *Yan*, no. 2.

CIUDAD REAL, A. DE
1873 Relación breve y verdadera de algunas cosas de las muchas que sucedieron al Padre Fray Alonso Ponce en las provincias de la Nueva España. . . . 2 vols. Madrid.
1930 Diccionario de Motul maya-español atribuído a Fray Antonio de Ciudad Real y arte de la lengua maya por Fray Juan Coronel. J. Martínez Hernández, ed.

CLAVIJERO, F. J.
1780–81 Historia antigua de México.

CLINE, H. F.
1944 Lore and deities of the Lacandon Indians, Chiapas, Mexico. *Jour. Amer. Folklore*, 57: 107–15.
1946 The terragueros of Guelatao, Oaxaca, Mexico: notes on the Sierra de Juarez and its XVIIth century Indian problems. *Acta Amer.*, 4: 161–84.
1947 Civil congregations of the Indians of New Spain, 1598–1606. *Hispanic Amer. Hist. Rev.*, 29: 349–69.
1953a Una subdivisión tentativa de los chinantecos históricos. *Rev. Mex. Estud. Antr.*, 12: 281–86.
1953b The United States and Mexico. Cambridge, Mass. (3d printing, 1966.)
1955 Civil congregation of the western Chinantla, New Spain, 1599–1604. *The Americas*, 12: 115–37.
1956 The Chinantla of northeastern Oaxaca, Mexico: bio-bibliographical notes on modern investigations. *In* Estudios antropológicos, pp. 635–56.
1957 Problems of Mexican ethno-history: the ancient Chinantla, a case study. *Hispanic Amer. Hist. Rev.*, 37: 273–95.
1960 *See* Barreda, 1730
1961a Mapas and lienzos of the colonial Chinantec Indians, Oaxaca, Mexico. *In* Homenaje Townsend, pp. 49–77.
1961b Re-edición con notas y apéndices . . . Espinosa, 1910 [q.v.]. *Mus. Nac. Antr., Ser. Cien.*, 7. *Papeles de la Chinantla*, 3. Mexico.
1962 Mexico: revolution to evolution, 1940–1960. London.

CÓDICE DEHESA
See Belmar, 1892

CÓDICE MARIANO JIMÉNEZ
1903 Códice Mariano Jiménez. Nómina de tributos de los pueblos Otlazpan y Tepexic. En jeroglífico azteca y lengua castellana y nahuatl, 1549. N. León, ed. Mexico.

CÓDICE MONTELEONE
1925 Códice del archivo de los duques de Monteleone. Declaración del indio Delmas en el juicio seguido por Hernan Cortés contra Nuño de Guzmán y otros sobre títulos de Huexotzingo. *An. Mus. Nac. Mex.*, ep. 2–3, pp. 58–64.

CÓDICE PÉREZ
1949 Códice Pérez. Merida.

COE, M. D.
1961 La Victoria: an early site on the Pacific coast of Guatemala. *Papers Peabody Mus., Harvard Univ.*, vol. 53.

COGOLLUDO, D. LÓPEZ DE
See López de Cogolludo, D.

COLBY, B. N.
1960 Social relations and directed culture change among the Zinacantan. *Practical Anthr.*, 7: 241–50.
1961 Indian attitudes toward education and inter-ethnic contact in Mexico. *Ibid.*, 8: 77–85.
1964 Elements of a Mesoamerican personality pattern. *Proc. 35th Int. Cong. Amer.*, pp. 125–29.
1966 Ethnic relations in the Chiapas highlands. Santa Fe.

—— AND P. L. VAN DEN BERGHE
1961 Ethnic relations in southeastern Mexico. *Amer. Anthr.*, 63: 772–92.

COLLIER, J. F.
1968 Courtship and marriage in Zinacantan, Chiapas, Mexico. *Tulane Univ., Middle Amer. Research Inst.*, Pub. 25.

COMAS, J.
1944 Contribución al estudio antropométrico de los indios triques de Oaxaca. *An. Inst. Etnol. Amer.*, 5: 159–241.
1950 Bosquejo histórico de la antropología en México. *Rev. Mex. Estud. Antr.*, 11: 99.
1953 El problema social de los indios triques de Oaxaca. *In* Ensayos sobre indigenismo, pp. 1–9. Inst. Indig. Inter-Amer.

CONQUISTADOR ANÓNIMO, EL
1556 Relación de algunas cosas de la Nueva España y de la gran ciudad de Temestitlan, México. *In* García Icazbalceta, 1858–66, 1: 368–98.

CONTRERAS ARIAS, A.
1959 Bosquejo climatológico. *In* Los recursos naturales del sureste y su aprovechamiento, ch. 3. 3 vols. Inst. Mex. Recursos Naturales Renovables. Mexico.

COOK, C.
See Cook de Leonard, C.

COOK, S. F.
1937 The extent and significance of disease among the Indians of Baja California, 1697–1773. *Ibero-Amer.*, no. 12.
1958 Santa Maria Ixcatlan: habitat, population, subsistence. Univ. California Press.

—— AND W. BORAH
1960 The Indian population of central Mexico, 1531–1610. *Ibero-Amer.*, no. 44.
1963 The aboriginal population of central Mexico on the eve of the Spanish conquest. *Ibid.*, no. 45.

—— AND L. B. SIMPSON
1948 The population of central Mexico in the sixteenth century. *Ibid.*, no. 31.

COOK DE LEONARD, C.
1953 Los Popolocas de Puebla. *Rev. Mex. Estud. Antr.*, 13: 423–45.

—— AND D. LEONARD
1949 Costumbres mortuarias de los indios huaves: un viaje. *El Mex. Antiguo*, 7: 439–513.

CÓRDOBA, J. DE
1578a Arte en lengua zapoteca. Mexico. (2d ed., 1886.)
1578b Vocabulario en lengua zapoteca. Mexico. (Reprinted 1942.)

CORDRY, D. B., AND D. M. CORDRY
1940 Costumes and textiles of the Aztec Indians of the Cuetzalan region, Puebla, Mexico. *SW. Mus. Papers*, no. 14.
1941 Costumes and weaving of the Zoque Indians of Chiapas, Mexico. *Ibid.*, no. 15.

CORRAL, R.
1887 José María Leyva Cajeme: apuntes biográficos. *La Constitución* (official organ of state government of Sonora), vol. 9, nos. 16–28.

CORRIEDO, J. B.
1852 Leyenda zapoteca. *Ilustración Mex.*, 3: 336–45.

CORTÉS, H.
1870 Cartas de relación dirigidas al emperador Carlos V. Five letters. *Bib. Hist. Iberia*, I. Mexico.

COSIO VILLEGAS, D., ed.
1956 Historia moderna de México. 4 vols. Mexico.

COVARRUBIAS, M.
1946 Mexico south: the Isthmus of Tehuantepec. New York.

COWAN, F. H.
1946 Notas etnográficas sobre los mazatecos de Oaxaca, México. *Amer. Indig.*, 6: 27–39.
1952 A Mazateco president speaks. *Ibid.*, 12: 323–41.

COWAN, G. M.
1946 Mazateco house building. *SW. Jour. Anthr.*, 2: 375–90.
1947 Una visita a los indígenas amuzgos de México. *An. Inst. Nac. Antr. Hist.*, 2: 293–302.
1948 Mazateco whistle speech. *Language*, 24: 280–86.
1954 La importancia social y política de la faena mazateca. *Amer. Indig.*, 14: 67–92.

COWAN, M. M.
1962 A Christian movement in Mexico. *Practical Anthr.*, 9: 193–204.

CREFAL
1959 CREFAL, its nature and purpose. [Centro Regional de Educación para la América Latina.] Patzcuaro, Michoacan, Mexico.

CRUZ, E. T.
1939 Aun se practica la idolatría en Oaxaca. *Oaxaca en México*, vol. 2, no. 14.

CRUZ, W. C.
1935 El tonalamatl zapoteco. Oaxaca.
1936 La hechicería entre los antiguos zapotecas. *Neza*, 2 (14): 3, 5.
1939 Conceptos fundamentales de la civilización zapoteca. *Proc. 27th Int. Cong. Amer.*, 2: 390–98.
1946 Oaxaca recóndita. Mexico.

CUEVA, P.
1607 Arte de la gramática de la lengua zapoteca conforme a la que de la gramática latina escribió Antonio de Lebrija. Mexico.

DAHLGREN DE JORDAN, B.
1954 La mixteca: su cultura e historia prehispánica. *Serie Cultura Mex.*, no. 11. Mexico.

DARK, P.
1958 Mixtec ethnohistory. London.

DECICCO, G.
1959 Ceremonias fúnebres de los chatinos. *Tlatoani*, 12: 22–24.

—— AND F. HORCASITAS
1962 Los cuates. *Tlalocan*, 4: 74–79.

DECORME, G.
1941 La obra de los jesuítas mexicanos durante la época colonial, 1572–1767. 2 vols. Mexico.

DE LA FUENTE, J.
1938 Yalalag. *Indoamérica*, vol. 1, no. 6.
1939 Las ceremonias de la lluvia entre los zapotecos de hoy. *Proc. 27th Int. Cong. Amer.*, 2: 479–84.
1947a Los zapotecos de Choapan, Oaxaca. *An. Inst. Nac. Antr. Hist.*, 2: 143–205.
1947b Notas sobre lugares de Oaxaca, con especial referencia a la toponimia zapoteca. *Ibid.*, 2: 279–92.
1949a Documentos para la etnografía e historia zapoteca. *Ibid.*, 3: 175–97.
1949b Yalalag: una villa zapoteca serrana. Mexico.
1952 Algunos problemas etnológicas de Oaxaca. *An. Inst. Nac. Antr. Hist.*, 4: 241–52.
1960 La cultura zapoteca. *Rev. Mex. Estud. Antr.*, 16: 233–46.

DENSIDAD
1950 *See* Instituto Nacional Indigenista (Mexico), 1950.

DESARROLLO CULTURAL DE LOS MAYAS
1964 Desarrollo cultural de los mayas. E. Z. Vogt and A. Ruz Lhuillier, eds. Univ. Nac. Autónoma Mex.

DÍAZ DEL CASTILLO, B.
1632 Historia verdadera de la conquista de la Nueva España. Madrid.
1912 *Idem.* A. P. Maudslay, tr. London.
1928 *Idem.* London.
1939 *Idem.* Mexico.
1944 *Idem.* P. Robredo, ed. Mexico.

DIEBOLD, A. R., JR.
1960 Determining the centers of dispersal of language groups. *Int. Jour. Amer. Ling.*, 26: 1–10.
1961 Incipient bilingualism. *Language*, 37: 97–112.
1966 The reflection of coresidence in Mareño kinship terminology. *Ethnology*, 5: 37–39.

DIESELDORFF, E. P.
1928–29 Religión y arte de las mayas. *An. Soc. Geog. Hist.*, vol. 4, nos. 1–4. Guatemala.
1940 Las plantas medicinales del departamento de Alta Verapaz. *Ibid.*, vol. 16, no. 3.

DIGUET, L.
1899 La sierra de Nayarit et ses indigènes. Paris.
1903 Le Chimalhuacan et ses populations avant la conquête Espagnole. *Jour. Soc. Amer. Paris*, 1: 1057.

DOCTRINA CRISTIANA
1944 Doctrina cristiana en lengua española y mexicana por los religiosos de la orden de Santo Domingo. Madrid. (Facsimile ed. of 1548 ed.)

DOCUMENTOS HISTÓRICOS DE CHIAPAS
1956 Documentos históricos de Chiapas. *Archivo General del Estado*, Bol. 6. Tuxtla Gutierrez.

DOMINGUEZ, F.
1939a Dos sones zapotecas. *Neza*, 4 (1): supplement.
1939b Telayuu (melodía de la madrugada). *Ibid.*
1939c Trío de músicos zapotecas. *Ibid.*, 4 (1): 9–15.

DONDÉ Y LÓPEZ, T.
1941 Costumbres cuitlatecas. *El Mex. Antiguo*, 5 (7–10): 233–38.

DOWNING, T.
1940 The marigolds of Mitla. *Mex. Life*, 16 (7): 21–23, 53–59.

DRIVER, H. E., AND W. DRIVER
1963 Ethnography and acculturation of the Chichimeca-Jonaz of northeast Mexico. *Indiana Univ. Research Center in Anthr., Folklore, Ling.*, Pub. 26.

—— AND W. C. MASSEY
1957 Comparative studies of North American Indians. *Trans. Amer. Phil. Soc.*, 47: 165–456.

DRUCKER, P.
1941 Culture element distributions: XVII Yuman-Piman. *Univ. California, Anthr. Rec.*, vol. 6, no. 3.

DRUCKER, S.
1963 Cambio de indumentaria. *Col. Antr. Social.* Inst. Nac. Indig. Mexico.

DUBY, G.
1944 Los lacandones: su pasado y su presente. *Bib. Enciclopedica Popular*, no. 30. Mexico.

1955 Los lacandones: el mundo y su influencia sobre ellos. *Novedades,* Aug. 14.
1961 Chiapas indígena. Univ. Nac. Autónoma Mex.

DURÁN, D.
1867–80 Historia de las Indias de Nueva España. 2 vols. Mexico.
1951 *Idem.,* another ed.

DURÁN OCHOA, J.
1955 Población. Fondo de Cultura Económica. Mexico.
1961 La explosión demográfica. *In* México: 50 años de revolución, 2: 3–28.

DUTTON, B. P.
1939 All Saints' Day ceremonies in Todos Santos, Guatemala. *El Palacio,* 46: 169–82, 205–17.

DYEN, I.
1956 Language distribution and migration theory. *Language,* 32: 611–26.

DYK, A.
1959 Mixteco texts. *Ling. Series,* no. 3. Norman.

ELSON, B. F.
1947 The Homshuk: a Sierra Popoluca text. *Tlalocan,* 2: 193–214.
1948 Sierra Popoluca personal names. *Int. Jour. Amer. Ling.,* 14: 191–93.

EMBER, M.
1959 The nonunilinear descent groups of Samoa. *Amer. Anthr.,* 61: 573–77.

ENGELHARDT, Z. (O.F.M.)
1929 The missions and missionaries of California. Vol. 1, Lower California. (2d ed.) Santa Barbara.

ERASMUS, C. J.
1948 The economic life of a Mayo village. MS in Dept. Anthropology, Univ. Arizona.
1955 Work patterns in a Mayo village. *Amer. Anthr.,* 57: 322–33.
1961 Man takes control: cultural development and American aid. Univ. Minnesota Press.

ESCALANTE, R.
1958 Field notes. MS. Mexico.

ESPINOSA, M.
1910 Apuntes históricos de las tribus chinantecas, matzatecas, y popolucas. Recuerdo del centenario. Mexico. [For re-edition see Cline, 1961b.]

ESPLENDOR DEL MÉXICO ANTIGUO
1959 Esplendor del México antiguo. R. Noriega and C. Cook de Leonard, eds. 2 vols. Centro Invest. Antr. Mex. Mexico.

ESQUIVEL, D. DE
1579 Relación de la chinantla. *In* Paso y Troncoso, 1905–06, 4: 58–68. [Tr. in Bevan, 1938, pp. 135–44.]

ESSAYS IN ANTHROPOLOGY
1936 Essays in anthropology, presented to A. L. Kroeber. Univ. California Press.

ESTUDIOS ANTROPOLÓGICOS
1956 Estudios antropológicos publicados en homenaje al doctor Manuel Gamio. Univ. Nac. Autónoma Mex.

EWALD, R. H.
1954 San Antonio Sacatepequez: culture change in a Guatemalan community. Doctoral dissertation, Univ. Michigan.

EZELL, P. H.
1955 Indians under the law: Mexico, 1821–1847. *Amer. Indig.,* 15: 199–214.

FABILA, A.
1940 Las tribus yaquis de Sonora: su cultura y anhelada autodeterminación. Depto. Asuntos Indígenas. Mexico.
1949 Sierra norte de Puebla. Mexico.
1959 Los huicholes de Jalisco. Inst. Nac. Indig. Mexico.

—— AND OTHERS
1962 Problemas de los indios nahuas, mixtecos y tlapanecos de la parte oriental de la Sierra Madre del Sur del estado de Guerrero. MS. Inst. Nac. Indig. Mexico.

FAULHABER, J.
1947 Análisis de algunos caracteres antropológicos de la población de San Miguel Totolapan, Guerrero. Mexico.

FAVRE, H.
1964 Notas sobre el homicido entre los chamulas. *Estud. Cultura Maya,* 4: 305–22.

FENOCHI, A.
1913 Villa Alta. *Bol. Soc. Mex. Geog. Estad.,* 6: 212–20.

FERNÁNDEZ DE MIRANDA, M. T.
1959 Fonémica del ixcateco. Inst. Nac. Antr. Hist. Mexico.

——, M. SWADESH, AND R. J. WEITLANER
1959 Some findings on Oaxaca language classification and cultural terms. *Int. Jour. Amer. Ling.,* 25: 54–58.

—— AND R. J. WEITLANER
1961 Sobre algunas relaciones de la familia Mangue. *Anthr. Ling.,* 3 (7): 1–99.

FORD, S. L.
1948 Informe sobre la tribu chinanteca, región de Yólox, Ixtlán de Juárez, Oaxaca. *Bol. Indig.*, 8: 290–98.

FOSTER, G. M.
1940 Notes on the Popoluca of Veracruz. *Inst. Panamer. Geog. Hist.*, Pub. 51. Mexico.

1942a A primitive Mexican economy. *Amer. Ethnol. Soc.*, Monogr. 5.

1942b Indigenous apiculture among the Popoluca of Veracruz. *Amer. Anthr.*, 44: 538–42.

1943 The geographical, linguistic, and cultural position of the Popoluca of Veracruz. *Ibid.*, 45: 531–46.

1945 Sierra Popoluca folklore and beliefs. *Univ. California Pub. Amer. Archaeol. Ethnol.*, 42: 177–250.

1946 Expedición etnológica de la región del lago de Pátzcuaro. *An. Mus. Michoacano*, ep. 2, no. 4, pp. 65–67.

1948 Empire's children: the people of Tzintzuntzan. *Smithsonian Inst., Inst. Social Anthr.*, Pub. 6.

1949 Sierra Popoluca kinship terminology and its wider implications. *SW. Jour. Anthr.*, 5: 330–44.

1951 Some wider implications of soul-loss illness among the Sierra Popoluca. *In Homenaje Caso*, pp. 167–74.

1952 Relationships between theoretical and applied anthropology: a public health program analysis. *Human Organization*, 11: 5–15.

1953a Cofradía and compadrazgo in Spain and Spanish America. *SW. Jour. Anthr.*, 9: 1–28.

1953b Relationships between Spanish and Spanish-American folk medicine. *Jour. Amer. Folklore*, 66: 201–17.

1955 Contemporary pottery techniques in southern and central Mexico. *Tulane Univ., Middle Amer. Research Inst.*, Pub. 22, pp. 1–48.

1960a Culture and conquest: America's Spanish heritage. *Viking Fund Pub. Anthr.*, no. 27.

1960b Life expectancy of utilitarian pottery in Tzintzuntzan. *Amer. Antiquity*, 25: 606–09.

1961 The dyadic contract: a model for the social structure of a Mexican peasant village. *Amer. Anthr.*, 63: 1173–92.

FOUGHT, J. G.
1967 Chorti (Mayan) phonology, morphophonemics and morphology. Doctoral dissertation, Yale Univ.

FRANCO MARTÍNEZ, R.
1951 Informe sanitario del municipio de San Gabriel Chilac, estado de Puebla. Mexico.

FRIAS, H.
1898 Páginas nacionales. Cosijoopii: leyenda zapoteca. *El Imparcial*, 5: 562.

FRIED, J.
1952 Ideal norms and social control in Tarahumara society. Doctoral dissertation, Yale Univ.

1953 The relation of ideal norms to actual behavior in Tarahumara society. *SW. Jour. Anthr.*, 9: 286–95.

1961 An interpretation of Tarahumara interpersonal relations. *Anthr. Quar.*, 34: 110–20.

FRIEDRICH, P.
1957 Community study of a Tarascan community. Doctoral dissertation, Yale Univ.

1958 A Tarascan cacicazgo: structure and function. *In* V. F. Ray, ed., Systems of political control and bureaucracy in human societies, pp. 23–39. *Proc. Amer. Ethnol. Soc.*

FUENTE, J. DE LA
See De la Fuente, J.

GAGE, T.
1648 The English American or a new survey of the West Indies. London.

1702 A survey of the Spanish West Indies, being a journal of 3000 and 300 miles on the continent of America. London.

1908 Viajes de Tomás Gage en la Nueva España, sus diversas aventuras. 2 vols. Paris.

GALLENKAMP, C.
1959 Maya: the riddle and rediscovery of a lost civilization. New York.

GÁMEZ, E.
1955 El valle del Fuerte. Los Mochis.

GAMIO, M.
1922 La población del valle de Teotihuacán. 2 vols. Sec. Agricultura y Fomento, Dirección Antr. Mexico.

GÁMIZ, E.
1948 Monografía de la nación tepehuana que habita en la región sur del estado de Durango. Mexico.

GANN, T. W. F.
1918   The Maya Indians of southern Yuca-
        tan and northern British Honduras.
        Smithsonian Inst., Bur. Amer. Ethnol.,
        Bull. 64.

GARCÍA GRANADOS, R.
1938   Contribución para la geografía etno-
        gráfica y lingüística del estado de
        Oaxaca. *Bol. Soc. Mex. Geog. Estad.*,
        44: 401–10.

GARCÍA ICAZBALCETA, J.
1858–66 Colección de documentos para la
        historia de México. 2 vols. Mexi-
        co.
1886   Bibliografía mexicana del siglo XVI:
        catálogo razonado de libros impresos
        en México de 1539 a 1600 con bio-
        grafías de autores y otras ilustraci-
        ones. [Index by C. A. Janvier,
        1890.] Mexico.
1889–92 Nueva collección de documentos
        para la historia de México. 5 vols.
        Mexico.

GARCÍA PÉREZ, H.
1943   Exploración sanitaria de Altepexi, dis-
        trito de Tehuacan, Puebla. Mexico.

GARCÍA PIMENTEL, L.
1904   Relación de los obispados de Tlaxca-
        la, Michoacan, Oaxaca y otros lugares
        en el siglo XVI. *In* Doc. Hist. de
        Mexico, vol. 2.

GARVIN, P. L.
1953   *Review of* Preliminaries to speech
        analysis: the distinctive features and
        their correlates, by R. Jakobson, C.
        G. M. Fant, and M. Halle. *Lan-
        guage*, 29: 472–81.

GATES, W. E.
1920   Distribution of the several branches
        of the Mayense linguistic stock. *In*
        Morley, 1920, pp. 605–15.

GAY, J. A.
1881   Historia de Oaxaca. 2 vols. Mexi-
        co. (Another ed. 1933.)

GERHARD, P., AND H. E. GULICK
1958   Lower California guidebook: a de-
        scriptive traveler's guide. Glendale.

GESSAIN, R.
1938   Contribution à l'étude des cultes et
        des cérémonies indigènes de la region
        de Huehuetla, Hidalgo: les "muñe-
        cos," figures rituelles. *Jour. Soc.
        Amer. Paris*, 30: 323–70.
1953   Les Indiens Tepehuas de Huehuetla.
        In Huastecos, Totonacos, pp. 187–
        211.

GIBSON, C.
1952   Tlaxcala in the sixteenth century.
        Yale Univ. Press.
1960   Aztec aristocracy in colonial Mexico.
        *Comparative Studies in Society and
        History*, 2: 169–96.

GIDDINGS, R. W.
1959   Yaqui myths and legends. *Univ.
        Arizona, Anthr. Papers*, no. 2.

GIFFORD, E. W.
1933   The Cocopa. *Univ. California Pub.
        Amer. Archaeol. Ethnol.*, vol. 31, no.
        5.
——— AND R. H. LOWIE
1928   Notes on the Akwa 'ala Indians of
        Lower California. *Ibid.*, vol. 23.

GILL, M.
1957   La conquista del valle del Fuerte.
        Mexico.

GILLIN, J.
1943   Houses, food, and the contact of cul-
        tures in a Guatemalan town. *Acta
        Amer.*, 1: 344–59.
1945   Parallel cultures and the inhibitions
        to acculturation in a Guatemalan
        community. *Social Forces*, 24: 1–
        14.
1948a   "Race" relations without conflict: a
        Guatemalan town. *Amer. Jour. So-
        ciol.*, 53: 337–43.
1948b   Magical fright. *Psychiatry*, 11: 387–
        400.
1951   The culture of security in San Carlos:
        a study of a Guatemalan community
        of Indians and Ladinos. *Tulane
        Univ., Middle Amer. Research Inst.*,
        Pub. 16.
1957   San Luis Jilotepeque: 1942–55. *In*
        R. N. Adams, 1957, pp. 23–27.
1958   San Luis Jilotepeque. Tr. by J.
        Noval. *Seminario de Integración
        Social Guatemalteca*, no. 7. Guate-
        mala.
——— AND G. NICHOLSON
1951   The security function of cultural
        systems. *Social Forces*, 30: 179–84.

GILLOW, E. G.
1889   Apuntes históricos. Mexico.

GIRARD, R.
1949   Los chortis ante el problema maya:
        historia de los culturas indígenas de
        América, desde su origin hasta hoy.
        5 vols. Col. Cultura Precolombiana.
        Mexico.

GÓMEZ MAILLEFERT, E.
1923   Folklore de Oaxaca. *Jour. Amer.
        Folklore*, 36: 199–200.

GÓMEZ ROBLEDA, J.
1943 Pescadores y campesinos tarascos. Mexico.

GONZÁLEZ BONILLA, L. A.
1939 Los huastecos. *Rev. Mex. Sociol.*, 1: 29–56.

GONZÁLEZ CASANOVA, P.
1925 Los idiomas popolocas y su clasificación. *An. Mus. Nac. Arqueol. Hist. Etnog.*, 3: 497–538.
1927 El Tapachulteca no. 2, sin relación conocido. *Rev. Mex. Estud. Hist.*, 1: 18–26.

GONZÁLEZ TENORIO, G.
1941 Informe general sobre la exploración sanitaria del municipio de Acaxochitlan, distrito de Tulancingo, estado de Hidalgo. Mexico.

GOODENOUGH, W. H.
1959 A problem in Malayo-Polynesian social organization. *Amer. Anthr.*, 55: 557–72.

GOUBAUD CARRERA, A.
1946 Distribución de las lenguas indígenas actuales de Guatemala. *Bol. Inst. Indig. Nac.*, 1 (2, 3): 63–76. Guatemala.
1949 Notas sobre los indios de la finca Nueva Granada. *Univ. Chicago, Micro. Coll. MSS Middle Amer. Cult. Anthr.*, no. 21.

——, J. DE DÍOS ROSALES, AND S. TAX
1947 Reconnaissance of northern Guatemala, 1944. *Ibid.*, no. 17.

GOULD, H. N.
1946 Anthropometry of the Chol Indians of Chiapas, Mexico. *Tulane Univ., Middle Amer. Research Inst., Records*, 1: 91–110.

GRIFFEN, W. B.
1959 Notes on Seri Indian culture, Sonora, Mexico. *Univ. Florida, School Inter-Amer. Studies, Latin Amer. Monogr.*, no. 10.

GRIMES, J. E.
1955 Style in Huichol structure. *Language*, 31: 31–35.
1959 Huichol tone and intonation. *Int. Jour. Amer. Ling.*, 25: 221–32.
1960 Spanish-Nahuatl-Huichol monetary terms. *Int. Jour. Amer. Ling.*, 26: 162–65.
1961 Huichol economics. *Amer. Indig.*, 21: 281–30.
1964 Huichol syntax. The Hague.

—— AND B. F. GRIMES
1962 Semantic distinctions in Huichol (Uto-Aztecan) kinship. *Amer. Anthr.*, 64: 104–14.

GROLLIG, F. X. (S.J.)
1959 San Miguel Acatan, Huehuetenango, Guatemala: a modern Mayan village. Doctoral dissertation, Indiana Univ.

GUERRERO, RAÚL G.
1939a La fiesta tradicional de Juchitan. *Rev. Mex. Estud. Antr.*, 3: 242–56.
1939b La música zapoteca. *Neza*, 4 (1): 16–20.
1950a Alfajayucan, etnografía y folklore de un grupo otomí del valle del Mezquital, estado de Hidalgo. MS. Bib. Inst. Indig. Interamer. Mexico.
1950b Etnografía y folklore de la zona otomí del estado de Hidalgo. MS. *Ibid.*

GUERRERO, ROSALÍA
1950 La mujer otomí. MS. *Ibid.*

GUITERAS HOLMES, C.
1947 Clanes y sistema de parentesco de Cancuc, México. *Acta Amer.*, 5: 1–17.
1948a Organización social de tzeltales y tzotziles, México. *Amer. Indig.*, 8: 45–62.
1948b Sistema de parentesco huasteco. *Acta Amer.*, 6: 152–72.
1951 El calpulli de San Pablo Chalchihuitan. *In* Homenaje Caso, pp. 199–206.
1952 Sayula. Soc. Mex. Geog. Estad. Mexico.
1956 Background of a changing kinship system among the Tzotzil Indians of Chiapas. MS.
1961a La magia en la crisis del embarazo y parto en los actuales grupos mayances de Chiapas. *Estud. Cultura Maya*, 1: 159–66.
1961b Perils of the soul: the world view of a Tzotzil Indian. Univ. Chicago Press.
1961c Informe sobre Bachajon. MS.

GUTIÉRREZ GARCÍA, D.
1946 Exploración sanitaria del municipio de Acaxochitlan, estado de Hidalgo. Mexico.

HACKETT, C. W., ed.
1923–37 Historical documents relating to New Mexico, Nueva Vizcaya and approaches thereto, to 1773, collected by Adolph F. A. Bandelier and Fanny R. Bandelier. 3 vols. *Carnegie Inst. Wash.*, Pub. 330.

904

HALE, K.
1958 Internal diversity in Uto-Aztecan: I. *Int. Jour. Amer. Ling.*, 24: 101–07.

HAMP, E. P.
1954 Componential restatement of syllable structure in Trique. *Ibid.*, 20: 206–09.

HARRIS, M.
1946 An introduction to the Chontal of Tabasco, Mexico. *Amer. Indig.*, 6: 247–55.

HARRISON, W. R.
1952 The mason: a Zoque text. *Tlalocan*, 3: 193–204.

HASKINS, W. C.
1940 In the land of the Zapotecs. *Mex. Life*, 16: 14–15.

HASLER, J. A.
1960 El mundo físico-espiritual de los mazatecos de Ichcatlan. *Rev. Mex. Estud. Antr.*, 16: 257–69.

HAY, C. L., ed.
1940 *See* The Maya and their neighbors.

HAYNER, N.
1944 Oaxaca, city of old Mexico. *Sociol. and Social Research*, 29: 87–95.

HEIM, R., AND R. G. WASSON
1958 Les champignons hallucinogènes du Mexique: études ethnologiques, taxonomiques, biologiques, physiologiques et chimiques. *Archives du Mus. Nat. d'Histoire Naturelle*, vol. 6.

HELBIG, K. M.
1964 La cuenca superior del Río Grijalva: un estudio regional de Chiapas, sureste de México. Inst. Cien. y Artes de Chiapas. Tuxtla Gutierrez.

HENDERSON, R.
1952a Lost silver ledge of Santa Catarina. *Desert Mag.*, vol. 15, no. 11.
1952b Tribesmen of Santa Catarina. *Ibid.*, vol. 15, no. 7.

HENDRICHS PÉREZ, P.
1939 Un estudio preliminar sobre la lengua cuitlateca de San Miguel Totolapan, Guerrero. *El Mex. Antiguo*, 4: 329–62.
1945 Por tierras ignotas: viajes y observaciones en la región del Río de las Balsas. Vol. 1. Mexico.
1946 *Idem*, vol. 2.

HENESTROSA, A.
1936a Estudios sobre la lengua zapoteca. *Neza*, 2: 19.
1936b Los sones zapotecas. *Ibid.*, vol. 2.
1936c Vini-gundah-zaa. *Ibid.*, 2 (10): 1, 5, 6.

1947 La viva raíz de Juchitan. *Univ. Mexico*, 1 (9): 16–17.

HENNING, P.
1919 Palangónen en zapoteco, que se usa en Zaachila, distrito de Zimatlan, estado de Oaxaca, para pedir la novia. *El Mex. Antiguo*, 1: 91–96.

HERAS, N.
1940 Yugo de uso entre los zapotecos. *El Nacional*, May 10.

HERNÁNDEZ, F.
1902 Las razas indígenas de Sonora y la guerra del yaqui. Mexico.

HERRERA Y TORDESILLAS, A. DE
1601–15 Historia general de los hechos de los castellanos en las islas y tierra firme del mar océano. . . . 4 vols. Madrid.
1945 *Idem*, another ed. Buenos Aires.

HIGBEE, E.
1947 The agricultural regions of Guatemala. *Geog. Rev.*, 37: 177–201.

HINSHAW, R.
1966 Structure and stability of belief in Panajachel. Doctoral dissertation, Univ. Chicago.

HINTON, T. B.
1955 The Seri girls' puberty rite at Desemboque, Sonora. *Kiva*, vol. 20, no. 4.
1959 A survey of Indian assimilation in eastern Sonora. *Univ. Arizona, Anthr. Papers*, no. 4.
1961 The village hierarchy as a factor in Cora Indian acculturation. Doctoral dissertation, Univ. California, Los Angeles.
1964 The Cora village: a civil-religious hierarchy in northern Mexico. *In* Culture change and stability: essays in memory of Olive Ruth Barker and George C. Barker, Jr., pp. 44–62. Univ. California, Los Angeles.

—— AND R. C. OWEN
1957 Some surviving Yuman groups in northern Baja California. *Amer. Indig.*, 17: 87–102.

HOHENTHAL, W. D.
1951 The mountain tribes of northern Baja California, Mexico. MS.
1960 The Tipai and their neighbors of northern Baja California, Mexico. MS.

HOLDEN, W. C., AND OTHERS
1936 Studies of the Yaqui Indians of Sonora, Mexico. *Texas Tech. College Bull.*, vol. 12, no. 1.

HOLLAND, W. R.

1961a Relaciones entre la religión tzotzil contemporánea y la maya antigua. *An. Inst. Nac. Antr. Hist.*, 13: 113–31.

1961b El tonalismo y el nagualismo entre los tzotziles. *Estud. Cultura Maya*, 1: 167–81.

1963a Medicina maya en los altos de Chiapas: un estudio del cambio sociocultural. *Inst. Nac. Indig., Col. Antr. Social*, no. 2.

1963b Psicoterapia maya en los altos de Chiapas. *Estud. Cultura Maya*, 3: 261–77.

1965 Contemporary Tzotzil cosmological concepts as a basis for interpreting prehistoric Maya civilization. *Amer. Antiquity*, 29: 301–06.

—— AND R. G. THARP

1964 Highland Maya psychotherapy. *Amer. Anthr.*, 66: 41–52.

HOMENAJE CASO

1951 Homenaje al Doctor Alfonso Caso. Nuevo Mundo. Mexico.

HOMENAJE TOWNSEND

1961 A William Cameron Townsend en el vigésimoquinto aniversario del Instituto Lingüístico del Verano. B. F. Elson, ed. Mexico.

HOMENAJE WEITLANER

See Pompa y Pompa, 1966.

HOOGSHAGEN, S. A.

1959 Notes on the sacred (narcotic) mushroom from Coatlan, Oaxaca, Mexico. *Bull. Oklahoma Anthr. Soc.*, 7: 71–74.

1960 Elección, instalación y aseguramiento de los funcionarios en Coatlan. *Rev. Mex. Estud. Antr.*, 16: 247–55.

—— AND W. R. MERRIFIELD

1961 Coatlan Mixe kinship. *SW. Jour. Anthr.*, 17: 219–25.

HOPPE, W. A.

1960 Field notes. MS. Mexico.

1961 Field notes. MS. Mexico.

HRDLIČKA, A.

1903 The region of the ancient "Chichimecs," with notes on the Tepecanos and the ruin of La Quemada, Mexico. *Amer. Anthr.*, 5: 385–440.

1904a Notes on the Indians of Sonora. *Ibid.*, 6: 51–89.

1904b Cora dances. *Ibid.*, 6: 744–45.

1905 A Cora cradle. *Ibid.*, 7: 361–62.

HUASTECOS, TOTONACOS Y SUS VECINOS

1953 Huastecos, Totonacos y sus vecinos. I. Bernal and E. Dávalos Hurtado, eds. *Rev. Mex. Estud. Antr.*, vol. 13, nos. 2 and 3.

HUMBOLDT, A. VON

1810 Vues de cordillères et monuments des peuples indigènes de l'Amérique. Paris.

IGLESIAS, A.

1856 Soteapan. *In* M. Orozco y Berra, ed., Apéndice al diccionario universal de historia y de geografía, 3: 433–38.

IGLESIAS, J. M.

1831 Los departamentos de Acayucan y Jalapa. Cuaderno segundo, Estadística del estado libre y soberano de Veracruz.

INDIANIST YEARBOOK

1962 Indians in the hemisphere today: Guatemala. Guide to the Indian population. *Inter-Amer. Indian Inst.*, vol. 22. Mexico.

INSTITUTO DE INVESTIGACIONES SOCIALES

1957 Etnografía de México. Mexico.

INSTITUTO INDIGENISTA NACIONAL (GUATEMALA)

1948a Chuarrancho. *Special publications, Inst. Indig. Nac.*, no. 2.

1948b San Juan Sacatepequez. *Ibid.*, no. 3.

1948c Chinautla. *Ibid.*, no. 4.

1948d Parramos. *Ibid.*, no. 5.

1948e San Antonio Aguas Calientes. *Ibid.*, no. 6.

1948f Santa Catarina Barahona. *Ibid.*, no. 7.

1949a Santo Domingo Xenacoj. *Ibid.*, no. 8.

1949b San Bartolomé Milpas Altas. *Ibid.*, no. 9.

INSTITUTO NACIONAL INDIGENISTA (MEXICO)

n.d.,*a* La deuda del sol, y otros cuentos. *Nuestros Cuentos*, no. 1.

n.d.,*b* El muchacho en la cueva, y otros cuentos. *Ibid.*, no. 2.

n.d.,*c* La casa de los tigres, y otros cuentos. *Ibid.*, no. 3.

1950 Densidad de la población de habla indígena en la República Mexicana (por entidades federativas y municipio, conforme al censo de 1940). Prologo de A. Caso. Introducción de M. G. Parra. *Mem. Inst. Nac. Indig.*, vol. 1, no. 1.

REFERENCES

INVENTARIO DE ASUNTOS PENALES
1953–63 Inventario de asuntos penales. Archivos del distrito de Villa Alta.

ISLAS, L.
1912 El hogar del indio zapoteca. *Bol. Mus. Nac.*, 2: 4–10. Mexico.

ITURRIBARIA, J. F.
1941 Historia de Oaxaca. Mexico.
1955 Oaxaca en la historia: de la época precolombina a los tiempos actuales. Mexico.

IXTLILXOCHITL, F. DE A.
See Alva Ixtlilxochitl, F. de

JENKINS, J.
1946 San Gregorio, an Otomi village of the highlands of Hidalgo, Mexico. *Amer. Indig.*, 6: 345–49.

JIMÉNEZ MORENO, W.
1937 Materiales para una etnografía de la América Latina. *Bol. Bibliog. Antr. Amer.*, vol. 1, nos. 1 and 2. Mexico.
1942a El enigma de los olmeca. *Cuad. Amer.*, 5: 113–45.
1942b Fr. Juan de Córdova y la lengua zapoteca. Mexico.
1944 Tribus e idiomas del norte de México. *In* El Norte de México, vol. 3.
1958 The Indians of America and Christianity. *In* History of religion in the New World, pp. 75–95.

JOHNSON, F.
1940 The linguistic map of Mexico and Central America. *In* The Maya and their neighbors, pp. 88–114.

JOHNSON, I. W.
1936 A Chinantec calendar. *Amer. Anthr.*, 38: 197–201.
1953 El quechquemitl y el huipil. *In* Huastecos, Totonacos, pp. 241–57.

JOHNSON, J. B.
1939a The elements of Mazatec witchcraft. *Ethnol. Studies*, 9: 128–50. Göteborg.
1939b Oaxaca market. [San Lucas, Zoquiapan.] *SW. Rev.*, 24: 333.
1939c Some notes on the Mazatec. *Rev. Mex. Estud. Antr.*, 3: 142–56.
1950 The Opata: an inland tribe of Sonora. *Univ. New Mexico Pub. Anthr.*, no. 6.

JOSEPH, A., R. B. SPICER, AND J. CHESKY
1949 The desert people: a study of the Papago Indians. Univ. Chicago Press.

KAPLAN, B. A.
1951 Changing functions of the Huanancha dance at the Corpus Christi festival in Paracho, Michoacan, Mexico. *Jour. Amer. Folklore*, 64: 383–92.

1960 Mechanization in Paracho: a craft community. *In* Leslie, 1960b, pp. 59–65.

KEANE, H. A.
1908 Veytia's "Calendarios mexicanos." *Atheneum*, 1: 193–94. London.

KELLY, I. T.
1953 The modern Totonac. *In* Huastecos, Totonacos, pp. 175–86.
1966 World view of a highland Totonac pueblo. *In* Pompa y Pompa, 1966, pp. 395–411.

—— AND A. PALERM
1952 The Tajin Totonac. Part 1: History, subsistence, shelter and technology. *Smithsonian Inst., Inst. Social Anthr.*, Pub. 13.

KELLY, W. H.
1942 Cocopa gentes. *Amer. Anthr.*, 44: 675–91.
1944 A preliminary study of the Cocopa Indians, with an analysis of the influence of geographical position and physical environment on certain aspects of the culture. Doctoral dissertation, Harvard Univ.
1949 Cocopa attitudes and practices with respect to death and mourning. *SW. Jour. Anthr.*, 5: 151–64.

KING, A. R.
1952 Changing cultural goals and patterns in Guatemala. *Amer. Anthr.*, 54: 139–42.

KINGSBOROUGH, E. K.
1831–48 Antiquities of Mexico. 9 vols. London.

KINO, E. F.
1913–22 Las misiones de Sonora y Arizona, comprendiendo la crónica titulada "Favores celestiales" y la "Relación diaria de la entrada al noroeste." *Archivo General de la Nación*, Pub. 8.

KIRCHHOFF, P.
1954 Gatherers and farmers in the greater Southwest: a problem in classification. *Amer. Anthr.*, 56: 529–61.
1956 La relación de Michoacan como fuente para la historia de la sociedad y cultura tarascas. *In* Relación de Michoacan.

KLINEBERG, O.
1934 Notes on the Huichol. *Amer. Anthr.*, 36: 446–60.

KROEBER, A. L.
1915 Serian, Tequistlatecan and Hokan. *Univ. California Pub. Amer. Archaeol. Ethnol.*, 11: 279–90.

1931 The Seri. *SW. Mus. Papers*, no. 6.

1934 Uto-Aztecan languages of Mexico. *Ibero-Amer.*, no. 8.

1939 Cultural and natural areas of native North America. Univ. California Press.

1958 *Idem*, 2d ed.

KUBLER, G.

1961 Chichen-Itza y Tula. *Estud. Cultura Maya*, 1: 47–80.

KURATH, W., AND E. H. SPICER

1947 A brief introduction to Yaqui, a native language of Sonora. *Univ. Arizona Social Sci. Bull.*, no. 15.

LaFARGE, O.

1927 Adaptations of Christianity among the Jacalteca Indians of Guatemala. *Thought*, December. New York.

1930 The ceremonial year at Jacaltenango. *Proc. 23d Int. Cong. Amer.*, pp. 656–60.

1940 Maya ethnology: the sequence of cultures. *In* The Maya and their neighbors, pp. 281–91.

1947 Santa Eulalia: the religion of a Cuchumatan Indian town. Univ. Chicago Press.

—— AND D. BYERS

1931 The year bearer's people. *Tulane Univ., Middle Amer. Research Inst.*, Pub. 3.

LANDA, D. DE

1864 Relación de las cosas de Yucatan. Paris.

1938 *Idem*. Pérez Martínez, ed. Merida.

1941 Landa's Relación de las cosas de Yucatan. Tr. and ed. with notes by A. M. Tozzer. *Papers Peabody Mus., Harvard Univ.*, vol. 18.

LAS CASAS, B. DE

1875–76 Historia de las Indias. Col. doc. inéditos para la historia de España. 5 vols. Madrid.

LAUGHLIN, R. M.

1962 El símbolo de la flor en la religión de Zinacantan. *Estud. Cultura Maya*, 2:123–39.

LAW, H. W.

1960 Linguistic acculturation in Mexico. *Univ. Texas, Dept. Anthropology, Student Papers Anthr.*, 3: 1–31.

LEAL, M.

1950 Patterns of tone substitution in Zapotec morphology. *Int. Jour. Amer. Ling.*, 16: 132–36.

1954 Noun possession in Villa Alta Zapotec. *Ibid.*, 20: 215–16.

LECHE, S. M.

1936 Dermatoglyphics and functional lateral dominance in Mexican Indians. III: Zapotecas and Mixtecas; IV: Chamulas. *In* Measures of Men, pp. 225, 287–314. *Tulane Univ., Middle Amer. Research Inst.*, Pub. 7.

LEHMANN, W.

1905 Les peintures Mixteco-Zapotèques et quelques documents apparentés. *Jour. Soc. Amer. Paris*, 2: 241–80.

1910 Ergebnisse einer Forschungsreise in Mittelamerika und Mexiko, 1907–09. *Zeit. für Ethnol.*, 42: 687–749.

1915 Ueber die Stellung und Verwandtschaft der Subtiaba-Sprache der Pazifischen Kuste Nicaraguas. *Ibid.*, 47: 1–34.

1920 Zentral-Amerika. 2 vols. Berlin.

1928 Ergebnisse einer mit Unterstützung der Notgemeinschaft der Deutschen Wissenschaft in den Jahren 1925–26 ausgeführten Forschungsreise nach Mexiko und Guatemala. *Anthropos*, 23: 749–91.

LEIGH, H.

1960a Notes on Mitla lore and language. *Bol. Estud. Oaxaqueños*, no. 18, pp. 1–3.

1960b The Zapotec name for the Zapotecs. *Ibid.*, no. 18, pp. 4–7.

LEMLEY, H. V.

n.d. Unpublished material.

1949 Three Tlapaneco stories from Tlacoapa, Guerrero. *Tlalocan*, 3: 76–82.

LEMOINE V., E.

1954 Ensayo de división municipal del estado de Oaxaca. *Yan*, no. 3, pp. 69–74.

LEÓN, F. DE P.

1939 Los esmaltes de Uruapan. Mexico.

LEÓN, N.

1887a Nombres de algunos vegetales, en tarasco, con su correspondiente clasificación científica. *El Monitor Médico-Farmacéutico e Industrial*, December. Morelia.

1887b Nombres de animales, en tarasco y castellano, con su correspondiente clasificación científica. *Ibid.*

1889a El matrimonio entre los tarascos precolombianos y sus actuales usos. *An. Mus. Michoacano*, 2: 155–65.

1889b Adición al estudio "Matrimonio entre los tarascos." *Ibid.*, 2: 135–86.

1901 Los huavi: estudio etno-antropológico.

Rev. Cien. Bibliog. Soc. Antonio Al-zate, 16: 103–29.

1902a Carta lingüística de México. An. Mus. Nac. Mexico.

1902b La caza de aves con el tzipaqui en el lago de Patzcuaro. *In* Lumholtz, 1902.

1903a Familias lingüísticas de México. *An. Mus. Nac.*, 7: 279–335.

1903b Los tarascos. *An. Mus. Nac.*, 11: 298–478.

1903c Vocabulario en lengua cuitlateca de San Miguel Totolapan, Guerrero. Mexico.

1904 Catálogo de la colección de antigüe-dades huavis del estado de Oaxaca, existente en el Museo Nacional de México. Mexico.

1905 Los popolocas. *An. Mus. Nac.*, 2: 103–20.

1906 Los tarascos: etnografía postcortesiana y actual. Part 3. *An. Mus. Nac.*, ep. 2, vol. 3.

1912 Vocabulario de la lengua popoloca chocha. *An. Mus. Nac.*, 3d ser., 3: 1–48.

1934 Los indios tarascos del lago Patzcuaro. *Ibid.*, ep. 5, 1: 149–68.

LEÓN M., A. F., AND H. CONTRERAS A.

1944 Pastorela de viejos, para el año 1912. *Tlalocan*, 1: 169–93.

LEÓN-PORTILLA, M.

1959 Panorama de la población indígena de México. *Amer. Indig.*, 19: 43–73 (2d ed.). Mexico.

LE PLONGEON, A. D.

1886 Here and there in Yucatan. New York.

LESLIE, C. M.

1960a Now we are civilized. Wayne State Univ. Press.

1960b [ed.] The social anthropology of Middle America. *Alpha Kappa Del-tan*, vol. 30, no. 1 (special issue).

LEWIS, O.

1951 Life in a Mexican village: Tepoztlan restudied. Univ. Illinois Press.

1960 Tepoztlan, village in Mexico. New York.

LIEKENS, E.

1952 Los zapotecas no son zapotecas sin itzaes Villahermosa, Tabasco.

LINCOLN, J. S.

1939 The southeastern Chinantla of Mex-ico. *Sci. Monthly*, 69: 57–65.

LOMBARDO, N.

1702 Arte de la lengua teguima llamada vulgarmente opata. Mexico.

LONGACRE, R. E.

1952 Five phonemic pitch levels in Trique. *Acta Ling.*, 7: 62–82.

1955 Rejoinder to Hamp's componential restatement to syllable structure in Trique. *Int. Jour. Amer. Ling.*, 21: 189–94.

1959 Trique tone morphemics. *Anthr. Ling.*, 1: 5–42.

—— AND R. MILLON

1961 Proto-Mixtecan and Proto-Amuzgo-Mixtecan vocabularies: a preliminary cultural analysis. *Ibid.*, 3 (4): 1–44.

LÓPEZ CHIÑAS, G.

1936 El paisaje en la vida de Juchitan. *Neza*, 2 (12): 1, 5.

1937 Los parientes: antecesores zapotecas. *Ibid.*, 3 (1): 33–37.

1939 La música aborigen de Juchitan. *Ibid.*, 4 (1): 21–24.

1945 El concepto de la muerte entre los zapotecas. *Anuario Soc. Folklórica Mex.*, 4: 485–91.

1949 Breve estudio sobre la evolución so-cial y jurídica de la familia zapoteca. Tésis, Escuela Nac. Jurisprudencia. Mexico.

1958 Vinni Gulasa: cuentos de Juchitan. (2d ed.) Mexico.

LÓPEZ CHIÑAS, J.

1936 La vida militar zapoteca. *Neza*, 1 (9): 2.

1937 Algunos animales y plantas que co-nocierón los antiguos zapotecas. *Ibid.*, 3 (1): 12–24.

1939 La música zapoteca en la capital. *Ibid.*, 4 (1): 25–27.

LÓPEZ DE COGOLLUDO, D.

1955 Historia de Yucatan. 3 vols. Cam-peche.

LÓPEZ VERA, T.

1935 Juchitan y Tehuantepec. *Neza*, 1 (1): 2.

LÓPEZ Y LÓPEZ, G.

1947 En pos de la filosofía zapoteca. *Filo-sofía y Letras*, 27: 9–20, 57–59, 85–98 (1955).

LOTHROP, S. K.

1928 Santiago Atitlan, Guatemala. *Mus. Amer. Indian, Heye Found., Indian Notes*, vol. 5, no. 4.

LOWE, G. W.

1959 Archaeological exploration of the up-per Grijalva River, Chiapas, Mexico.

Papers New World Archaeol. Found., no. 2.

LUMHOLTZ, C.

1891 Explorations in the Sierra Madre. *Scribner's Mag.*, vol. 10, no. 5.

1898 The Huichol Indians of Mexico. *Bull. Amer. Mus. Natural Hist.*, 5 (10): 1–14.

1900 Symbolism of the Huichol Indians. *Amer. Mus. Natural Hist., Mem. Anthr.*, vol. 2, no. 1.

1902 Unknown Mexico. 2 vols. New York.

1904 Decorative art of the Huichol Indians. *Amer. Mus. Natural Hist., Mem. Anthr.*, 2: 279–326.

1912 New trails in Mexico. New York.

McBRIDE, G. M.

1923 The land systems of Mexico. *Amer. Geog. Soc., Research Ser.*, no. 12.

McBRYDE, F. W.

1934 Solola: a Guatemalan town and Cakchiquel market center. *Tulane Univ., Middle Amer. Research Inst.*, Pub. 5, pp. 45–152.

1947 Cultural and historical geography of southwest Guatemala. *Smithsonian Inst., Inst. Social Anthr.*, Pub. 4.

McGEE, W J

1898 The Seri Indians. *Smithsonian Inst., Bur. Amer. Ethnol.*, 17th ann. rept.

MACÍAS, C.

1912 Los tehuantepecanos actuales. *Bol. Mus. Nac.*, 2: 18–29. Mexico.

McINTOSH, J. B.

1945 Huichol phonemes. *Int. Jour. Amer. Ling.*, 11: 31–35.

—— AND J. GRIMES

1954 Niuqui 'iquisicayari: vocabulario huichol-castellano, castellano-huichol. Inst. Ling. Verano. Mexico.

McKAUGHAN, H. P.

1954 Chatino formulas and phonemes. *Int. Jour. Amer. Ling.*, 20: 23–27.

—— AND B. McKAUGHAN

1951 Diccionario de la lengua chatino. Inst. Ling. Verano. Mexico.

McKINLAY, A.

1945 Visits with Mexico's Indians. Mexico.

McMAHON, A.

1967 Phonemes and phonemic units of Cora (Mexico). *Int. Jour. Amer. Ling.*, 33: 128–34.

—— AND M. J. McMAHON

1959 Vocabulario Cora. Ser. Vocabularios Indígenas Mariano Silva y Aceves, no. 2. Inst. Ling. Verano. Mexico.

MacNEISH, R. S.

1961 First annual report of the Tehuacan archaeological-botanical project. Robert S. Peabody Found. for Archaeology, Phillips Academy. Andover.

1962 Second annual report of the Tehuacan archaeological-botanical project. *Ibid.*

McQUOWN, N. A.

1941 La fonémica del cuitlateco, Mexico. *El Mex. Antiguo*, 5: 239–54.

1955 The indigenous languages of Latin America. *Amer. Anthr.*, 57: 501–70.

1956 The classification of the Mayan languages. *Int. Jour. Amer. Ling.*, 22: 191–95.

1959 [ed.] Report on the "Man-in-Nature" project of the department of anthropology of the University of Chicago in the Tzeltal-Tzotzil-speaking region of the state of Chiapas, Mexico. 3 vols. Hectographed.

1964 Los orígines y la diferenciación de los mayas según se infiere del estudio comparativo de las lenguas mayanas. *In* Desarrollo cultural de los Mayas, pp. 49–80.

MADSEN, W.

1955a Shamanism in Mexico. *SW. Jour. Anthr.*, 11: 48–57.

1955b Hot and cold in the universe of San Francisco Tecospa, valley of Mexico. *Jour. Amer. Folklore*, 68: 123–39.

1956 Aztec morals. *In* Encyclopedia of Morals, pp. 41–45. Philosophical Library of New York.

1957 Christo-paganism: a study of Mexican religious syncretism. *Tulane Univ., Middle Amer. Research Inst.*, Pub. 19, pp. 105–80.

1960 The Virgin's children: life in an Aztec village today. Univ. Texas Press.

MAK, C., AND R. E. LONGACRE

1960 Proto-Mixtec phonology. *Int. Jour. Amer. Ling.*, 26: 23–40.

MALER, T.

1901 Researches in the central portion of the Usumatsintla valley. *Mem. Peabody Mus., Harvard Univ.*, vol. 2, no. 1.

MALINOWSKI, B., AND J. DE LA FUENTE

1957 La económica de un sistema de mercados en México. *Acta Anthr.*, ser. 2, vol. 1, no. 2. Mexico.

MANN, C. E., AND R. CHADWICK

1960 Present-day use of ancient calendars

among the lowland Mixe. *Bol. Estud. Oaxaqueños,* no. 19.

MANRIQUE CASTAÑEDA, L.

1957 Notas de campo sobre el área pame. Inst. Nac. Antr. Hist., Depto. Invest. Antr. Mexico.

1959 Field notes. MS.

1961 La organización social de Jiliapan, Hidalgo. *An. Inst. Nac. Antr. Hist.,* 13: 95–111.

1967 Jiliapan Pame. *In* Handbook of Middle American Indians, vol. 5, Art. 7G.

MANZO DE CONTRERAS, C.

1661 Relación cierta y verdadera de lo que sucedió y ha sucedido en esta villa de Guadalcazar, provincia de Tehuantepec. . . . Mexico.

MARÍN TAMAYO, F.

1960 La división racial en Puebla de los Angeles bajo el régimen colonial. Puebla.

MARINA ARREOLA, A.

1961 Población de los altos de Chiapas durante el siglo XVII e inicios del XVIII. *In* Los Mayas del sur, pp. 247–64.

MARINO FLORES, A.

1963 Distribución municipal de los hablantes de lenguas indígenas en la República Mexicana. Inst. Nac. Antr. Hist. Mexico.

MARROQUÍN, A. D.

1954 Tlaxiaco: una ciudad mercado. *Inst. Nac. Indig., Mimeo. Ser.,* no. 4. Mexico.

1957 La ciudad mercado (Tlaxiaco). Mexico.

MARTÍNEZ, P. L.

1956 Historia de Baja California. Mexico.

1958 El magonismo en Baja California: documentos. Mexico.

MARTÍNEZ GRACIDA, M.

1883a Catálogo etimológico de los nombres de los pueblos, haciendas y ranchos del estado de Oaxaca. Oaxaca.

1883b Colección de cuadros sinópticos. Anexo no. 50 a la memoria administrativa. Oaxaca.

1910a Historia antigua de la chontalpa oaxaqueña. Mexico.

1910b La civilización chontal. Mexico.

MASON, J. A.

n.d. Notes and observations on the northern Tepehuan Indians. MS. [See his 1952.]

1912 The fiesta of the pinole at Azqueltan. *Mus. Jour.,* 3: 44–50. Philadelphia.

1913 The Tepehuan Indians of Azqueltan. *Proc. 18th Int. Cong. Amer.,* pp. 344–51.

1918 Tepecano prayers. *Int. Jour. Amer. Ling.,* 1: 91–153.

1936 Classification of the Sonoran languages. *In* Essays in anthropology, pp. 183–98.

1940 The native languages of Middle America. *In* The Maya and their neighbors, pp. 52–87.

1948 The Tepehuan and other aborigines of the Mexican Sierra Madre Occidental. *Amer. Indig.,* 8: 289–300.

1952 Notes and observations on the Tepehuan. *Ibid.,* 12: 33–53.

1959 The Tepehuan of northern Mexico. *Mitteilungen aus dem Museum für Völkerkunde in Hamburg,* 25: 91–96.

—— AND D. M. BRUGGE

1958 Notes on the lower Pima. *In* Misc. Paul Rivet. Mexico.

MASSEY, W. C.

1949 Tribes and languages of Baja California. *SW. Jour. Anthr.,* 5: 272–307.

MATSON, G. A., AND J. SWANSON

1959 Distribution of hereditary blood antigens among the Maya and non-Maya Indians in Mexico and Guatemala. *Amer. Jour. Physical Anthr.,* 17: 49–74.

MATUS, V. E.

1935a Nuestro istmo zapoteca. *Neza,* 1 (4): 1, 5.

1935b Tópicos de mi tierra. *Ibid.,* 1 (5): 1, 5.

1939a Comentarios sobre zapoteco y nahuatl. *El Universo Gráfico,* 18 (7677): 8, 15.

1939b Lecciones de escritura comparada zapoteca. *Ibid.,* 18 (7659): 8, 19.

1939c ¿Zapoteco moderno? *Ibid.,* 18 (7749): 9, 13.

1940a Sandunga tehuantepecana. *Oaxaca en México,* special issue, October, pp. 32–34.

1940b El verbo zapoteco. *El Universo Gráfico,* 19 (8024): 11.

1941 El zapoteco. *Istmo,* 2 (2, 12): 4–5.

1942 Poesía zapoteca. *Ibid.,* 2 (2, 13): 4.

1945 Zapotecos del istmo de Oaxaca. *In* L. Alvárez y Alvárez de la Cadena, ed., Leyendas y costumbres, trajes y danzas, pp. 359–65. Mexico.

MAUDSLAY, A. C., AND A. P. MAUDSLAY
1899 A glimpse at Guatemala. London.

MAYA AND THEIR NEIGHBORS, THE
1940 The Maya and their neighbors. C. L. Hay and others, eds. New York.

MAYAS DEL SUR, LOS
1961 Los mayas del sur y sus relaciones con los nahuas meridionales. VIII mesa redonda, San Cristobal de las Casas, Chiapas. Soc. Mex. Antr. Mexico.

MAYERS, M. K.
1960a The linguistic unity of Pocomam-Pocomchi. Int. Jour. Amer. Ling., 26: 290–300.
1960b The phonemes of Pocomchi. Anthr. Ling., 2: 1–39.
1966 Languages of Guatemala.

MAZA, A. DE LA
1947 La nación pame. Bol. Soc. Mex. Geog. Estad., vol. 63, no. 2.
1953 La Pamería a través de los tiempos. In Huastecos, Totonacos, pp. 269–80.

MEADE, J.
1942 La huasteca: época antigua. Mexico.

MECHLING, W. H.
1912 Indian linguistic stocks of Oaxaca, Mexico. Amer. Anthr., 14: 643–82.

MEDINA, A.
1960 Field notes. MS.

MEDINILLA, M.
1883 Una idea de los idiomas . . . caminos, ríos, hamacas . . . [district of Tuxtepec]. In Martínez Gracida, 1883b.

MEDIONI, G.
1952 L'art tarasque du Mexique: Mexique occidental. Paris.

MEGGERS, B.
1954 Environmental limitation on the development of culture. Amer. Anthr., 56: 801–24.

MEIGS, P.
1935 The Dominican mission frontier of Lower California. Univ. California, Pub. Geog., no. 7.
1939 The Kiliwa Indians of Lower California. Ibero-Amer., no. 15.

MENDELSON, E. M.
1958 A Guatemalan sacred bundle. Man, 58 (art. 170): 121–26.
1959 Maximón: an iconographical introduction. Ibid., 59 (art. 87): 57–60.
1962 Religion and world-view in Santiago Atitlan. Univ. Chicago, Micro. Coll.

MSS Middle Amer. Cult. Anthr., no. 52.

MENDIETA, G. DE
1869 Historia eclesiástica indiana. Mexico. (Another ed. 1945.)

MENDIETA HUERTA, E.
1939 La economía de los pueblos indígenas huastecos de San Luis Potosi. Rev. Mex. Sociol., 1: 57–68. Mexico.

MENDIETA Y NÚÑEZ, L.
1940 [ed.] Los tarascos: monografía histórica, etnográfica y económica. Inst. Invest. Sociales. Mexico.
1949 Los zapotecos: monografía histórica, etnográfica y económica. Mexico.

MENDIZÁBAL, M. O. DE
1939 La demografía mexicana: época colonial 1519–1810. Bol. Soc. Mex. Geog. Estad., 48: 301–41.
1946a La evolución del noroeste de México. In his 1946–47, 3: 7–86.
1946b Charts at end of vol. 5 in his 1946–47.
1946–47 Obras completas. 6 vols. Mexico.
1947a Evolución económica y social del valle de Mezquital. In his 1946–47, vol. 6.
1947b Industrias de los otomíes contemporáneos. In his 1946–47, vol. 6.

—— AND W. JIMÉNEZ MORENO
1936 Mapa lingüístico de Norte y Centro-América. Inst. Panamer. Geog. Hist. Mexico.
1937 Distribución prehispánica de las lenguas indígenas de México. Ibid.

——, ——, AND E. ARANA OSNAYA
1959 Linguistic map. In Esplendor del México antiguo, p. 97.

MENGET, P.
1968 Death in Chamula. Natural Hist., 67: 48–57.

MERRIAM, C.
1932 Zapotecan funeral. Mex. Life, 8 (9): 11–13.

MERRIFIELD, W. R.
1959 The Chinantec kinship system in Palantla, Oaxaca, Mexico. Amer. Anthr., 61: 875–81.
1966 Linguistic clues for the reconstruction of Chinantec prehistory. In Pompa y Pompa, 1966, pp. 579–96.

METZGER, B.
1959 The social structure of three Tzeltal communities: Omaha systems in

912

change. *In* McQuown, 1959, sec. 25.

1960   Notes on the history of Indian-Ladino relations in Chiapas. MS. Laboratory Social Relations, Harvard Univ.

METZGER, D.
1960   Report on Aguatenango. MS.

MEXICO
1943   Sexto censo de población (1940). Dirección General de Estad.

1944   Mapas lingüísticos de la República Mexicana. Depto. Asuntos Indígenas. Mexico.

1953   Séptimo censo . . . (1950).

1963   Octavo censo . . . (1960).

MICHELSEN, R.
1967   Pecked metates of Baja California. *Masterkey*, 41 (2): 73–77.

—— AND R. C. OWEN
1967   A keruk ceremony at Santa Catarina, Baja California, Mexico. *Pacific Coast Archaeol. Soc. Quar.*, vol. 3, no. 1.

MILES, S. W.
1948   A comparative analysis of the survivals of the ancient Maya calendar. Master's thesis, Univ. Chicago.

1952   An analysis of modern Middle American calendars: a study in conservatism. *In* Tax, 1952b, pp. 273–84.

1957   The sixteenth-century Pokom-Maya: a documentary analysis of social structure and archaeological setting. *Trans. Amer. Phil. Soc.*, 47: 731–81.

MILLA, J. D.
1879   Historia de la América Central desde los primeros españoles (1502) hasta su independencia de la España (1821). Guatemala.

MILLER, F. C.
1960   The influence of decision-making on the process of change: the case of Yalcuc. *In* Leslie, 1960b, pp. 29–35.

1964   Tzotzil domestic groups. *Jour. Royal Anthr. Inst.*, 94: 172–82. London.

1965   Cultural change as decision-making: a Tzotzil example. *Ethnology*, 4: 53–65.

MILLER, W. S.
1956   Cuentos mixes. *Inst. Nac. Indig., Bib. Folklore Indig.*, no. 2.

1961   Notes on the Mixe. MS.

MIRAMBELL, L.
1961   Evangelización y organización eclesiástica en la época colonial. *In* Los Mayas del sur, pp. 221–32.

MIRANDA, F.
1952   La vegetación de Chiapas. Ed. Gobierno del estado, depto. prensa y turismo. Tuxtla Gutierrez.

1959   Estudios acerca de la vegetación. *In* Los recursos naturales del sureste y su aprovechamiento, ch. 6. 3 vols. Inst. Mex. Recursos Naturales Renovables. Mexico.

MIRANDA, J.
1952   El tributo indígena en la Nueva España durante el siglo XVI. Colegio de México. Mexico.

MODIANO, N.
1968   A Chamula life. *Natural Hist.*, 67: 58–63.

MOLINA, A. DE
1944   Vocabulario en lengua castellana y mexicana. Ed. Cultura Hispánica. Mexico.

MOLINA, A. G.
1892   El jazmín del istmo: principios generales para aprender a leer, escribir y hablar la lengua zapoteca. Oaxaca.

1894   La rosa de amor: frases en español y zapoteca. San Blas Tehuantepec.

MONTAGU, R.
1958   Preliminary summary of a survey in the Tojolabal region, Chiapas, Mexico. MS.

—— AND E. HUNT
1962   Nombre, autoridad y el sistema de creencias en los altos de Chiapas. *Estud. Cultura Maya*, 2: 141–47.

MONTEMAYOR, F.
1950–56   La población de Veracruz; historia de las lenguas; culturas actuales; rasgos físicos de la población. Mexico.

MONTOYA, J. J., J. M. VÁZQUEZ, AND M. E. MORALES
1961   Informe sobre el trabajo de campo en San Pablito, Puebla. MS en Depto. Invest. Antr., Inst. Nac. Antr. Hist. Mexico.

MONZÓN, A.
1945a   Restos de clanes exogámicos entre los cora de Nayarit. *Escuela Nac. Antr.*, Pub. 4, pp. 12–16. Mexico.

1945b   Teogonía trique. *Tlalocan*, 2: 3–9.

1949   El calpulli en la organización social de los tenochca. Mexico.

MORALES, S. A.
1950   Modos de vida otomí. MS en Bib. Inst. Indig. Interamer. Mexico.

MORALES HENESTROSA, B.
1936   Semblanzas zapotecas: fiestas y ropaje. *Neza*, 2 (15): 2, 5.

1937 Semblanzas zapotecas: perfiles de la sandunga. *Ibid.*, 3 (2): 57–59.

MORGADANES, D.
1940 Similarity between the Mixco (Guatemala) and the Yalalag (Oaxaca, Mexico) costumes. *Amer. Anthr.*, 42: 359–64.

MORLEY, S. G.
1920 The inscriptions at Copan. *Carnegie Inst. Wash.*, Pub. 219.
1946 The ancient Maya. Stanford Univ. Press.
1947 *Idem*, 2d ed.
1956 *Idem*, 3d ed., revised by G .W. Brainerd.
1963 *Idem*, reprinted.

MOSCOSO PASTRANA, P.
1961 El complejo ladino en los altos de Chiapas. *In* Los Mayas del sur, pp. 265–78.

MOTA Y ESCOBAR, A. DE LA
1939–40 Memoriales del obispo de Tlaxcala Fray Alonso de la Mota y Escobar. *An. Inst. Nac. Antr. Hist.*, 1: 191–306.
1940 Descripción geográfica de los reinos de Nueva Galicia, Nueva Viscaya y Nuevo León. Intro. by J. Ramírez Cabanas. Mexico.

MOTOLINIA, T. DE B.
1541 Historia de los indios de la Nueva España. Barcelona. (Other eds. 1914, 1950.)

MÜLLERRIED, F. K. G.
1957 La geología de Chiapas. Gobierno constitucional del estado de Chiapas. Tuxtla Gutierrez.

MUÑOZ, M.
1950 Notas preliminares sobre el municipio Tasquillo, estado de Hidalgo, México. MS en Bib. Inst. Indig. Interamer. Mexico.

MUÑOZ CAMARGO, D.
1892 Historia de Tlaxcala. Mexico.

MURDOCK, G. P.
1949 Social structure. New York.
1957 World ethnographic sample. *Amer. Anthr.*, 59: 664–87.

NADAILLAC, J. F. DE
1899 Les Zapotecs. *La Nature*, 27: 177–79.

NADER, L.
1964 Talea and Juquila: a comparison in Zapotec social organization. *Univ. California Pub. Amer. Archaeol. Ethnol.*, 48: 195–296.

1966 Variations in Zapotec legal procedure. *In* Pompa y Pompa, 1966.
—— AND D. METZGER
1963 Conflict resolution in two Mexican villages. *Amer. Anthr.*, 65: 584–92.

NAHMAD, S., AND L. BEVILLE
1959 Field notes. MS.

NASH, J.
1959 The social structure of Oxchuc. MS.
1960 Protestantism in an Indian village in the western highlands of Guatemala. *In* Leslie, 1960b, pp. 49–58.

NASH, M.
1955 The reaction of a civil-religious hierarchy to a factory in Guatemala. *Human Organization*, 13: 26–28.
1956 Recruitment of wage labor and development of new skills. *Ann. Amer. Acad. Political and Social Sci.*, 305: 23–31.
1957 Cultural persistences and social structure: the Mesoamerican calendar survivals. *SW. Jour. Anthr.*, 13: 149–55.
1958a Machine age Maya: the industrialization of a Guatemalan community. *Amer. Anthr. Assoc.*, Mem. 87.
1958b Political relations in Guatemala. *Social and Economic Studies*, 7: 65–75.

NAVARRO Y NORIEGA, F.
1943 Catálogo de los curatos y misiones de la Nueva España. (1st ed. 1813.) Mexico.

NELLIS, J. G.
1947 Sierra Zapotec forms of address. *Int. Jour. Amer. Ling.*, 13: 231–32.

NEZA
1935–39 Organo mensual de la sociedad nueva de estudiantes juchitecos.

NOGUERA, E.
1940 Tribu: yalaltecos. *In* Basauri, 1940c, 2: 467–96.

NOLASCO A., M.
1965 Los Papagos, habitantes del desierto. *An. Inst. Nac. Antr. Hist.*, 45 de la colección. Mexico.

NORIEGA, R., AND C. COOK DE LEONARD, eds.
1959 *See* Esplendor del México antiguo.

NORIEGA HOPE, C.
1922 Apuntes etnográficos. *In* Gamio, 1922, 2: 207–81.

NORTE DE MÉXICO, EL
1944 El norte de México y el sur de Estados Unidos. Tercera reunión de mesa redonda sobre problemas antropológicos de México y Centro América. Soc. Mex. Antr. Mexico.

NORTH, A. W.
1908 The native tribes of Lower California. *Amer. Anthr.*, 10: 236–50.
1910 Camp and camino in Lower California. New York.

NÚÑEZ CABEZA DE VACA, A.
1906 Relación de los naufragios y comentarios, ilustrados con varios documentos inéditos. *In* Doc. referentes a la historia de América. 2 vols. Madrid.

NUTINI, H. G.
1961 Clan organization in a Nahuatl-speaking village of the state of Tlaxcala, Mexico. *Amer. Anthr.*, 63: 62–78.

OAKES, M.
1951a Beyond the windy place: life in the Guatemalan highlands. New York.
1951b The two crosses of Todos Santos: survivals of Mayan religious festivals. *Bollingen Ser.*, no. 27.

OAXACA
1956 División territorial del estado de Oaxaca. Oaxaca.

OCAMPO, M.
1950 Historia de la misión de la tarahumara. Mexico.

OCCIDENTE DE MÉXICO, EL
1948 El occidente de México. Cuarta reunión de mesa redonda sobre problemas antropológicos de México y Centro América. Soc. Mex. Antr. Mexico.

OGLESBY, C.
1938 The potters of Mexico. *Mex. Life*, 15 (8): 20–22.
1940 Weavings for use and sale. *Ibid.*, 16 (2): 17–20, 54–56.

OLMSTED, D. L.
1958 Tequistlatec kinship terminology. *SW. Jour. Anthr.*, 14: 449–53.
1961 Lexicostatistics as 'proof' of genetic relationship: the case of "Macro Manguean." *Anthr. Ling.*, 3 (6): 9–14.
1967 Tequistlatec ceremonies and the analysis of stereotypy. *In* Studies in Southwestern ethnolinguistics, D. H. Hymes and W. E. Bittle, eds., pp. 68–88. The Hague.

O'NEALE, L. M.
1945 Textiles of highland Guatemala. *Carnegie Inst. Wash.*, Pub. 567.

OROZCO, G.
1946 Tradiciones y leyendas del istmo de Tehuantepec. Mexico.

OROZCO Y BERRA, M.
1858 San Juan Yalalag. *In* Diccionario Universal, app. 2. Mexico.
1864 Geografía de las lenguas y carta etnográfica de México. Mexico.
1880 Historia antigua y de la conquista de México. 4 vols. and atlas. Mexico.

ORTEGA, J. DE
1754 Conquista de Nayarit. Barcelona. (Mexico, 1944.)
1887 Historia de Nayarit, Sonora, Sinaloa y ambas Californias. Mexico.

OSBORNE, L. DE J.
1945 Costumes and wedding customs at Mixco, Guatemala. *Carnegie Inst. Wash., Notes Middle Amer. Archaeol. Ethnol.*, no. 48.

OVIEDO Y VALDÉS, G. F. DE
1851–55 Historia general y natural de las Indias, islas y tierra-firme del mar océano. 4 vols. Madrid.
1943–45 *Idem*, another ed. Paragua.

OWEN, R. C.
1957 Paddle and anvil appearance of some Sonoran pottery. *Amer. Antiquity*, 22: 291.
1958 Easter ceremonies among Opata descendents of northern Sonora, Mexico. *Kiva*, vol. 23, no. 4.
1959 Marobavi: a study of an assimilated group in northern Sonora. *Univ. Arizona, Anthr. Papers*, no. 3.
1960a Paipai ethnography. MS.
1960b Concepts of disease and the curing practices of the Indians of ex-Mission Santa Catarina, Baja California Norte, Mexico. MS.
1962 The Indians of Santa Catarina, Baja California, Mexico: concepts of disease and curing. Doctoral dissertation, Univ. California at Los Angeles.
1963a Indians and revolution: the 1911 invasion of Baja California, Mexico. *Ethnohistory*, 10: 373–95.
1963b The use of plants and non-magical techniques in curing illness among the Paipai, Santa Catarina, Baja California, Mexico. *Amer. Indig.*, 23: 319–44.
1965 The patrilocal band: a linguistically and culturally hybrid social unit. *Amer. Anthr.*, 67: 675–90.

PACHECO DA SILVA, F.
1686 Doctrina cristiana en lengua zapoteca nexitza. Mexico.
1687 Doctrina cristiana traducida de la

lengua castellana en lengua zapoteca nexitza. Mexico.

PAINTER, M. T.
1960 Easter at Pascua village. Univ. Arizona Press.

——, R. SAVALA, AND I. ALVÁREZ
1955 A Yaqui Easter sermon. Univ. Arizona, Social Sci. Bull., no. 26.

PALACIOS, E. J.
1940 El simbolismo del chacmool: su interpretación. Rev. Mex. Estud. Antr., vol. 4, nos. 1, 2.

PANIAGUA, F. A.
1876 Catecismo elemental de historia y estadística de Chiapas. San Cristobal de las Casas.

1908 Documentos y datos para un diccionario etimológico, histórico, y geográfico de Chiapas. 3 vols. San Cristobal de las Casas.

PAPALOAPAN, EL
1949 El Papaloapan: obra del presidente Alemán. Sec. Recursos Hidráulicos. Mexico.

PAPELES DE NUEVA ESPAÑA
See Paso y Troncoso, 1905–06.

PARSONS, E. C.
1930a La institución de la mayordomía. Mex. Folkways, 6: 72–78.

1930b Entierro de un angelito. Ibid., 6: 141–45.

1930c Ritos zapotecos de año nuevo. Ibid., 6: 38–46.

1931 Curanderos in Oaxaca, Mexico. Sci. Monthly, 32: 60–68.

1932a Las varas. Mex. Folkways, 7: 81–86.

1932b Zapotecan and Spanish tales of Mitla, Oaxaca. Jour. Amer. Folklore, 45: 277–317.

1932c Casándose en Mitla, Oaxaca. Mex. Folkways, 7: 129–37.

1936 Mitla: town of the souls. Univ. Chicago Press.

PASO Y TRONCOSO, F. DEL
1905 Las guerras con las tribus yaqui y mayo del estado de Sonora. Mexico.

1905–06 Papeles de Nueva España. 2d ser. 8 vols. Madrid.

1928–31 Indice de documentos de Nueva España existentes en el archivo de Indias de Seville. 4 vols. Monogr. Bibliográficas Mexicanas, nos. 12, 14, 22, 23.

1939–42 Epistolario de Nueva España. 16 vols. Comp. by J. P. Robredo. Mexico.

PASSIN, H.
1942 Tarahumara prevarication: a problem in field method. Amer. Anthr., 44: 235–47.

1943 The place of kinship in Tarahumara social organization. Acta Amer., 1: 361–89, 469–95.

PATIÑO, L. R., AND H. CÁRDENAS
1955 Informes agroeconómicos de la mixteca de la costa. Inst. Nac. Indig., Mimeo. Ser., no. 8. Mexico.

PATTIE, J. O.
1905 See Thwaites, 1905.

PAUL, B. D.
1950a Symbolic sibling rivalry in a Guatemalan Indian village. Amer. Anthr., 52: 205–18.

1950b Life in a Guatemalan Indian village. In Patterns for modern living, division 3: cultural patterns, pp. 469–515. Delphian Soc. Chicago.

—— AND L. PAUL
1952 The life cycle. In Tax, 1952a, pp. 174–92.

1962 Ethnographic materials on San Pedro la Laguna, Solola, Guatemala. Univ. Chicago, Micro. Coll. MSS Middle Amer. Cult. Anthr., no. 54.

PAUL, L., AND B. D. PAUL
1963 Changing marriage patterns in a highland Guatemalan community. SW. Jour. Anthr., 19: 131–48.

PEÑA, M. T. DE LA
1950 Problemas sociales y económicos de las mixtecas. Inst. Nac. Indig., Mem. 2. Mexico.

1951 Chiapas económico. 4 vols. Gobierno del estado de Chiapas, depto. prensa y turismo. Tuxtla Gutierrez.

PEÑAFIEL, A.
1887 Gramática de la lengua zapoteca por un autor anónimo (con bibliografía de la lengua zapoteca de tierra caliente o de Tehuantepec). Mexico.

PENNINGTON, C. W.
1963 The Tarahumar of Mexico: their environment and material culture. Salt Lake City.

PÉREZ DE RIBAS, A.
1645 Historia de los triunfos de nuestra santa fe entre gentes las más bárbaras y fieras del nuevo orbe. Madrid.

1944 Idem, another ed. Mexico.

PÉREZ GARCÍA, R.
1956 La sierra Juárez. 2 vols. Mexico.

PÉREZ SERRANO, M.
1942 Leyenda zapoteca: el "betooc" o se-

ñor de los bosques. *Anuario Soc. Folklórica Mex.*, 3: 173–175.

PICKETT, V. B.
1946   Cartillas I and II. Inst. Ling. Verano. Mexico.
1948   Problems in Zapotec tone analysis. *Int. Jour. Amer. Ling.*, 14: 161–70.
1953   Isthmus Zapotec verb analysis I. *Ibid.*, 19: 292–96.
1955   Isthmus Zapotec verb analysis II. *Ibid.*, 21: 217–32.
1959   Castellano-zapoteco, zapoteco-castellano. Inst. Ling. Verano. Mexico.
1960   The grammatical hierarchy of isthmus Zapotec. *Language,* suppl. 56.

PIKE, E. V.
1948   Head-washing and other elements in the Mazateco marriage ceremony. *Amer. Indig.*, 8: 219–22.

PIKE, K. L.
1947   Phonemics. *Univ. Michigan Pub. Ling.*, no. 3.

PIMENTEL, F.
1875   Cuadro descriptivo y comparativo de las lenguas indígenas de México. 3 vols. 2d ed. Mexico.

PIMENTEL S., J.
1954   Narración tradicional. *Anuario Soc. Folklórica Mex.*, 9: 9–24.
1957   Miscelánea de creencias en la congregación de los angeles, Simojovel, Chiapas. *Ibid.*, 11: 207–24.

PIÑA CHAN, R.
1959   Museo de la cultura huasteca. Guía oficial. Inst. Nac. Antr. Hist. Mexico.

PINEDA, E.
1845   Descripción geográfica de Chiapas y Soconusco. Mexico.

PINEDA, V.
1888   Historia de las sublevaciones indígenas habidas en el estado de Chiapas. San Cristobal de las Casas.

PLANCARTE, F. M.
1954   El problema indígena tarahumara. *Inst. Nac. Indig.*, Mem. 5. Mexico.

POMAR, J. B.
1891   Relación de Tezcoco. *In* García Icazbalceta, 1889–1902, 3: 1–69.

POMPA Y POMPA, A., ed.
1966   Summa anthropologica: en homenaje a Roberto J. Weitlaner. Inst. Nac. Antr. Hist. Mexico.

PONCE, A.
    See Ciudad Real, A. de.

PONCE, P.
1892   Breve relación de los dioses y ritos de la gentilidad. *An. Mus. Nac. Mex.*, ep. 1–6, pp. 3–12.

POZAS, I. H. DE
1949   Notas etnográficas de Eloxochitlan, Oaxaca. MS.

POZAS A., R.
1945   El fraccionamiento de la tierra por el mecanismo de herencia en Chamula. *Rev. Mex. Estud. Antr.*, 7: 187–97.
1949   La alfarería de Patambam. *An. Inst. Nac. Antr. Hist.*, 3: 115–45.
1952a   Juan Pérez Jolote: biografía de un Tzotzil. Fondo de Cultura Económica. Mexico. (3d ed. 1959.) [See his 1962.]
1952b   El trabajo en las plantaciones de café y el cambio socio-cultural del indio. *Rev. Mex. Estud. Antr.*, 13: 31–48.
1959a   Chamula: un pueblo indio de los altos de Chiapas. *Mem. Inst. Nac. Indig.*, vol. 8.
1959b   El mundo mágico de los chamulas. *Acad. Mex. Pediatría*, no. 16, pp. 3–10. Mexico.
1960   Etnografía de los mazatecos. *Rev. Mex. Estud. Antr.*, 16: 211–26.
1962   Juan the Chamula: an ethnological re-creation of the life of a Mexican Indian. Tr. from the Spanish by L. Kemp. Univ. California Press. [Tr. of Pozas, 1952a.]

PRESCOTT, W. H.
1844   History of the conquest of Mexico, with a preliminary view of the ancient Mexican civilization and the life of the conqueror Hernando Cortés. 3 vols. London.

PREUSS, K. T.
1912   Die Nayarit-Expedition, Textaufnahmen und Beobachtungen unter mexikanischen Indianern. Leipzig.

PRICE, S. H.
1966   I was Pashku and my husband was Telesh. *Radcliffe Quar.*, May-June, pp. 4–8.

PRIDE, K.
1961   Numerals in Chatino. *Anthr. Ling.*, 3: 1–10.

PROCESOS . . .
1912   Procesos de indios idólatras y hechiceros. *Archivo General de la Nación*, Pub. 3. Mexico.

QUIJADA, H.
1579   Relación de Usila. *In* Paso y Troncoso, 1905–06, 4: 45–52. [Tr. in Bevan, 1938, pp. 129–34.]

RABASA, R.
1895 El estado de Chiapas: geografía y estadística. Mexico.

RADIN, P.
1915 Folktales from Oaxaca. *Jour. Amer. Folklore*, 28: 390–408.
1916 On the relationship of Huave and Mixe. *Amer. Anthr.*, 18: 411–23.
1917 El folklore de Oaxaca. New York.
1925 The distribution and phonetics of the Zapotec dialects: a preliminary sketch. *Jour. Soc. Amer. Paris*, 17: 27–76.
1930 Preliminary sketch of the Zapotec language. *Language*, 6: 64–85.
1931 Mexican kinship systems. *Univ. California Pub. Amer. Archaeol. Ethnol.*, 31: 1–14.
1933 Notes on the Tlappanecan language of Guerrero. *Int. Jour. Amer. Ling.*, 8: 45–72.
1935 An historical legend of the Zapotecs. *Ibero-Amer.*, no. 9.
1940 Notes on Schultze-Jena's Tlappanec. *Bol. Bibliográfico Antr. Amer.*, 4: 70–74.
1943–44 Cuentos y leyendas de los zapotecos. *Tlalocan*, 1: 3–30, 134–54, 194–226.
1946 Zapotec texts: dialect of Juchitan-Tehuano. *Int. Jour. Amer. Ling.*, 12: 152–72.

RAMÍREZ, J. F.
1949 Noticias sacadas de un manuscrito intitulado Relaciones de todas las cosas que en el Nuevo México . . . desde el año 1538 hasta el de 1626 por Fr. Gerónimo de Zárate S. . . . Mexico.

RAVICZ, R.
1958 A comparative study of selected aspects of Mixtec social organization. Doctoral dissertation, Harvard Univ.
1961 La mixteca en el estudio comparativo del hongo alucinante. *An. Inst. Nac. Antr. Hist.*, 13: 73–92.
1962–65 Field notes on Mixtec. MS.

—— AND A. K. ROMNEY
1955 Sixteen centuries of Mixtec kinship. MS.

RECINOS, A.
1913 Monografía del departamento de Huehuetenango, República de Guatemala. Guatemala. (2d ed. 1954.)
1947 El Popol Vuh: las antiguas historias del Quiché. Fondo de Cultura Económica. Mexico.

REDFIELD, R.
1930 Tepoztlan: a Mexican village. Univ. Chicago Press.
1938 Primitive merchants of Guatemala. *Quar. Jour. Inter-Amer. Relations*, 1 (4): 42–56.
1941 The folk culture of Yucatan. Univ. Chicago Press.
1946a Ethnographic materials on Agua Escondida. *Univ. Chicago, Micro. Coll. MSS Middle Amer. Cult. Anthr.*, no. 3.
1946b Notes on San Antonio Palopo. *Ibid.*, no. 4.
1953 The primitive world and its transformations. Ithaca, N.Y.

—— AND S. TAX
1952 General characteristics of present-day Mesoamerican Indian society. *In* Tax, 1952a, pp. 31–39.

—— AND A. VILLA ROJAS
1939 Notes on the ethnography of the Tzeltal communities of Chiapas. *Carnegie Inst. Wash.*, Pub. 509, Contrib. 28.
1962 Chan Kom: a Maya village. Rev. ed. Univ. Chicago Press.

REED, N.
1964 The caste war of Yucatan. Stanford Univ. Press.

REINA, R. E.
1957a Chinautla: 1944–53. *In* R. N. Adams, 1957, pp. 32–37.
1957b Chinautla, a Guatemalan Indian community: a field study in the relationship of community culture and national change. Doctoral dissertation, Univ. North Carolina.
1958 Continuidad de la cultura indígena en una comunidad guatemalteca. *Rev. Cien. Sociales*, 2: 243–59. Puerto Rico.
1959a Continuidad de la cultura indígena en una comunidad guatemalteca. *Cuad. Seminario Integración Social Guatemalteca*, no. 4.
1959b Two patterns of friendship in a Guatemalan community. *Amer. Anthr.*, 61: 44–50.
1959c Political crisis and cultural revitalization: the Guatemalan case. *Human Organization*, 17: 14–18.
1960 Chinautla, a Guatemalan Indian community: a study in the relationship of community culture and national change. *Tulane Univ., Middle Amer. Research Inst.*, Pub. 24, pp. 55–130.

1963a Chinautla, comunidad indígena guatemalteca: estudio de las relaciones entre la cultura de comunidad y el cambio nacional. *Guatemala Indig.*, 3: 31–150.

1963b The potter and the farmer: the fate of two innovators in a Maya village. *Expedition*, 5 (4): 18–31.

1967 The law of the saints: a Pokomam pueblo and its community culture. New York.

REKO, B. P.

1945 Mitobotánica zapoteca. Tacubaya.

REKO, V. A., AND F. HESTERMANN

1931 Quellenschriften zur mexikanischen Linguistik. Das verschollene Manuskript des Gaspar de los Reyes, "Gramática zapoteca del valle" (1700). *Mitteilungen der Anthr. Gesellschaft in Wien*, 61: 331–50.

RELACIÓN DE AJUCHITLAN

1579 Relación de Ajuchitlan. *Papeles de Nueva España*, 5: 81–98.

RELACIÓN DE MICHOACAN

1869 Tomo 3 de la colección de documentos inéditos para la historia de España. Madrid.

1875 *Idem*, reissued fraudulently with new covers.

1903 Relación de las ceremonias y ritos y población y gobernación de los índios de la provencia, de Mechuacán, hecho al Ilmo. Señor don Antonio de Mendoza, viery y gobernador de Nueva España (1541). Morelia.

1956 *Idem*, limited new edition with analysis by P. Kirchhoff. Madrid.

RELACIÓN DE TETELA DEL RÍO

1579 Relación de Tetela del Río. *Papeles de Nueva España*, 5: 124–73.

RELACIÓN DE TEZCOCO

See Pomar, 1891.

RELACIÓN DE TLACOLULA Y MITLA

1955 Notes and trans. by F. Horcasitas and R. George. Mexico City College, *Mesoamer. Notes*, 4: 13–24.

RELACIONES DE YUCATAN

1898–1900 Incluidas en la colección de documentos inéditos relativos al descubrimiento, conquista y organización de las antiguas posesiones españoles de ultramar. 2a ser., vols. 11 and 13. Madrid.

REMESAL, A. DE

1908 Historia de San Vicente de Chiapas y Guatemala. Madrid.

1932 Historia general de las Indias occidentales y particular de la gobernación de Chiapa y Guatemala. 2 vols. Guatemala.

RENDÓN, S.

1947 La alimentación tarasca. *An. Inst. Nac. Antr. Hist.*, 2: 202–27. Mexico.

1950 Aspectos de ceremonias civiles tarascas. *Amer. Indig.*, 10: 91–98.

RENDÓN MONZÓN, J.

1960 Relaciones internas de la familia zapoteca-chatina. *In* Gloto-cronología y las lenguas oto-mangues. Cuad. Inst. Hist., Univ. Nac. Autónoma Mex.

REYES, A. DE LOS

1593 Arte en lengua mixteca. Mexico.

REYES, G. DE LOS

1891 Gramática de las lenguas zapoteca-serrana y zapoteca del valle. Oaxaca.

RICARD, R.

1933 La "conquête spirituelle" du Mexique. *Univ. Paris, Inst. Ethnol., Travaux et Mem.*, no. 20.

RICKETSON, O. G.

1939 Municipal organization of an Indian township in Guatemala. *Geog. Rev.*, 29: 643–47.

RILEY, C. L., AND J. HOBGOOD

1959 A recent nativistic movement among the southern Tepehuan Indians. *SW. Jour. Anthr.*, 15: 355–60.

—— AND H. D. WINTERS

1963 The prehistoric Tepehuan of northern Mexico. *Ibid.*, 19: 177–85.

ROBLES URIBE, C., AND OTHERS

1967 Los Lacandones: bibliografía y reseña crítica de materiales publicados. Inst. Nac. Antr. Hist. Mexico.

RODAS N., F., O. RODAS CORZO, AND L. F. HAWKINS

1940 Chichicastenango: the Kiche Indians. Guatemala.

RODRÍGUEZ GIL, A.

1907 Los indios ocuiltecas actuales. MS en Depto. Invest. Antr., Inst. Nac. Antr. Hist. Mexico.

ROHRSHEIM, L.

1928 Una visita a los huavis. *Mex. Folkways*, 4: 49–65.

ROJAS GONZÁLEZ, F.

1949a Los zapotecos en la época prehispánica. *In* Mendieta y Núñez, 1949, pp. 35–102.

1949b Los zapotecos en la época colonial. *Ibid.*, pp. 105–56.

1949c Los zapotecos en la época indepen-
diente. *Ibid.*, pp. 157–95.

1957 Los huastecos. *In* Cerda Silva,
1957a, pp. 581–91.

—— AND R. DE LA CERDA SILVA

1941 Los tzotziles. *Rev. Mex. Sociol.*, 3:
113–42.

1949 Etnografía general de los zapotecos.
In Mendieta y Núñez, 1949, pp.
201–61.

ROMERO ALVÁREZ, J.

1952 Estudio de las principales parásitos
intestinales en el municipio de Jaltocan, Hidalgo. Mexico.

ROMNEY, A. K.

1957 The genetic model and Uto-Aztecan
time perspective. *Davidson Jour.
Anthr.*, 3: 35–41.

1967 Kinship and family. *In* Handbook
of Middle American Indians, vol. 6,
Art. 11.

—— AND R. ROMNEY

1963 The Mixtecans of Juxtlahuaca, Mexico. *In* Six cultures; studies of child
rearing, B. B. Whiting ed., pp. 541–
692.

ROSALES, J. DE D.

1949 Notes on San Pedro la Laguna.
*Univ. Chicago, Micro. Coll. MSS
Middle Amer. Cult. Anthr.*, no. 25.

ROSENZWEIG, F.

1959 Demografía de la peninsula de Yucatan. MS en Depto. Invest. del Banco
de México.

ROUAIX, FR., G. DECORME, AND A. G. SARAVIA

1952 Manual de historia de Durango.
Editorial Jus, S.A. Mexico.

ROYS, R. L.

1932 Antonio de Ciudad Real, ethnogra-
pher. *Amer. Anthr.*, 34: 118–26.

1939 The titles of Ebtun. *Carnegie Inst.
Wash.*, Pub. 505.

1940 Personal names of the Maya of Yucatan. *Ibid.*, Pub. 523, Contrib. 31.

1943 The Indian background of colonial
Yucatan. *Ibid.*, Pub. 548.

RUBEL, A. J.

1955 Ritual relationships in Ojitlan, Mexico. *Amer. Anthr.*, 56: 1038–40.

RUBÍN DE LA BORBOLLA, D. F., AND
R. L. BEALS

1940 The Tarascan project: a cooperative
enterprise of the National Polytechnic
Institute, Mexican Bureau of Indian
Affairs, and the University of California. *Amer. Anthr.*, 42: 708–12.

RUIZ DE ALARCÓN, H.

1892 Tratado de las supersticiones y costumbres gentílicas que hoy viven entre los indios naturales de esta Nueva
España. *An. Mus. Nac.*, 1–6: 123–
224. Mexico.

RUZ LHUILLIER, A.

1962 Chichen-Itza y Tula: comentarios a
un ensayo. *Estud. Cultura Maya*, 2:
205–20.

SÁENZ, M.

1936 Carapan: bosquejo de una experien-
cia. Lima.

SAHAGÚN, B. DE

1829 Historia general de las cosas de Nueva
España. 3 vols. Ed. Bustamante.
Mexico.

1938 *Idem*, ed. Robredo. 5 vols. Mexico.

1950–63 Florentine codex: general history
of the things of New Spain. Tr.
from the Aztec into English, with
notes and illustrations, by A. J. O.
Anderson and C. E. Dibble. Univ.
Utah and School of American Research. Santa Fe. Book 1 (1950):
The gods. Book 2 (1951): The ceremonies. Book 3 (1952): The origin of the gods. Book 4 (1957):
The soothsayers. Book 5 (1957):
The omens. Book 7 (1953): The
sun, moon, and stars, and the binding
of the years. Book 8 (1954): Kings
and lords. Book 9 (1959): The
merchants. Book 10 (1961): The
people. Book 11 (1963): Earthly
things. Book 12 (1955): The conquest of Mexico.

SALER, B.

1962a Migration and ceremonial ties among
the Maya. *SW. Jour. Anthr.*, 18:
336–40.

1962b Unsuccessful practitioners in a bicul-
tural Guatemalan community. *Psy-
choanalysis and the Psychoanalytic
Rev.*, 49: 103–18.

1964 Nagual, witch, and sorcerer in a
Quiche village. *Ethnology*, 3: 305–
28.

1965a The departure of the dueño. *Jour.
Folklore Inst.*, 2: 31–42.

1965b Religious conversion and self-aggran-
dizement: a Guatemalan case. *Practical Anthr.*, 12: 107–14.

SALOVESH, M.

1965 Pautas de residencia y estratificación
entre los Mayas: algunas perspectivas

de San Bartolomé, Chiapas. *Estud. Cultura Maya*, 5: 317–38.

SANDERS, W. T.
1953 The anthropogeography of central Veracruz. *Rev. Mex. Estud. Anthr.*, 13: 27–78.

SAPPER, C.
1927 La lengua tapachulteca. *El Mex. Antiguo*, 2: 259–68.

SAPPER, D. E.
1925 Costumbres y creencias religiosas de los indios kekchis. *An Soc. Geog. Hist.*, vol. 2, no. 2.

SAPPER, K.
1891 Ein Besuch bei den östlichen Lacandonen. *Ausland*, 64: 892–95.
1897a Die Gebraunche und religiosen Anfechaungen der Kikchi Indianer.
1897b Das nördliche Mittel-Amerika. Nebst einem Ausflug nach dem Hochland von Anahuac. Reisen und Studien aus den Jahren 1888–95. Brunswick.
1901 Speise und Trank der Kekchi-Indianer. *Globus*, 80: 259–63.
1904 Independent Indian states of Yucatan. *Smithsonian Inst., Bur. Amer. Ethnol.*, Bull. 28, pp. 623–24.
1912 Die Indianer und ihre Kultur einst und jetzt. Leipzig.
1913 Das tägliche Leben der Kekchi-Indianer. *Proc. 18th Int. Cong. Amer.*, pp. 362–71.

SAUER, C.
1934 The distribution of aboriginal tribes and languages in northwestern Mexico. *Ibero-Amer.*, no. 5.
1935 Aboriginal population of northwestern Mexico. *Ibid.*, no. 10.

SCHMIEDER, O.
1930a Oldest democracy in Mexico. *El Palacio*, 29: 292–93.
1930b The settlements of the Tzapotec and Mije Indians, state of Oaxaca, Mexico. *Univ. California Pub. Geog.*, 4: 1–184.
1931 Kulturgeographische Studien im Staate Oaxaca: summary. *El Mex. Antiguo*, 3: 73–74.
1934 Der Einfluss des Agrarsystems der Tzapoteken, Azteken und Mije auf die Kulturentwicklung dieser Völker. *Proc. 24th Int. Cong. Amer.*, pp. 109–11. Hamburg.

SCHOLES, F. V., C. R. MENÉNDEZ, J. I. RUBIO MAÑÉ, AND E. B. ADAMS, eds.
1936–38 Documentos para la historia de Yucatan. 3 vols. Merida.

—— AND R. L. ROYS
1948 The Maya Chontal Indians of Acalan-Tixchel: a contribution to the history and ethnography of the Yucatan peninsula. *Carnegie Inst. Wash.*, Pub. 560.

SCHULLER, R.
1923–24 Die ehemalige und die heutige Verbreitung der Huaxteka-Indianer. *Anthropos*, 19: 793–803.
1924–27a Notes on the Huaxteca Indians of San Luis Potosi. *El Mex. Antiguo*, 2: 129–40.
1924–27b La posición etnológica y lingüística de los huaxtecos. *Ibid.*, 2: 141–50.

SCHULTES, R. E.
1940 Plantae mexicanae V: *Desmoncus chinantlensis* and its utilization in native basketry. *Bot. Mus. Leafl., Harvard Univ.*, 8: 134–40.
1941a A contribution to our knowledge of *Rivea corymbosa*, the narcotic *Ololiuqui* of the Aztecs. Bot. Mus., Harvard Univ.
1941b The meaning and usage of the Mexican place-name 'Chinantla.' *Bot. Mus. Leafl., Harvard Univ.*, 9: 101–16.
1941c Plantae mexicanae IX: *Aechmea magdalenae* and its utilization as a fibre plant. *Ibid.*, 9: 117–22.

SCHULTZE-JENA, L. S.
1933 Leben, Glaube und Sprache der Quiche von Guatemala. Indiana, vol. 1.
1938 Bei den Azteken, Mixteken und Tlapaneken der Sierra Madre del Sur von Mexiko. Indiana, vol. 3.

SCHULZ, R. P. C.
1942 Apuntes sobre cálculos relativos al calendario de los indígenas de Chiapas. *El Mex. Antiguo*, 6: 6–14.
1953 Nuevos datos sobre el calendario tzeltal y tzotzil de Chiapas. *Yan*, 2: 114–16.
1955 Dos variantes nuevas del calendario chinanteco. *El Mex. Antiguo*, 8: 233–46.

SEAFORD, H. W.
1953 Un breve resumen de la economía chocha. *Rev. Mex. Estud. Antr.*, 13: 235–40.
1955 Observaciones preliminares de los ritos funerarios chochos. *El Mex. Antiguo*, 8: 323–45.

Séjourné, L.
1952 Los otomís del Mezquital. *Cuad. Amer.*, 66: 17–34.

Seler, E.
1892 Notice sur les langues zapothèque et mixtèque. *Proc. 8th Int. Cong. Amer.*, pp. 550–55.
1901a Die Huichol-Indianer des Staates Jalisco in Mexiko. *Gesammelte Abhandlungen*, 3: 355–91.
1901b Die Huichol-Indianer des Staates Jalisco in Mexiko. *Mitteilungen der Anthr. Gesellschaft in Wien*, 31: 138–63.
1904 The Mexican chronology, with special reference to the Zapotec calendar. *Smithsonian Inst., Bur. Amer. Ethnol.*, Bull. 28, pp. 13–55.

Serna, J. de la
1892 Manual de ministros de indios para el conocimiento de sus idolatrías y extirpación de ellas. *An. Mus. Nac.*, 1–6: 261–480. Mexico.

Shattuck, G. C.
1933 The peninsula of Yucatan: medical, biological, meteorological and sociological studies. *Carnegie Inst. Wash.*, Pub. 431.

Shor, G. G., and E. Roberts
1956 San Miguel, Baja California Norte, earthquakes of February 1956: a field report. *Seismological Soc. Amer. Bull.*, 48: 101–16.

Siegel, M.
1941a Religion in western Guatemala: a product of acculturation. *Amer. Anthr.*, 43: 62–76.
1941b Resistance to culture change in western Guatemala. *Sociol. and Social Research*, 25: 414–30.
1941c Problems of education in Indian Guatemala. *Jour. Experimental Education*, 9: 285–94.
1942a Horns, tails, and Easter sport: a study of a stereotype. *Social Forces*, 20: 382–86.
1942b Effects of culture contact on the form of the family in a Guatemalan village. *Jour. Royal Anthr. Inst.*, 72: 55–68.
1943 The creation myth and acculturation in Acatan, Guatemala. *Jour. Amer. Folklore*, 56: 120–26.
1954a Culture change in San Miguel Acatan, Guatemala. *Phylon*, pp. 165–76.
1954b Perspective in Guatemala. *New Republic*, July 19.

Siliceo Pauer, P.
1923 Los indios de Yalalag. *Mag. Geog. Nac.*, 1: 3–45.
1927 La población indígena de Yalalag, Oaxaca, con algunas notas sobre el tsapoteco-mixteco. *Anthropos*, 22: 45–65.

Silvert, K. H., and A. R. King
1957 Coban: 1944–53. *In* R. N. Adams, 1957, pp. 44–47.

Siverts, H.
1955 Informe sobre Oxchuc. MS.
1960 Political organization in a Tzeltal community in Chiapas, Mexico. *In* Leslie, 1960b.

Slocum, M.
1956 Cultural changes among the Oxchuc Tzeltals. *In* Estudios antropológicos, pp. 491–95.

Smith, R. E.
1949 Cerámica elaborada sin torno, Chinautla, Guatemala. *Pub. Inst. Antr. Hist.*, 1 (2): 58–61. Guatemala.

Solien, N. L.
1959 The nonunilineal descent group in the Caribbean and Central America. *Amer. Anthr.*, 61: 578–83.

Solis, J. de
1945 Estado en que se hallaba la provincia de Coatzacoalcos en el año de 1599. *Bol. Archivo General de la Nación*, 16: 195–246, 429–79. Mexico.

Soustelle, G.
1958 Tequila: un village nahuatl du Mexique oriental. *Univ. Paris, Inst. Ethnol., Travaux et Mem.*, no. 62.
1959 Observations sur la religion des Lacandons du Mexique méridional. *Jour. Soc. Amer. Paris*, 48: 141–96.

Soustelle, J.
1933 Notes sur les Lacandon du Lac Peljá et du Rio Jetzjá (Chiapas). *Ibid.*, 25: 153–80.
1935a Les idées religieuses des Lacandons. *La Terre et La Vie*, 5: 170–78.
1935b Le totémisme des Lacandons. *Maya Research*, 2:325–44.
1936 Mexique: terre Indienne. Paris.
1937a La culture matérielle des Indiens Lacandons. *Jour. Soc. Amer. Paris*, 29: 1–95.
1937b La famille Otomi-Pame du Mexique central. *Univ. Paris, Inst. Ethnol., Travaux et Mem.*, no. 26.

SPICER, E. H.
1940 Pascua, a Yaqui village in Arizona. Univ. Chicago Press.
1943 Linguistic aspects of Yaqui acculturation. *Amer. Anthr.*, 45: 410–26.
1945 El problema yaqui. *Amer. Indig.*, 5: 273–78.
1947 Yaqui villages past and present. *Kiva*, 13: 2–11.
1954a Spanish-Indian acculturation in the southwest. *Amer. Anthr.*, 56: 663–84.
1954b Potam, a Yaqui village in Sonora. *Amer. Anthr. Assoc.*, Mem. 77.
1961 [ed.] Perspectives in American Indian culture change. Univ. Chicago Press.

SQUIER, E. G.
1852 Nicaragua: its people, scenery, monuments, and the proposed interoceanic canal. New York.

STADELMAN, R.
1940 Maize cultivation in northwestern Guatemala. *Carnegie Inst. Wash.*, Pub. 523, Contrib. 33.

STANISLAWSKI, D.
1947 Tarascan political geography. *Amer. Anthr.*, 49: 46–55.
1950 The anatomy of 11 towns in Michoacan. *Univ. Texas, Inst. Latin Amer. Studies*, Pub. 10.

STARR, B.
1951 The Chorti and the problem of survival of Maya culture. *Amer. Anthr.*, 53: 355–69.

STARR, F.
1899a Catalogue of a collection of objects illustrating the folklore of Mexico. London.
1899b Indians of southern Mexico: an ethnographic album. Chicago.
1900–02 Notes upon the ethnography of southern Mexico. 2 parts. *Proc. Davenport Acad. Natural Sci.*, vols. 8, 9.
1902 The physical characters of the Indians of southern Mexico. Univ. Chicago.
1908 In Indian Mexico: a narrative of travel and labor. Chicago.

STAUB, W.
1919 Some data about the pre-Hispanic and the now living Huastec Indians. *El Mex. Antiguo*, 1: 1–65.
1926 Le nord-est du Mexique et les Indiens de la Huaxtèque. *Jour. Soc. Amer. Paris*, 18: 279–96.
1933 Zur Uebereinanderschichtung der Völker und Kulturen an der Ostküste von Mexiko. *Mitteilungen Geog.-Ethnog. Gesellschaft*. Zurich.
1939 Algunos datos acerca de los indios huastecas prehispánicos y de los contemporáneos. *Divulgación Hist.*, 1: 423–32.

STAVENHAGEN, R.
1960 Descendencia y nombres entre los mazatecos. *Rev. Mex. Estud. Antr.*, 16: 231–32.

STEGGERDA, M.
1932 Anthropometry of adult Maya Indians: a study of their physical and physiological characteristics. *Carnegie Inst. Wash.*, Pub. 434.
1941 Maya Indians of Yucatan. *Ibid.*, Pub. 531.

STEININGER, G. R., AND P. VAN DE VELDE
1935 Three dollars a year: being the story of San Pablo Cuatro Venados, a typical Zapotecan Indian village. New York.

STEPHENS, J. L.
1841 Incidents of travel in Central America, Chiapas, and Yucatan. 2 vols. New York. (Another ed. 1949.)
1843 Incidents of travel in Yucatan. 2 vols. New York.

STEWARD, J. H.
1955 Theory of culture change. Univ. Illinois Press.

STORM, M.
1945 Enjoying Uruapan: a book for travelers in Michoacan. Mexico.

STOLL, O.
1884 Zur Ethnographie der Republik Guatemala. *An. Soc. Geog. Hist. Guatemala*, 11: 191–216 (1934).
1889 Die Ethnologie der Indianerstämme von Guatemala. *Internat. Archiv für Ethnog.*, 1: 112, supplement.
1894 Suggestion und Hypnotismus in der Völkerpsychologie. Leipzig.
1901 Die ethnische Stellung der Tzutijil Indianer. *Festschrift Geog.-Ethnog. Gesellschaft*, Jahresbericht für 1900–01, pp. 27–59. Zurich.
1908 Das Geschlechtsleben in der Völkerpsychologie. Leipzig.
1928 Das Vokabular der Sprache von Aguacatan, no. 2 (Guatemala). *Mitteilungen Geog.-Ethnog. Gesellschaft*. Zurich.
1958 Etnografía de Guatemala. Ministerio de Educación Pública. Guatemala.

STRESSER-PÉAN, G.

1944–46 La danse des barbares et la danse des démons dans la religion des Indiens Huastèques. *Inst. Français Anthr., comptes rendus sommaires des séances*, 21–41: 8–9.

1948 Danse des aigles et danse des jaguars chez les Indiens Huastèques de la région de Tantoyuca. *Proc. 28th Int. Cong. Amer.*, pp. 335–38.

1953 Les Indiens Huastèques. *In* Huastecos, Totonacos, pp. 213–34.

1955 Mission au Mexique (1950–1955). *Jour. Soc. Amer. Paris*, 44: 245–52.

1959 Ixtab, Maximón et Judas: croyances sur la pendaison chez les Mayas de Yucatan, du Guatemala et de la Huasteca. *Proc. 33d Int. Cong. Amer.*, 2: 456–61.

SWADESH, M.

1940 Orientaciones lingüísticas para maestros en zonas indígenas. Depto. Asuntos Indígenas. Mexico.

1947 The phonemic structure of Proto-Zapotec. *Int. Jour. Amer. Ling.*, 13: 220–30.

1949 El idioma de los zapotecos. *In* Mendieta y Núñez, 1949.

1959a Mapas de clasificación lingüística de México y las Américas. *Univ. Nac. Autónoma Mex., Inst. Hist.*, Pub. 51, Antr. Ser., no. 8.

1959b Indian linguistic groups of Mexico. Escuela Nac. Antr. Hist. Mexico.

1959c Linguistics as an instrument of prehistory. *SW. Jour. Anthr.*, 15: 20–35.

1960 The Oto-Manguean hypothesis and Macro-Mixtecan. *Int. Jour. Amer. Ling.*, 26: 79–111.

1961 Interrelaciones de las lenguas mayances. *An. Inst. Nac. Antr. Hist.*, 13: 231–68. Mexico.

TABOADO, E.

1962 Desarrollo económico integral de la cuenca del Grijalva: planeación agrícola. MS. Sec. Recursos Hidráulicos. Mexico.

TAMAYO, J. L.

1949a Geografía general de México. 2 vols. Mexico. (Rev. ed. 1960.)

1949b Atlas geográfico general de México. Mexico.

1960 Geografía moderna de México. Mexico.

TAPIA, A. DE

1866 Relación hecha por el Sr. Andrés de Tapia, sobre la conquista de México. *In* García Icazbalceta, 1858–66, 2: 554–94.

TAPIA ZENTENO, C. DE

1767 Noticia de la lengua huasteca. Mexico.

TAX, SOL

1937 The municipios of the midwestern highlands of Guatemala. *Amer. Anthr.*, 39: 423–44.

1941 World view and social relations in Guatemala. *Ibid.*, 43: 27–42.

1944 Information about the municipio of Zinacantan, Chiapas. *Rev. Mex. Estud. Antr.*, 6: 181–95.

1946 The towns of lake Atitlan. *Univ. Chicago, Micro. Coll. MSS Middle Amer. Cult. Anthr.*, no. 13.

1947a Notes on Santo Tomas Chichicastenango. *Ibid.*, no. 16.

1947b Miscellaneous notes on Guatemala. *Ibid.*, no. 18.

1949 Folk tales in Chichicastenango: an unsolved puzzle. *Jour. Amer. Folklore*, 62: 125–35.

1950 Panajachel: field notes. *Univ. Chicago, Micro. Coll. MSS Middle Amer. Cult. Anthr.*, no. 29. (Contains autobiography of Santiago Yach from Panajachel.)

1951 [ed.] The civilizations of ancient America. Selected papers of the 29th Int. Cong. Amer. Chicago.

1952a [ed.] Heritage of conquest: the ethnology of Middle America. Viking Fund seminar on Middle American ethnology. Glencoe.

1952b [ed.] Acculturation in the Americas. Selected papers of the 29th Int. Cong. Amer. Chicago.

1953 Penny capitalism: a Guatemalan Indian economy. *Smithsonian Inst., Inst. Social Anthr.*, Pub. 16.

1964 Cultural differences in the Maya area: a 20th century perspective. *In* Desarrollo cultural de los mayas, pp. 279–328.

TAX, SUSAN

1964 Displacement activity in Zinacantan. *Amer. Indig.*, 24: 111–21.

TERMER, F.

1930 Zur Ethnologie und Ethnographie des Nördlichen Mittel-Amerika. *Ibero-Amer. Archiv*, 4: 303–492.

1957 Etnología y etnografía de Guatemala. Seminario de Integración Social Guatemalteca. Guatemala. (Tr. of his 1930.)

TEZOZOMOC, H. A.
See Alvarado Tezozomoc, H.

THOMAS, C., AND J. R. SWANTON
1911 Indian languages of Mexico and Central America and their geographical distribution. *Smithsonian Inst., Bur. Amer. Ethnol.*, Bull. 44.

THOMAS, N. D.
1967 The nexus of envy, witchcraft, and ceremonial organization in a Zoque Indian pueblo. Doctoral dissertation, Univ. California, Berkeley.

THOMPSON, J. E. S.
1930 Ethnology of the Mayas of southern and central British Honduras. *Field Mus. Natural Hist., Anthr. Ser.*, 17: 23–214.
1954 The rise and fall of Maya civilization. Univ. Oklahoma Press.

THWAITES, R. G.
1905 The personal narrative of James O. Pattie of Kentucky. *In* Early western travels, 1784–1846, vol. 18.

TIBÓN, G.
1961 Pinotepa nacional: mixtecos, negros y triques. *Univ. Nac. Autónoma Mex.*, pp. 129–54.

TOOR, F.
1925 The passion play at Tzintzuntzan. *Mex. Folkways*, 1: 21–25.
1926 I am cured of fright. *Ibid.*, 2: 31–32.
1928 Gentes y escuelas de la sierra de Juárez. *Ibid.*, 4: 119–29.
1947 [ed.] A treasury of Mexican folkways. Mexico.

TOQUERO, R.
1946 Los zapotecas, los "beniguelaza." *Ex-Alumnos*, 2 (75): 5–6.

TORO, A.
1924–27 Una creencia totémica de los zapotecas. *El Mex. Antiguo*, 2: 123–28.

TORQUEMADA, J. DE
1943–44 Monarquía indiana. 3 vols. Mexico.

TOZZER, A. M.
1907 A comparative study of the Mayas and the Lacandones. New York.
1913 A Spanish manuscript letter on the Lacandones in the archives of the Indies in Seville. *Proc. 18th Int. Cong. Amer.*, 2: 497–509.
1921 A Maya grammar, with bibliography and appraisement of the works noted.

Papers Peabody Mus., Harvard Univ., vol. 9.
1941 [ed.] Landa's Relación de las cosas de Yucatan. Tr. and ed. with notes. *Ibid.*, vol. 18.

TRENS, M. B.
1942 Historia de Chiapas: desde los tiempos más remotos hasta la caída del segundo imperio. Mexico.
1957 *Idem*, 2d ed.

TREUTLEIN, T.
1949 Sonora: a description of a province. Albuquerque.

TUMIN, M.
1945a Culture, genuine and spurious: a re-evaluation. *Amer. Sociol. Rev.*, 10: 199–207.
1945b Some fragments from the life history of a marginal man. *Character and Personality*, 13: 261–95.
1946 San Luis Jilotepeque: a Guatemalan pueblo. *Univ. Chicago, Micro. Coll. MSS Middle Amer. Cult. Anthr.*, no. 2.
1949 Reciprocity and stability of caste in Guatemala. *Amer. Sociol. Rev.*, 14: 17–25.
1950a The dynamics of cultural discontinuity in a peasant society. *Social Forces*, 29: 135–41.
1950b The hero and the scapegoat in a peasant community. *Jour. Personality*, 19: 197–211.
1952 Caste in a peasant society: a case study in the dynamics of caste. Princeton Univ. Press.

TURNER, J. K.
1911 Barbarous Mexico. Chicago.

TURNER, P. L., AND D. L. OLMSTED
1966 Tequistlatecan kinship and limitations on the choice of spouse. *Ethnology*, 5: 245–50.

TYLOR, E. B.
1861 Anahuac, or Mexico, and the Mexicans, ancient and modern. London.

UNDERHILL, R. M.
1939 Social organization of the Papago Indians. *Columbia Univ., Contrib. Anthr.*, vol. 30.
1946 Papago Indian religion. *Ibid.*, vol. 33.
1948 Ceremonial patterns in the greater southwest. *Amer. Ethnol. Soc.*, Monogr. 13.
1954 Intercultural relations in the greater southwest. *Amer. Anthr.*, 56: 645–62.

UPSON, J.
1956 Some Chatino riddles analyzed. *Int. Jour. Amer. Ling.*, 22: 113–16.
1960 A preliminary structure of Chatino. *Anthr. Ling.*, 2: 22–29.

U'REN, M. R.
1940 From Coatzacoalcos to Salina Cruz. *Mex. Life*, 16 (5): 24–26, 41–42.

VALDIVIESO, E. R.
1929 El matrimonio zapoteco. *Quetzalcoatl*, 1: 21–22, 89.

VALLADARES, L. A.
1957 El hombre y la maíz: etnografía y etnopsicología de Colotenango, Guatemala.

VALLE, R. H.
1937 Bibliografía zapoteca. *Neza*, 3 (2): 72–87.

VAN DE VELDE, P.
1933 Breve vocabulario comparado del idioma zapoteca. *Invest. Ling.*, pp. 251–57.

VARA GÓMEZ, C.
1948 Exploración sanitaria e incidencia del bocio endémico en el municipio de Xatatlaco, Mexico. Univ. Nac. Antr. Mex.

VÁSQUEZ RAMÍREZ, I.
1946 Estudio médico sanitario de villa de Chalco. Mexico.

VELASCO RAMOS, J.
1950 Informe general sobre la exploración sanitaria del municipio de Chiconcuac, estado de México. Mexico.

VEYTIA, M.
See Keane, 1908.

VILLA ROJAS, A.
1945 The Maya of east central Quintana Roo. *Carnegie Inst. Wash.*, Pub. 559.
1946 Notas sobre la etnografía de los indios tzeltales de Oxchuc. *Univ. Chicago, Micro. Coll. MSS Middle Amer. Cult. Anthr.*, no. 7.
1947 Kinship and nagualism in a Tzeltal community, southeastern Mexico. *Amer. Anthr.*, 49: 578–87.
1948 Breve noticia acerca de las investigaciones antropológicas en la cuenca del Papaloapan. *Bol. Indig.*, 8: 130–34. Mexico.
1955 Los mazatecos y el problema indígena de la cuenca del Papaloapan. *Inst. Nac. Indig.*, Mem. 7. Mexico.
1956 Notas introductorias sobre la condición cultural de los mijes. *In* W. S. Miller, 1956, pp. 13–69.

1962 Distribución y estado cultural de los grupos mayances del México actual. *Estud. Cultura Maya*, 2: 45–77.
1963 El nagualismo como recurso de control social entre los grupos mayances de Chiapas, México. *Ibid.*, 3: 243–60.
1964 Barrios y calpules en las comunidades tzeltales y tzotziles del México actual. *Proc. 35th Int. Cong. Amer.*, 1: 321–34.
1967 Los Lacandones: su origen, costumbres y problemas vitales. *Amer. Indig.*, 27: 25–54.

VILLACORTA C., J. A.
1926 Monografía del departamento de Guatemala. Guatemala.

VILLAGUTIERRE SOTO-MAYOR, J. DE
1933 Historia de la conquista de la provincia de el Itza (1701). Guatemala.

VILLA-SEÑOR Y SÁNCHEZ, J. A. DE
1746–48 Teatro americano, descripción general de los reynos, y provincias de la Nueva España, y sus jurisdicciones. 2 vols. Mexico.

VILLAVICENCIO, D.
1692 Luz y método de confesar idólatras y destierro de idolatrías. Puebla. (Reproduced in Gillow, 1889, pp. 77–88.)

VIQUIERA, C., AND A. PALERM
1954 Alcoholismo, brujería y homocidio en dos comunidades rurales de México. *Amer. Indig.*, 14: 7–36.

VIVÓ, J. A.
1941 Razas y lenguas indígenas de México, su distribución geográfica. *Inst. Panamer. Geog. Hist.*, Pub. 52.
1954 La integración de Chiapas y su agregación a la nación mexicana. *Bol. Soc. Mex. Geog. Estad.*, 78: 389–505.
1958 Geografía de México. (4th ed.) Fondo de Cultura Económica. Mexico.
1961 Esbozo de geografía física humana de Chiapas. *In* Los Mayas del sur, pp. 11–20.

VOGT, E. Z.
1955 Some aspects of Cora-Huichol acculturation. *Amer. Indig.*, 15: 249–63.
1961 Some aspects of Zinacantan settlement patterns and ceremonial organization. *Estud. Cultura Maya*, 1: 131–46.
1964a Ancient Maya concepts in contemporary Zinacantan religion. *6th Int.*

Cong. Anthr. Ethnol. Sci., Mus. de l'Homme, 2: 497–502.

1964b Ancient Maya and contemporary Tzotzil cosmology: a comment on some methodological problems. *Amer. Antiquity,* 30: 192–95.

1964c Cosmología maya antigua y tzotzil contemporánea: comentario sobre algunos problemas metodológicas. *Amer. Indig.,* 24: 211–19.

1964d The genetic model and Maya cultural development. *In* Desarrollo cultural de los mayas, pp. 9–48.

1964e Some implications of Zinacantan social structure for the study of the ancient Maya. *Proc. 35th Int. Cong. Amer.,* 1: 307–19.

1965a Ceremonial organization in Zinacantan. *Ethnology,* 4: 39–52.

1965b Structural and conceptual replication in Zinacantan culture. *Amer. Anthr.,* 67: 342–53.

1965c Zinacanteco 'souls.' *Man,* no. 29, pp. 33–35.

1966 [ed.] Los zinacantecos: un pueblo tzotzil de los altos de Chiapas. Inst. Nac. Indig. Mexico.

1967 Tendencia de cambio en las tierras altas de Chiapas. *Amer. Indig.,* 27: 199–222.

1968 Zinacantan: a Maya community in the highlands of Chiapas. Harvard Univ. Press.

——— AND A. RUZ LHUILLIER, eds.
1964 Desarrollo cultural de los Mayas. Univ. Nac. Autónoma Mex.

WAGLEY, C.
1941 Economics of a Guatemalan village. *Amer. Anthr. Assoc.,* Mem. 58.

1949 The social and religious life of a Guatemalan village. *Ibid.,* Mem. 71.

1957 Santiago Chimaltenango: estudio antropológico-social de una comunidad indígena de Huehuetenango. Seminario de Integración Social Guatemalteca. Guatemala. (Tr. of his 1941 and 1949, with new preface.)

WAGNER, P. L.
1959 Precipitation in the transect area. *In* McQuown, 1959, fig. 7.

WALDECK, F. DE
1838 Voyage pittoresque et archéologique dans la province d'Yucatan (Amérique Centrale) pendant les années 1834 et 1836. Paris. (Tr. into Spanish, 1930, Merida.)

WARWICK, A. W.
n.d. A report of the Los Angeles mining district, state of Chihuahua, Mexico. MS prepared for Messrs. F. Stallforth, Hnos., Sucs. y Cía.

WASSON, V. P., AND R. G. WASSON
1957 Mushrooms, Russia and history. 2 vols. New York.

WATERHOUSE, V.
1949 Learning a second language first. *Int. Jour. Amer. Ling.,* 15: 106–09.

——— AND M. MORRISON
1950 Chontal phonemes. *Ibid.,* 16: 35–39.

WAUCHOPE, R.
1938 Modern Maya houses: a study of their archaeological significance. *Carnegie Inst. Wash.,* Pub. 502.

WEATHERS, K.
1946 La agricultura de los tzotzil de Nabenchuac, Chiapas, México. *Amer. Indig.,* 6: 315–19.

WEITLANER, I.
See Johnson, I. W.

WEITLANER, R. J.
1939a Los chinantecos. *Rev. Mex. Estud. Antr.,* 3: 195–216.

1939b Notes on the Cuitlatec language. *El Mex. Antiguo,* 4: 363–73.

1940a Notes on Chinantec ethnography. *Ibid.,* 5: 161–75.

1940b Field notes. MS.

1945 Parentesco y compadrazgo coras. *Escuela Nac. Antr.,* Pub. 4, pp. 3–11.

1948a Lingüística de Atoyac, Guerrero. *Tlalocan,* 2: 377–83.

1948b Situación lingüística del estado de Guerrero. *In* El occidente de México, pp. 129–33.

1948c Field notes. MS.

1951 Notes on the social organization of Ojitlan, Oaxaca. *In* Homenaje Caso, pp. 441–55.

1952a Curaciones mazatecas. *An. Inst. Nac. Antr. Hist.,* 4: 279–88.

1952b Sobre la alimentación chinanteca. *Ibid.,* 5: 177–95.

1958a Notas del campo sobre Tetzu, San Andres Jilotepec, etc. MS en Depto. Invest. Antr., Inst. Nac. Antr. Hist. Mexico.

1958b Un calendario de los zapotecos del sur. *Proc. 32d Int. Cong. Amer.,* pp. 296–99.

1960 Field notes on San Felipe Otlaltepec, Puebla. MS.

1961 Datos diagnósticos para la etnohistoria del norte de Oaxaca. *Inst. Nac. Antr. Hist., Dir. Invest. Antr.*, Pub. 6.

1963 Los zapotecos del sur. MS.

—— AND C. A. CASTRO

1954 Mayultianguis y Tlacoatzintepec. *Mus. Nac. Antr., Ser. Cien.*, 3. *Papeles de la Chinantla*, 1. (See Cline, 1961b.) Mexico.

—— AND G. DeCICCO

1962 La jerarquía de los dioses zapotecos del sur. *Proc. 34th Int. Cong. Amer.*, pp. 695–710.

—— AND S. HOOGSHAGEN

1960 Grados de edad en Oaxaca. *Rev. Mex. Estud. Antr.*, 16: 183–209.

—— AND I. W. JOHNSON

1943 Acatlan y Hueycantenango, Guerrero. *El Mex. Antiguo*, 6: 140–204.

1946 The Mazatec calendar. *Amer. Antiquity*, 11: 194–97.

WEST, R. C.

1948 Cultural geography of the modern Tarascan area. *Smithsonian Inst., Inst. Social Anthr.*, Pub. 7.

WHETTEN, N. L.

1948 Rural Mexico. Univ. Chicago Press.

1961 Guatemala: the land and the people. Yale Univ. Press.

WHORF, B. L.

1946 The Milpa Alta dialect of Aztec. *In* Linguistic structures of native America, H. Hoijer, ed., pp. 367–97. *Viking Fund. Pub. Anthr.*, no. 6.

WILDER, C. S.

1941 The Yaqui deer dancer: a study in cultural change. Master's thesis, Univ. Arizona.

WILLEY, G. R.

1964 An archaeological frame of reference for Maya culture history. *In* Desarrollo cultural de los Mayas, pp. 137–78.

WILLIAMS, A. F.

1946 Notes on the Popoloca Indians of San Felipe Otlaltepec, Puebla. *Amer. Anthr.*, 48: 683–86.

WILLIAMS, G. D.

1931 Maya-Spanish crosses in Yucatan. *Papers Peabody Mus., Harvard Univ.*, vol. 13, no. 1.

WILLIAMS GARCÍA, R.

1950a Informe preliminar sobre el municipio de Cardonal, Hidalgo. MS en Bib. Inst. Indig. Interamer. Mexico.

1950b Orizabita, etnografía y folklore de la zona árida del municipio de Ixmiquil-pan, estado de Hidalgo, México. *Ibid.*

1953 Un mito y los mazatecos. *Bol. Indig.*, 13: 360–65.

1961 Los huaxtecos: guión para la planeación e instalación del Museo Nacional de Antropología. Mexico.

1963 Los tepehuas. Univ. Veracruzana, Inst. Antr. Jalapa.

WILSON, C.

1966 Crazy February. New York.

WISDOM, C.

1940 The Chorti Indians of Guatemala. Univ. Chicago Press.

WOLF, E. R.

1959 Sons of the shaking earth. Chicago.

WONDERLY, W. L.

1946 Textos en zoque sobre el concepto del nagual. *Tlalocan*, 2: 97–105.

1947a *Review of* Mapas lingüísticos de la República Mexicana, Departamento de Asuntos Indígenas (1944). *Int. Jour. Amer. Ling.*, 13: 122–25.

1947b Textos folklóricos en zoque: tradiciones acerca de los alrededores de Copainala, Chiapas. *Rev. Mex. Estud. Antr.*, 9: 135–63.

1949a Some Zoquean phonemic and morphophonemic correspondences. *Int. Jour. Amer. Ling.*, 15: 1–11.

1949b Folklore zoque: cuento del weya-weya. *Hontanar*, vol. 1, no. 5. Tuxtla Gutierrez.

1951–52 Zoque: phonemics and morphology. Reprinted from *Int. Jour. Amer. Ling.*, vol. 17, nos. 1–4; vol. 18, nos. 1, 4.

XIMÉNEZ, F.

1720 Historia de la provincia de San Vicente de Chiapa y Guatemala de la orden de predicadores. 3 vols. Guatemala.

1929–31 *Idem*, another ed.

1944–45 El Popul Vuh. *Yikal Maya Than*, vols. 5–7. Merida.

ZABALA, M. T.

1961 Instituciones políticas y religiosas de Zinacantan. *Estud. Cultura Maya*, 1: 147–58.

ZANTWIJK, R. A. M. VAN

1960 Los indígenas de Milpa Alta. *Inst. Real Trópicos, Amsterdam no. 135, Sec. Antr. Cultural y Física*, no. 64.

ZAVALA, S. A.

1937 La "Utopia" de Tomás Moro en la Nueva España y otros estudios. Mexico.

1941   Ideario de Vasco de Quiroga. Fondo de Cultura Económica. Mexico.
—— AND J. MIRANDA
1954   Instituciones indígenas en la colonia. *In* Caso, 1954, pp. 31–94.

ZIMMERMAN, C.
1961   The religion of the Mayas of X-Cacal and Chunpom. MS. Detroit Univ.

ZINGG, R. M.
1938   The Huichols: primitive artists. *Univ. Denver, Contrib. Ethnog.*, no. 1.
1939   A reconstruction of Uto-Aztekan history. New York.

1942   Genuine and spurious values in Tarahumara culture. *Amer. Anthr.*, 44: 78–92.

ZUÑIGA, I.
1835   Rápida ojeada al estado de Sonora. Mexico.

ZUNO, J. G.
1952   Las llamadas lacas michoacanas de Uruapan no proceden de las orientales. *Cuad. Amer.*, 11: 145–65.

ZURITA, A. DE
1891   Breve relación de los señores de la Nueva España. *In* García Icazbalceta, 1889–92, 3: 71–227.

INDEX

abortion: methods of, 186, 365; prevention of, 352

abstinence. SEE Sexual behavior

Acaxee: language of, 779; subsistence of, 786

accordion: 131, 183

acculturation: aided by Hospital de Santa Fe, 727, 728; processes of, 582–583; of religion, 62, 584, 598–600—in central Mexican highlands, 579–580, 581–600, 727–730; in Chiapas highlands, 147–150, 197; in Guatemala, 41, 43, 45; of Pokomames, 118–120; of Popoloca, 489, 493; of Tarahumara, 846, 850, 851, 864; of Yucatec Maya, 244, 247. SEE ALSO Cofradía; Culture change; Mestizoization

acorns: consumption of, 875; for toy tops, 290, 296

adaptation. SEE Ecological adaptation

adobe: for house construction, 54, 61, 79, 109, 162, 227, 342, 362, 384, 425, 465, 546, 567, 590, 615 (fig. 10), 616, 617, 618, 696 (fig. 11), 697, 698, 738, 756 (fig. 31), 757, 797, 817, 836, 837, 855, 876, 881

adobe bricks: 110, 614, 753

adoption: by godparents, 58. SEE ALSO Godparents, duties of

adornment, personal: beads, 53, 163, 287, 856; bean necklaces, 125; body painting, 864, 865; Catholic medals, 800; coins, 53, 125, 163, 343; crosses, wooden, 125; crucifix pendant, 163; earrings, 111, 164, 208, 231, 235, 261, 287, 384, 396, 407, 425, 432, 518, 538, 620, 660 (fig. 17), 710, 800; face painting, 790, 801, 883–885 (figs. 5, 6); gold jewelry, 261, 343, 660 (fig. 17); of hair, 53, 54, 82, 111 (fig. 8), 164, 208, 231, 235, 238, 287, 303, 343, 484, 538, 620, 661, 710; mirrors as, 240, 575, 800; necklaces, 111, 125, 208, 231, 235, 261, 303, 343, 344 (fig. 6), 396, 407, 432, 441, 484, 518, 660 (fig. 17), 710, 800, 882 (fig. 2), 883; rings, 53, 163, 407, 800; squirrel tails, 801; of teeth, 709; wristbands, 800. SEE ALSO Hair styles

adultery. SEE Sexual behavior

adze: 285, 707 (fig. 35), 708, 746, 750, 751

agave: 286, 735, 753, 797, 800, 876. SEE ALSO Maguey

age-grades: as basis for community service, 36, 487, 542, 562; of unmarried men, 548, 549

agricultural calendar: of Amuzgo, 420, 421 n.; of Chatino, 363; of Chocho, 507 (fig. 2); of Chontal, 232; of Chorti, 130; of Huichol and Cora, 797, 813; of Kekchi, 238; of Lacandon, 280; in midwestern highlands (Guat.), 75; of Mixtec,

373, 398; in Nahuatl area, 634, 636; in northwestern Guatemala, 50, 52; of Otomi, 689, 690; of Pokomames, 107, 118 (Table 3); of Tarahumara, 869–870; of Totonac, 643, 645, 680; of Tzeltal, 199, 201; of Tzotzil, 157, 178–179

agricultural crops. SEE by individual name

agricultural rituals. SEE Rituals, agricultural

agricultural tools. SEE by individual name

agriculture: chinampa cultivation, 586; crop rotation, 101, 107–108, 159, 643, 735; European commercial, 34–35; flood-plain, 778, 787, 835, 881; history of, 24, 26; Ladino, 34; in proto-Maya community, 24, 26; in raised plots, 252; supernatural aspects of, 52. SEE ALSO Irrigation; Rituals, agricultural; and under subsistence of individual tribes

agrupación: Spanish policy of, 28, 40

agua loca: 610

Aguacatec: census of, 23, 48; distribution of, 23, 38, 48

Aguacatenango, town of: Tzeltal in, 195–225

Agua Escondida: Ladinos in, 70

aguardiente: consumption of, 66, 67, 98, 99, 123, 217, 218, 219, 224, 238, 241, 266, 355, 361, 374, 405, 414–415, 420, 432, 441, 444, 475, 489, 497, 499, 505, 514, 518, 521, 533, 546, 564, 567, 610, 721; sprayed in fields, 405

Aguilar, Francisco de: chronicle by, 4

ahpish: among Pokomames, 114–115, 119

Ahuacatlan, town of: 647, 665, 674, 676

Ahuiran, town of: 742 (fig. 15)

alcoholic beverages. SEE Beverages, alcoholic

Aleman dam: effect on Mazatec, 319

alfalfa: 373

alligator: mythology about, 473

Almolonga: onion cultivation in, 75

Altar de Sacrificios: location of, 27, 140; Mexicanoid influences at, 28

altars: Christian, 92, 202, 221; funeral, 130; native, 57, 92, 110 (fig. 7), 118, 123, 125, 128, 146 (fig. 10), 162, 202, 208, 222, 223, 231, 233, 237, 238, 239, 241, 269, 303, 307, 308, 309, 385, 425, 488, 493, 497, 501, 505, 512, 514, 537, 611, 618 (fig. 13), 626, 646, 657, 658 (fig. 15), 673, 677 (fig. 20), 681, 721, 738, 757, 820, 862, 863, 865

Alva Ixtlilxochitl, Fernando de: writings by, 6–7

Alvarado, Pedro de: ethnographic contribution by, 7

Alvarado Tezozomoc, Hernando: writings by, 6

amák: 887

806–810; settlement patterns of, 797–799; social organization of, 803–806; subsistence of, 786, 797; technology of, 799–801

cordage: making of, 707–708 (fig. 34), 800

coriander: use of, 161, 300, 508, 737

corn. SEE Maize

corn mill: 161, 279, 285, 287 (fig. 12), 584

corncob: in childbirth, 187, 223, 233; in olotera, 609; in pottery manufacture, 79

corncribs: 362, 608 (fig. 5), 612, 620, 689 (fig. 8), 690, 797, 798 (fig. 4). SEE ALSO Maize, storage of

cornet: 631

corral: for animals, 376, 385, 509 (fig. 4), 612, 617, 647, 798, 855

Cortés, Hernán: Spanish Conquest activities of, 143–144, 298, 334, 554; writings by, 4

cosmogony. SEE Creation; and under religion of individual tribes

cosmology. SEE under life cycle (death) and religion of individual tribes

costumes, ritual: renting of, 65, 674. SEE ALSO Clothing, ceremonial

cotense: 825

Cotorra phase: at Chiapa de Corzo, 26

cotton: clothing of, 53, 76, 79, 82–83, 161, 163, 208, 231, 235, 238, 260, 303, 343, 362–363, 381, 383, 406, 407, 424, 439, 463, 464 (fig. 13), 466, 493–494, 502, 510, 537, 564, 569, 620, 660, 709, 758–759, 801, 818, 825, 856; cultivation of, 76, 126, 201, 281, 373, 441, 482, 539, 567, 646, 835; weaving of, 53, 76–79, 161, 208, 341, 381, 406, 424, 463, 465, 569, 653, 706, 753, 800, 836

cotton mill: in Cantel, 71

courtship and marriage customs: bride price, 67, 98, 190, 217, 218, 242, 266, 297, 497, 558, 887; bride service, 127, 190, 266, 347, 392, 427, 475, 521, 544, 819; capture of girl, 218, 357, 415, 720, 767, 826; elopement, 57, 98, 218, 233, 544, 576, 668, 720; gift-giving during, 67, 98, 113, 190, 217, 218, 229, 232, 236, 242, 266, 309–310, 363, 365, 387, 392, 415, 427, 475, 497, 504, 505, 521, 544, 576, 593, 634, 667–668, 720, 767, 887; go-between, 98, 113, 190, 266, 357, 392, 393, 427, 432, 445, 475, 497, 504, 521, 544, 576, 593, 634; godparents role in, 309–310, 767; marriage "manager," 767; padrinos role in, 98, 357, 497, 505; parents role in, 67, 98, 113, 127, 189–190, 218, 229, 232, 236, 242, 266, 297, 309–310, 357, 365, 392, 415, 427, 445, 475, 497, 504, 514, 521, 544, 558, 633–634, 667–669, 720, 759, 812, 821, 887; trial marriages, 720—of Chatino, 365–366; of Chinantec, 544; of Chocho, 514; of Chol, 236; of Chontal, 232–233; of Chorti, 127, 130; of Cora, 812; of Huastec, 309–310; of Huichol, 812; of Ichcatec, 504–505; of

Kekchi, 242; of Lacandon, 288, 290, 296–297; of Mazatec, 521; in midwestern highlands, 96–98; of Nahua, 633–634; in northwestern Guatemala, 67; of Otomi, 720–721; in Panajachel, 96–97; of Pokomam, 113; of Popoloca, 497; of Tepehuan (northern), 826, 828; of Tepehuan (southern), 821; of Tequistlatec, 558–559; of Tojolabal, 229; of Totonac, 666–669; of Trique, 415–416; of Tzeltal, 217–219; of Yucatec Maya, 266–267; of Zapotec, 357. SEE ALSO Marriage

cow horn: 308, 352

cowhide: tanning of, 853–854; use of, 182 (fig. 13), 818

cows: 66, 160, 422, 623, 797, 824. SEE ALSO Cattle

Coxcatlan Cave: wild maize in, 26

coyote leather: 709

coyotes: 692

Cozumel: oracle on, 270

cradle: manufacture of, 653; use of, 303, 475, 561. SEE ALSO Crib

craft specialization. SEE under specific crafts

creation: mythology about, 115, 175, 295, 350, 364, 412, 473, 542, 671, 715, 864. SEE ALSO under religion of individual tribes

crib, hanging: 493. SEE ALSO Cradle

cristero revolt: 728, 770, 795

Cristos: worship of, 629

crop specialization: in central Mexican highlands, 607 (Table 1); of Chorti, 126; of Mazatec, 319; in midwestern highlands, 72, 75–76, 84; in northwestern Guatemala, 50; in San Antonio Palopo, 84; of Tzotzil, 157–159 (Table 1). SEE ALSO under specific crops

cross, cult of: in Kanhobalán-speaking area, 62

"Cross of our Fathers." SEE Sacred objects and places, family cross

"cross that speaks": in Quintana Roo, 270

crowbar: 301, 689, 853

Cuchumatanes Mountains: 21, 28, 30, 35, 46, 48, 49, 133, 230

cucumbers: 797

Cuicatec: census of, 318, 320 (fig. 2), 434, 435; distribution of, 318 (fig. 1), 434, 435 (fig. 1); economy of, 441–442; geographical area of, 434, 435 (fig. 1); history of, 434; life cycle of, 445; Mixtec contacts of, 369; recreational patterns of, 445; religion of, 444; settlement patterns of, 438; socio-political organization of, 442–444; subsistence of, 436–438; technology of, 438–441

Cuitlatec: aesthetic and recreational patterns of, 575; census of, 320 (fig. 2), 321, 567 (Table 1); distribution of, 318 (fig. 1), 321, 565, 566 (figs. 1, 2); economy of, 569–573; life cycle of, 575–576; political organization of, 573–575; religion of, 575; settlement patterns of, 567; subsistence of, 567; technology of, 567–569

cult of the saints. SEE Saints

6), 571 (fig. 7), 612, 649, 690, 738, 752 (fig. 28), 787, 838, 852, 869, 870

ferns: in sweat house, 659

fertility, folklore about: 91

fertilizer: in midwestern highlands, 75, 76; in Milpa Alta–Tepoztlan area, 609; in northwestern Guatemala, 52; by Tarascans, 736; by Zapotec, 339

fertilizers: animal dung, 851; ant excrement, 339; ashes, 157, 609, 645; coffee leaves, 76; coffee-bean shells, 339; corn stubble, 157, 645; human excrement, 339; manure, 52, 75, 157, 339, 636, 736

festivals. SEE Fiestas

fetishes, as protective objects: 790. SEE ALSO Amulets; Charms

fiddle: 414

fiestas: alcoholic beverages at, 95, 100, 117, 186, 374, 392–393, 396, 397, 399, 414–415, 420, 429, 474, 496, 544, 631, 676, 811, 820, 827, 852, 887; All Saints' Day, 95, 241, 636; All Souls' Day, 95, 99, 115, 186, 308, 636; of Black Christ of Tila, 236; Carnaval, 308, 443, 551; cofrades responsibilities for, 60, 117; cost of, 116, 221, 512; dances at, 65, 94, 95, 186, 356, 392, 397; fireworks at, 95, 186 (Table 5), 397, 399, 432, 496, 631, 676, 770; during Holy Week, 95, 186, 828, 887; horse racing at, 186, 233; importance attached to, 95, 186; markets at, 95, 167, 356, 623, 763, 765, 770, 771; of patron saint, 65–66, 95, 186, 221–222, 233, 241, 268, 269, 397, 399, 496, 542, 770, 772, 841; pilgrims to, 503; of San Francisco, 887; of Santa Cruz, 178; sponsorship of, 56, 95, 221, 347, 350, 356, 512, 520, 542, 562, 593, 597, 625–626, 676, 770–772, 827, 839 (SEE ALSO Officials, mayordomos). SEE ALSO aesthetic and recreational patterns, and religion, under individual tribes

fife: 355

fig-tree paper: significance of, 520

figurines: prehistoric, 373, 384, 388 n., 394, 418–419 n. SEE ALSO Idols

Fine Orange ware: rarity of, 141

fireplace: 54, 81, 110, 125, 162, 207, 224, 231, 237, 257, 258 (fig. 10), 259, 385, 425, 437, 465, 493, 501, 511 (fig. 6), 518, 537, 617 (fig. 12), 655, 657 (fig. 14), 702 (fig. 23), 705, 757–758, 797, 837, 855

fireworks: direction of, 166; at fiestas, 95, 186 (Table 5), 397, 399, 432, 496, 631, 676, 770; making of, 345, 388, 426, 495, 772. SEE ALSO Rockets

fish, consumption of: 72, 161, 236, 238, 339, 361, 405, 420, 437, 483, 532, 546, 561, 567, 737, 790, 797

fish basket: 567, 570 (fig. 6)

fishhook: 253, 281, 300, 567, 693, 800, 883

fishing: by Chinantec, 532; by Chontal, 231; by

Cora, 797, 800; by Cuitlatec, 567, 572; by Huastec, 300; by Huave, 483; by Huichol, 797, 800; by Kekchi, 240; by Lacandon, 281; in midwestern highlands, 84; by Mixtec, 372; by Otomi, 692–693; by Seri, 784, 881, 883; by Tarahumara, 851 (fig. 6), 852, 870; by Tarascans, 733, 734 (fig. 10), 737, 760; by Tzotzil, 161; by Yaqui, 835; by Yucatec Maya, 253; by Zapotec, 339

"Five Letters": of Cortés, 4

flageolet: 94

flashlight, used in hunting: 692

floods, in mythology: 115, 175, 671, 715, 789, 790, 840

flooring: of cement, 757; of planks, 757; of stone slabs, 567; of tile, 465

flowers: as altar decorations, 221, 238, 239, 307, 414, 436, 537, 618, 646, 657; for bride's family, 558; as clothing decoration, 801; growers of, 341, 646, 735; offerings of, 236, 308, 351, 394, 413, 415, 443, 503, 505, 560, 576, 631, 636; sellers of, 166, 167, 572, 623

flowers, artificial: for decoration, 365, 660

flute: manufacture of, 286; use of, 52, 65, 94, 131, 183, 202, 222, 228, 291 (fig. 15), 306, 355, 444, 445, 488, 543, 575, 631, 673, 820, 842, 854, 862, 864

flycatcher, in mythology: 352

folk culture: definition of, 605; integrated, of Yaqui, 834

folklore: municipio differences in, 91; paucity of, among Maxeños, 91. SEE ALSO under religion of individual tribes

food classification: "hot" and "cold," 53, 93, 94, 108–109, 181, 273, 340, 361, 437, 719, 827

food patterns: of Amuzgo, 420–421 n.; of Baja California Indians, 875; of Chatino, 361; of Chinantec, 532–533, 546; of Chocho, 508; of Chontal, 231; of Chorti, 123; of Cora, 797; of Cuicatec, 436–438; of Cuitlatec, 567; of Huastec, 300; of Huave, 483; of Huichol, 797; of Ichcatec, 499, 501; of Kekchi, 238; of Lacandon, 281; of Mazatec, 517; in midwestern highlands, 72; of Mixtec, 372, 373–374; of Nahua, 609–611; in northwestern Guatemala, 52–53; of Otomi, 691–693, 695; of Pokomames, 108–109; of Popoloca, 489, 493; of Seri, 881; of Tarahumara, 852; of Tarascans, 733, 735–738; of Tepehuan (northern), 824; of Tepehuan (southern), 816; of Tequistlatec, 555, 561; of Tlapanec, 563; of Totonac, 646–647; of Trique, 405; of Tzeltal, 199–201, 203; of Tzotzil, 161; of Yaqui, 835, 836; of Yucatec Maya, 254; of Zapotec, 339–340

foods, ceremonial: 52, 66, 67, 72, 117, 131, 161, 199–201, 238, 437, 483, 517, 558–559, 611, 691, 692, 695, 721, 735, 737, 797, 816, 824, 852

fowlhouse. SEE Chicken coops

medium of exchange: beans, 470; cacao, 230, 387, 425; coffee, 387, 391, 425, 442; eggs, 165, 202–203, 253, 263, 288, 405, 408, 483, 485, 692–693, 736; firewood, 442; hats, 510, 512; maize, 167, 264, 374, 387, 391; money, 50, 86, 166, 167, 211, 213, 264, 347, 387, 391, 425, 427, 442, 470; panela, 425

melons: 300

Mendieta, Gerónimo de: ethnographic contributions by, 5

men's groups. SEE Male friendship groups

men's houses: pre-Spanish organization of, 595

menstruation: restrictions during, 575, 679

merchants: hats of, 83; traveling by, 167, 263–264, 623. SEE ALSO Markets; Trade; Trade routes

Merida: founding of, 28

mescal: 355, 361, 489, 499, 505, 514, 555, 558, 567, 572, 610, 676, 803, 820, 821, 887

Messianism: of Mayo, 834

Mestizoization: of Huastec, 299; of Otomi, 684–685; in southern Mexican highlands, 327, 452; of Tarascans, 730; of Zoque, 452, 459

Mestizos: as compadres, 306; distribution of, 21, 317, 377, 579, 684, 727, 795, 799, 822, 824; in fiesta competitions, 719; Indian attitudes toward, 627; Indian exploitation by, 404; as ironworkers, 746; lacquerwork by, 755, 760; land purchase by, 641, 664, 745; in markets, 408, 665, 802; as officials, 304; settlement patterns of, 301, 377, 378, 422; as store owners, 377, 421, 423, 427 n., 765, 802; as teachers, 720; as traders, 363, 765, 802

metal: for rattle belts, 865; for roofs, 79, 109, 384, 518, 702

metallurgy, aboriginal: disappearance of, 590

metate: manufacture of, 162, 206; use of, 54, 79, 81, 108, 110, 123, 125, 161, 187, 207, 231, 235, 259, 285, 301, 303, 380, 385, 423, 437, 484, 493, 509 (fig. 3), 511 (fig. 6), 518, 535 (fig. 13), 613, 655, 657, 689 (fig. 8), 693, 705, 757, 799, 817, 852, 854

Mexican Bureau of Indian Affairs: 732

Mexican Revolution: land reforms after, 29

Mexico City: 579, 589, 614, 623

Michoacan: early ethnographies about, 7, 732

midwife. SEE Childbirth

migration, to United States: of Tarascans, 728, 730, 765

military theocracy: in Quintana Roo, 269–270

milk: consumption of, 374, 405, 737, 797; lack of consumption of, 253, 691; sale of, 160

mill. SEE Grinding mill; Sugar mill

milpa: communal lands for, 36; preparation of, 75, 157, 238, 249 (fig. 2), 252, 280, 339, 363, 372–373, 398, 405, 420, 458 (fig. 8), 460, 540 (fig. 22), 609, 634, 642 (fig. 2), 643, 645, 689,

690, 797, 852, 870. SEE ALSO Maize, cultivation of

Milpa Alta, area of: 604–636

miming. SEE Drama

miniature objects: as offerings, 202, 800

mining: of salt, 162

mining settlements: of Spanish, 340, 579, 683, 782, 822

mint: 161, 353, 508

Miraflores phase: cultural diversity of, 27

mirrors: ceremonial wearing of, 240, 575

miscarriage. SEE Pregnancy

missionary activities: in central Mexican highlands, 598, 599, 600, 629, 639–640, 683, 727; in Chiapas highlands, 145–146, 198; in Guatemalan highlands, 120; in northwestern Guatemala, 49, 62; in northwestern Mexico, 779–784, 787, 795, 814, 816, 822, 830, 832, 846, 850, 874, 877, 879, 881; in southern Mexican highlands, 318, 326, 334–335, 370, 403, 455, 481, 488, 506, 516, 542, 554

Mitla, town of: 319

Mitontic, town of: Tzotzil in, 155–194

mitote ceremonies: of Cora, 806; of Tepehuan (southern), 819, 820, 821

Mixco: acculturation of, 119–120

Mixe: aesthetic patterns of, 474–475; census of, 320 (fig. 2), 448; cultural borrowing from Zapotec, 466; distribution of, 318 (fig. 1), 324, 331, 448–450 (figs. 1, 2); economy of, 469–472; ethnographic studies of, 456–457; geographical area of, 448–449; history of, 335, 453–456; life cycle of, 475–476; religion and world view of, 472–474; settlement patterns of, 340, 448, 462–463; social organization of, 472; Spanish conquest of, 326–327, 335, 455; subsistence of, 459–462; technology of, 463–469

Mixe-Zoque: prehistory of, 26–27

Mixtec: aesthetic and recreational patterns of, 395–397; annual cycle of, 398–399; census of, 318, 320 (fig. 2); distribution of, 318 (fig. 1), 367, 368 (fig. 1), 417, 436, 489, 506; economy of, 387–391; ethnological studies of, 371–372; geographical area of, 367–369 (fig. 1); history of, 322, 325, 369–371; life cycle of, 397–398; religion and world view of, 394–395; settlement patterns of, 374–379 (figs. 2–5); social organization of, 391–394; subsistence of, 372–374; technology of, 379–387 (figs. 6–11); trading network of, 319, 369, 389–391, 427

mobility. SEE Seasonal mobility; Social mobility

modeling. SEE Pottery, manufacture of

"modified" Indians: definition of, 45

molding. SEE Pottery, manufacture of

molds: for adobes, 708; for clay tiles, 708; in hat manufacture, 232; in pottery manufacture, 109; for sugar cakes, 662

Tlapanec: aesthetic and recreational patterns of, 564; census of, 320 (fig. 2), 321, 563; distribution of, 318 (fig. 1), 321, 417, 563; economy of, 564; life cycle of, 564; religion of, 564; settlement patterns of, 563; social organization of, 564; subsistence of, 563; technology of, 564

Tlatelolco: history of, 5

Tlatilco: relationships with Monte Alban, 323

Tlaxcala, town of: 7, 602–636

Tlaxcala-Puebla area: early ethnography of, 5, 7

toads: consumption of, 567; folklore about, 863

tobacco: cultivation of, 126, 252, 281, 327, 518, 521, 539, 540, 797, 852; use of, 129, 185–186, 187, 203, 306, 355, 381, 397, 421, 424, 445, 493, 499, 520, 521, 533, 672, 675, 695, 867; weighing of, 290 (fig. 14). SEE ALSO Cigarettes; Cigars

Todos Santos, town of: 33 (fig. 3), 45, 46, 49, 51 (fig. 2), 54, 56, 59–61

Tojolabal: census of, 23, 226–227 (Table 1); distribution of, 133, 134, 138, 139, 140, 226; geographical area of, 226; history of, 133; integration of, 138, 227; linguistic history of, 25; location of, 23, 25; political-religious organization of, 228; prehistoric location of, 140; religion of, 228, 229; settlement pattern of, 138; subsistence of, 227

Toltec: Postclassic "invasions" of, 28

Toluca, city of: 686

tomatoes: 50, 252, 280, 300, 373, 420, 459, 508, 607, 636, 691, 735, 736

tombs: cruciform subterranean, 324

tonal (tono): concept of, 351, 394, 430, 445, 475, 679

Tonantzin. SEE Virgin of Guadalupe

tools, agricultural: in Guatemalan highlands, 35, 50; in midwestern highlands, 75; storage of, 55. SEE ALSO Coa; Dibble stick; Digging stick; Hoe; Machete; Plow; and under subsistence and technology of individual tribes

tools, for pottery manufacture: cane piece, 79; cloth, 79; corncob, 79; leather, 79; metal piece, 79; potter's wheel, 705; revolving base, 79; stone piece, 79

Torquemada, J. de: as chronicler, 7–8

tortoiseshell: objects made from, 259, 285

Totolapan, town of: Cuitlatec in, 567–576

Totonac: aesthetic and recreational patterns of, 673–678; annual cycle of, 680–681; census of, 641; distribution of, 580–581 (fig. 1), 582 (fig. 2), 638, 639 (fig. 1); economy of, 662–666; geographical area of, 638; life cycle of, 678–680; linguistic relationships of, 638, 641, 643; religion and world view of, 671–673; settlement patterns of, 647–649; social organization of, 666–671; Spanish conquest of, 639–641; subsistence of, 642–647 (figs. 2, 3); technology of, 649–662

Totonac Cempoala: Spanish missionizing at, 639–640

Totonicapan, Dept. of: economic specialization in, 71–72; ethnographic study in, 71; pottery manufacture in, 76, 79

Totonicapan, town of: 34 (fig. 4), 71, 73–75, 81, 84–86, 90, 98

toys: airplanes, wooden, 286, 290; balls, 631, 718; blowguns, 189, 380, 441; bows and arrows, 189, 296, 441, 561; of cane, 674; of clay, 674; dolls, 189, 286, 290, 296, 365, 475, 544, 561, 633, 674, 718, 868; flowers as, 188; hoops, 365; looms, 189; marbles, 189, 773; metates, 189; of palm, 495, 674; peashooters, 544; pots, 189; puppets, 445; sling shots, 65, 189, 718; string, 188; tops, 65, 189, 290, 296, 674; trucks, 189, 633; wood pieces, 188. SEE ALSO Games

Tozzer, Alfred M.: anthropological contributions by, 251, 280

tractor: in farming, 736, 746

trade: among Chocho, 510, 512; by Lacandon, 288; by Mixtec, 319, 369, 389, 391; in northwest Mexico, 788, 802, 818, 819, 825, 836, 857, 858, 877; by Tarahumara, 857, 858; by Yaqui, 836; by Zapotec, 319, 346–347, 363. SEE ALSO Markets; Trade routes

trade routes: geographical barriers to, 69; of traveling merchants, 263–264, 765. SEE ALSO Markets; Trade

trade unions: in Cantel, 71, 90; in Totonicapan, 90

trading system: of Tarascans, 733, 736–737, 761 (fig. 33), 763, 765

"traditional" Indians: definition of, 45

trait distributions: in Guatemalan highlands, 37–38

tranchete: 609, 613

transportation: by bicycles, 111, 386; by burro, 372, 386, 427, 557, 620, 621 (fig. 16), 692, 736, 759, 765, 816, 817, 836, 857; by bus, 61, 111, 164, 375 n., 386, 620, 621, 641, 661, 697, 711, 759; by canoe, 261, 278 (fig. 2), 287, 538, 711; by car, 641, 661; by cart, 344, 481 (fig. 4), 485, 759; by donkey, 303, 801; by flatboats, 569; by horse, 48, 363, 386, 620, 668, 759, 801, 817; by litter (shoulder-borne), 661; by mule, 48, 303, 386, 620, 759, 765, 801; by oxen, 620; by plane, 363, 422, 661, 801; of produce and crafts, 61, 83, 164, 208, 261, 303, 385, 408, 427, 518, 538, 711; by rafts, 538, 539 (fig. 21), 569; by trucks, 61, 164, 208, 261, 303, 344, 386, 422, 494, 510, 518, 623, 661, 711, 729, 759, 822, 881; by wagons, 822. SEE ALSO Tumpline

traps: 161, 206, 236, 253, 300, 339, 372, 380, 406, 420, 422, 423, 459 (fig. 9), 825, 854

treadle loom. SEE Loom, foot

trees: as private property, 346, 470

Tres Zapotes: relationships with Monte Alban, 323

tribute: paying of, 591, 640. SEE ALSO Taxes